GEOGRAPHY
of
RELIGION

GEOGRAPHY

OF RELIGION

Where God Lives, Where Pilgrims Walk

SUSAN TYLER HITCHCOCK WITH JOHN L. ESPOSITO

NATIONAL GEOGRAPHIC

WASHINGTON, D.C.

OPPOSITE: Splendid mosaics glorifying Allah dwarf a veiled worshiper at Masjid-i-Jami in Herat, Afghanistan.
PREVIOUS PAGES: Looking to the heavens, people everywhere have long sought solace—and answers—in religion.

TABLE OF CONTENTS

OPPOSITE: *A young Orthodox Jew prays at Jerusalem's Western Wall—the remains of King Solomon's Temple.*

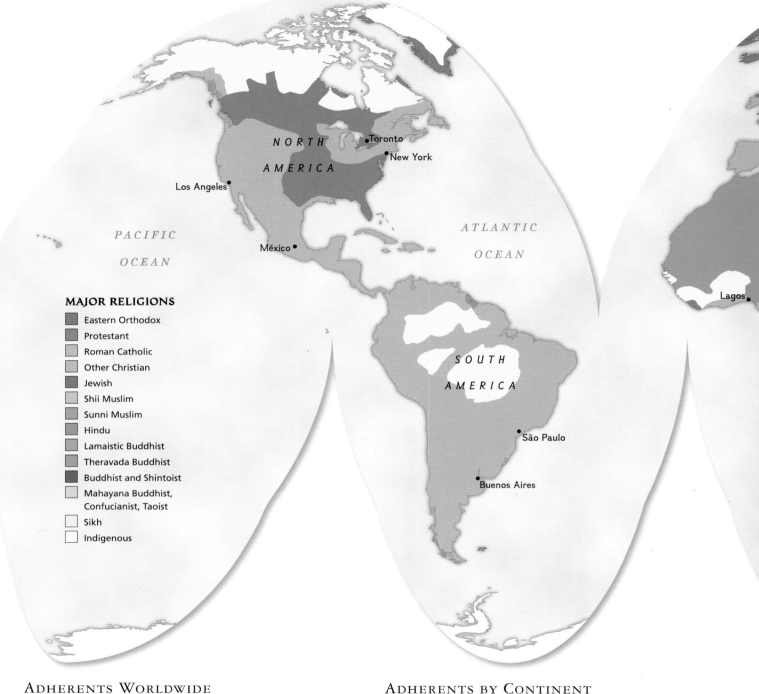

MAJOR RELIGIONS

- Eastern Orthodox
- Protestant
- Roman Catholic
- Other Christian
- Jewish
- Shii Muslim
- Sunni Muslim
- Hindu
- Lamaistic Buddhist
- Theravada Buddhist
- Buddhist and Shintoist
- Mahayana Buddhist, Confucianist, Taoist
- Sikh
- Indigenous

ADHERENTS WORLDWIDE

1900

Non-religious 0.2%
Buddhism 7.8%
Other 9.2%
Islam 12.3%
Chinese traditional 23.5%
Hinduism 12.5%
Christianity 34.5%

2000

Other 6.7%
Buddhism 5.9%
Chinese traditional 6.3%
Non-religious 15.1%
Islam 19.6%
Christianity 33.0%
Hinduism 13.4%

The growth of Islam and the decline of Chinese traditional religion stand out as significant changes over the past one hundred years. Christianity, largest of the world's main faiths, has remained largely stable in number of adherents. Today more than one out of six people claim to be atheistic or nonreligious.

ADHERENTS BY CONTINENT

In terms of religious adherents, Asia ranks first. This is not only because half the world's people live on that continent but also because three of the five major faiths are practiced there: Hinduism in South Asia; Buddhism in East and Southeast Asia; and Islam from Indonesia to the Central Asian republics to Turkey. Australia, Europe, North America, and South America are overwhelmingly Christian. Africa, with many millions of Muslims and Christians, retains large numbers of animists.

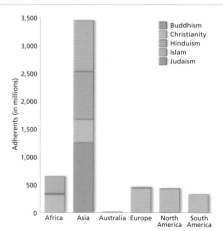

Buddhism
Christianity
Hinduism
Islam
Judaism

Adherents (in millions)

Africa | Asia | Australia | Europe | North America | South America

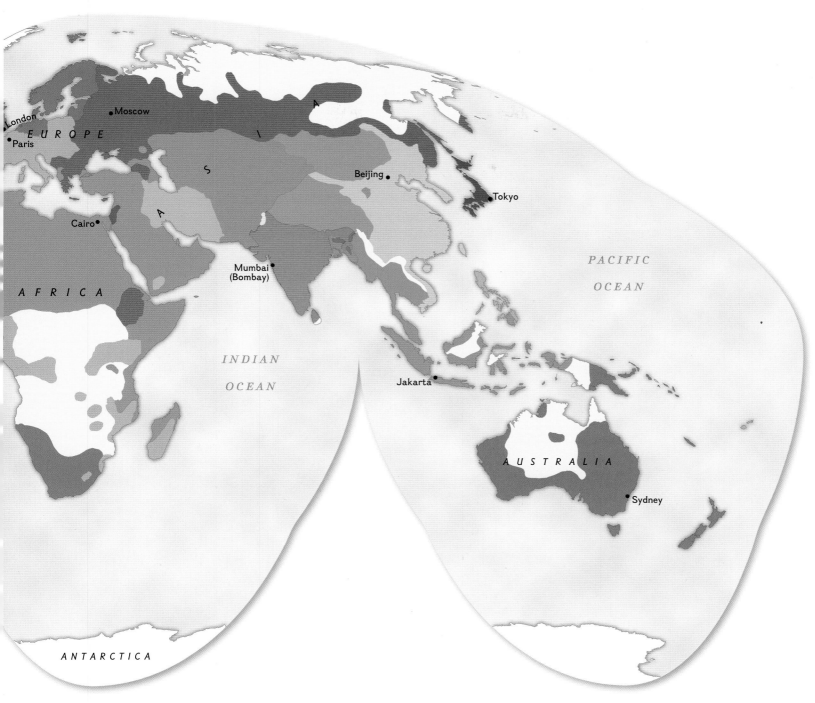

ADHERENTS BY COUNTRY

COUNTRIES WITH THE MOST BUDDHISTS

Country	Buddhists
1. China	105,829,000
2. Japan	69,931,000
3. Thailand	52,383,000
4. Vietnam	39,534,000
5. Myanmar	33,145,000
6. Sri Lanka	12,879,000
7. Cambodia	9,462,000
8. India	7,249,000
9. South Korea	7,174,000
10. Taiwan	4,686,000

COUNTRIES WITH THE MOST CHRISTIANS

Country	Christians
1. United States	235,742,000
2. Brazil	155,545,000
3. Mexico	95,169,000
4. China	89,056,000
5. Russia	84,308,000
6. Philippines	68,151,000
7. India	62,341,000
8. Germany	62,326,000
9. Nigeria	51,123,000
10. Congo, Dem. Rep.	49,256,000

COUNTRIES WITH THE MOST HINDUS

Country	Hindus
1. India	755,135,000
2. Nepal	18,354,000
3. Bangladesh	15,995,000
4. Indonesia	7,259,000
5. Sri Lanka	2,124,000
6. Pakistan	1,868,000
7. Malaysia	1,630,000
8. United States	1,032,000
9. South Africa	959,000
10. Myanmar	893,000

COUNTRIES WITH THE MOST MUSLIMS

Country	Muslims
1. Indonesia	181,368,000
2. Pakistan	141,650,000
3. India	123,960,000
4. Bangladesh	110,805,000
5. Turkey	65,637,000
6. Egypt	65,612,000
7. Iran	65,439,000
8. Nigeria	63,300,000
9. China	38,208,000
10. Algeria	30,690,000

COUNTRIES WITH THE MOST JEWS

Country	Jews
1. United States	5,621,000
2. Israel	3,951,000
3. Russia	951,000
4. France	591,000
5. Argentina	490,000
6. Canada	403,000
7. Brazil	357,000
8. Britain	302,000
9. Palestine*	273,000
10. Ukraine	220,000

*Nonsovereign nation

All figures are estimates based on data for the year 2000.
Countries with the highest reported nonreligious populations include China, Russia, United States, Germany, North Korea, Japan, India, Vietnam, France, and Italy.

FOREWORD

AT THE START of the 21st century, the world is torn by war and terrorism, often in the name of faith. Indeed, throughout much of recorded history different faiths have clashed in their efforts to defend and advance their beliefs.

This is not a book about religious warfare. Rather, it was conceived as an antidote to it. The key to its mission is in its title: *The Geography of Religion: Where God Lives, Where Pilgrims Walk.* The book traces the geography and spread of the five major world religions and takes the reader through their histories. By revealing where each faith was born, what barren and rocky or lush and fertile landscape spawned its tenets, what nomads or kings or enlightened prophets spread its word, we have tried to identify common threads running through all faiths: belief in a higher being, belief that acts of kindness reward both the giver and the recipient, belief in an afterlife. Each religion has handed down a code of conduct for its society that is surprisingly similar to all the others.

It is naïve to think that by identifying these common threads, we will all say, "Aha, now I understand you." But our hope is that these common elements will be the foundation for educating each of us about the other. Perhaps with knowledge comes tolerance, with tolerance, peace.

In the journey that follows we invite you to discover the realms where God lives and to walk with the pilgrims of each faith. The book is multifaceted but easy to use. A board of advisers has worked closely with us, guiding our words and our layout, our approach to modern topics, and our interpretation of the most ancient philosophies and texts.

Author Susan Tyler Hitchcock in consultation with university professor John L. Esposito wrote with insight and reverence. Archbishop Desmond Tutu, Anglican priest and Nobel laureate for world peace joins his daughter, the Reverend Mpho A. Tutu, to open the book with their views of the part religion has played in world history.

The first chapter, "Origins," looks at the beginnings of human belief in a higher being. Inspired by natural forces such as thunder and lightning, floods and volcanoes, and the mysteries within the landscape around them, humans gradually journeyed toward worship of beings they termed divine.

The subsequent chapters explore the five major religions: Hinduism, Buddhism, Judaism, Christianity, and Islam. The story of each faith begins in its original landscape and develops its character based on the culture that conceived it; it spreads by the will of humans who sense divine guidance; and it changes in its evolving environment, adding the effects of its new culture.

In each chapter a map reveals the religion's birthplace and important sites. A sidebar gives excerpts from the faith's sacred texts. Another sidebar addresses daily practice. A major essay by a member of the Board of Advisers, each a scholar of his or her faith, reveals a personal view of that faith in modern times.

In conclusion, His Holiness the Dalai Lama delivers a message of hope that this book will play a part in bringing readers to recognize that there are many ways of "generating a good heart and a positive mind."

—THE EDITORS

OPPOSITE: *Angkor Wat, Cambodia's 12th-century temple complex, is reflected in its moat at sunrise.*

INTRODUCTION

—ARCHBISHOP DESMOND TUTU AND THE REV. MPHO A. TUTU

WE WRITE as a father and daughter, two Christian priests, one at the beginning of her ordained ministry, the other with a lifetime of experience from which to draw. Each of us has a distinct role in our faith community, and yet we are bound in a common mission and ministry in the world. Our task is to address the importance of religion in the world today and the importance of understanding something of faiths other than our own for promoting world peace. We write as Christians, with all the gifts and limitations that perspective can imply. Each of us has drawn our friends from and formed alliances across religious lines among people of many faiths. Those who are not our co-religionists have deepened, rather than undermined, our faith, for people who do not believe as we believe prod us into a closer examination of the tenets of our faith.

We human beings are, fundamentally, worshiping creatures. Our response to our religious impulse is either to worship God or to worship something that is less than God. As Christian author C.S. Lewis observed: "What Satan put into the hand of our remote ancestors was the idea that they could be like gods, could set up on their own as if they had created themselves, be their own master, invent some sort of happiness for themselves outside God, apart from God. And out of that hopeless attempt has come nearly all that we call human history—money, poverty, ambition, war, prostitution, classes, empires, slavery—the long terrible story of man trying to find something other than God which will make him happy."

At our best, however, we worship God, the Supreme Being. On remote mountain peaks and windswept prairies, in lush jungles and barren deserts, in rural outposts and teeming cities, humans worship the divine and erect monuments to the glory of God. And despite the variety of their geographical beginnings, the differences in their political contexts, and the diversity of their followers, religions have certain essential elements in common.

Whether Hindu or Christian, Buddhist, Muslim or Jew, it is our religion that gives us direction, a sense of self-worth, and a feeling of oneness with the universe. It is our faith that undergirds our morality. Our religious beliefs prompt us to acts of genuine altruism: People of every religious stripe abandon the comforts of home and family to offer their services in refugee camps, in hospitals, and in schools. Through the financial contributions of the faithful, the hungry are fed,

ABOVE: *The Shrine of Aaron stands atop Jebel Haroun in Jordan. Aaron, a high priest, was brother to Moses, prophet of three religions.*

the homeless are housed, and the naked are clothed. The imperatives of religious belief send men and women the world over to minister to those marginalized by modern society: the aged and infirm, prisoners and prostitutes. Religion assures us that no part of life is arbitrary or chaotic; religion makes meaning out of human experience. For the believer, prayer has the power to alter physical circumstance. Studies show that people who pray, and are prayed for, experience better medical outcomes than those who do not pray and for whom no prayers are offered.

Every religion assumes that we have the capacity to be ethical beings; none teaches that it is good to steal, to murder, or to be vicious. Violence and war are aberrations from the high ideals of our faiths, yet each faith's tradition has the capacity for destruction. Christians countenanced the crusades, slavery, the holocaust, apartheid, and the continuing turmoil in Northern Ireland. Hindus were responsible for the bloody expulsion of Muslims to Pakistan at the time of partition. Jews raze the homes of Palestinians and mount raids on refugee camps. Muslims waged holy wars into Byzantium, Persia, North Africa, and Spain; some Muslims strap munitions to their bodies and become suicide bombers

All faiths have the potential to create saints and breed fanatics. Hinduism brought us the wisdom of Gandhi and the madness of his assassin. Buddhism has shown us the tranquil face of the Dalai Lama and the brutality of Pol Pot. Judaism has given us the courage of young Anne Frank and the insanity of fundamentalist Baruch Goldstein. Christianity was the religion of Mother Theresa and of Adolf Hitler. Islam is the faith of both the mystic and poet Rumi and of terrorist Osama bin Laden.

Yet it is also within each faith that the paths to redemption lie. It was Christianity that sustained America's slaves and enlivened her abolitionists. It was their Christian faith that encouraged many of those oppressed by apartheid; Christianity, Islam, and Judaism animated many leaders of the anti-apartheid struggle. And it was men and women of all faiths who had the courage to oppose the Nazi holocaust.

Each religion offers a true path to God. It behooves us to hear what members of other faiths have to say about their seeking. In their exploration we may find the keys to doors heretofore closed against us. Contrary to our own Scripture, Christians have been quick to dismiss the notion that other faiths have any insights into truth and have reveled in the luxury of remaining ignorant of the beliefs of other religions. Yet the God who created us is bigger than any single religion. The paths to the knowledge of God may be many more than we can imagine. God is too big to fit into our box.

In the human frame we, and our interests, are central; and poverty, war, injustice, and oppression are born from human self-centeredness. In the religious frame human beings are not the center. Religion is the hope of the world for peace because each religion forces us to look beyond our personal good, beyond our local or national aspirations to the service of a God who is greater than we are. All the major religions look forward to a time when creation is reunited with the divine. All look forward to a time when goodness will prevail over evil; when hope will overcome fear; when light will banish the darkness; when joy will dry every tear; when justice will be as a flood to drown injustice and oppression, and God, the Supreme, will be all in all.

We invite you to learn more about religions in the following pages and hope that what you discover can bring you to a deeper understanding of your own religion and of the beliefs of others. Understanding between the faiths is ultimately understanding between individual people of faith.

ORIGINS

There is a Power by which we are surrounded, like the atmosphere in which some motionless lyre is suspended, which visits with its breath our silent chords, at will. . . . This Power is God.

— Percy Bysshe Shelley

ORIGINS

ON EASTER Island, 2,300 miles west of the South American mainland, stone heads five times the size of a human figure gaze out across the Pacific Ocean, their tight-lipped faces exuding fierceness, wonder, and mystery. In New Zealand, Maoris wear jade good-luck charms of Hei Tiki, to some the first man, to others a fertility god. In South Africa, rock paintings portray the age-old Bushman trance dance, led by a man wearing leg rattles and a mask with antelope horns.

OPPOSITE: Shadowed in mystery, a stony sentinel called a moai *guards the secrets of Easter Island.*
PRECEDING PAGES: Nature's awesome power, in Zaire's Virunga Mountains, may have spurred spiritual quests.

IN EVERY culture and every age humans have sensed in the natural world a power greater than themselves. Surrounded by phenomena they cannot understand and forces they cannot control, they have apprehended a sacred presence. Humans responded to this supernatural force with fear and respect and attempts to understand or gain favor from these unknowables. They developed forms of worship, recognized certain phenomena as sacred, and kept them apart from ordinary activities. In art and ceremony, they have given this feeling expression and sought connection with the supernatural.

Some cultures recognized sacred spirits in every part of their surroundings. Others developed a belief in gods, superhuman beings who interested themselves in the affairs of humans and with whom they could have a relationship through worship. Of these, some worshiped multiple gods, and still others believed in one supreme being.

In all these traditions, humankind has sought to understand its place in the universe, both in the natural world and in the divine order. Human beings had to determine the rules on how to relate to the divine being, how to behave to gain protection in this life, to be spared from tribulations, and how to achieve salvation in the afterlife. They fulfilled these requirements with incantations and ceremonial dances. They offered promises, gifts, and sacrifices and developed rituals to beseech the gods or spirits. Above all, they understood that there is a power greater than themselves, and therefore that they must seek salvation through requests for divine assistance.

FORCES OF NATURE

THE FORCES present in the natural landscape are formative and necessary to human life. They can evoke fear and awe, dependency and anxiety: the ocean that pounds up on shore; the rain, whether gentle and nutritive, torrential, or parchingly absent; fire, beneficent for cooking, yet a ferocious antagonist when out of control; thunder and lightning storms; earthquakes, volcanoes, dust, and wind. The landscape and its shapes prompt universal responses: a mountain, soaring above the horizon, appears to touch the heavens; a cave or grotto, dark and deep, presents a hideaway filled with ominous foreboding; a major river, coursing with power, maps out the possibilities and the limits of daily life.

Humans depend on plants for food, yet must work hard to gather or sow, harvest and prepare them. They cannot direct but can only respond to the climate, the weather, and annual variations in light, heat, and moisture. Human beings depend as well on animals, reckoning with their ferocity when wild or their dependency when herded. Certain cycles cannot be interrupted, reversed, or denied: the seasons of the natural world and the seasons of human life, from birth to death with landmarks in between such as puberty, marriage, childbirth, and the death of elders. Dreams and states of delirium present places and people, feelings and phantasms that are very real yet never present in waking life.

Every one of these powerful experiences in the human landscape has inspired religious beliefs and practices— words of prayer and attitudes of worship, whether in supplication, praise, or communion.

Human consciousness raises questions that cannot be answered through fact, reason, or observation. *Who am I, and why am I here?* No simple answer exists. Cultures share myths —narratives dramatizing the origin, destiny, and interactions of humans, nature, and the divine, especially narratives that provide defining characteristics about the gods' importance to the culture. Those myths provide a common and authoritative groundwork from which to derive answers to these questions. Long before writtten language, myths passed on the experiences, revelations, beliefs, and promises of ancestors.

What can I do to gain control over the elements? In the face of cataclysmic forces, humans often addressed spirit beings,

OPPOSITE: Arms raised, evil spirits called Quinkans *stand guard on cave walls in Cape York, Australia.*

hoping to gain a sympathetic ear, secure their guardianship, and gain some sort of comfort in a world beyond their understanding or control.

They explained the forces and phenomena of nature in myths, in concepts that humans can grasp and discuss and in forms with which they can interact. Ritual practices allow people to face the unknown together. Rituals are patterned activities with prescribed rules and outcomes. These practices can include words—spoken or chanted—rhythm and music, dance or processionals, and a whole host of sensory stimuli to fully engage the participants. Special acts apart from the flow of everyday life, rituals are designed to gain the attention and good will of forces and beings other than human. As these practices are taught from generation to generation, they form bonds in the present and connect to an earlier time beyond individual memory. Conceptually, the ritual ceremonies repeat and reinforce the beliefs that unite a people.

What can I do to improve this life for myself and others of my beloved circle? For a community or culture to unite, all people within it must share rules of morality. Even before the organization of states and nations, religions provided laws of right and wrong and the boundaries of behavior within the community.

Does it really matter how I behave? Myths and cautionary tales have served to answer this question, whether

ABOVE: *Australian Aborigines thought ancestors called Wandjina came back to leave their image on rocks.*

narrating ideals, portraying final rewards and punishments, or expressing the concern of divine beings for humankind.

Recognizing that death is our ultimate fate, what happens next? Some of the earliest proof of a religious sense—a sense of meaning beyond the human being's physical existence—can be found in the care with which bodies tens of thousands of years ago were placed in graves. What comes after death is the unanswerable question, the experience all humans share yet can never know. Myths, ceremonies, and intricate constellations of belief arise from looking deep into this mystery, central yet antithetical to human life, and finding in it the inspiration for an entire system of beliefs and practices that declare human life, individually and collectively, to have meaning.

EARLIEST SIGNS

THE DAWN of religion, tens of thousands of years ago, accompanied many other significant developments: the making of tools, clothing, and ornaments; construction of shelter; control of fire; the beginning of a symbol system, which allowed the development of language; and the imaginative projections that resulted in art and religion. While we may never fully understand the inspiration that created them, graves and paintings from this period, the Paleolithic era, hint at practices and ritual that might be called religious.

Human remains dating back 70,000 years suggest that both Neandertal man and Paleolithic-era *Homo sapiens* may have placed objects in graves with the deceased. Around the bones of a Neandertal child buried in Teshik Tash, a cave site in Uzbekistan, lay a wild goat's horn and bone scrapers. This practice may simply indicate generosity toward a departed loved one, but later burial configurations suggest a larger system of beliefs. The so-called Red Lady of Paviland —ultimately identified as a young male—was buried in Goat's Hole Cave in southern Wales about 26,000 years ago. He wore rings and waist ornaments of mammoth bone and a pouch full of periwinkle shells to the grave. His bones and accoutrements were all stained red with ocher.

His remains were carefully extended and stone slabs laid at head and feet. An abundance of plant remains was found near the grave, suggesting that his people worked to express respect for his body after death. Historians interpret such artifacts and activities as evidence of the earliest stages of a belief in the afterlife and the influence of ancestral spirits among the living.

Cave paintings at Trois Frères, in the French foothills of the Pyrenees, date from about 10,000 years ago. Among paintings of bison and horses, a fantastical biped with antlers, paws, and tail stares down. His round eyes gaze straight out of his furry, bearded head. He seems entranced. Perhaps he embodies the strength and cunning that the hunters of that place and time hoped to achieve, thus an ally god; or perhaps he embodies the dangers of the hunt, thus an antagonistic god. Art historians call him the Sorcerer, seeing in him the prototype of a man honored in his community for a special connection to the unknown power beyond.

Archaeologists also have discovered evidence of early worship of female beings that had power over the natural world. In western Romania, for instance, the people of the Vinca civilization created terra-cotta statuettes of the Vegetation Goddess, whose blessings would ensure a bountiful harvest.

BEGINNINGS

THE FOUNDATIONS of religious practice are often shrouded in mystery, their ancient origins covered over by time. In many cultures, myths grew up to explain the society's rituals and beliefs, as in the Blackfeet story relating a hero's tale of quest and successful return.

The Blackfeet Indians of the North American Plains told of Scarface, the young hunter wounded on his face early in life. He fell in love with a maiden already claimed by the Person Above, the Sun. Devoted to her, Scarface went on a journey, hoping to find the great power and get the Sun's permission to marry. He asked people and animals, none of whom could help, until two swans carried him across deep

water filled with monsters. On the other shore, Scarface met a young man named Early Riser—the morning star, which we now identify as the planet Venus. This man said his mother was the Moon, his father the Sun. Scarface grew fond of the celestial family and lived with them for a long time. Finally he got permission to marry.

Saying goodbye, the Sun instructed him on how to build and use a medicine lodge. The Sun demonstrated the power of medicine and removed the scar from the young Blackfeet's face, a narrative element symbolizing the health and fertility that this practice would bring to all his people. Returning home, Scarface built and tended a medicine lodge, a place for religious observance and spiritual healing. When inside the lodge, he always wore two raven feathers given to him by the Sun. When he grew old, Scarface passed those feathers and their power on to a new keeper of the medicine lodge. This myth explained the origin of the Blackfeets' religious practice, centered on the medicine lodge and its rituals, and assured them of connection to—and care, and affection from—the great uncontrollable forces, the Sun and the Moon, highest beings in heaven.

Many variations exist in the broad tradition of myths about gods of nature's primal elements and their creation. Many of these are told in the context of the creation of the universe. Such tales may come to be seen as cultural constructs, or—as in the biblical account, in Genesis, of the creation of the world in seven days—may be accepted literally by believers.

Sculptural reliefs dating from before 2,000 B.C. were found in Susa, near today's Dezful, Iran, representing two primary gods of Sumer, the world's first civilization and seedbed for the cultures and religions that arose in Mesopotamia. In this panel the Sumerian sky god, An, emerges from the sea, rays of light emanating from his shoulders. As An steps out of the water, his foot rests on the shoulder of a kneeling human, and the god climbs stair steps up the world mountain. Enki, the water god, remains in the briny depths.

Sumerian cuneiform texts tell creation myths of Nammu, a goddess and the mother of *amu tu an-ki,* Heaven-and-Earth, a single universal being made of two parts: An and Ki, male and female. From their union came Enlil, god of the air, "who brings up the seed of the land from the earth" and whose blowing separates An and Ki, heaven and earth. As in heaven, so on earth: The Sumerians watched kings mount steps to the peak of their ziggurats, the mountain-shaped temples whose ruins still stand in Iraq near the site of Ur. Planting seed and hoping for the blessings of Enlil to bring bountiful weather to their crops, they saw the progression of life as a series of steps from sea to earth to heaven.

Strands of early Hinduism pictured the creation of the world in the form of a goddess rising up out of the waters, perched on a lotus blossom. An Indian relief sculpture dating from the third century B.C. shows the goddess flanked by elephants whose trunks grip large pitchers from which they pour the waters of heaven, so the blessing of

OPPOSITE: Pebbles tossed into the sky? Gifts from the gods? Early peoples explained the stars in myriad and wonderful ways.
ABOVE: The fierce face of the Sun, principal god of the Aztecs, shines from a stone calendar.
FOLLOWING PAGES: The mysterious megaliths known as Stonehenge form a circle on England's Salisbury Plain.

23

water rests below her and falls upon her, like river and rain. Other Hindu myths from the Vedas—ancient sacred texts—tell of the cosmic giant Purusha whose dismemberment and sacrifice gave rise to all creation.

In the Kimberley region of northwestern Australia, the Unumbal people told a myth about how their rugged, rocky landscape got its water. Their cosmos began with a sky god, Wallanganda, their name for the galaxy we now call the Milky Way, and an earth god, Ungud, who took the form of a great snake. Wallanganda scattered water on the earth; Ungud deepened it. They slept, and out of their dreams arose the creatures that inhabit the earth. In the watery depths, Ungud discovered Wandjina, spirit-forms with wide, hollow eyes, long arms, and no mouths. When they emerged from underwater, they spread across the land, forming the hills and plains and refreshing them with falling rain. Then the Wandjina lay down on certain rocks in the landscape, leaving their impressions to watch over lakes, rivers, and springs. In a cave near a gorge formed by a tributary of the Chapman River, a vast tableau of red and black rock paintings of these and other fantastic figures was discovered in the 1950s. Archaeologists estimate them to be 17,000 years old.

The Haida people, of the Queen Charlotte Islands in the Canadian province of British Columbia, took the opposite position on the creation of the world. They believed the universe began with water, as told in the story of Raven, He-Whose-Voice-Is-Obeyed:

"Not long ago, there was no land to be seen. Then there was a little thing on the ocean, the rest was all open sea. Raven sat upon this little thing. 'Become dust!' he said, and it became the earth."

In the creation myth told among the Pima Indians of the southwestern United States, primeval man emerged out of darkness to make the earth and the heavens. He put his hand into his heart and drew out a stone, then divided the stone into pebbles and tossed them into the sky to light the darkness. Wanting the world even brighter, he drew another rock from his heart and made the Milky Way.

At the other extreme, Kung Bushmen in Botswana saw falling stars as gifts from the great god who had ordered things at the very beginning. This god continued to give gifts to believers: ostrich eggs, bees and honey, giraffes, aardvarks, blood, the sun, and especially the medicine songs uttered ceremonially by tribal healers. The Kung named the power in all these gifts *ntum.* They could not pray for or to ntum, though. In the human realm, they associated it with death and fighting. Only a select few, the healers among them, could come into contact with ntum.

PROPITIATING THE GODS

THROUGH RELIGION, human beings established a relationship with the gods they named and envisioned within the powerful forces of the landscape. In prayer and ritual, they communicated with their gods, hoping thereby to win their blessings and gain some control over the natural environment. In modern times, too, although science has discovered much about natural phenomena, in every corner of the planet, at every moment of the day, millions of people are at prayer or attending religious services, seeking divine intervention in the workings of the weather, and in the health, safety and happiness of living creatures, animal and human.

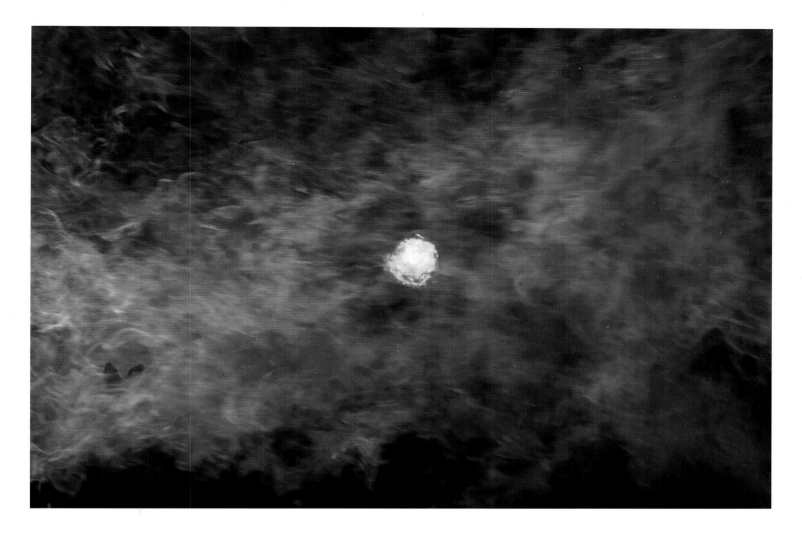

Some people may promise physical sacrifice—fasting, for instance, or temporarily forgoing a favorite food, or undertaking strenuous pilgrimages. Others promise to reform a personal habit, such as smoking or gambling or sleeping too late. Still others make offerings in the form of flowers, food, and water provided for temple or household gods; monetary donations to churches, mosques, and synagogues; and good deeds performed on the behalf of the less fortunate.

Throughout much of the first millennium, the Maya of Mexico's Yucatan Peninsula believed that to receive the blessings of rain, they should propitiate Chac, the god who lived in the depths of Chichen Itza's sacred cenote. This freshwater pool is traditionally considered the dwelling place of the gods. Portrayed in Maya art with fangs, bulging eyes, and a long, curved nose, Chac was later known as the famous *chacmool*, the reclining figure who has come to symbolize Chichen Itza, one of the principal centers of ancient Maya civilization. Staring to one side, the stone statue balances a bowl for offerings on his stomach between his chest and bent knees.

Explorations four miles east of Chichen Itza in 1959 revealed a cave whose depths had not been plumbed for centuries. In it lay more than 600 artifacts of pottery—bowls, figurines, incense holders, some dating back to 1000 A.D. Details of design and construction suggested that the cache

OPPOSITE: The Minoans of ancient Crete may have revered the snake goddess as the mother who renews life.
ABOVE: Fire—which early people sought to control through religion—rages in Yellowstone National Park.
FOLLOWING PAGES: Creator and destroyer, water—seen here, the Zambezi River in Zambia—inspired rituals and myths.

represented gifts left in the cave for Tlaloc, a rain god of the Toltec people who defeated the Maya at Chichen Itza at the end of the first millennium. When citizens from the nearby village heard the news of the discovery, they conducted special ceremonies before archaeologists dismantled the cave. The modern-day Maya told an archaeologist working at the site that the chacs, gods of rain, whose precincts had been violated, and the *balams,* guardians of the cave and the water sources, must be propitiated, not only to avoid retaliation on the individuals who had entered, but to ensure against possible suffering on the part of the entire population of the region.

Other Maya gods have been more voracious in their demands, their believers understanding that they must make ultimate sacrifices, often surrendering their own life or the life of a dear one, in order to placate them and secure their blessings for future generations. According to an account by a 16th-century observer, the powerful men living at Chichen Itza "had the custom, after sixty days of abstinence and fasting, of arriving by daybreak at the mouth of the cenote and throwing into it Indian women belonging to each of [them], at the same time telling these women to ask for their masters a year favorable to his particular needs and desire."

Some of the women, who had been pulled back up from the cenote, reported that they were received below by "many people of their nation" who gave them information as to whether the year would be a favorable one. Some of them, however, never reemerged from the cenote. In the early 19th century, archaeologists explored its depths and brought up copal incense balls—made from the resin of tropical trees—and incense burners, artifacts and jewelry of copper and gold, jade effigies, ceremonial knives, and human bones of men, women, and children: precious people and objects sacrificed in the hope of securing good favor from the gods.

Forces in nature often seem huge, malevolent, and oblivious to human concerns. Dotted across the planet, volcanoes exhibit all the fearsome strength of the natural world in its most awesome and terrifying aspect. On the Big Island of Hawaii, volcanoes have spewed their fiery lava across the landscape and into the surrounding ocean for hundreds of thousands of years. Kilauea, on the southeast slopes of the volcano Mauna Loa, is one of the largest and most active craters in the world.

According to island beliefs it is the home of Madam Pele, a violent and punishing goddess. The sister of a sea goddess and a shark god, Pele was exiled from her birthplace of Tahiti by her father, who could not abide her anger. She set off through the Pacific in a canoe, hounded by her vengeful sister, Namaki.

The two sisters' endless contests formed the Hawaiian Islands. Pele would plunge a stick into the sea, release the lava, and make a fiery pit in which to live. Jealous Namaki would create tidal waves,

dowse the fire, and turn the lava to rock. Pele traveled from one place to another and finally settled on the Big Island. Its massive mountain, Mauna Loa, was so tall that there she could live untouched by Namaki's waves.

Now deep in Kilauea, Pele remains a watchful goddess, ever ready to erupt in anger. She moves among humans on the island, dancing and flirting, often accompanied by her white dog, but she becomes furious when a lover spurns her. She wrangles especially with Poliahu, goddess of snow, who dwells on the nearly 14,000-foot peaks of Mauna Kea and Mauna Loa. Pele has come to embody the social conscience of the island's human culture, and may erupt in response to human cruelty, greed, or pride, and especially to the misconception that humans can equal or surpass the gods in understanding or power. To such hubris, according to island myths, she responds with an outburst of fiery lava, dense smoke, and smothering ash. The people of Hawaii place leis of tropical ferns and flowers on the lava rock all over the island, especially near active steam vents. With these gifts they express their humble respect for the goddess and the hope that Madam Pele will respond compassionately and spare them.

This link between the natural world, the moral order, and divine power is expressed in the story of Thor, the god of thunder, from the Norse sagas of Scandinavia and Iceland. Every roll of thunder meant that he was in heaven, wielding his hammer against his foes. Thrown far by Thor to strike down an enemy, the magical hammer would circle back and return to the hand of its owner. He also used it honorifically, hallowing things and people with its touch. Thor battled endlessly with Jörmungand, the world serpent and symbol of evil. The sagas predict that they will kill each other in Ragnarök, Old Norse for the Doom of the Gods, a coming time of darkness, winter, and chaos, when the sun will dim, the stars will vanish, and the earth will sink burning into the sea. Only the just will survive, living in a great hall of gold. For the time

OPPOSITE: *Greek gods dwelt on a mythic mountain called Olympus, possibly Mytikas in northern Greece.*

ABOVE: *Lord of the seas, the Greek god Poseidon was thought to stir the waves into storms and shake the earth.*

FOLLOWING PAGES: *Undulating along a rocky ridge in Ohio, the Great Serpent Mound probably dates from the 11th century.*

being, though, the universe is characterized by the constant strife between Thor and evil, and the thunder made by Thor's hammer still reverberates through the skies.

SPIRIT ANIMALS

FROM THE earliest of times, humans have respected the animals living around them as embodiments of a greater power. Individual animals were often seen as expressions of a unique spirit. An eagle embodies the spirit of Eagle, a bear the essence of Bear. Each spirit animal is the source and ultimate realization of qualities found in the living animal. To win these spirits as allies in the struggle against the unknown, humans have sought to establish sacred relationships with them and their animal forms. The Kwakiutl and other American Indian tribes of the Pacific Northwest are famous for carving totems—stout, straight logs cut into an imposing stack of stylized animal heads: raven, frog, mink, whale, fox, bear. Among them often stand fantastical animal characters, such as Sisiutl, out of whose antennaed head sprang two serpents.

In Kwakiatl rituals, dancers covered their bodies with fur or woven grass robes and wore painted wooden masks that echoed the animal faces on the poles. By wearing a mask, the believer moved into the identity of the spirit or god, thus accessing its power.

A Kwakiutl crane mask collected by the American anthropologist Franz Boas measured more than five feet to the end of its narrow beak. The dancer performed complex footwork while working the mask, opening and closing the huge beak in time with the beat of the drum. The crane spirit was feared as a cannibal hunter of men, and its central place in winter ceremonials provided an opportunity for the tribe to accept the fate of death.

The dancer performed the part of the cannibal crane for the sake of his tribe. By taking on its threatening nature, he enacted a reconciliation between death and the living, who gained strength as a community by witnessing the ceremony.

The raven played an important role in those cultures where it shared the landscape, especially in the northern reaches of North America and Asia. In Raven these native cultures saw both a creator and a trickster—a reasonable interpretation of the bird itself, whose call sounds intelligent but whose behavior can be pesky.

The Koryaks, who lived on the Kamchatka Peninsula of far northeastern Siberia, told a myth that explained the darkness of the winter solstice through Raven's behavior. Raven Man and Little Bird Man were vying for the hand of Big Raven's daughter, Yinyé-a-nyúet. When Little Bird Man won her heart, Raven Man swallowed the sun. Yinyé-a-nyúet went to Raven Man, who greeted her with a shut beak. She tickled him under the wing. When he laughed, his mouth opened and out popped the sun.

Ravens inhabit spirit worlds all along the North Pacific coast of North America, as evidenced by artifacts—dance rattles, masks, and drums, for example—from the Haida of the Queen Charlotte Islands, including one remarkable rattle carved in the shape of a man reclining on the back of a raven and sticking his tongue into the mouth of a frog. Frogs, considered allies to both ravens and humans, helped the two species communicate. They also conveyed magic tokens and potions to tribal leaders, as this one was doing—mouth-to-mouth.

Domesticated animals have embodied spiritual power in the religions of humankind as well. Egyptians associated cats with the sun god, Ra, who was constantly on the look-out for another attack from Apophis, the demon serpent. Each time the serpent captured Ra and dragged him into the underworld, the world cycled through another night of darkness. Wall paintings represented their cosmic struggle with an image of a cat attacking a snake. The ancient

OPPOSITE: Buried with its owner, this bird-shaped vessel was found in a tomb of the Moche people of Peru.
FOLLOWING PAGES: On a temple wall in Chiapas, Mexico, a Maya ruler and his warriors lord it over captives.

Egyptians also revered Bastet, a goddess with a cat's head and a woman's body, representing the radiant strength of the sun, fearsome and protective at the same time. Along the trade routes to the Middle East and Asia stood Bubastis—near today's Zagazig in Lower Egypt—where devotees gathered at a splendid red granite temple for the annual festival in honor of Bastet. A cat necropolis was situated near the temple. There mummified cats, some laid in ornamented sarcophagi, were entombed.

SPIRIT BEINGS

VISIONARY EXPERIENCES often came about through animal guidance into the spirit world. Into the 19th century, the Yahgan people of Tierra del Fuego, Chile, had never seen visitors from other cultures. They lived in simple grass huts and paddled canoes out into the rough Pacific Ocean, living on fish and mussels, gulls and their eggs, porpoises, seals, and, occasionally, whales. They first saw civilization in the form of the *Beagle,* which brought not only naturalist Charles Darwin but also a Catholic priest, Martin Gusinde, to their shores. "A man could be strolling alone along the seashore, lost in dreamland, without thought or purpose," recorded Father Gusinde,

when he would suddenly find himself in the midst of a visionary spectacle of what are known as asikaku, *"apparitions." Around him crowds an immeasurable company of herrings, whales, swordfish, vultures, cormorants, gulls, and other creatures. All are addressing him in flattering terms, respectfully, in the most friendly way; and he is beside himself, has no idea what is happening. His whole body numb, he drops to the ground and lies there without moving.*

ABOVE: *Fending off evil spirits, Ainu men and women of northern Japan imitate the dancing of cranes.*

His soul (his kespix), is consorting with the spirits, and feeling, while among them, an inordinate joy.

Returning home, still somewhat in a daze, the man would fall into bed, Father Gusinde related. The animals approached him in his dream as well. "There is one that is being especially amiable, in the most extravagantly attentive way," wrote Gusinde. That one animal becomes the shaman's familiar, his special guide into the world of the spirits of nature.

Historians use the word "animism," from the Latin *anima* or soul, to describe the religious beliefs of those who feel that spirits live in the phenomena of nature. That state of mind was clearly expressed in the conversation, recorded by Alexander von Humboldt in 1795, between a Christian missionary and an Indian in the Orinoco Valley of Venezuela. "Your God keeps himself shut up in a house, as if he were old and infirm," said the Indian. "Ours is in the forest, in the fields, and on the mountains of Sipapu, whence the rains come."

The Celtic people of pre-Christian Northern Europe revered the power dwelling in trees and associated particular deities with indigenous plant species. Cerridwen, the white moon goddess, inhabited the pale-barked birch. The fruit-bearing rowan was sacred to the goddess Brigit. The Celts saw the oak as a tree of male strength, the abode of the god of thunderstorms.

By the third century B.C., the Druids, a sect of male magic-workers, grew out of these Celtic traditions. The coming of Christianity meant the decline of Celtic rites, although early Christians found ways to weave its symbolism into their rituals. Canterbury Cathedral, built and rebuilt on a Celtic worship site in southeastern England, contains as many as 70 sculptural interpretations of the Green Man, a central Celtic spirit-figure represented as a man with a face and body sprouting leaves. To celebrate the birth of Jesus, Christians borrowed the symbols of holly—Celtic tree of the waning year, honored for its evergreen leaves—and ivy, the Celtic vine of resurrection, since it quickly revives after winter. In modern times, the Christmas traditon of decorating an evergreen tree with lights and ornaments also grew out of Celtic tree worship.

The Hopi Indians of the American Southwest believe in a world populated by hundreds of kachina, or spirits, each associated with a plant, animal, natural phenomenon, or legend. Examples include Mongwa, the great horned owl; Palik Mana, the butterfly; and Honan, the badger. Others are Koyemsi or Mudhead, symbolizing the earth, and Koshari, the Hano Clown. For religious ceremonies, dancers wear brilliant costumes matching the characteristics of each kachina. Dancers wearing Hano's headdresses and his black and white stripes painted on their bodies are at liberty to spoof and jostle, in keeping with his trickster personality. The Hopi give their children kachina dolls in traditional dress as good-luck charms. The dolls hang from the rafters of Hopi pueblo homes, guaranteeing blessings from the spirits for the whole family.

CLEANSING RITUALS

RELIGIOUS CEREMONIES often began—and still do—with special preparations that distinguish a sacred act from the ordinary routine and express respect for the spiritual realm. Everyday garments must be removed and replaced with special clothing or headgear. These may take the form of vestments worn by the officiant, such as a priest's white surplice. Worshipers may don veils or skullcaps, prayer shawls or fine clothing. Special marks or colors may be put on the body. Sometimes these are temporary—chalk, flour, or plant dyes. Sometimes they are permanent—tattoos applied, scars inflicted, as part of the ceremony—and will remain for the rest of that individual's lifetime as reminders of that sacred ceremony.

Often worshipers begin services with cleansing rituals, based on systems of belief that see human life as limited, dependent, and impure compared with powerful and transcendent forces, which stand forth as ideals of perfection and purity beyond human reach.

In the Catholic faith, worshipers entering a church dip fingers in holy water blessed by a priest, a purifying act before making the sign of the cross and asking God's blessing. In many Christian denominations, the body must be baptized, a form of spiritual rebirth in which the individual is cleansed of sin before being formally accepted into the faith. This sacrament may occur shortly after birth, in a ceremony in which the infant's head is sprinkled with baptismal water, or may take place later in life, in some faiths involving full immersion of the body in a sacred font or blessed river.

Muslims wash before entering a mosque and ensure that the area for prayer is clean at home and elsewhere by using a prayer rug.

Ancient precursors to modern-day Hinduism regarded both bathing in water and burning in fire as methods of ritual purification and preparation for approaching the gods. The ruins of the Indus Valley city of Mohenjo Daro include a large bathing pool in a central location, presumed by archaeologists to be a place for cleansing the body in preparation for worship in the temple.

Later, the Aryans laid fires in which they sacrificed animals. Invoking Agni, the mouth of the sacred flame, they watched the smoke rise from the offerings and the glowing incense. In that smoke they saw their gifts and prayers ascending to the gods. Their first sacrifice, though, was Purusha, the giant creator god. After creating the world and all its beings, he consumed himself in the fire of creation. Priests reenacted his sacrifice in rituals to renew and sustain the world order.

SACRED PLACES

IN MANY religious traditions, among them those of the Hindus, early Greeks, Chinese, and the Shintos of Japan, the earth is considered sacred in and of itself. In the western prophetic traditions, certain places on the earth must be consecrated, made holy, and then be commemorated as such with the building of a temple, church, or shrine upon the site. In still other traditions, particular places were respected as sacred—geographical configurations where humans sensed a closer contact with the divine. Certain springs, rivers, grottoes, caves, rocks, and mountains took on special significance. Profane attributes could not be allowed in such places.

At the foot of Greece's Mount Parnassus, rising 2,000 feet above the Gulf of Corinth, an abundant spring feeds a tributary of the Cephissus River. Those who worshiped there considered themselves to be at the navel of the earth. Traces of religious activity at this site date back to the Mycenaeans early in the first millennium B.C. They believed that Python, the serpent son of Mother Earth, guarded the central cave.

Athenians took over the shrine in the eighth century B.C., believing that their god Apollo had killed Python and reenacting the battle between them every eight years. They built a temple to Apollo nearby and inside erected a hive-shaped omphalos, a stone symbol indicating that this site, called Delphi, was the center of the world. Worshipers cleansed themselves ritually, brought sacrifices to Apollo, and consulted the famous oracle there, a priestess whose ecstatic states connected her with the divine. Returning to the human realm, she revealed the gods' will in prophecies about the fates of citizens and rulers.

Perhaps the oracle's most famous prophecy was that of Oedipus, the legendary king of Thebes, who was fated to kill his father and marry his mother. Familiar to all in ancient Greece, his tragic story is known to us today through the plays of Sophocles.

At the border between today's Israel and Syria, at the base of Mount Hermon, a nature preserve protects the forested streams and waterfalls, primary headwaters of the Jordan River, which were likely honored in times before

OPPOSITE: *Carved from red cedar, the totem poles of America's Northwest Indians proclaimed status and honored ancestors.*
FOLLOWING PAGES: *With smoke and frenzy, Kwakiutl Indians dance to make a monster give back the eclipsed moon.*

THE GLOBAL RESURGENCE OF RELIGION

—JOHN L. ESPOSITO, *Georgetown University*

FROM EARLIEST times, religion—its beliefs, rituals, prophets, scriptures, and traditions—has played a significant and often critical role in human history. Originally, all major religions were holistic in approach, not restricting themselves to individuals, but assuming a powerful role in society as well. In the Post-Enlightenment period, the tendency developed to restrict religion to private life. By the mid-20th century, there were those who not only believed in the separation of church and state, a principle embraced by America's Founding Fathers, but who also saw secularization of society—politically, economically, legally and educationally—as necessary for modernization. Theologians

spoke of demythologizing the Scriptures for the modern age. Intellectual sophistication often was judged according to a secular liberalism that seemed antithetical to religion. The choice faced by developing countries appeared limited to the polar dichotomies of tradition and modernity.

All of this changed in the late 20th century. A global resurgence of religion and the impact of politicized religion, reversing what many had seen as an inexorable process of modernization, have been evident in most parts of the world. Christianity, for example, which has witnessed a steep decline in some European countries, such as Great Britain, Germany, and France, is growing rapidly in Asia, Africa, and Latin America. In the United States, presidents, corporate leaders, and athletes freely discuss their faith in the media; and prayer breakfasts sponsored by legislators and titans of industry are commonplace.

This resurgence of faith has been especially evident in international politics. A potent mix of religion, nationalism, and ethnicity has proved to be an enduring source of both unity and conflict, polarizing populations and fueling discord, from Northern Ireland to Bosnia and Kosovo, Somalia and Rwanda, Iran, Iraq, Lebanon, Kashmir, and Sri Lanka. Indeed, much is now made of a "desecularization of society" as religion is recognized ever more as a key factor in domestic, transnational, and international relations.

Iran's Islamic revolution in 1978-79 spotlighted a contemporary Islamic revival. From North Africa to Southeast Asia, Islam reemerged as a major force in both political and

ABOVE: *In a candlelight service, worshipers express reverence to God.*

social development. Radical Islamic movements engaged in a campaign of violence to destabilize or overthrow governments. Moderate Islamists, espousing the desecularization of society, emerged as major social and political activists.

In Israel, religious leaders and parties have been courted by and critical of prospective prime ministers and ruling governments. Orthodox rabbis have sought to expand their influence over Israeli laws and society. Religion informed claims to territory and settlements, and governments have had to deal with fundamentalists and violent extremists.

In Latin America, Catholic liberation theology, with its emphasis on "preferential option for the poor," informed attempts at social and political reform. Christian base communities sprouted across Brazil, Nicaragua, El Salvador, Columbia, and Venezuela. In Poland and Eastern Europe, Christian churches were also instrumental in reform, where they played a significant role in the fall of Communism.

The challenge of religious nationalism has also been evident in the conflict between Buddhist Sinhalese and Hindu Tamils in Sri Lanka. India, a secular state, has experienced multiple conflicts that are motivated by religious nationalism, from Sikh demands for independence in Punjab to a Muslim uprising in Kashmir. A Hindu nationalist party, the BJP, became the dominant Indian political party, governing until 2004. In Central Asia a reemerging Muslim nationalism has been matched by new religio-political impulses in the Russian Orthodox Church.

This resurgence is not only a religious, but also a social and political awakening; it is a quest for identity, authenticity, and community, and a desire to establish meaning in personal and public life. Many have returned to their religious tradition, reaffirming the relevance not only for the next life, but also for this one. Revivalists of the three Abrahamic faiths hope to re-Islamize, re-Christianize, or re-Judaize their societies. Similar movements can be found in Hinduism, Buddhism, and other faiths.

Most religious revivalist movements share a return to the cornerstones of faith. They reemphasize the primacy of divine sovereignty and the divine-human covenant, the centrality of faith, human stewardship, and the equality of all within the community of believers. They reread Scripture, and look to the lives of founders and to the example of the early faith community. Social injustice, repression, and violence drives many to houses of worship, where the message of Scripture speaks to their desperate situation. Major religious events are reinterpreted— to demonstrate their relevance to modern conditions—and serve as sources for divine guidance and liberation from oppression.

Our world continues to reveal the two faces of religion, its transcendent side and its dark reflection. Religion continues to grow and to become more relevant in the lives of individuals. Yet, religion has caused division within its traditions, fueling debates over social policies. Its dark side, violence and terror, has been apparent in conflicts from Egypt to Indonesia. The terrorist attacks of September 11, 2001 and their aftermath have revealed the depth of hate and its global implications. It is critical to appreciate the extent to which religion is coupled with political and economic issues, often used to legitimize and mobilize. Theologies of hate exist in many faiths today and threaten the moral and social fabric of societies. They are evident in the rise of anti-Semitism, Islamaphobia, and conflicts between religious communities in many parts of the world.

In a matter of decades, Islam, Hinduism, and Buddhism have become prominently woven into the tapestry of Western society. The realities of globalization require mutual understanding and respect, informed by knowledge of the faiths and religious histories of our fellow citizens.

recorded history. Uniquely refreshing even in the summer heat, this area in the third century B.C. was renowned as a center for worshiping Pan, a god of the Greeks, half-man, half-goat, able to provide fertility among the flocks and evoke fear—"panic" comes from his name—among humans. At this site, springs burst out of rock grottoes and pooled up inside the shadowy caves. Worshipers offered their sacrificial gifts to Pan by throwing them into the primary grotto. Niches carved in nearby rock walls can still be seen today. They once held statuary of Pan, his lover, Echo, and his father, Hermes, messenger of the gods. The name of today's nearby village of Banias, Syria, is a variation on his name.

SACRED TIMES

WITH THE turn of the seasons, certain times came to be held as sacred, the holy days on which ordinary business ceased and all people concentrated on their relationship with the powers in the spirit world. In regions far enough from the equator to notice the changing of the seasons, the spring and autumn equinoxes, and the summer and winter solstices have been observed since ancient times. Stonehenge, the monumental stone circle on England's Salisbury Plain, was built between 2500 and 1900 B.C. with stones imported to a site already in ritual use for as long as a thousand years before. The complicated layout appears to have been designed to make the most of the light at the time of the summer equinox, when the sun at dawn creates a remarkable interplay of rocks and shadows.

The Celts, inheritors of the Stonehenge tradition, divided a calendar into eight parts: the two equinoxes, the two solstices, and halfway points in between—Samhain, summer's end, November 1; Imbolc, winter's end, time for the storyteller, February 1; Beltane, May Day; and Lughnasadh, the festival of light, August 1. Each one of the eight holidays was celebrated with a different ritual feast or ceremony.

The ancient Greeks explained the change of seasons in the story of Demeter, the goddess of the harvest, especially responsible for grain. From her Roman name, Ceres, comes the English word "cereal." She lived with Zeus and the pantheon of gods who inhabited Mount Olympus. Some people see in her Greek name the root word for mother, suggesting she evolved from an even earlier goddess, a type of Mother Earth.

Demeter's daughter, Persephone—also called Kore, the virgin—was kidnapped by a god who did not live on Olympus. Hephaestus, god of the forge and lord of the dead, lived in Hades, the shadowy underworld on the far side of the River Styx. According to the ancient Greeks, the boatman Charon ferried the dead from this side of the world across the river to the underworld. Mythologically, Styx was the eldest child of Oceanus, the ancient river that circled the world and whose underground channels formed the known rivers. Geographically, the Styx was today's Krathis River, which plunges 600 feet down rocky Mount Chelmos and courses wildly through a gorge in the northern Peloponnesus. "The stream that falls from the crag by Nonakris drops first of all on to a high rock and down through the rock into the river Krathis," wrote the second-century author Pausanias in his *Description of Greece.* "Its water is death to men and all animals." Across this river and into his nether realm, Hephaestus carried his new bride.

Grieving for the loss of her daughter, Demeter lost interest in the crops and the seasons, so no grain grew. She wandered to Eleusis, an ancient Attican city with an unnavigable bay to the south and rich fields all around. In the time that this myth was held to be true, around 1000 B.C., Eleusis was the most important Greek city after Athens and its port of Piraeus.

Zeus, anxious to see mortals harvesting the fields once again, persuaded Hephaestus to allow Persephone to spend two-thirds of the year with her mother. During that time, the plants grew, blossomed and bore fruit. In the

OPPOSITE: Hammurapi (right) believed he ruled Babylon with a mandate from ancient gods to enlighten the land.

months when Persephone returned to the underworld, the earth grew cold, and the plants withered, lying dormant until the following year, when she again returned to the land of the living.

At Eleusis, an annual cycle of Demeter-focused rituals developed to mark the important points in a year in agriculture: plowing, planting, sprouting, full growth, harvest, and threshing. This cycle has marked the seasons of human life for ten thousand years.

Nature's turning points of each day—morning, noon, afternoon, sunset, and evening—are also important markers in ritual, especially for prayer, reminding Mulims, for example, to make their devotions five times a day, Jews three times—morning, noon, and evening—and Christians in the morning and at night.

THE SEASONS OF LIFE

SEASONAL CEREMONIES provide a sense of control and a promise of return. Ceremonies marking the seasons of human life delineate passages in the progress of a person's relationship to the community and the divine powers. When a child is born, the instinct in any social circle is to welcome her or him into the community. In most cultures, there is also a special ceremony to ask God for protection of the child.

Among the Blood Indians of Saskatchewan, Canada, part of the Blackfeet Federation, a male elder performed a naming ceremony when a child was born. He purified himself with fragrant burning sweetgrass, then marked the infant's face with tribal signs, red ocher lines below the eyes and above the lips. He lifted the baby up ceremonially and showed it to the sun, chanting and singing songs that ask for the sun's radiant light to guide and protect the new member of the tribe.

Coming-of-age celebrations mark the passage from childhood into adulthood in many societies. Adult males

among the Pende people of Zaire led the boys coming to manhood each year to an initiation camp, set apart from the village. The men donned striped costumes woven of bark and raffia, with full skirts of straw surrounding neck, waist, wrists, and ankles. Some wore horned headdresses, some exaggerated artificial eyes. The costumes of these *minganji*, as the presiding elders are called, emphasized their special connection to the spirits of the dead. They danced ominously with and around the initiates, finally leading them back into the village and pronouncing them men.

Followers of Candomblé, a tradition brought to Brazil by Africans who practiced Yoruba Voodoo, believe that only when an *orixa*, a spirit, calls a young man, is it time to initiate him into the religion. Then the young man is isolated for six months. Believers say that he enters a trance world, becoming a horse ridden by a god. In a designated cult house, male and female priests pour the blood of a goat and scatter the feathers of seven fowl over his shaved head. After these chastening ceremonies, the community greets the young man with a festival that celebrates the renewed communion of Brazilians with their African past.

Many rituals around the world mark women's coming of age as well. One of the most glorious is the Apache sunrise ceremony, performed by Native Americans in the Southwest, who celebrate by supporting the young woman as she reenacts their myth of the origin of the world. During the 96-hour ritual, the young woman wears splendid robes with long white fringe, a colorful scarf, and a neckpiece of beads and feathers. Her family selects a godmother —an elder woman to guide her through this passage. They prepare a mix of white clay and cornmeal and pour it over the young woman's head, caking her hair and staining her dress for the entire ceremony. She is later dowsed with bright yellow cattail pollen, symbol of fertility. Dancing, chanting, and praying go on for four nights. At certain points in the ceremony, the young initiate runs in the four cardinal directions; at dawn she runs toward the rising sun.

OPPOSITE: *The Inca carved Machu Picchu, a ceremonial city in the sky, from the gray granite of the Andes in Peru.*

Her godmother kneads her body, singing of its changes. "Now you are entering the world," she sings. "You become an adult with responsibilities.… Walk with honor and dignity…for you will become the mother of a nation."

In Bali, where Hinduism mingles with ancient local tradition, puberty is the time of life when young women and men undergo tooth filing. The ceremony called *mepandes* or *metatah,* performed by a man born into the priestly caste, is a necessary preparation for marriage. Male and female participants are dressed elegantly for the occasion, in colorful fabric brocaded with gold. Boys wear a sword; girls wear flowers; both wear special makeup. To begin, the priest cracks open a yellow coconut and sanctifies it as the ceremonial spittoon. Incense and floral essence fill the air. The priest uses a file to flatten the fanglike upper canines and remove the evil beast inherent in humanity. He chisels and files the four upper teeth between the canines. All attending understand that the six teeth symbolize the six human weaknesses—lust, greed, anger, drunkenness, ignorance, and jealousy—and that after the tooth-filing ceremony, the young people have been cleansed, and are ready to take on adult responsibilities. The boys and girls spit the filing dust into the sacred coconut, which is later buried in the family temple, its power still close at hand.

Other rites of passage include the Christian Confirmation, the Jewish Bar Mitzvah and Bat Mitzvah, and the Hindu thread initiation ceremony, in which young people accept the religious duties and obligations of an adult.

The union of two people in marriage has required since earliest times a blessing in a religious ceremony and sanction by the community. Wedding rituals are always joyous and elaborate. The bride is often dressed in white, symbolic of her sexual purity. The bridal veil has been traced back at least to the time of ancient Rome, where brides covered their whole body with a red veil before they arrived at their wedding. To remove the veil is to reveal and give herself to her husband. In many ceremonies, it is the husband who lifts the veil. History records the presence of flowers and other symbols of fecundity.

Muslim brides in Syria carried bouquets of fragrant orange flowers. In ancient Greece, brides held sheaves of wheat and wore crowns of holly. Another recurrent theme is the community's wish for fertility: Rice, wheat, corn, or other dried grains are tossed upon the couple as they emerge from the wedding ceremony. A wedding cake or pie has been central to the celebration for centuries. Middle Eastern accounts from the first millennium B.C. describe the newlyweds sharing a sesame-seed pie. Or, family members would strew bits of wedding cake in the marriage bed.

During the complex marriage rituals of Java, where Islam mingles with native spirit religions, the couple receives two bowls, one with white rice and one with yellow. Together they combine the two kinds of rice and then feed each other.

DEATH AND ITS MEANING

RELIGIOUS CEREMONIES mark each step in the progress of a human life, but none so solemnly and extravagantly as death, the ultimate mystery and the fueling force of many devotional practices. Whether seen in dreams, conjured up through belief, or witnessed through actual contact, the spirits of the dead play vivid roles in many cultures of the past and the present. Many indigenous religions ascribe their own wisdom and power to their ancestors.

The Manu people of the Bismarck Archipelago, northeast of Papua New Guinea, called the spirit of the male head of the household "Sir Ghost" during his lifetime. After his death, they mounted his skull at the door, so he could continue to protect and judge the household. The burial practices of the Thonga people in Mozambique and South Africa include ceremonies within the village which introduce the deceased to the ancestors.

OPPOSITE: *Offerings to the rain god were placed in the bowl held by* chacmool *at Mexico's Chichen Itza.*

The neighboring Zulu believe that for a time after his burial, an old man's spirit wanders in the veldt, then reappears as a snake in the village, a sign that he has joined the ancestors. It is to the ancestors that the Zulu dance and give offerings, believing that they are the source of barrenness or fertility, drought or rain, pestilence or a good harvest.

The first day of November, a time in the Northern Hemisphere when nature itself has begun to die, is a traditional time to remember the spirits of the dead. The American holiday of Halloween, quite disconnected from religious ceremony, is a vestige of early Samhain observations by which the Celts defended against the coming dark with bonfires blazing into the night. Roman conquerors extended the holy day to two days, combining respect for the dead with a harvest festival in honor of Pomona, the goddess of fruits and trees. As Christians gained control of the British Isles, they reinterpreted the pagan holidays by calling November 1 All Saints' Day, honoring the saints and martyrs of their religion, followed by All Souls' Day. Many still observed October 31 as All Hallows' Evening—shortend to Halloween.

Similarly, on the first two days of November, Mexicans observe the Day of the Dead, *Dia de los Muertos.* Believing that at this time of the year the spirits of the dead return to their households, Mexican families set out lavish altars with candles, wreaths, flowers, and an array of food prepared only for this holiday, especially *pan de muertos,* the bread of the dead, kneaded into the shape of bones and human figures representing souls. Other families picnic at relatives' graves. Gleeful fireworks call the faithful to a solemn mass.

While the Mexican Day of the Dead incorporates Christian symbols and celebrations, it probably represents, like Halloween, an assimilation of earlier local practices.

Many cultures refined the use of fragrant embalming spices and resins, as much for the sake of the living as the dead, so that the bodies of deceased family members could be enshrined in homes for a period of time. In some cultures, relatives returned in a certain number of months or years, performing a second ceremony of respect to store the bones. Cremation practices in India and Europe date from the Neolithic era or earlier. In ancient Rome, the bodies of the noble dead were displayed for a few days or as long as a week before cremation, while those of the lower classes were usually cremated a day after death. In the fifth century B.C., the Roman senate banned cremation within the city limits, but the practice continued, with a procession of mourners and musicians carrying the corpse outside city walls to burn it on a pyre. The ashen remains were saved in a jar. Wealthy Romans subscribed to funeral societies, paying monthly dues to ensure that their funerary urns would end up in *columbaria,* protected underground vaults where the family could install a memorial plaque.

Middle Eastern cultures tended to prefer underground burial to cremation, an inclination that influenced Judaism, Christianity, and Islam. One exception arose among the Zoroastrians of ancient Persia, whose descendants, Iranian and Indian Parsees, followed ancient practices with the bodies of their dead. In 1895, the American author Samuel Clemens—better known as Mark Twain—traveled to Africa, India, and beyond. In India, he witnessed a Parsee crowd of mourners who watched a procession of corpse-bearers, clad in white, carrying their beloved's body to its final resting place, the Tower of Silence. "We have the Grave, the Tomb, the Mausoleum, God's Acre, the Cemetery," Twain wrote in *Following the Equator,* "but we have no name that is so majestic as

that one, or lingers upon the ear with such deep and haunting pathos.

"When the mourners had reached the neighborhood of the Tower—neither they nor any other human being but the bearers of the dead must approach within thirty feet of it—they turned and went back to one of the prayer-houses within the gates, to pray for the spirit of their dead. The bearers unlocked the Tower's sole door and disappeared from view within. In a little while they came out bringing the bier and the white covering-cloth, and locked the door again. Then the ring of vultures rose, flapping their wings, and swooped down into the Tower to devour the body. Nothing was left of it but a clean-picked skeleton when they flocked out again a few minutes afterward."

The bones are left in the Tower of Silence for weeks, washed by rain and bleached by equatorial sun. Then the corpse-bearers return and throw the bones down into the tower's well. A skeleton is "never seen again, never touched again, in the world." Twain explains that, to the Zoroastrians, corpses were unclean. None but those assigned the lifelong job of corpse-bearer were allowed to touch them, and even those men wore all-new garments every time they performed their job. Death levels all in society: "The bones of the rich, the poor, the illustrious and the obscure are flung into the common well together," wrote Twain.

Some traditions tell that the human race was once immortal and that death itself is a judgment pronounced by the gods for some basic wrongdoing. A Pygmy tribe of Central Africa told the story that in the beginning there was one man, Masupa, who had two sons and one daughter. From one son descended the Pygmies; from the other descended a neighboring tribe. The daughter was assigned the household tasks of fetching water and wood. They lived happily, commanded by their father to follow just one rule: They must never look upon him, never see him. His daughter delivered water and wood, routinely leaving it just outside

OPPOSITE: *Passed over a ritual fire, an Australian Aborigine child is baptized with pungent smoke.*

FOLLOWING PAGES: *Dancers representing spirits from the grave distract Zambian boys from the pain of circumcision, a coming-of-age rite.*

his door, until one day her curiosity got the better of her. She hid behind a post at her father's doorstep, and as he reached out to grab the water pot, she saw his arm, richly ornamented as no ordinary man's would be.

Masupa was furious. He called his three children to his house and, still unseen, informed them that he must now depart, leaving them to a life of hard work and misery. He gave them tools and weapons and taught them how to forge iron. He told his daughter that of the three of them, she would experience the most pain, suffering through childbirth. Masupa left secretly, still unseen, moving down the river. Soon the daughter gave birth to her first child. She named him Death-Is-Coming. He died two days later. From then on, no one escaped the fate of death.

REALMS BEYOND DEATH

SOME CULTURES invented ways to preserve the bodies of the dead. The Egyptians in the third millennium B.C., the Inca in the 15th century A.D., the Aborigines in Australia's Torres Strait in recent times—all practiced their own procedures of mummification. Of all the world's civilizations, the ancient Egyptians most vividly represent a people who honored their dead with complex burial rites and awe-inspiring tombs. The Egyptian pantheon included a host of interconnected gods. Ra, god of the sun, created Shu, god of the air, and Tefnut, goddess of moisture. They in turn gave birth to Geb, god of the earth, and Nut, goddess of the sky, whose children included Isis and Osiris. The pharaoh stood between humans and gods, responsible to bring divine order to the world below. In his lifetime, he was seen to be the incarnation of Horus, son of Isis and Osiris, often portrayed with a falcon's head. After death the pharaoh merged with Osiris, considered not only the god of fertility but also the god of the dead.

An individual was composed of several parts, the ancient Egyptians believed, including the *ren* or name,

the *ba* or soul, the *ka* or internal life force, and the *akh*— the eternal spirit, which left the body after death and returned to live among the gods in the stars. The ka remained behind and therefore deserved special treatment after death, especially on behalf of an elevated personage such as the pharaoh or a member of the royal family. The body was mummified following procedures that blended technical knowhow with religious belief. When Osiris was killed by his jealous brother, Seth, his sister and wife, Isis, gathered the pieces of his body, wrapped them together in linen, and brought him back to life. Every time Egyptian high priests embalmed and wrapped the body of a pharaoh, they reenacted the myth, believing that the resident akh would soon live again with the gods.

By the 13th century B.C., during Egypt's New Kingdom, a text called the *Book of the Dead,* inscribed on the walls of a tomb, codified the progress from death into the afterlife. The dead travel on a river through the underworld. The jackal-faced god, Anubis, weighs the soul of the deceased against the feather of truth. Only those souls light of heart—that is, righteous and honest in their earthly behavior—will proceed to the heavenly realm. Those who are judged worthy and survive the perils of the voyage through the underworld will rise at the next day's dawn with Ra, the sun god—perhaps civilization's earliest promise of an eternal life after death. In images of the scene of judgment, there is always a little bird with a human face—the ba, or soul, of the person being judged—perched on the scales, waiting for the verdict.

Other cultures prepared for the unknown after death by describing the passages the departed travel through and the experiences they undergo. According to Daoist traditions, dead souls descended to hell and had to endure hardships to atone for their sins. During the Northern and Southern dynasties of China, in the fifth and sixth centuries A.D., the Daoist hell was the realm of the Emperor Fengdu, a netherworld of incredible dimensions where mountains

OPPOSITE: *The mummy of an Inca boy, sacrificed to the gods, carried gifts and extra sandals on his journey to the next world.*

rose 2,600 miles high and spread 30,000 miles around. There the souls of the dead traveled to face the judgment of the great emperor. He paid attention to the activities of the dead person's living relatives, for their ritual offerings could incline him to judge a soul more leniently and exact less hard work before allowing it to go to heaven.

A century later, during the Tang dynasty, a new and even more complicated tradition emerged, very likely an elaboration of a Hindu myth. According to this belief, the future of the dead was determined by ten kings, the Yamas of the Ten Halls, each one responsible for one sector out of the full panoply of souls arriving. An overarching Yama-King—represented in Tibetan Buddhist iconography with a ferocious fanged face, hair aflame, and six arms—greets the dead in the first hall and, making a first judgment, sends each on to the proper hall of reckoning. One soul, judged a dishonest intermediary in his former life, may go to Ice Hell, the second hall. Another, judged lustful, might be sent to the Wailing Hell, the fifth hall. Those lacking in filial piety file into the eighth hall, Grand Noisy Hell.

Only those whom the Lord Yama-King recognizes as truly virtuous may go to the tenth hall, where they begin to prepare for transmigration, the movement of a soul back into a new life and body. On the way, a deity named Mongpo feeds the soul bound for a new life a magic potion to erase all memories of the past. During the Ming and Qing dynasties, from the 14th to the 19th century, these visions of hell and judgment so moved the Chinese people that they would address their worship and bountiful offerings to the Yamas upon the death of any loved one, since the efforts of their supplication might improve the future lot of the deceased.

RELIGION AND CULTURE

THROUGHOUT THE ages, groups of people united by a sense of shared identity and history have approached the unknown or transcendent through their common myths, beliefs, and ritual practices. Normative rules for morality and behavior mold community. From the narrative tableaux that depict the births, life adventures, unions, conflicts, and deaths of gods, human beings learn about the world and their place in it.

Effective answers to those questions intrinsic to human consciousness lie in the mythic cycles of indigenous practices, but also in the oral and scriptural traditions of the world's religions.

The characteristics of God, gods, or spirits mirror the fears and hopes of humans in society. Leaders of the community play central roles, often assuming the part of intermediary between the human and spirit worlds. Ritual celebrations engage all the senses with color, movement, music, rhythm, and fragrance. Some ceremonies occur in reverent, mournful, or ominous silence, while others boil over with noise and energetic activity, joyous or frightful. Intricate masks and costumes are created or passed through generations just for these special occasions. In religious ceremony, people join together to gain new energy and renew shared identities in a circle of believing.

When Spanish conquistadores arrived in the New World, they encountered not only treasures, fertile land, and indigenous people but also complex cultures beyond their ken, woven together with myths and ritual practices like nothing they had ever seen in Europe or the Middle East. Troops led by Francisco Pizarro entered Cajamarca, Peru, in 1532. The Incan culture that they encountered was only 300 years old. Atahuallpa, the leader captured by Pizarro, was counted as the 13th in the Inca royal lineage, descending from Inti, the omnipotent sun god, and Pachamama, the earth goddess. Every king inherited the title *Sapan Intiq Churin,* Only Son of the Sun, along with royal headdresses, robes, and objects made from the gold found in regions of western and southern Peru and still being mined today. The Inca king sat on a throne of gold in the dazzling Temple of the Sun, also plated with gold. Priests tended the temple and performed frequent rituals. Women took vows of chastity and joined in the priestly rites. They were called virgins of the sun.

Inti Raymi, the feast of the sun, was celebrated each year at the winter solstice, which in the Southern Hemisphere represents the time when the sun rises highest and stays longest in the sky (as the seasons are reversed from those of the Northern Hemisphere). As the Inca people gathered around, singing songs of ceremony and praise, the Son of the Sun lifted golden tumblers filled with *chicha,* maize beer. He poured some out as a gift to Inti, drank some himself, then offered some to the nobles of his court.

Next he witnessed his high priest performing a holy sacrifice, using a golden knife to slice open the chest of a chosen all-black or all-white llama and divine the fortunes of the next year in the animal's still-throbbing heart. The high priest then used a brilliantly polished gold medallion to focus the sun's rays and light a sacramental fire. Conquering Spaniards banned the festival of Inti Raymi in 1572. Today the Quechua, Peru's Inca descendants, reaffirm their kinship with the sun by reenacting the ceremony in Cuzco every summer.

A poignant example of how religious vision and ceremony can build a sense of community is found in the North American Indian Ghost Dance of the early 20th century. At a time when native cultures across the West were being decimated by hostile white settlers and the United States military, a leader rose up named Wovoka, a Paiute Indian in Nevada. During a solar eclipse in 1889, he fell into a trance. Returning to consciousness, he explained that he had visited heaven, where the Indian ancestors lived in plenitude and peace. He returned with instructions for his people: They were to live harmoniously, work hard, and perform a religious ceremony called the Ghost Dance. "I want you to dance every six weeks," read a transcript of his message, written down at a school for Indian children in Carlisle, Pennsylvania. "Do not refuse to work for the whites and do not make any trouble with them until you leave them," he advised. "When the time comes there will be no more sickness and everyone will be young again."

Wovoka's mystical promise spread quickly through the tribes of the American West, most of whom were by that time living on government-run reservations. The Lakota of the Dakota Territory recast the message in a militant way. By performing the Ghost Dance, they believed, they could make all whites disappear, bring the ancestors back to Earth, and replenish the buffalo—a sacred animal, source of food, clothing, shelter—brought nearly to extinction within a few decades after the arrival of the white man.

Z. A. Parker, a teacher from the Pine Ridge Reservation in the Dakota Territory, recorded her observations of a Ghost Dance ceremony there in June 1890. As many as 300 tents formed a circle around a central dance ground, in the middle of which grew a large pine tree "which was covered with strips of cloth of various colors, eagle feathers, stuffed birds, claws, and horns—all offerings to the Great Spirit."

The dance was led by medicine men and by those "who had been so fortunate as to have had visions" in which they spoke to departed friends and ancestors. Men and women wore special ceremonial robes hung with feathers and painted with "birds, bows and arrows, sun, moon, and stars, and everything they saw in nature." Between 300 and 400 people, Parker counted, danced in a ring to the sound of drumbeats. They laid their hands on the shoulder of the next person in the circle, singing the words, "Father, I come." Next, she recorded,

> *they stopped marching, but remained in the circle, and set up the most fearful, heart-piercing wails I ever heard—crying, moaning, groaning, and shrieking out their grief, and naming over their departed friends and relatives, at the same time taking up handfuls of dust at their feet, washing their hands in it, and throwing it over their heads. Finally, they raised their eyes to heaven, their hands clasped high above their heads, and stood straight and perfectly still, invoking the power of the Great Spirit to allow them to see and talk with their people who had died.*

This was just the beginning. The ceremony continued for five days, punctuated by ritual cleansing in a nearby river. Many participants swooned into unconsciousness.

The others eagerly awaited their return to waking life to see if they, like Wovoka, had reached the heavenly land of the dead. The frenzy of the dance, its anti-white implications, and the powerful sense of community that it mustered, all threatened U.S. government officials, who responded by staging the final act in their takeover of Indian Territory: the massacre at Wounded Knee.

RELIGIONS
PAST AND PRESENT

THE HUMAN family shares many experiences, no matter what the period of history, no matter what the culture or country. As a man looks out into the world, he sees things he does not control or understand, forces that can overwhelm him with their strength and inexorability. As a woman looks into past and future, she recognizes that she and all the members of her family will face the inevitabilities of human life: joy and sorrow, pain and pleasure, sickness and health, birth and death. So many givens in the human condition lie beyond our ken, yet it is the nature of the human consciousness to seek knowledge and to establish patterns that make the future more predictable.

Since the dawn of humankind, religion has been a source of comfort and provided answers for many of the fundamental existential questions posed by thinking human beings: *Who am I? Why am I here? How should I behave? Does it matter how I behave? Do I matter? What can I hope for in this lifetime? What can I hope for after I die?* Many of these drives and satisfactions, found in all religions from all times, connect intimately with those essential to the established religions now predominant in the world today.

The religious impulse accompanied the earliest of developments that make human beings what they are today: language, social organization, the use of symbols to express and record thought. Momentous changes in religious practice parallel the major shifts in human civilization. The transition from nomadic and hunter-gatherer cultures to settled agricultural life took place between 4000 and 3000 B.C., notably in the fertile river valleys of the Tigris and Euphrates in Mesopotamia, the Nile in Egypt, and the Indus in Asia. As humans clustered in an agricultural existence, cities grew, and trade developed, generating written records, city-focused leadership and administration, a code of law, public works—and centralized religious institutions. Artifacts from ancient Sumer, considered the world's first civilization, reveal the intertwining of these new features of human life. A clay tablet impressed with cuneiform marks dated to about 2350 B.C. records the pilgrimage of one ruler's wife from her city of Girsu—now called Tello, an Iraqian site much excavated by archaeologists. She visited six temples, honored 13 gods, and to them offered goats, sheep, and lambs.

The ancient Mesopotamian ruler of Babylon, Hammurapi, anchored the authority of his code of law, written around 1780 B.C., to the ancient gods. He traced his power back to Anu the Sublime and Bel, the lord of heaven and earth, through Marduk, granted dominion over earthly man by Ea, God of righteousness. It was Anu and Bel who founded the city of Babylon as "an everlasting kingdom, whose foundations are laid so solidly as those of heaven and earth," and it was Anu and Bel who "called by name me, Hammurapi, the exalted prince, who feared God, to bring about the rule of righteousness in the land, to destroy the wicked and the evil-doers . . . and enlighten the land."

Thus all the laws expressed in Hammurapi's famous code—regarding crime, divorce, adoption, inheritance, military obligations, interest rates, scales for fees and wages—all come from the primeval gods through the worldly leader. Through much of early history, religion and state entwined inextricably. Many scholars believe that the rising eminence of solitary rulers in cities with vast wealth and territorial dominion encouraged the emergence of monotheism, the belief in one supreme divine being.

Religions and their moral code have shaped the history of the world. This book concentrates on five of the world's great religions: Hinduism, Buddhism, Judaism, Christianity, and Islam. While exact numbers are difficult to ascertain, authoritative estimates suggest that as of the year 2000, those practicing these religions represented about 77 percent of the nearly six billion people in the world, and nearly 90 percent of those who practice any religion whatsoever. An exploration of their histories and beliefs begins in the river valleys considered the cradles of civilization. From these regions, through thousands of years, the great religions emerged, evolving through twists and turns and changes also to be understood through the interactions of human beings and their physical environments.

From earliest times, human beings have sought to understand the forces of nature, the dynamics of their interactions with the environment, and the larger meaning of the life they live. In many ways, they have sought a map of reality—grounded in, harmonious with, but never limited to the geography of the world around them.

Contemporary religious beliefs and practices also arose in specific times and places. Just as the beliefs and rituals of indigenous traditions clearly connected with their place of origin, responding to their historical, social and geographic contexts, so too the religions featured in this book are rooted in the particular places in which they began and developed. An appreciation of the geography of religion, its origins and development, reveals important insights and lessons about the enduring significance of religious beliefs and cultures in so many parts of our world. □

OPPOSITE: Ladders to heaven, the Pyramids at Giza were meant to help entombed pharaohs join the sun god after death.
FOLLOWING PAGES: Heads of Greco-Persian gods stand sentinel at a royal funeral mound at Nemrud Dagi, Turkey.

A SPECIAL PLACE

ITS JUTTING chin personifying power, a massive *moai,* one of nearly 900, rises against the stark landscape of one of the most isolated places on earth—Easter Island, or Rapa Nui, in the South Pacific *(above).* Who carved these statues, and why? And how did these people transport the megaliths, which weigh an average of 14 tons? Although the answers are still somewhat shrouded in mystery, archaeologists think that the island's Polynesian inhabitants shaped the giant statues from rough volcanic rock to honor their ancestors, and that the moai helped mediate between people and the gods, earth and sky.

Rock art *(right)* decorates the entrance to an Easter Island cave. Seven moai *(following pages)* look down on an *ahu,* a plaza where rituals and dancing were performed.

Like tombstones on a hill, giant statues dot the slopes of a defunct volcano *(below)*. Easter Islanders chipped at the volcano's soft rock with heavy stone picks to shape the moai, leaving some unfinished at the volcano's

summit. Beneath rocks carved with the image of a creature half bird and half man *(opposite)*, young men from each clan would scramble down steep cliffs for an annual swimming race to the small isle of Motu Nui. On the islet, they competed to find the season's first egg from the Sooty Tern. The winner presented the egg to his clan representative, who assumed the status title of Birdman, or *Tangata Manu*, the creator god's surrogate on earth.

HINDUISM

Who is without beginning or end, in the midst of disorder;

who is the creator of the universe displaying various forms;

who, alone, encompasses the universe—when someone

recognizes him as God, he is freed from all fetters.

— SVETASVATARA UPANISHAD

HINDUISM

FOR THOUSANDS of years, the Hindu faithful have started the
day by greeting the river. Mindful of its history, its symbolism,
its life-giving force, the Hindu steps into the cool, fresh water,
pressing palms together and uttering an ancient prayer, seeking
a state of cleanliness in body, mind, and spirit. That water—
an element that can be neither made nor destroyed by human
hands—links the Hindu of today back to the beginning of time
and the beginning of belief.

OPPOSITE: *Where the Ganges River meets the Bay of Bengal, a devotee greets sunrise with a prayer.*
PRECEDING PAGES: *Mist hangs over the sacred Ganges, obscuring Varanasi, a spiritual center for Hindus.*

TWO OF the world's great religions, Hinduism and Buddhism, came into being on the Asian subcontinent of India. Of the five major religions, Hinduism is the oldest. Versatile, flexible, and absorbent, it has adapted to people's needs in different landscapes, times, and cultures.

In so many ways, the Hindu religion is like the land from which it sprang: a massive whole, yet within itself containing many diverse parts. The Indian subcontinent is bounded to the north by an arc of daunting mountains and to the south by one of the great oceans. Two river systems dominate the geography of the interior. Both figure prominently in the history of Hinduism: the Indus River to the west, ancient birthplace of the religion, and the Ganges River to the east, greatest of all rivers to Hindus.

The territory of the Indian subcontinent has been divided many ways over time, into tribal domains, princely states, and empires. The people living in these lands speak hundreds of languages. An age-old caste system divides the population into classes. Caste designations and regional origins are expressed in family names. For millions, though, the Hindu religion unites them.

Of the population of India, estimated at just over one billion people in 2003, more than 800 million practice the many paths of Hinduism—a population representing the vast majority of Hindus worldwide. Hinduism is also practiced in regions near India and in those to which Indians have migrated, such as the southeastern Caribbean, East Africa, Southeast Asia, the cities of Europe and North America, and Austral-Asia. Through millennia, the Hindu tradition has proved capable of incorporating within itself many divergent beliefs and practices. It has always been a religion of many gods, many colors, many festivals. The soul itself, in the Hindu tradition, cycles through several lives, and the spark of divinity shows itself in many different living beings, from the lowliest insect to a great spiritual leader. Amid all these vectors of diversity, Hinduism has the power to unify believers with each other, the world in

which they live, and the divinity found within, around, and beyond them—called Brahma, the One.

THE RIVER VALLEYS

THE STORY of Hinduism begins along the Indus River. ("Hindu," or "Sindhu," was originally a geographical term, meaning Indus River, later extended to mean the land around it and its people.) The Indus flows southwest from the heights of Kashmir through today's Pakistan and empties, 1,800 miles from its source, into the Arabian Sea. West of the river rises the Sulaiman Range and farther northwest the Hindu Kush. To the east stretches the Great Indian Desert. Nomads gravitated to the hospitable valley of the river, where fertile soil and reliable water sources supported permanent dwellings. Here—as in the Middle East at about the same time, in the valley of the Tigris and Euphrates Rivers—one of the world's early civilizations arose.

In the 1920s, archaeologists working in the Indus River Valley unearthed architecture and artifacts that revealed sophisticated cities and a culture dating back 4,500 years. More than 300 sites have since been identified, stretching from Allahdino, at the mouth of the Indus near modern-day Karachi, Pakistan, to Manda, more than 400 miles north on the Chenab River, west to Sutkagen Dor, near Iran, and east to Lothal, at the top of the Gulf of Cambay near the Sabarma River in India. The principal sites are the cities of Mohenjo Daro and Harappa, the latter giving its name to this early culture. All indicators suggest that the Harappan culture rose to a level of sophistication equaling that of Sumer and Egypt.

Ruins at Mohenjo Daro date to the third millennium B.C. There, paved streets are laid out in an organized grid around a central mound, called the Citadel by early discoverers. Designed to stand well above the flood level of the Indus, the complex was built of fired bricks and includes granaries, assembly halls, and a large raised reservoir

OPPOSITE: *Hindus, hoping for spiritual cleansing through the holy waters of the Ganges, bathe at the river's edge in Varanasi.*

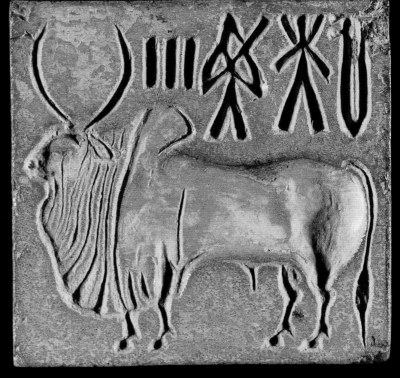

approached by wide stone walkways—archaeologists dubbed it the Great Bath—that was perhaps used for ritual purposes. The city's population is estimated to have peaked at 35,000 to 40,000. Wells and a drainage system suggest that the entire city was provided with water. Excavation finds at Harappa, 300 miles north, reveal a similarly complex culture, evolving over two millennia.

Artifacts unearthed at Harappan sites are intriguing. Tools and weapons were fashioned from stone, copper, and bronze. A four-inch bronze figurine of a girl, clad only in a necklace and arm bangles, poses on long, slender legs. Other figurines sit with legs crossed and hands touching knees symmetrically, suggesting a pose later formalized in Hindu and Buddhist meditative practice. Most fascinating are the thousands of seals, one to two inches square, made of steatite, or soapstone. Presumably they were used to stamp soft clay as a signature or mark of ownership. The Harappan seals are carved with lettering not yet deciphered by linguists, and with images, primarily of animals—ox, bull, elephant, tiger, rhinoceros—but occasionally a human figure. No objects or structures that can be unambiguously associated with religion have been discovered in the Harappan sites along the Indus River, but cultural clues lead archaeologists to interpret their finds as precursors to later well-known imagery and beliefs.

Drastic change affected the Harappan cities in the middle of the second millennium B.C. Historians have long believed that invaders decimated the populations or drove them east, but it is also possible that changes in climate caused drought, altered the course of rivers, disturbed irrigation networks, and forced a migration out of the Indus River Valley. Earthquakes may have caused severe upheavals and interrupted the flow of the Indus. Whatever happened, by 1500 B.C. new waves of people had moved into the region from Central Asia. They called themselves Aryan, the word for "noble" or "pure" in the precursor to Sanskrit.

The Aryan culture mingled with the vestiges of existing Harappan civilization and spread east into the valley of India's other great river, the Ganges. Much of what we know about these people and their way of life has been learned from the Vedas, an ancient canon of hymns and recitations considered the world's first holy scripture. Flowering throughout central and northern India for most of the first millennium B.C., Vedic civilization forms an underlayer of Hindu belief and practice.

THE FIRST HOLY BOOKS

HINDUS BELIEVE that the Vedas, their ancient holy books, have existed eternally. They reveal eternal truths and wisdom passed down through the ages. Scholars consider them a composite work dating from 1200 B.C. or earlier and surviving by oral tradition until being written down nearly two thousand years later. There are four Vedas. The Rig Veda, oldest of all, and the Sama Veda are collections of laudatory hymns to deities. The Yajur Veda is a manual for performing rituals. The Atharva Veda, compiled later, contains prayers and charms for health and good fortune.

"In the beginning the Golden Embryo stirred and evolved," reads one of the creation hymns of the Rig Veda. "Once born he was the one Lord of every being; this heaven and earth did he sustain.... What god shall we revere with the oblation?" *Recognize many gods,* appears to be the answer to this rhetorical question: Varuna, who "by the power of his pure will upholds aloft the cosmic tree's high crown"; Indra, "who created the sun, the dawn, and who guides the waters"; Rudra, "wielder of the bolt"; Vishnu, associated with the sun; and Agni, associated with fire, "well kindled, nobly fed." The rivers of India appear as goddesses; reigning above them is Sarasvati, "whose limitless unbroken flood, swift-moving with a rapid rush, comes onward with tempestuous roar." This now nonexistent river may have

OPPOSITE: Animals, people in meditative poses, and early forms of writing adorn tiles made by the Harappans of 2000 B.C.
FOLLOWING PAGES: Rows of ruins at Mohenjo Daro reflect the rigid social order of the ancient culture of the Indus Valley.

been a tributary of the Indus, originating in the Himalaya, flowing westerly, and skirting the Great Indian Desert.

Hymn after hymn names and distinguishes the many gods and goddesses of the Vedic universe, frequently associated with things and forces of the natural world. The rain and the floods are often addressed, reflecting the life-and-death powers of the South Asian rivers, swelling over their banks in monsoon season. "May the Floods' Child accept my songs with favor," pleads one hymn of the Rig Veda. "Will not the rapid Son of Waters make them lovely?" Another beseeches "mighty Heaven and Earth" to "stand pouring out their rain, exhaustless."

Many Vedic hymns address Soma, a god associated with an intoxicating plant juice. Out of the ten books of the Rig Veda, one is devoted entirely to hymns to Soma. "O Soma flowing on thy way," reads one, "make us better than we are." Lengthy recitations, expressing devotion and aspirations for greater wisdom, were spoken as the celebrant prepared and ingested the soma or put it into the fire as a gift to the gods. While the poetry about soma has come down through time from the ancient Vedic priesthood, the botanical identity of this plant remains a mystery. Numerous hypotheses have been offered, including rhubarb, marijuana, grain distilled into brandy, and the hallucinogenic Amanita mushroom.

Less debatable in the Vedic ritual world is the role of fire, which transports offerings to the gods. Hundreds of hymns in the Rig Veda address Agni, the fire god. "O Agni, radiant One, to whom the holy oil is poured, burn up our enemies whom fiends protect," the Vedic priests intoned. Judging from its prominence in this holy canon, sacrificial ritual was central to ancient Vedic practices. Oil, sap-rich plants, straw, and animals—even dogs and horses— were offered as food to the gods to gain their favor for peacetime harvests and wartime victories. Placed into a ceremonially prepared fire, the physical bulk of these gifts would be consumed, their essence carried as smoke to the gods above. Detailed rules are laid out in the Yajur Veda: To ask for offspring, a hornless goat should be sacrificed; for cattle, one of a triplet of goats; for prosperity, a spotted beast. Often, the Vedas advise that sacrifices be made to specific gods for specific purposes. "He who is long ill from an unknown cause should offer to Prajapati a beast without horns," directs one, referring to the god whose name comes from the Sanskrit for "lord of creatures." Echoes of these ancient practices remain today. Although Hindus concentrate their daily attentions on a local or household deity, they celebrate other gods as well. For instance, they may visit the shrine of Lakshmi, goddess of wealth and beauty, when hoping to conceive a child.

Indra is the creator god of the Vedas: Aggressive, fierce, and terrifying, yet he is the source of light and water for the world of humans. More hymns are addressed to Indra than to any other of the dozens of gods named in the Rig Veda. Indra is the mighty warrior, riding upon the white elephant, Airavata, who with a dart to the belly slew Vrtra, the Dragon, described as encompassed with darkness. In that same blow, Indra cleaved the rock that Vrtra guarded, out of which flowed the waters of the earth. This one thundering blow separated the heavens from the earth.

Indra and Agni, power and fire, rule over an entire pantheon of gods and demons in the ancient Vedas. This was the worldview transported eastward into the Ganges River Valley by the first millennium B.C., the seedbed from which Hinduism sprang. (Despite its early beginnings, the term Hinduism was not coined until the 19th century.)

THE GANGES RIVER

HINDUS HAVE for ages revered the Ganges as the holiest river. "The Ganga, especially, is the river of India," wrote Jawaharlal Nehru, the country's first prime minister, using the river's ancient name. "She has been a symbol of India's age-long culture and civilization, ever changing, ever

OPPOSITE: *Elephant-headed Ganesha, sitting in relief in the Shiva Temple at Prambanan, helps faithful Hindus start new projects.*

flowing, and yet ever the same Ganga." The river's headwaters originate in an icy cave called Gaumukh, the "Cow's Mouth," downstream from the Gangotri Glacier, which glistens amid the Bhagirathi Peaks of the Himalaya. From an altitude of 13,000 feet, the stream called Bhagirathi plunges through gorges and tumbles down slopes.

Where the Alaknanda merges with the Bhagirathi in the mountains, the Ganges's main stream begins. The Ghaghara, Gandak, Kosi, and Brahmaputra Rivers from the Himalayan highlands, and the Yamuna from central India—all join in. The Ganges measures more than 1,500 miles from headwaters to mouth. The river plunges through its initial one hundred miles, but from Haridwar on it

broadens out into a gently rolling floodplain, its elevation dropping no more than a foot a mile from there all the way to the Indian Ocean. This fertile band is known as the Indo-Gangetic Plain.

Three thousand years ago, those dwelling along the Ganges began the slow process of clearing the forest and turning the soil. Migration to the Ganges and settlement locations may have been guided by the search for deposits of iron ore, which came into use in this area around 700 B.C. With crude metal tools these people cultivated rice, a crop that tolerates the extremes of the monsoon climate. Household devotions amplified their practical successes in the fields. Following the rules laid down by the priests who

ABOVE: *Pilgrims draw warmth from a fire along the Bhagirathi, a revered glacial stream that feeds the Ganges.*
OPPOSITE: *Sunrise strikes icicles at Gaumukh, or "Cow's Mouth," the Himalayan source of the holy Ganges.*

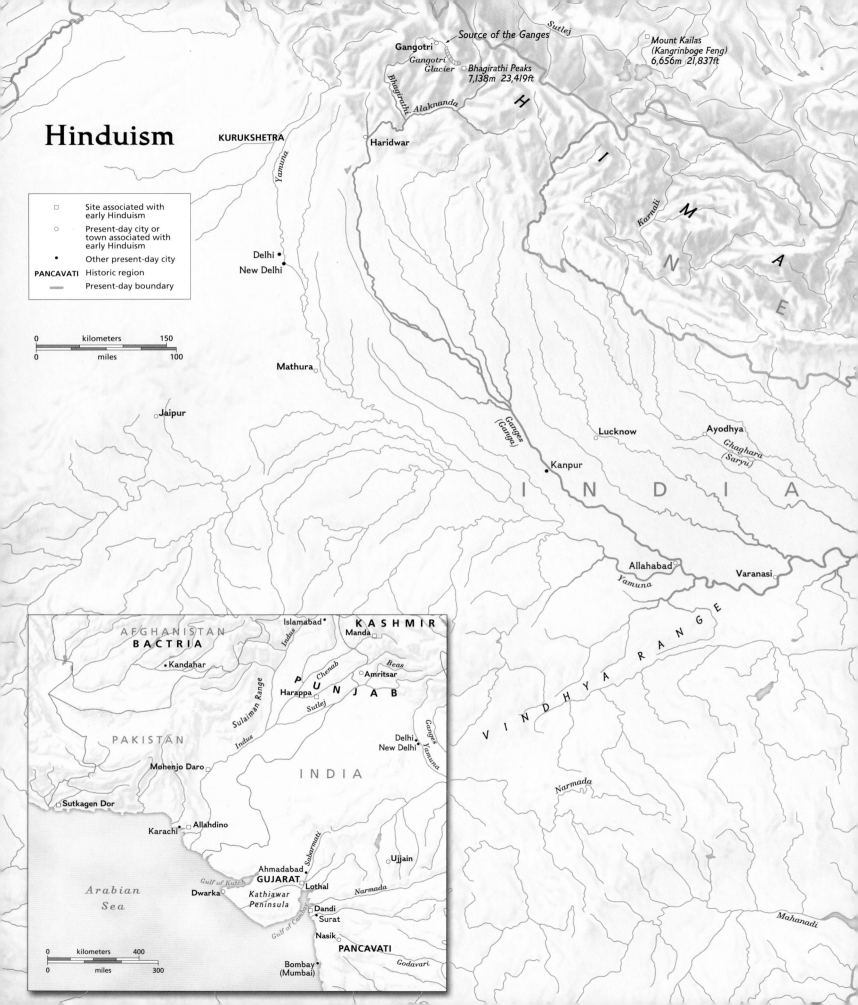

Hinduism

Source of the Ganges

Sutlej

Gangotri

□ Mount Kailas
(Kangrinboge Feng)
6,656m 21,837ft

*Gangotri
Glacier*
□ Bhagirathi Peaks
7,138m 23,419ft

Bhagirathi

Alaknanda

H

KURUKSHETRA

I

Haridwar

M

A

Karnali

L

A

Y

A

□ Site associated with
early Hinduism

○ Present-day city or
town associated with
early Hinduism

• Other present-day city

PANCAVATI Historic region

Present-day boundary

• Delhi
New Delhi

E

0   kilometers   150

0   miles   100

Mathura

Ganges
(Ganga)

○ Lucknow

○ Ayodhya

*Ghaghara
(Saryu)*

• Jaipur

• Kanpur

I

N

D

I

A

Allahabad

Varanasi

Yamuna

V

I

N

D

H

Y

A

R

A

N

G

E

Narmada

Mahanadi

AFGHANISTAN
BACTRIA

• Islamabad

KASHMIR

Indus

Manda □

• Kandahar

Chenab

P

Beas

U

Harappa

N

○ Amritsar

J

A

B

PAKISTAN

Sulaiman Range

Sutlej

Ganges

• Delhi
New Delhi

Yamuna

Indus

• Mohenjo Daro □

I N D I A

• Sutkagen Dor

• Ujjain

□ Allahdino

Karachi •

Narmada

Ahmadabad •

GUJARAT

Sabarmati

□ Lothal

*Arabian
Sea*

Gulf of Kutch

Dwarka ○

*Kathiawar
Peninsula*

Narmada

□ Dandi
• Surat

Gulf of Cambay

Nasik •

0   kilometers   400

PANCAVATI

0   miles   300

Bombay
(Mumbai) •

Godavari

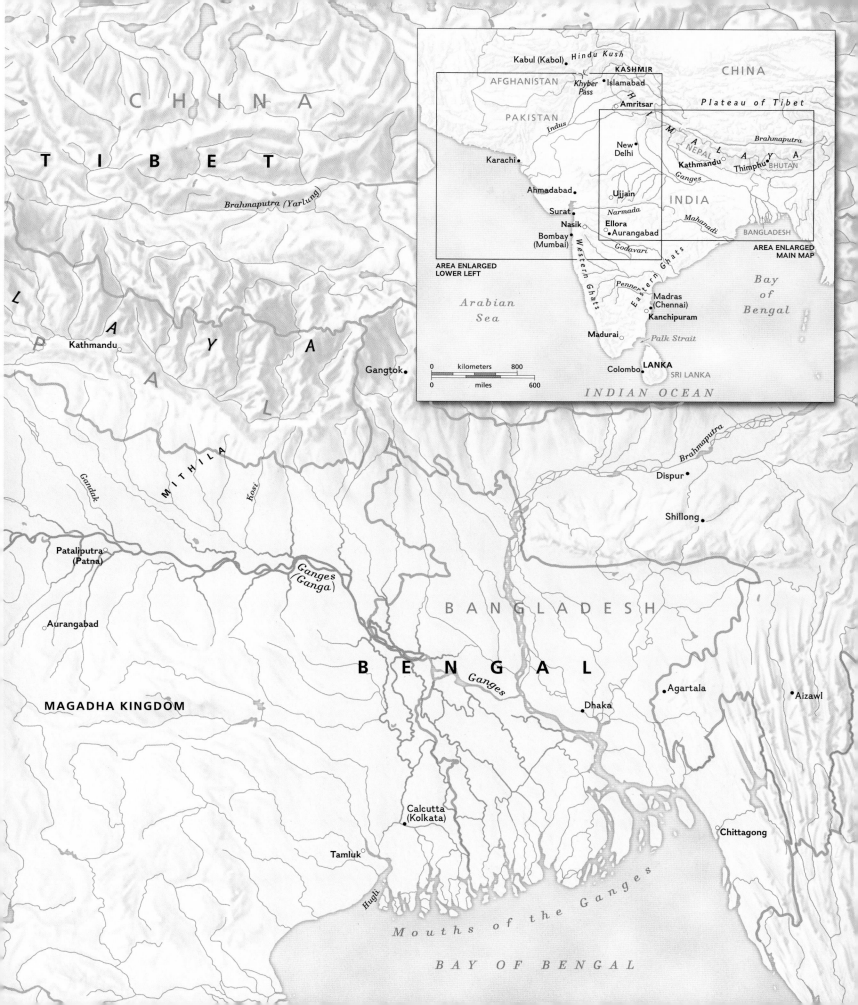

CHINA

TIBET

Brahmaputra (Yarlung)

H I M A L A Y A

Kathmandu

Gangtok

MITHILA

Gandak

Kosi

Pataliputra
(Patna)

Ganges
(Ganga)

Aurangabad

MAGADHA KINGDOM

B A N G L A D E S H

Brahmaputra

Dispur

Shillong

B E N G A L

Ganges

Dhaka

Agartala

Aizawl

Calcutta
(Kolkata)

Tamluk

Chittagong

Hugli

Mouths of the Ganges

BAY OF BENGAL

Kabul (Kabol)   *Hindu Kush*

KASHMIR   CHINA

AFGHANISTAN   *Khyber* Islamabad
                   Pass

PAKISTAN   Amritsar   *Plateau of Tibet*

Indus   *Brahmaputra*

                   New   H I M A L A Y A
Karachi   Delhi   NEPAL
                          Kathmandu Thimphu   BHUTAN
                          Ganges

Ahmadabad   Ujjain   INDIA

Surat   *Narmada*
Nasik   **Ellora**   *Mahanadi*
Bombay   Aurangabad
(Mumbai)   BANGLADESH
                                   Godavari
                    Western Ghats   AREA ENLARGED
AREA ENLARGED   MAIN MAP
LOWER LEFT

Arabian   *Penner* *Eastern Ghats*
Sea   Madras
                             (Chennai)
                   Kanchipuram   *Bay*
                                              of
         Madurai   *Palk Strait*   *Bengal*

0   kilometers   800
                              Colombo **LANKA**
0   miles   600   SRI LANKA

                              INDIAN OCEAN

knew the Vedas, people along the Ganges performed household sacrifices at each turning of the season. The Ganges provided water for crop irrigation but also for drinking, cooking, bathing, laundering—without the river, there would not be life. The cleansing of the body in the river grew beyond a mundane daily obligation into a sacred ritual still performed today.

THE HINDU WAY OF LIFE

THE VEDAS explained the universe in terms of a grand cosmic sacrifice. When the creator god Purusha, "all that yet hath been and all that is to be," was sacrificed, the world of things came forth. This great event resulted in the creation of all animals. Different parts of the sacrificed body became parts of the visible world: The moon came from Purusha's mind, the sun from his eye, the sky from his head, and the earth from his feet. According to this hymn, the four fundamental constituents of the Hindu class system that would for centuries characterize Hinduism and Indian culture also emerged as a result of the sacrifice. When they divided Purusha, how many portions did they make?

> *What do they call his mouth, his arms?*
> *What do they call his thighs and feet?*
> *The Brahman was his mouth, of both his arms*
> *was the Rajanya {Kshatriya} made.*
> *His thighs became the Vaishya, from his feet*
> *the Sudra was produced.*

Holy scripture thereby decreed that there was a hierarchy among people. An individual was born into one of four classes or *varnas,* a Sanskrit word meaning both "class" and "color," which has led some scholars to suggest that age-old racial distinctions underlie India's ancient caste system, but this view is under challenge. Brahmans, or priests, made up the highest varna. Agni, representing fire and sacrifice, was their special god. Brahmans conducted religious rituals, received sacrificial gifts on behalf of the gods, and shared their knowledge of the Vedas. Born to a life of responsibility and privilege, the ancient Brahmans traveled from place to place or attached themselves to wealthy households. There were no designated places of worship, but simple shrines, designating holy ground, often developed into the hub of the community. Rock-cut sanctuaries in caves followed. Public shrines and household altars could be quite simple, always including some lingam, or symbolic focal center. The tradition of the lingam probably took root in a time of phallocentric worship. The word can mean "phallus," and some ancient artifacts are appropriately shaped. It can also mean "sign" or "symbol," and in Hindu practice over the centuries, the lingam evolved into a monolithic rounded shaft set into a cradle, male and female combined, associated with the life-giving force of the god Shiva. An entire repertoire of variations in size, material, and ornamentation has evolved through time, and the lingam remains the focal point in daily worship, or *puja,* of a devotee of Shiva. On a family altar today, as in a household of the Vedic period, even an unusual river stone can serve.

The next highest varna, the Kshatriyas (or Rajanyas), were the men born to be warriors and nobility, specially linked to the god Indra. By the middle of the first millennium B.C., many small kingdoms and even a few republics had developed along the Ganges Valley. Wealth, status, and religious favor went hand in hand. As a member of the Kshatriya class garnered more power, he often contributed capital to build a shrine or temple, thus gaining not only the goodwill of the gods but also of the priests in attendance.

Riverbank cities flourished, chief among them Varanasi. Situated on an auspicious riverbend, this ancient Hindu city has gone by many other names: Kashi, "city of light," or Anandavana, "forest of bliss," in early times;

OPPOSITE: *Smiles greet monsoon rains that bring annual floods to the farming regions of India's river valleys.*

FOLLOWING PAGES: *Cows—sacred to Hindus—ignore pilgrims rowing to Jahangira, a temple to Shiva on an outcropping in the Ganges.*

Benares, in its anglicized form. Settlement grew naturally at this site, just upstream from the confluence of the Varuna and the Ganges. A levee formed by flood deposits along the river's outside curve creates a natural amphitheater. The landform invites worship, so pleasing is it to stand on the western bank of the Ganges and watch the sun rise over the water, so refreshing is it to wade into the slow-moving water, to drink and bathe. More than 70 ghats, or sets of steps, guide the faithful down into the river. Many of these broad stone stairways, with landings big enough to hold shrines and shopkeepers' carts, date back to the 18th century. Daily ablutions, both satisfying and necessary, became codified as religious ritual centuries ago. Throngs still salute the dawn daily by bathing in the Ganges to purify body and soul and to shed all sin. They hope to die in Varanasi in old age and have their ashes strewn in the river to find release from the cycle of rebirth.

According to the ancient caste divisions, most people belonged to the third varna, the Vaishyas. These were the farmers, merchants, and craftsmen. Like the thighs of Purusha, they were the motive and muscle of society. Slaves and serfs belonged to the fourth varna, the Sudra, along with peoples living in conquered territories. Without them, society could not stand or move, and yet like feet, they were unclean and lowly. Two social groups complicate this picture of the universe: Women, who assumed the class status of their fathers and husbands, and those so low that they fell beneath the Sudra. In centuries to come, this group would be called "untouchable;" the preferred term today is Dalit (oppressed).

Boys born into the three higher classes were expected to follow an exemplary life path through four stages of life, or *ashramas*. In the student stage, they learned the ancient physical discipline of yoga—from the Sanskrit "to yoke"—a practice by which one's physical being might be joined with the larger cosmic body. Boys dedicated themselves to study, reciting not only the ancient Vedas but also the growing body of philosophical commentary on those holy books. At the end of this first stage, a boy underwent a coming-of-age ceremony, symbolized by a thread given to him to drape over his left shoulder forever after. This thread-investiture marked a second, spiritual birth. The boy had become a "twice-born" and was entitled to study the Vedas.

Now a young man embarked on his second phase of life, that of the householder. In ancient practice, a wife was selected for him by his family from among the unmarried women in their varna. Hindu marriage ceremonies used by many today recall ancient ritual. Bride and bridegroom are anointed for the event with sandalwood paste and the fragrant yellow oil of turmeric, reputed to aid in fertility. Under a flower-strewn canopy, where a nuptial fire burns, the priest ties a knot, joining bride and groom together by their garments. To invoke the blessing of the gods, he places a gift of *samagree*—an aromatic paste made of crushed sandalwood, herbs, sugar,

OPPOSITE: Burnt offerings rise with the smoke from fire during worship and celebrations as a Hindu priest chants a prayer to the gods.

ABOVE: A phallic lingam exudes the life-giving force of Shiva, the Hindu god of destruction and creation.

FOLLOWING PAGES: A yoga practitioner, holding the tree posture, meditates to a backdrop of peaceful waters and sunrise.

rice, and ghee—into the fire. As the groom faces west and the bride east, the priest utters hymns from the Veda. The couple pours grain into the fire, then walks around it—usually seven times, but in some areas just four—singing the vows. In the most important part of the service, the bride and groom take seven steps together, either forward or around the fire, with each step asking for a different blessing. A prayer for their union concludes the ritual and the couple are husband and wife.

Many Hindu traditions seem designed to be practiced by men, but women have their own rituals as well. In one region of northern India, for example, married women gather at a certain banyan tree, said to be the place where

a devoted wife named Savitri defended her husband from the clutches of Yama, or Death. When Yama insisted it was time for the man to release his soul, Savitri argued heartily. Death, so daunted by her persistence, finally gave Savitri her way. He also granted her three wishes, among them that she give birth to many sons. Hindu women hoping for more children make a pilgrimage to Savitri's banyan tree. They encircle it with cotton thread a sacred 108 times in the hope that Savitri's fortune will be their own.

Once a family was established, the patriarch ideally passed into his third stage of life, called the "forest-dwelling" stage. Now he left his family in the hands of his oldest son and directed his attention entirely to studying the sacred

OPPOSITE: A young man receives a sacred thread, an initiation ceremony, representing the second stage of a life dedicated to Hinduism.

ABOVE: A wedding party brings New Delhi streets to a halt on November 27, a revered date on which thousands of Hindus marry.

texts. While he may never have gone into a forest, his devotion mirrored those great sages who did choose to leave the comfort of a civilized agricultural town and return to the wilderness where, it was believed, they might better commune with the gods.

In the fourth stage of life, he might take this conviction even further, choosing the path of the sadhu, the holy man, renouncing worldly ties to seek Brahman, or God, through asceticism and meditation. (Twice-borns who underwent a special renunciation ritual were called *sannyasis.*) Sadhus walked from town to town, village to village, having forsaken home and family, wealth and possessions. They ate meagerly, depending on donations of food, and found shelter in hermitages. Some wore robes, but others remained naked. Some shaved their hair, others let their locks and beards grow long. Some shaved all but one strand, which was wound up in a knot atop the head.

Several hundred thousand men, and some women, follow the path to become Hindu sadhus in modern times. Their presence on the streets of Indian cities is an everyday reminder of ultimate devotion to one's religion. Not all modern sadhus pass through the householder life-stage: Many are young men electing a monastic lifestyle. Depending on the sect, they follow a prescribed initiation ritual. For

example, one sect's initiates cut staffs from the forest and carry them for the next two days, finally burning them in a sacrificial fire. Others make new clothes together, laying aside their street wear and dying their robes saffron orange, a color said to signify the mind purified of all passions. Some initiation rites deliberately mirror Hindu funeral rituals, for to become a sadhu is to be dead to the everyday world.

When a person died, he or she became destined for the realm of the departed. Those of the higher classes prepared a corpse with oil and herbs and cremated it with meticulous ceremony, returning the body's elements to their cosmic source. Public cremation still predominates as the Hindu world's chosen funerary form. It is considered the last of a lifetime of *samskaras,* or rites of passage. To follow the tradition, a Hindu family prepares the body for cremation at home. They prepare themselves as well: Often the chief mourner, usually the oldest son of the family, shaves his head in respect for the departed. Then, carrying the remains on a wooden frame, the mourners proceed to a publicly designated cremation site. There the body is laid on a pyre, and the chief mourner lights the fire. Participants circle the pyre, chanting mantras from the Vedas. All that remains—bits of bone and ash—is collected afterward and strewn into the holy river. Ten days

ABOVE: *Seeking enlightenment through ritual mortification, a Hindu sadhu, or holy man, meditates while buried in Ganges Delta mud.*
OPPOSITE: *Orange robe and saffron-colored ash on his forehead signify a sadhu, whose life is given to asceticism and meditation.*

after the cremation, the family offers ten *pindas,* or rice balls, to the river, to feed the spirit of the deceased on its travels into the next incarnation.

A belief in reincarnation infuses the entire system of Hinduism. Every living thing, the Hindu believes, has a spirit cycling through many body forms, undergoing a rhythm of repeating births and deaths that could be endless. Through karma, which means "action" in Sanskrit, the deeds of the present life shape the character of the next. A life of generous devotion to the gods will be rewarded in the next incarnation. "As a man acts, as he behaves, so does he become," says one ancient Hindu text. "Whoso does good, becomes good: whoso does evil, becomes evil. By good works a man becomes holy, by evil he becomes evil."

During the first millennium, this doctrine of reincarnation began to emerge in the Ganges Valley. Some historians see it as a response to the growing power of priests and the sacrifices they performed. Men of power and wealth wanted to bank more than one life's share of divine favor, goes one theory, and the promise of future lives offered them that comfort. The promise of life after death began to appear in holy writings in India by about 500 B.C. The doctrine of karma, which came to function as a moral rule guiding present-day life and promising reincarnation, was one of a bundle of new religious ideas now reshaping the ancient Vedic traditions.

As trade and economic stability enriched life in the Ganges Valley, a religious countermovement began. "Frail, in truth, are those boats, the sacrifices," reads one commentary on the Vedas. "Nothing that is eternal can be gained by what is not eternal." Denouncing wealth and sacrificial objects, followers of this new faith chose poverty and turned inward for spiritual reward. The turnabout signals a step toward the Hinduism of today and also marks the starting point for two new religions: Jainism and Buddhism.

Brahmans traveled throughout the Ganges Valley, leading ritual events by reciting and commenting on the ancient texts. Their teachings have come down through history as the next great chapter of Hindu scripture, the Upanishads. Written between 700 and 200 B.C., the Upanishads all share the new concept of one cosmic spirit, infusing the universe and the individual. This cosmic spirit is called Brahma.

"Let a man meditate on mind as Brahma," reads one of the Upanishads, linking what is inside the individual with what pervades the vast universe. "He is my self within the heart, smaller than a corn of rice, smaller than a corn of barley, smaller than a mustard seed, smaller than a canary seed or the kernel of a canary seed. He also is my self within the heart, greater than the earth, greater than the sky, greater than heaven, greater than all these worlds." The seed of Brahma inside each human being is called atman, the soul. The ultimate goal is to experience atman and Brahma as one, which would lead to *moksha,* or ultimate liberation from the cycle of birth, death, and reincarnation.

Under the influence of the Upanishads and other late-first-millennium commentaries, Hinduism developed with an emphasis on spiritual rather than material riches. Animal sacrifice was abandoned under the new concept of ahimsa, which forbade injury to any creature, either by word, thought, or deed. Many ritual practices remained, however: the importance of fire and water, the acts of cleansing and lifting up symbolic gifts to the gods. Brahma, set above the many particular gods of the Vedas, did not replace those gods. Nor did attention to the atman within mean an end to physical ritual. These new ideas represented a larger cosmos within which the wheel of living beings—gods, demons, and humans alike—kept turning. A household deity, a local god, or the many emanations of Shiva simply provided the Hindu with different pathways by which to approach the divine. Even today, the Hindu believer chooses among four paths to spiritual fulfillment: karma yoga, the path of righteous action in the world; jnana yoga, or intellectual inquiry; raja yoga, meditation through physical

OPPOSITE: *Stone stairs leading to the Ganges, the "burning ghats," at Varanasi hold funeral pyres ready to send the dead to their next life.*

WHAT HINDUISM MEANS TO ME

—ARVIND SHARMA, *McGill University*

I MUST have been about eight years old at the time, in India. Throughout the night I had heard the crackling of wireless messages and, when not asleep, vaguely felt the hushed presence of people speaking in whispers. When morning came I witnessed a spurt of activity, especially on the part of people wearing small white caps.

I saw my mother exchange nods with one of them. Thereupon all the children were made to sit around the dining table. We were then told that a great man, who stood for love of God and human-

ity, had been killed the previous night on his way to a prayer meeting and that we should pray that his soul might find peace. We prayed in silence for one serene minute.

At that age one is innocent enough to believe in prayer, and I remember that prayer as the sincerest prayer I have offered either before or since.

Now, with the benefit of hindsight and adulthood, I can put a definite date to that day otherwise lost in the unde-fined expanse of childhood: January 31, 1948. On the pre-vious day, January 30, Mahatma Gandhi had been shot dead on his way to a prayer meeting in Delhi. The white caps, popularized by Gandhi in the 1920s, were made of home-spun cloth to symbolize India's desire for economic and polit-ical independence. Known as Gandhi caps, they were worn by his supporters and members of the Indian National Congress Party.

Hinduism, ever in-definable, is redefined by each generation of Hindus for itself. For my generation its defining figure was Mahatma Gandhi. Our generation shared with him a vision of the future of India, which he articulated as follows:

I should like to see all men, not only in India but in the world, belonging to different faiths, become better people by contact with one another and, if that happens, the world will be a much better place to live in than it is today. I plead for the broadest toleration, and I am working to that end. I ask people to examine every religion from the point of the religionists themselves. I do not expect the India

ABOVE: *Sunset at India's Pushkar Lake silhouettes the roof of the Brahma Temple, dedicated to the Hindu god of creation.*

of my dream to develop one religion, i.e., to be wholly Hindu or wholly Christian or wholly Mussalman, but I want it to be wholly tolerant with its religions working side by side with one another.

An integral part of this vision, then, was religious tolerance. One hears a lot about Hindu tolerance as a Hindu growing up in India, so much so that one begins to take it for granted without even quite understanding its implications. The Gandhian vision was granted a surprising vivacity to me when I read a newspaper account of a conversation between the late Sri Chandrasekhara Bharati, Swami of Sringeri Pitha, near Madras, and an American tourist. The tourist professed a desire to convert to Hinduism, because Christianity had left him unfulfilled.

" 'Indeed, it is unfortunate,' the swami replied, 'but tell me honestly whether you have given it a real chance. Have you fully understood the religion of Christ and lived according to it? Have you been a true Christian and yet found the religion wanting?'

" 'I am afraid I cannot say that, Sir.'

" 'Then we advise you to go and be a true Christian first; live truly by the word of the Lord, and if even then you feel unfulfilled, it will be time to consider what should be done.'

"To put the puzzled American at his ease the sage explained:

" 'It is no freak that you were born a Christian. God ordained it that way because by the *samskara* [improvements] acquired through your actions [karma] in previous births, your soul has taken a pattern which will find its richest fulfillment in the Christian way of life. Therefore your salvation lies there and not in some other religion. What you must change is not your faith but your life.'

" 'Then, Sir', exclaimed the American, beaming with exhilaration, 'your religion consists in making a Christian a better Christian, a Muslim a better Muslim and a Buddhist a better Buddhist. This day I have discovered yet another grand aspect of Hinduism, and I bow to you for having shown me this. Thank you indeed.' "

I thought that this conversation had helped me achieve a deep insight into what was meant by tolerance. I came to realize, however, during my sojourn in the United States that my understanding had not been deep enough, when I heard about Rabbi Richard Rubenstein's encounter with Swami Muktananda, who has numerous followers in the United States. At the time Rabbi Rubenstein had begun to feel dissatisfied with the brand of Judaism he had been following as too limiting for him.

After the rabbi described his situation, the swami turned to him and said: "I hope you don't believe in your religion; I don't believe in mine." He then explained that one's specific religious identity is like a trellis one sets up around a tender plant to protect it. But when the plant becomes a tree, then that trellis might itself begin to come in the way of the tree attaining its full growth. So one should not feel too upset when that happens.

This, however, does not mean that anything goes. When one feels buffeted by the currents of change to which being a Hindu leaves one particularly open, perhaps even vulnerable, one thinks of the following words of Mahatma Gandhi, which remain valid wherever and whenever cultures or civilizations come in contact and even clash: "I want the cultures of all lands to be blown about my house as freely as possible. But I refuse to be blown off my feet by any."

Hinduism will continue to hold me in its spell so long as it shares Gandhi's vision of a "wholly tolerant" India, "with its religions working side by side with one another."

and mental discipline; and bhakti yoga, the path of devotion—the choice of most, focused on Vishnu or Shiva.

Stories spun out over the centuries enriched the tradition by offering further adventures among the gods and goddesses and more accessible discussions of how those stories illuminate the ethics of human life. These diverse texts came to be grouped together as the 18 Puranas, Sanskrit for "ancient lore," and helped to codify Hindu ceremonies, seasonal cycles, and sacred sites.

JAINISM AND THE BIRTH OF BUDDHISM

ABOUT 600 B.C., a son was born into a Kshatriya household in Kundagama, a small town north of the Ganges in the growing Magadha kingdom—the modern state of Bihar. Trained in the ancient religion, Vardhamana must have received the thread of hemp granted ceremonially to a young man of his caste as he reached spiritual maturity. He married, and he and his wife were blessed with a daughter. When he reached the age of 30 it was time to leave his family behind, in the care of his brother, and set out on the next phase of his spiritual path. Wearing just a simple swatch of cotton cloth, he set out south into the dense forests. He found caves for shelter and ate fruits for sustenance. After 12 such years, so it is told, he attained enlightenment. For the next 30 years, this holy man walked barefoot—and, by some versions, naked—through northeast and central India, teaching his beliefs: Renounce worldly goods and pleasures, never harm any living thing, and find spiritual truth by fasting and meditating.

This teacher, later given the name Mahavira, or "great hero," became one of the pivotal figures of the religion called Jainism. A rich body of literature developed during the next few centuries, codifying the beliefs embodied in the life of Mahavira: self-discipline and meditation, vegetarianism, renunciation of worldly goods, and ahimsa—nonviolence.

Jains believe that Mahavira was the 24th in a line of *tirthankaras,* or "ford-builders," who form the bridge from this world into the state of spiritual enlightenment. With no supreme deity, the world of Jainism is populated with a rich and colorful array of tirthankaras and spiritual beings, including the mother goddess Ambika.

The kingdom of Magadha rose in power by expanding into north and central India. Since the sixth century B.C., the Indus River Valley up into the Himalaya had been controlled by Persia. In 327 B.C., Alexander the Great invaded the region from Bactria (today's Afghanistan), but when his troops mutinied he was forced to retreat. Armies under Emperor Chandragupta Maurya followed in 322 B.C., traveling the newly built roadway that would later become the foundation for the Grand Trunk Road from Calcutta to the Khyber Pass, and Mauryan forces conquered the northwestern territories.

Chandragupta's rule signaled the start of a family dynasty that lasted nearly a century and united most of the subcontinent of India. Chandragupta himself, it is said, retired from the throne to a Jain monastery in Svravana Belgola in southwestern India. By then, wandering ascetics had carried the religion down the Eastern Ghats, the ridge of hills overlooking the country's southeastern coastline. They probably dwelt in the caves of southern India, centuries later ornamented with arched entryways and wall sculptures.

Svravana Belgola remains a key pilgrimage site for Jains today, one of four in the south Indian state of Karnataka, where powerful leaders espoused Jainism in the Middle Ages. Overlooking each site is a giant statue of Gommateshvara Bahubali, son of the first tirthankara. He is always represented nude, his legs often entwined with snakes or vines to indicate how long he sat meditating in the wild. The largest of the statues stands above the burial site of Chandragupta, in Svravana Belgola, high in the Western Ghats at the far southern tip of the Indian subcontinent. The single block of granite rises 57 feet and is considered

OPPOSITE: Offerings of milk and spices cascade down the statue of Gommateshvara, a Jain hero of spiritual perfection and fertility.

HINDUISM

SELECTED SCRIPTURES

HINDU SCRIPTURES are divided into *shruti*, what is heard or revealed—the most sacred—and *smirti*, what is remembered. Shruti includes the Vedas, or sacrificial hymns, the Brahmanas that explain them, and the Aranyakas and Upanishads, philosophical and metaphysical speculations about the sacrifice. The Upanishads include the words of Manu, a sage whose ethical code set down the duties of each caste and delineated the stages of life. These texts are collectively called the Vedas. Each sacred book, Hindus believe, holds truth by which men can lead their lives.

THE BRHADARANYAKA UPANISHAD 4:5-8

Every action has its consequence in the concept of karma and rebirth, or transmigration. Traveling through many bodies, a soul reaps in each life what it has sown in the past.

A man who's attached goes with his action,
To that very place to which
His mind and character cling.
Reaching the end of his action
Of whatever he has done in this world—
From that world he returns back to this world,
Back to action.

That is the course of a man who desires. Now a man who does not desire—who is without desires, who is freed from desires, whose desires are fulfilled, whose only desire is his self—his vital functions do not depart. Brahman he is, and to Brahman he goes. On this point there is the following verse:

When they are all banished,
Those desires lurking in one's heart;
Then a mortal becomes immortal,
And attains Brahman in this world.

THE CHANDOGYA UPANISHAD 4:15.5

Now, whether they perform a cremation for such a person or not,
people like him pass into the flame,
from the flame into the day,
from the day into the fortnight of the waxing moon,
from the fortnight of the waxing moon into the six months when the sun moves north,
from these months into the year, from the year into the sun,
from the sun into the moon, and from the moon into the lightning.
Then a person who is not human—he leads them to Brahman.
This is the path to the gods, the path to Brahman.
Those who proceed along this path do not return to this human condition.

THE LAW CODE OF MANU

Wound not others, do no one injury by thought, or deed, utter no word to pain thy fellow creatures.
He who habitually salutes and constantly prays reverence to the aged obtains an increase of four things:
length of life, knowledge, fame, and strength.... Depend not on another, but lean instead on thyself.
True happiness is born of self-reliance.... By falsehood a sacrifice becomes vain; by self-complacency the
reward for austerities is lost; by boasting the goodness of an offering is brought to naught.

the tallest freestanding sculpture in India and perhaps the world. Every 12 years, Svravana Belgola is the site of Mahamastakabhisheka, the principal Jain festival. Thousands of pilgrims climb 700 steps up the hillside to the statue and douse it from head to foot with ghee (clarified butter), vermilion powder, milk, coconut water, turmeric paste, poppy seeds, honey, saffron, gold dust, and silver coins.

About a hundred years after the founder of Jainism began his spiritual wanderings, another young Indian nobleman, named Siddhartha Gautama, left his home to seek new meaning. After years of meditation, he achieved enlightenment and spent the rest of his life traveling and instructing others with his wisdom. His teachings mark the beginning of Buddhism (see Chapter 3).

The two new religions, Jainism and Buddhism, swiftly rose to prominence among those of wealth and influence in India. The Mauryan Empire continued to flourish during the 35-year reign of Chandragupta's grandson, Ashoka, in power from 268 to 233 B.C. A passionate convert to Buddhism, Ashoka's commitment and wealth propelled that religion as it spread from the Mauryan capital of Pataliputra west and south across much of the Indian subcontinent. Temples were built, schools and monasteries established, diminishing the power of the Vedic priesthood.

Trade and invasion continued to bring influences into India from parts of the world never before seen. Mediterranean seafarers brought copper, gold, and slaves from Africa and the Middle East in exchange for Indian gems and tortoiseshell. Traders followed overland routes through Anatolia, Persia, and Afghanistan into India from the West; a pass through China penetrated the Himalaya, leveled off near the mouth of the Ganges, and ended at Tamluk.

The city of Mathura, located on the Yamuna River about 50 miles southeast of Delhi, was a crossroads and resting place on trade routes linking East and West. Mathura saw the constant exchange of wealth and cultures. Craftsmen carved icons out of the indigenous red sandstone. They shifted subject matter to suit customers' beliefs, and Mathura gained fame as a center for religious sculpture. Mathura is considered the place where the first representations of the Buddha became popular. Pieces from this region date back to the first century B.C., and later sculptures represent three religions: Jainism, Buddhism, and Hinduism.

After Ashoka's death, the empire splintered into smaller territories and faced invasions, particularly from the northwest. Amid this ferment, strong voices rose anew, revitalizing the ancient religion with the philosophy central to Hinduism today.

HINDU GODS AND HEROES

MANY BATTLES were waged among tribal warlords in the upper reaches of the Ganges during the first millennium B.C., but one has gripped the Hindu imagination ever after. According to the Sanskrit epic the *Mahabharata,* the Pandavas and the Kauravas, rival factions within one family, met in battle near the town of Kurukshetra, in northwest India. The 18-day war pitted family ties against state obligation and spawned thousands of lines of poetry and philosophy central to the Hindu religion.

As Arjuna, a young warrior on the side of the Pandavas, approached the battlefield in his chariot, he hesitated,

ABOVE: *Carved in stone, a wheel of the solar chariot of Surya, the sun god, adorns the foundation of his temple at Konark.*

horrified to think that he was about to kill family and friends. "Krishna, Krishna," he said to his charioteer, "now as I look on these my kinsmen arrayed for battle, my limbs are weakened.... How can I care for power or pleasure, my own life, even, when all these others, teachers, fathers, grandfathers, uncles, sons and brothers, husbands of sisters …stand here ready to risk blood and wealth in war against us?" He threw down his weapons and refused to fight. As Krishna answered, he revealed himself to be not a lowly charioteer but a divine being. His words on the battleground, urging Arjuna to action with a clear mind, form the poetry of the *Bhagavad Gita,* one of the most accessible and popular holy books of Hinduism. The *Bhagavad Gita* is part of the *Mahabharata,* which consists of more than 100,000 verses and is probably a compilation of multiple works written between 300 B.C. and 300 A.D.

The other great epic of classical Hinduism, the *Ramayana,* is an Indian odyssey, significant for the geography it encompasses. Prince Rama, its main character, leaves his home of Ayodhya, a small northern plains town, just east of today's Faizabad. He ultimately travels 200 miles east to Mithila, a region now straddling the India-Nepal border. Known as the Forest of Honey for its lush abundance, Mithila is also celebrated for its women, who to this day create colorful murals and tapestries. In Mithila, Rama meets the lovely Sita and brings her home to be his wife.

ABOVE: *Sea nymphs plead for mercy from god-hero Krishna as he battles Kaliya, a poisonous serpent in this 14th-century miniature.*
OPPOSITE: *Northern Indians revere Hanuman, the monkey-warrior whose likeness is thought to bring luck to any community.*

Exiled from home by his conspiring stepmother, Rama embarks on a 14-year journey, accompanied by Sita and his brother. Along the way, they frequently take shelter in ashrams, hermitages built for roaming sadhus. In Pancavati, at the northeasternmost reach of Central India's Vindhya Range, a demoness is attracted to Rama and attacks Sita out of jealousy. When Rama's brother lops off the jealous woman's ears and nose, her brothers retaliate, backed by a force of demons. The vengeful ten-headed Ravana, worst of all demons, disguises himself as a wandering ascetic and kidnaps Sita.

Searching for Sita, Rama earns the loyalty of Sugriva, the monkey king of Kishkindhya, which was a place name used both in central India, near Pancavati, and farther southeast, along the Penner River. Sugriva's simian military commander, Hanuman, son of the wind, joins the search for Sita and discovers her in a location named Lanka, far across the sea. Hanuman can fly there, but a bridge must be built so Rama and his army of monkey followers can cross over. Rama rescues Sita and returns to Ayodhya, marking the beginning of the Ram Rajya, a time of peace and harmony considered India's mythical golden age.

Hindus throughout the world relive the story of Rama's search for and successful rescue of Sita in annual festival reenactments, often dramatized with colorful masks or larger-than-life puppets. During the ten-day festival called Dusserah, which takes place in the early fall, pageants climax with the burning of an effigy of Ravana. Diwali, the festival of lights, celebrated as the culmination of Dusserah, commemorates Rama's return to Ayodhya and Krishna's victory over a demon of darkness. Houses throughout India are scrubbed clean and strung with lights in the belief that Lakshmi, the goddess of wealth and prosperity, will bless those that are clean and well lit. Arising in the wee hours, celebrants light candles placed throughout the house in auspicious symbolic designs. They burn sparklers, set off fireworks, visit friends and relatives, and share sweets all around in this time of good cheer, considered the last night of the Hindu year.

It is tempting to interpret Rama's destination as the island of Sri Lanka, reached via the chain of shoals and an ancient bridge across the Palk Strait. That journey would have taken him the length of the Indian subcontinent. Some scholars believe, more conservatively, that the story refers to the town of Lanka in central India. Whichever the case, the *Ramayana* epic intertwines myth and geography, gods and heroes, in an intriguing tale. The text had assumed its final shape by the rise of the Gupta dynasty, which again unified India, from the fourth to the seventh century. Praised as India's classical age for its wealth and commerce, its art and literature, and the influence of its culture on the east, Gupta India remained diverse religiously. Particular regions represented strongholds of Jainism, Buddhism, or current forms of Hinduism. Men of power, instead of choosing one religion, supported several.

In 350 A.D. the glorious Gupta dynasty began when Chandragupta I, of the old Mauryan capital of Pataliputra, acquired territory through marriage and conquest. Soon his realm extended as far west as Allahabad. His son, the great warrior Samudragupta, continued the conquests in all directions, from the Himalaya to the Narmada River and east to the Bay of Bengal. He is said to have performed the ancient horse sacrifice from the Vedas to thank the gods for his defeat of nine kings in the north and twelve kings in the south. The next king in line, Chandragupta II, conquered land to the west and extended the hegemony of the Gupta Empire over the Indian subcontinent.

The Gupta dynasty remained in power until about 600 A.D. Those three centuries represented a time of great cultural flowering and a period during which the multitude of Hindu gods settled into patterns of hierarchy and relationship that continue to this day. Hinduism became a dense fabric of many strands, weaving together mythic stories and cosmic personalities distinguished by their physique, dress,

OPPOSITE: Colorful murals that depict scenes from the Ramayana—*a Hindu heroic epic—are a specialty of the women artists of Mithila.*

accoutrements, and actions. To list the primary gods is to barely begin to reveal the full Hindu pantheon.

Brahma, the supreme deity, possesses four heads. It is said that one day for Brahma is equivalent to 2,160,000,000 human years. Vishnu, who embodies kindness and mercy, often is depicted as a blue-skinned prince whose four hands hold symbolic items: a conch shell; a golden *chakra,* or disk; a jeweled club; and a lotus blossom. Another depiction of Vishnu shows him as a blue-skinned butter thief, gleefully dancing among the lotus blossoms. Vishnu incarnates himself as a fish, a tortoise, a boar, and a man-lion; a dwarf and a warrior; King Rama, Krishna, the Buddha, and Kalki, his incarnation to come. These ten incarnations are also iconographically represented. Shiva, embodying grace and good fortune, often has a third eye in his forehead, snakes wrapped around his waist or neck, and a trident by his side. He can also appear as Nataraja, Lord of the Dance, drumming the universe into existence with one hand and destroying it by fire with another. Ganesha, remover of obstacles, has an elephant head and a rotund belly. Hanuman, Rama's lieutenant, has a red monkey face and a long monkey tail.

Hindu goddesses are equally colorful in character and appearance. Sarasvati, consort to Brahma, is the goddess of learning and wisdom. She sits on a lotus blossom surrounded by swans. Two of her four arms carry symbolic objects—a string of beads and a book—and two play a *vina,* predecessor to the sitar. Lakshmi, goddess of wealth, holds a conch shell, a bowl of ambrosia, and two lotus flowers in her four hands. Durga, one of the many emanations of Shiva's consort, rides a fierce lion. Terrible Kali—blue skin gleaming, red tongue protruding, wearing a necklace of skulls and a skirt of severed arms—embodies the principle of darkness yet ruthlessly seeks out and destroys all evil.

Thousands of other gods, goddesses, demons, and supernatural figures populate the Hindu religion. Many are local gods, gracefully absorbed into the larger religion. Gods and goddesses die and return in new configurations —Sati, for instance, wife of Shiva, walked into the sacrificial fire, was reborn as Parvati, and married Shiva again.

Likewise, gods and goddesses can show themselves in different embodiments. Vishnu appears in ten different incarnations; Shakti, the Mother Goddess, manifests herself as Bhuvaneswari, Durga, Chandika, or Kali. She herself is considered an aspect of Shiva. It is a complicated, shifting, and intertwining cast of characters, another way in which the Hindu religion thrives on diversity.

Humble household shrines and grand public temples alike house figurines of gods and goddesses. The deities themselves are believed to reside in the idols, which are treated with the utmost care, bathed and dressed, garlanded with flowers, and anointed with fragrant oils. In many ways, the Hindu temple is more a home for the resident god than a gathering place for worshipers, who may not approach the idol directly but must circle it counterclockwise, thus showing respect and humility. Worshipers walk and stand but do not sit. Many Hindu temples have a pathway designed around the inner sanctum, and some of the more complex temples place as many as seven layers of architectural distance along the path. Temple doors are traditionally shut briefly at midday so that the deities within may rest.

During the Gupta Empire, sects formed that focused their reverence on either Vishnu or Shiva, raising them to levels of prominence higher than other gods. A third sect emphasized the worship of Hindu goddesses, embodied in Shakti. The distinction between Vaisnavas (followers of Vishnu), Saivas (followers of Shiva), and Shaktas (followers of the goddess in her various aspects, including Kali, Durga and Devi) still holds true today, especially among sadhus. Vaisnava sadhus often mark their foreheads with vertical lines, Saiva sadhus with horizontal lines, and Shakta sadhus with a dot. Vaisnavas wear white robes, Saiva saffron, and Shakta red.

Each of these distinguishing features has a philosophical reason behind it. The various sects emphasize different strands of scripture and thought, yet by and large they coexist harmoniously. This early division into sects explains why most temples, many of which date back to medieval India, are dedicated to one of these three deities.

THE MUSLIM ERA AND SIKHISM

INCURSIONS FROM the west, first from Arabia, then through Afghanistan, brought Muslims into India from the 7th century on. By the 16th century, Muslim rule predominated politically and religiously in northern India. The result was the great Mughal Empire, which continued to the early 18th century and derived legitimacy from an Islamic ideology, yet relied on an intimate knowledge of Hindu culture and patronage of Hindu temples. Hinduism proper lay fallow at best during the Mughal centuries, but one important offshoot resulted from the interaction between Muslims and Hindus: the religion of Sikhism.

In the late 15th century, a Hindu boy named Nanak, from a Punjab village in northern India, refused the thread of investiture. "Let mercy be the cotton, contentment the thread, continence the knot, and truth the twist," he is said to have proclaimed. After becoming an accountant for the Muslim authorities, Nanak went one day with his friends to bathe in the Beas River. His friends surfaced but he did not. For three days he stayed underwater, where God had revealed himself. Nanak finally reemerged, radiant with light and inspired to a new belief, neither Hindu nor Muslim. He traveled extensively, criticizing the formalist features of both religions, renouncing physical rites and icons, and preaching inner purity. It is said that before he died, his followers questioned whether he should be buried, in the

ABOVE: *Multiple exposures create a many-armed dancer at the Durga Puja, a Hindu festival in Waisghat honoring the goddess Durga.*

Muslim tradition, or cremated, as in Hindu practice. He asked that both the Muslims and the Hindus place flowers beside his dead body. The group whose flowers lasted longest would prevail in the matter. They did so, covering both his body and the flowers with a cloth. The next day they lifted the cloth and found only the flowers.

Nanak was the first of ten gurus, the holy men of the Sikh religion, who lived between the 15th and the 18th centuries. Their influence became both religious, through exemplary lives and extensive writings, and political, through leadership and diplomacy in the Punjab region. By the 17th century, the Sikh leaders represented such a threat to Muslim authorities that they were driven from their villages. They hid in the Himalayan foothills for several generations, then rose with military ferocity and, led by Ranjit Singh, declared Punjab a Sikh kingdom.

Punjab today is a state within the nation of India, and Sikhs maintain a significant religious and political presence there. The Golden Temple of Amritsar, at the edge of Hari Mandir, a lake in northern Punjab, is the Sikhs' most holy shrine. Originally erected in the late 16th century, it is the summation of generations of rebuilding and ornamentation that extols the sanctity of the Adi Grantha, the holy sculpture that the temple protects. In 1984 animosity between the Sikhs and the government of Indira Gandhi erupted in violence, resulting in an attack on the temple to root out a group of Sikh holy men and armed insurgents. Seven months later Indira Gandhi was assassinated by two Sikh bodyguards in retaliation. It took more than a decade to repair the Golden Temple. Bullet holes were left in the walls of one of the temple halls as a memorial to those who died.

SACRED SITES

CITIES AND temples, rivers and mountains, are intimately associated with particular Hindu gods. Associations arise out of geography, history, or mythology. The exquisite Jagat Mandir Temple, located near Dwarka, a seaside town in far western India, is a case in point.

Dwarka sits on the outer rim of the Kathiawar Peninsula, less than 150 miles from where the Indus River drains into the Arabian Sea. As a sacred site, Dwarka may predate the Gupta Empire. Tradition says the town was founded by Krishna, who moved to this region after helping Arjuna in battle. In the *Mahabharata,* a passage describes Arjuna's visit to Krishna's new home, which coincides with a massive tidal wave that innundates the town. Marine archaeologists working near Dwarka since the 1980s have found both artifacts and submerged masonry that appear to confirm the story of a drowned city from the Harappan age.

The ancient city may have gone under, but the site rose again. In the eighth century, the Vedic philosopher Shankaracharya identified four key monasteries—one for each of the cardinal directions—to connect Hindu practitioners throughout India. He called them the Four *Dhams,* or divine abodes. To represent the west, he chose Dwarka, apparently already an established holy place. The town was busy with ships traveling down the Persian Gulf, and its prime location as a trade gateway to India insured the wealth needed to build temples. During a period of Muslim dominance in this part of India, Hindu buildings at Dwarka were torn down. The grand temple now on the site dates from 1730, although it is claimed that its predecessor was built 2,500 years ago by Sambha, grandson of Krishna. This intricate building, 1,800 feet square and 180 feet tall at the highest spire, is supported by 72 sandstone and granite pillars. It protects the idol Sri Ranchhodrayji, an emanation of Krishna. Other temples and shrines cluster nearby, and just off the coast is the island of Bet Dwarka, where another temple marks the place where Krishna is said to have died.

To go from one of the homes of Krishna, incarnation of Vishnu, to one of the homes of Shiva, the other high god,

OPPOSITE: The 16th-century Golden Temple of Amritsar, in Punjab, protects the Adi Grantha, a statue held sacred by the Sikhs. FOLLOWING PAGES: Legend holds the 180-foot towers of the temple at Dwarka, in western India, once housed Krishna.

Hindu pilgrims must travel from sea level to one of the highest mountains in the world. Mount Kailas, tallest in Tibet's Kailas Range, stands apart from other peaks and soars to 22,028 feet, its four sheer slopes facing the cardinal directions. The mountain is regarded by Hindus as a dwelling-place of Lord Shiva. Buddhists consider it a holy place as well, home to one of their respected bodhisattvas. Jains believe it to be the place where their first tirthankara attained enlightenment. It has been called the center of the universe, the navel of the Earth, the jewel of the snow, the land of the gods.

To secular eyes, Mount Kailas is a stark and lifeless place, with snow sifting over black rock, reached only by an arduous climb. Yet Hindu art and literature is full of stories of Shiva making boundless love with his divine consort, Parvati, in these Himalayan hinterlands. Simply reaching Mount Kailas does not satisfy the spiritual quest, though. As if entering a temple, pilgrims circumambulate the peak at an altitude of about 19,000 feet, following a well-worn 32-mile path on a trek that can take one to three days.

Few leave without a plunge into the cold waters of Lake Manosaravar, the lake said to be divine. "When Manosaravar touches your body, you shall go to paradise and shall be released from the sins of one hundred births," wrote the poet Kalidasa. Close by is a twin lake, Rakshastal, called in contrast the lake of the demon, perhaps for its saline waters, perhaps because it is more treacherous to visit. Near these lakes spring the headwaters for four great rivers: the Indus and the Sutlej, flowing west into modern-day Pakistan; the Karnali and the Brahmaputra, flowing east into India's Ganges. Modern pilgrims to Kailas and Manosaravar find evidence that people not only reached these spots but made them into their hermitage homes. Eight Buddhist monasteries circle the lake, eerily vacant since the Chinese occupation of Tibet in 1950.

Nearly one thousand miles south, the devout of three religions—Hinduism, Buddhism, and Jainism—mirrored the natural marvels of Mount Kailas with marvels of their own. In a remarkable effort of art and engineering over many generations during the Gupta Empire, architectural monuments were carved out of a high basalt cliff at Ellora, near Aurangabad in west central India. All told, 34 edifices were sculpted out of stone, plus incidental statuary, both standing and relief. As if to provide Shiva with a dwelling when he travels south, the Hindu craftsmen of Ellora created an intricate temple by removing rock, not building it up. As much as 400,000 tons of stone had to be removed to result in the structure, which covers 60,000 square feet and reaches a height of 90 feet with its tallest tower. Another nearby cave, the Sita-ki-Nahani, includes a 15-foot-tall relief sculpture of Shiva engaged in one of his favorite pastimes: dancing. He waves his many arms in the air, displaying his coterie of symbols. The busyness of this image represents one of Shiva's many characteristics. As the mediator who can balance the battling dualities of existence, the spiritual assistance he can offer is so universally useful that temples in his honor have been erected not only all over India but wherever Hinduism has spread.

Temples cluster at the mouth of the Mahanadi River, the fertile rice-growing region on the east coast of India. In the third century B.C., Ashoka conquered this area. Jain ascetics carved out cave dwellings in its stony hills. Layer upon layer of control, religion, and artistry has resulted in more than one hundred temples that stand within one hundred miles of one another. It is called the Golden Triangle of Orissa in honor of the three most grand: Bhubaneswar, Konark, and Puri. Bhubaneswar and its attendant temples surround the Bindu Sagar Lake, said to have been formed by Shiva to quench the thirst of his consort, Parvati. At Konark, twelve wheels carved of stone appear to support the temple, creating the illusion that the building is a chariot of the sun god to whom it is dedicated. At Puri, a 20-foot wall encircles a complex containing 120 temples and shrines, many of their broad, pyramid-shaped

OPPOSITE: Sunset lights the stone spire of Shiva's Kailasa Temple, cut deep into the hillside of Ellora in western India.

SEEING THE DIVINE
A Daily Practice

MOST HINDU families make room for an altar in their home where they perform *puja,* or worship. There a statue or image of a special household god is surrounded by depictions of other deities, saints, gurus, or ancestors. A pitcher of water, incense, a bell, and a lamp or candle are at the ready. The family brings offerings of flowers, fruit, and food—especially *bhog,* a sweet, spicy rice ball—to the altar.

Once a day, the family gathers there. The head of the household rings the bell, lights the incense, and requests the deity to descend into their presence. Feeling the god's presence in the central statue, the *murti,* is called *darshana,* seeing the divine. Then the family lights the lamp or candle and passes it before the deity in praise. They show consideration for the divine presence by washing the statue, clothing it anew, presenting their gifts, and offering food and water. When the deity has partaken of the offering, the family shares the food, called *prasada.*

Hindus may visit a temple for puja to magnify their tribute to a deity. In so doing, they gain karma, or merit, and hope for a better afterlife. Underlying a Hindu temple's design is the idea that, with each step, a person progresses into a sacred space, moving further away from everyday illusions and deeper into the ultimate reality of the divine. Passing through an archway adorned with scenes of Hindu myths and historical events, worshipers enter a square, pillared hallway, often used during festivals for dancing and singing. They proceed into the small, dark *garbhagriha,* or womb chamber, the sanctuary, where the temple murti is enshrined. The resident god might be Shiva, Vishnu, or Shakti, Hinduism's three central deities, or a god worshiped locally. After offering gifts to the god, which the priest delivers, the worshipers maintain a prayerful state of mind as they circumambulate the inner chamber clockwise.

One or more priests live in a Hindu temple, caring for the murti and assisting worshipers. Unlike a household murti, the temple statue is the god's permanent dwelling place. It is installed with ancient rites of honorific cleansing, culminating with the recitation of a mantra, a sacred incantation, praying that the breath of life infuse the statue. Priests perform puja at sunrise, noon, sunset, and midnight to create a hospitable dwelling place for the god.

The same ritual acts form the basis of all Hindu puja. By summoning, praising, and giving gifts to a god or goddess, Hindus connect with the divine.

towers painted bright red. Rath Yatra, the chariot festival, takes place each year in Puri. Celebrants hoist a huge painted chariot above their heads and parade it through the city streets. Inside rides Jagannath, the Lord of the Universe, another embodiment of Vishnu. His masklike face and bulging eyes suggest that he might originally have been an animistic deity, now absorbed into the Hindu faith.

REVIVAL AND SPREAD

WITH THE end of the Gupta Empire, around 600 A.D., the Hindu religion and culture slid into a centuries-long period of quietude. Other religions, first Buddhism and then Islam, dominated among the ruling classes. From the 16th century into the 18th, the Indian subcontinent was the domain of the Mughal Empire, with its capital in the city of Delhi. Islam was the state religion in northern India, but Hinduism did not die. Worship continued in households. Hermits still meditated austerely in caves and monasteries, and begged for alms in the city streets. Scholars added to the rich lore of Hindu philosophy and some of the greatest Hindu devotional poetry in the north was written. Hindu leaders maintained territorial power in the south and in out-of-the-way places, harking back to the days when a warrior class maintained India's wealth and power. The caste system became more and more elaborate, dividing far beyond the four ancient varnas.

During this period, Portuguese traders established strongholds on the west coast. Dutch frigates carried Indian cotton out of Gujarat, India's westernmost province, heading out of the port city of Surat either across to the Red Sea or south to Africa and around the Cape of Good Hope. When British imperialists began to eye India, the Dutch presence on the west coast discouraged them, but they were welcomed by the local Hindu ruler of a little southeastern fishing village called Madraspatam, 400 miles up the Coromandel Coast from the tip of India. In 1644, supported by the British crown, the English Company built Fort Saint George and established the city of Madras there. In 1661,

through a royal marriage, the British acquired islands in a western bay 160 miles south of Surat. King Charles II donated the holdings to the English in India, who founded the city of Bombay there. In 1674 Bombay became headquarters for the company now called East India. A Muslim potentate agreed that the British could also establish a trade center near the mouth of the Hugli River on the east coast. Fort William was built there in 1702, and the nearby village of Kalikata soon became Calcutta.

The establishment of these three cities—Madras, Bombay, and Calcutta (now Kolkata)—signified the beginning of modern India, dominated by Western culture but steeped in its Hindu identity. Hinduism, as a culture and a religion, played a central role in India's 20th-century independence movement, as embodied by Mohandas Gandhi. Gandhi devoutly assumed the lifestyle of a sadhu. Wearing only a loincloth, he lived austerely, articulated the principles of non-violence and self-sufficiency, and was passionately dedicated to helping the Indian people regain control of their land's resources. To epitomize his message, he focused on one of the land's indwelling minerals, essential to human life, abundant in his homeland, and yet strictly controlled by the British colonial powers: salt.

Salt had long been a mainstay product in two regions of India, west and east: the Gujarat marshlands north of the Gulf of Kutch and the Orissa salt flats along the eastern coastline. Orissa salt especially was valued throughout India and in Europe. As British colonialists moved into India, they sought control of the Indian salt market in large part to protect trade in the lower-quality salt produced at home. An 1804 proclamation by the East India Company declared Orissa salt a British monopoly, banned the private harvest of it, and forbade its transport. The action resulted in starvation and epidemics among those Indians for whom the salt harvest had been their livelihood for generations. First they revolted violently against British salt agents; then their business went clandestine. The British responded bureaucratically, establishing a customs line between Orissa and Bengal, the center of colonial authority. They planted a 14-foot-high, 12-foot-thick hedge at the boundary between the two Indian states to deter salt smugglers. To maintain the boundary line and harvest wood for fuel, the British cleared jungle land in southern Bengal, disturbing the habitat of tigers, bears, and leopards. A massive famine swept Orissa in 1866. By 1888, native Indians began to organize politically in protest over British salt policy.

In March 1930, Gandhi conducted his historic Salt March, at once a religious pilgrimage and a political act of civil disobedience. He focused his protest in the western salt-producing region of India, his homeland. Beginning his pilgrimage from the Sabarmati Ashram, his headquarters in Ahmadabad in the east of Gujarat, Gandhi and 78 others traveled from village to village in what he called a "salt satyagraha," using the Sanskrit word for "a grasping of the truth." The march took on all the trappings of a Hindu pilgrimage, each day beginning with the dawn ritual of cleansing in a river. By the time Gandhi reached his destination, 240 miles and

25 days later, thousands of people had joined the march. He stood at dawn at the edge of the Arabian Sea, on the beach of Dandi, on April 6, 1930, and repeated the simple steps of primitive salt harvest performed over centuries. Then he picked up a flake of sun-encrusted salt, symbolically defying British law. At the same time, on the Orissa coastline, more than a thousand miles away, other protesters leaned down and scooped up handfuls of salt. Sympathizers trumpeted praise with conch shells and tossed flower petals into the air in celebration.

These acts sparked violence. Gandhi and other leaders were arrested and imprisoned. Demonstrations were

bravely continued, and on March 5, 1931, the British ended their salt campaign, releasing the harvest back into the hands of those who lived on that land. Sixteen years later, as India won its independence, the Salt March was seen as a turning point in the efforts to help the Indian people reclaim their land and its resources.

With independence in 1947, however, came new troubles. Instead of an all-India government, the country split into the secular state of India, with a Hindu majority, and a separate Muslim state—Pakistan (East and West)—despite assurances by Gandhi and other leaders that Muslims would be protected in an independent India. Seventeen million people were displaced and a million killed in the bloody riots that accompanied the event. In 1948 Gandhi was assassinated. In 1971 East Pakistan seceded from West Pakistan and became the independent nation of Bangladesh. In 1990, a member of the Bharatiya Janata Party (BJP) led a *Rath Yatra,* or chariot march, through north India to highlight the Hindu demand for a temple at the birthplace of the god-hero Rama. Protestors traveled by car and rail along a circuitous path to Ayodhya in the Himalayan foothills, the legendary birthplace of Rama and the presumed site of a Hindu temple razed by a Mughal emperor in the 16th century. Militant Hindu nationalists returned in 1992 and destroyed a mosque at the site. Ayodhya continues to be a flashpoint in the ongoing antagonism between Hindus and Muslims in 21st-century India. Mountainous Kashmir is a volatile issue between India and Pakistan as well, each nation insisting since partition that the predominantly Muslim territory should be part of its nation.

ABOVE: *Forgers of independence, Mohandas Gandhi, civil rights leader, and Jawaharlal Nehru* (left), *India's first prime minister, confer.*

HINDUISM TODAY

WITHIN A religion that so reveres its bodies of water, environmental concerns of the 21st century take on a bitter edge. Simple irrigation ditches have borrowed water from the Ganges for millennia, but the British were the first to engineer real canals. New plans to dam and redirect Indian rivers, to irrigate the dry Deccan Plain of central India, are drawing criticism for both political and ecological reasons.

Pollution poses a massive threat to the rivers of India. Thousands, even millions, of Hindus flock to the Ganges River at many points along its course, using the flowing water to bathe, drink, cook, wash clothing, dispose of refuse, and cast the ashes of the dead. Curiously enough, recent studies done in collaboration with the Indian Institute of Technology in Kanpur verify the ancient claims for the river's powers of purification: Organic matter is decomposed 15 to 25 times faster in the Ganges than in other rivers. Nevertheless, Mother Ganga is faltering under the weight of human use. Water tests done at the most populous spots along the river have revealed fecal coliform counts thousands of times higher than the acceptable level. Waterborne diseases such as cholera, typhus, hepatitis, and amoebic dysentery are ravaging the Indian people.

In 1985, the Indian government established the Ganga Action Plan, building sewage treatment plants along the Ganges River and enacting regulations against industrial runoff. The privately organized Sankat Mochan Foundation, concerned by what it considers the ineffectiveness of government efforts, has proposed alternative strategies and technologies. Foundation leader Veer Bhadra Mishra, a Hindu priest and civil engineer, emphasizes the need to balance ancient beliefs with present-day solutions. "There is a struggle and turmoil inside my heart," he said recently. "I want to take a holy dip— I need it to live. The day does not begin for me without the holy dip." But at the same time, as a scientist, he knows the dangers of biochemical oxygen demand (BOD) and fecal coliform. One way to relieve the pressure on the environment would be to redesign some of the most ancient rites of Hinduism. An estimated 40,000 cremations take place in Varanasi alone each year, creating a constant demand for firewood and raising concern over deforestation. The Indian government has built electrical crematoria, but many Indians still hold the ancient belief that only a wood fire's flame will carry the spirit of the dead to the gods.

The insistent pulse of Hindu worship still brings tens of thousands of worshipers daily into the waters of the Ganges and India's other sacred rivers. At no time is that pulse felt as overwhelmingly as during Kumbh Mela, the mass immersion that now brings millions of devout Hindus to Allahabad, where the Yamuna—and, it is believed, the mythical Sarasvati—pour their sacred waters into the Ganges. Legend has it that as Vishnu's winged carrier, Garuda, carried holy nectar across the skies, defending it against the onslaught of demons, four drops escaped, sanctifying those places where they fell to earth: Allahabad, Haridwar, Ujjain, and Nasik. At all of them Kumbh Mela is celebrated, but Allahabad is considered the holiest of the four. The precise time for gathering is calculated according to the planets, the auspicious date recurring about every 12 years. In February 2001, perhaps as many as 70 million people over the course of the three-week festival converged on the riverbanks near Allahabad, creating a temporary tent city that spread across 18 square miles. City officials set up 20,000 temporary latrines for the event. Sadhus from all sects and every direction immersed themselves en masse in the river waters, joined by other Hindus from all walks of life. The 2001 Kumbh Mela in Allahabad was the largest religious gathering in world history.

Four out of five Hindus today live in India, but Hinduism is represented on every continent of the globe. It has spread mainly through migration and cultural contact, not missionary conversion. Hindu practice spread from eastern India during the Gupta Empire and later along southeastward sea trade routes. Traces of that migration remain today in Bali, an island whose Hindu culture

sets it apart from the rest of Indonesia, which is nearly 90 percent Muslim. Bali was an enclave of escape for Javanese Hindus in the 16th century, and it remained relatively isolated from both Java and India in the succeeding centuries, developing a Hinduized culture all its own. Bali Hinduism intertwines with strands of Buddhist and indigenous religion, resulting in a colorful and energetic religion renowned for its gamelan music and *wayang,* or shadow puppet, theater. Pura Besakih, built on the slopes of Mount Agung, is considered the holiest of Bali's nearly 20,000 temples. It is a complex of 30 different temples, chief among them Pura Panataran Agung, which holds in its inner sanctum a three-seated shrine to Vishnu, Shiva, and Brahma.

Once every hundred years, as tradition has it, Balinese Hindus celebrate the ritual called Eka Dasa Rudra, enacting the struggle between demons in the underworld, gods in the heavens above, and humans in the balance between

them. Effigies of the gods are carried from all over the island down to the sea, where they are ceremonially cleansed. Men in native outriggers sacrifice a water buffalo calf, ornamented in gold and silver, to the demons of the sea. In a grand climax, the entire population converges at Besakih, bestowing gifts to the gods and sacrificing all sorts of animals, from snake to eagle, to appease Rudra, fiercest demon of all, and ensure health and prosperity for another century.

Modern impatience and an eye for commercial possibilities have stepped up the frequency of ceremonies linked to Eka Dasa Rudra. The first jolt to tradition came in 1963 when Indonesia's President Sukarno persuaded priests to schedule the ritual early. Preparations were under way when Mount Agung erupted, the first time since 1350, killing 2,000 people and forcing tens of thousands to evacuate. Some said the gods were expressing their anger at the Sukarno regime. Finally, 16 years later, the 20th-century Eka

Dasa Rudra took place. Although the next date for the ceremony has not been set, it may occur before 2079.

Hinduism's westward spread began in the early 1800s. Once their countries banned slavery, European sugar companies looked to Africa and Asia for low-cost labor on their West Indies plantations. Between 1841 and 1847, nearly 50,000 indentured workers were brought into British Guiana, on the north coast of South America. Some 12,000 came from India, and by 1883, one-quarter of the population was Indian. On the nearby island of Trinidad, another British colony, one-third of the population of 153,000 was recently from India. Such significant population groups carried their religion with them, leading today to lively Hindu cultures, influenced by African, Anglo, and indigenous traditions, in these Caribbean nations.

The spring festival called Holi has become Phagwa in Trinidad and Tobago. In Hindu tradition, Holi celebrates the triumph of good over evil as portrayed in the story of Prahlada, a boy whose devotion to god made his own father jealous. The father sent the boy's aunt, Holika, to burn him to death, but the fire engulfed her and left Prahlada unscathed. Similar to celebrations in India, the island version dates back to 1845. Phagwa festivalgoers burn an image of Holika one night, and the next day strew bright paints called *abir* over one another in a raucous festival of color. Musicians travel through village streets, singing *chowtals*—joyful songs with lyrics that blend Hindi and English—to the accompaniment of instruments that in themselves tell a story: the *dholak,* a classical Indian drum, and the *dhantal,* a percussion instrument unique to Trinidad that began as a crowbar and horseshoe. Phagwa celebrations culminate in Pichakaaree, a performance extravaganza reminiscent of Caribbean calypso competitions.

Hindu temples now stand on every continent of the world, from Lansing, Michigan, U.S.A., to Johannesburg, South Africa, from Basel, Switzerland, to Canberra, Australia,

signifying the broad spread of small constituencies of practicing Hindus. Meanwhile, the influence of Hindu faith and practice has made its way into the everyday life of many a non-Hindu man and woman, few of whom would recognize the spiritual source. Through the late 20th century and into the 21st, Hindu-inspired practices of meditation and yoga infused modern culture around the world, presenting an escape from the fast-paced materialism of the Western world. One sect with an especially broad reach in the 20th century was the International Society for Krishna Consciousness (ISKCON). Established in the mid-1960s by Bhaktivedanta Swami Prabhupada, an Indian devotee of Krishna who had moved to the United States, ISKCON attracted many American and European youths, including Beatle George Harrison. Other Hindu gurus gained worldwide followings and notoriety, such as the Maharishi Mahesh Yogi, Bhagwan Shree Rajneesh, and Swami Satchidananda. Born in India in 1914 and initiated into the Hindu priesthood in 1949, Satchidananda moved to the United States in the 1960s. He ultimately founded the Yogaville ashram in the Virginia countryside 150 miles southwest of Washington, D.C. There his following engineered a finger of land stretching out into the nearby James River, on which they built a pink-and-white lotus-shaped temple which includes a meditation room and a shrine to the world's religions.

Meanwhile, spiritual seekers journey to India itself. Today a map of the Hindu nation is speckled with shrines, temples, holy places, ashrams, and bathing sites. Holy destinations tend to be concentrated down the eastern and western coastlines and along the river valleys from high in the Himalaya to the edge of the sea. Pilgrimage tourism is booming in India. This onslaught of curious newcomers does not stop the native Hindu faithful from quietly following the age-old practice of greeting the dawn at the edge of the river, hands clasped in communion with the gods. □

OPPOSITE: Pilgrims walk to the shrines of Palni, in southern India, where Hindus worship a son of Shiva.

FOLLOWING PAGES: A tent city rises for Kumbh Mela at Allahabad on the Ganges, as millions of celebrants arrive for soul-cleansing baths.

FESTIVALS

AMUSED YOUNG women *(above)* of the Bhil tribe, in central India, dress to impress prospective husbands during Bhagoriya, which can be translated as the festival of elopement. Any young man attending the dance who is interested in one of them, simply has to offer her a betel leaf. If she accepts, the young woman grabs him and dances with him *(right)*, signifying to all that they are engaged. The only thing left to resolve is the matter of a dowry, which the groom's family must pay.

Hindu festivals such as the Bhagoriya often serve several purposes. They unite religion with pageantry and magic and serve to purify and renew, or thwart evil influences on daily lives. Ancient in origin, the Hindu festivals are typical of the many celebrations that take place throughout the year in India.

Pilgrims bathe *(following pages)* in the spray of the Kapildhara Falls, near the source of the Narmada River.

SECOND IN importance only to the sacred Ganges, the Narmada is said to have been created from a drop of Shiva's sweat. Its waters are considered so spiritually powerful that simply gazing upon them can ensure eternal happiness.

The Narmada is a goddess, often referred to by locals as Narmada ma or "Mother Narmada." Its life-giving force is personified by the black basalt statue at left, which is housed at a temple near its source. During the Narmada Jayanti festival, an annual celebration of the river's creation, Hindus light thousands of oil lamps *(above)*, floating them on the river at night from the bathing steps at Hoshandgabad.

BUDDHISM

The mountain is the mountain and the Way is the same as of old. Verily what has changed is my own heart.

— Zen Buddhist Training Poem

BUDDHISM

SOMETIME IN the fifth century B.C. in the foothills south of the Himalaya, a son was born to Mayadevi, the wife of King Suddhodana. The king, a member of the Kshatriya, or warrior, caste, was a powerful patriarch in the ruling Shakya tribe, in the capital city of Kapilavastu. Legend has it that Queen Mayadevi had chosen the time of the full moon in May to travel to her parents in the capital of the neighboring clan, some 20 miles east.

OPPOSITE: *Drawing the spiritual energy of the Himalaya, the Tiger's Den monastery clings to a cliff in Bhutan.*
PRECEDING PAGES: *Dawn bathes Buddhist temples, clustered on the sacred plain of Bagan, Myanmar, in a soft glow.*

SHE KNEW she was soon to give birth. Some months before, in a dream, she was lying in a golden mansion when trumpets announced the coming of a great white elephant. Carrying a lotus blossom in its trunk, the animal circled her three times, then entered her body. At that moment, according to Buddhist scripture, "all the ten thousand worlds suddenly quaked, quivered, and shook." When the queen told the dream to her husband, wise men of the court predicted that the coming son would become either a universal monarch or a Buddha—an enlightened one.

Near Lumbini, Queen Mayadevi stopped in a grove of sal trees. In their shade, she found a spring-fed pool and paused to bathe. Stepping out of the pool, she clutched an overhanging branch and smiled at the wildflowers. At that moment two celestial figures appeared from out of the clouds, showering her with water and lotus blossoms. Mayadevi felt the pain of labor. She rested against a fig tree and a child emerged from her side, bright and shining, already able to walk and talk. "This is my last birth," he exclaimed. Because of this and other auspicious signs at his birth, the young prince was named Siddhartha, "the one who attains the goal."

All that is left of Siddhartha's royal city of Kapilavastu are brick remains suggesting city walls and an ancient moat on a 250-acre site in the Terai region. The Terai is a timber-rich subtropical plain along the southern border of Nepal. Excavations at Tilaurakot, a site now presumed to be the ancient Shakya capital, have unearthed artifacts and architectural remains revealing many layers of history. The oldest—mud walls and pottery—appear to date back as far as 600 B.C. Disturbed earth in mounds and trenches has been radiocarbon-dated to the beginning of the first millennium B.C., justifying the belief that even in the lifetime of the Buddha, this was an established city.

The young prince, whose mother had died a week after his birth, grew up in a palace, unaware of the larger world and the sufferings of those whose daily lives were spent in physical toil. The king pampered and indulged the prince with every sensual and artistic pleasure, in the hope that the perquisites of rule would persuade him to follow the path of the nobleman and assume a position of power within the tribe. As befit a future king, Siddhartha was also trained in the martial arts, and Suddhodana arranged for Brahmans to instruct the prince in the religion of the Vedas. The priests chanted holy words and conducted sacrifices on behalf of the tribe and its rulers. All were pleased when the young prince married and when his wife gave birth to a son.

Then Siddhartha's life changed dramatically. He ventured outside the palace walls and saw things he never knew existed: a man doubled over with sickness, a man decrepit with age, a corpse. Sickness, old age, and death had been hidden from him in his world of privilege and pleasure. Now these evidences of human suffering struck him deeply. They caused him to ponder the nature of this world and to question his place in it. A fourth passing sight appeared as if in answer. He saw a sadhu, a Hindu mendicant who had renounced all worldly pleasures to seek a greater wisdom. *This man, this way of life, can teach me,* Siddhartha realized.

At that, so it is said, he kissed his wife and son goodbye, opened the locked city gates, shaved off his long hair with his sword, and exchanged his princely clothing for the humble robe of a man of the forest. Assuming the name Gautama, he traveled south to the Ganges Plain, where he and other wandering ascetics lived in caves and begged for food. After six years of wandering and self-deprivation, Gautama was near death. He sat down under a fig tree beside the Nairanjana River near Uruvela, called Bodh Gaya today. It was the evening of the full moon of May—the same time of year in which he had been born. "There I saw a beautiful stretch of countryside, a clear flowing river, a lovely ford, and a village nearby for support," Gautama later wrote. He ate a bowl of rice, milk, and honey brought to him by a village woman, then withdrew into a meditation.

OPPOSITE: *A monk kneels in prayer at the Bodh Gaya shrine in northeastern India, the spot where the Buddha attained enlightenment.*

From that moonlit meditation, a religious movement sprang up and flourished, grew and divided, so that today it has become the fourth-largest organized religion in the world, embraced by nearly 375 million people. Despite its growth, Buddhism remains a religion primarily of the East, a living faith and an indelible cultural influence in India, China, Southeast Asia, Korea, and Japan. The story of its origin may be layered in myth, but this great world religion did begin with one historical person and at a place that can still be visited today.

THE BUDDHA'S PATH

SIDDHARTHA GAUTAMA achieved enlightenment at Bodh Gaya. After resisting the temptations and dangers sent by the demon Mara to assail him, he arose a Buddha—an awakened one. He lived another 45 years, traveling along trade routes in today's northern India and Nepal, teaching in cities no more than 150 miles from his birthplace. Politically, this region was divided into small principalities, mostly monarchies and oligarchies but also a few republics.

In these cities, such as Vaishali, Shravasti, Rajagrha, and Varanasi, the Buddha spread his word. "I have obtained deliverance by the extinction of self," the Buddha said. During his enlightenment experience he had arrived at the concept of *anatman,* or "non-self"—in contrast to the atman, the physically real and indestructible soul in Hinduism. All existence is subject to the law of impermanence and thus reality is a process, the Buddha taught. A human being has no permanent essence but is an ever-changing relationship of the five *skandhas* (aggregates): the physical body (made up of earth, fire, air, and water); feelings caused by sensory contacts; perceptions of those contacts as good, evil or neutral; habitual mental dispositions, which link mental activity and physical action; and consciousness, created through the experience of the external world by the mind and body.

The Buddha proposed a "Middle Way": not the indulgence of the wealthy, confident that by plying the priests with ample gifts, they would win the favor of the gods, nor the severe self-denial of ascetics, who torture themselves physically in the belief that it will bring spiritual rewards. Determined to share his insights with everyone—of high and low caste, men and women, old and young—the Buddha sought five friends from his days as a *bhikkhu,* a wandering mendicant. He found them north of Varanasi in a place for quiet meditation. This place was known as Mrigadaya, or deer sanctuary. Today it is called Sarnath. At first the bhikkhus mocked their friend, seeing his bright eyes, his serene countenance, his light-filled being. His response has come down through history as one of the central doctrines of Buddhism.

"Now this, O bhikkhus, is the Noble Truth concerning the way which leads to the destruction of sorrow.... By the practice of loving-kindness I have attained liberation of heart, and thus I am assured that I shall never return in renewed birth. I have even now attained nirvana."

And he counseled them on the Four Noble Truths, the heart of his teachings:

1. There is suffering in the world.
2. There is a cause of suffering.
3. By eliminating the cause, one can end suffering.
4. There is a path by which one can end suffering.

(In some traditions, the cause of suffering is deemed ignorance; in others, it is desire.) In form, the Buddha's message followed the protocol of ancient Indian physicians, who were expected to articulate, in this order, the symptoms, the cause, the possibility of a cure, and the remedy for a given ailment. His principles assumed a belief in reincarnation, the cycle of birth, death, and rebirth, which the Buddha called the wheel of life. Attachment to matters of this world—its thoughts and its things—keeps one chained to that never-ending cycle. The challenge the Buddha posed was to break free.

OPPOSITE: *A 19th-century Tibetan painting displays a three-eyed demon holding a mandala showing the wheel of life and rebirth.*

His solution suggests a progression of practices that the Buddhist can follow to move toward nirvana, a beatitude that ends the cycle of rebirth into life and its suffering. The steps have been codified over the years as the Noble Eightfold Path, which divides into three categories. Under the practice of wisdom come:

1. Right Views

2. Right Intent. The Buddhist sees the world with compassion and intends the best for it, without hatred or cruelty. Under the practice of morality come:

3. Right Speech

4. Right Conduct

5. Right Livelihood. The Buddhist speaks and acts thoughtfully toward others and devotes the efforts of daily life toward an improvement of the world, avoiding any meddling with magic or inflicting harm.

And under the practice of mental discipline come:

6. Right Effort

7. Right Mindfulness

8. Right Concentration. Central to the Buddhist practice is the diligent effort to clear and calm the mind, to cultivate detachment in both body and mind, and thereby to approach the higher states attainable only through advanced meditation. Those who follow this way of life may become *arhats,* "holy ones," in whom there is no longer desire and for whom there will be no further rebirth.

Inspired and convinced, those five friends became the first *sangha,* or community of the faithful, the prototype of Buddhist monasteries to this day. Together they agreed to

preach the dharma, the doctrine of truth and the path to enlightenment shown by the Buddha. Buddhists today express their faith with this holy chant:

> *I take refuge in the Buddha,*
> *I take refuge in the dharma,*
> *I take refuge in the sangha.*

To take refuge in the Three Jewels—the Buddha, his teachings, and his community—is to turn from material pleasures, mental annoyances, and worldly concerns in favor of mindful attention to the wisdom and way of life represented by the Buddha. These three commitments have their place in the daily life of every Buddhist, not just those who choose the monastic life.

Actions in this life directly influence future lives, according to the Buddhist concept of karma. Each positive action builds an individual's repository of merit, and ensures progress toward enlightenment in the next lifetime. Buddhists make merit in a variety of ways: by giving—to the poor or to monks, nuns, and their communities; by doing good deeds; and by worshiping. Worship can take place at a home altar or at a stupa or shrine. Placing palms together, bowing or kneeling, and circumambulating; offering a flower or lighting a candle; chanting or praying—all these acts of worship can make merit. Some worshipers spin prayer wheels—large or small metal cylinders with written prayers wound tightly inside that spin freely, each spin representing another devotion. Many Buddhists believe that merit can be transferred:

ABOVE: A 30-foot-tall golden Buddha, one of four in the Ananda Temple at Bagan, holds the pose of teaching the right path.

OPPOSITE: A teacher prays at the head of a statue of the Buddha in Orissa, India, a center for Buddhist study since ancient times.

FOLLOWING PAGES: Ancient irrigation methods are used within view of the Sri Jagannath Temple in Puri on the Bay of Bengal.

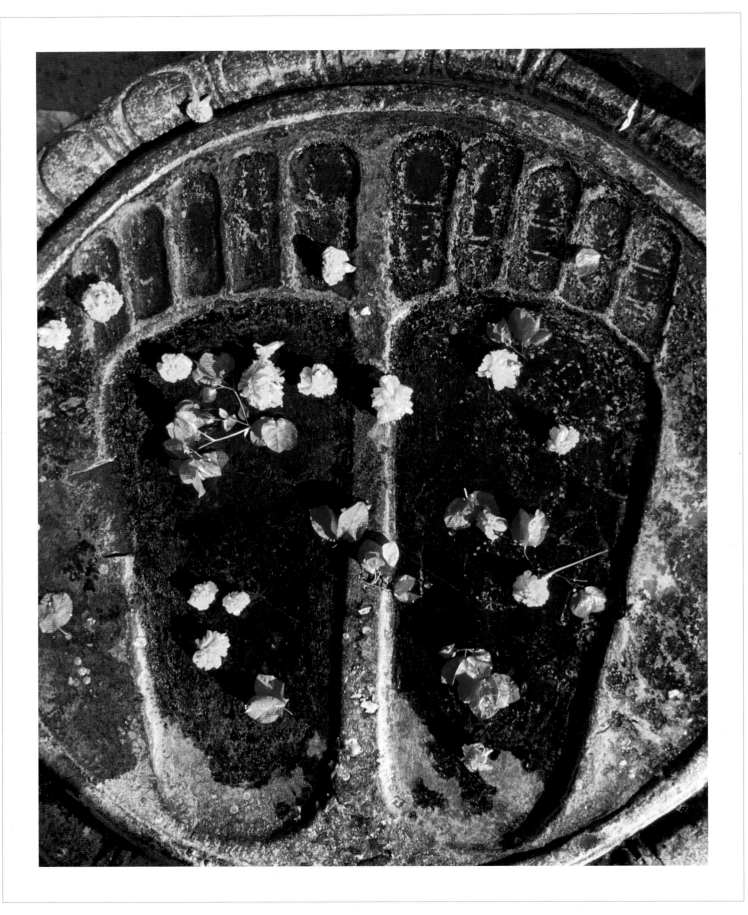

An act of charity or worship can be performed on behalf of another, the transfer itself being a way of making merit.

In his teachings, the Buddha emphasized the value of a loving life and the transience of worldly riches. Desire, hatred, and ignorance are the roots of all evil, he told his followers. "Lust, passion, and the thirst for existence that yearns for pleasure everywhere"—the Buddha's definition of selfishness—constitute the origin of all suffering, he taught. And he counseled all to go the way of the noble youth who "walks on the path that leads to the annihilation of suffering, radically forsaking passion, subduing wrath, annihilating the vain conceit of the 'I-am,' leaving ignorance, and attaining to enlightenment." This path is open to all, regardless of caste, the Buddha taught and related a parable about a girl of low caste who met Ananda, his revered disciple, on the road.

Ananda, who had been sent on a mission by the Buddha, was passing by a village when he came upon a well. Seeing a girl, he asked her for a drink of water. "O Brahman, I am too humble and mean to give thee water to drink," she answered, following the strict rules of the Vedic caste system. "Do not ask any service of me lest thy holiness be contaminated, for I am of low caste."

"I ask not for caste but for water," replied Ananda. The girl was filled with joy and gave Ananda a drink. After Ananda had gone, she went to the Buddha and declared her love for his disciple. He corrected her that it was not Ananda but his kindness that she loved. "Verily there is great merit in the generosity of a king when he is kind to a slave," he continued, "but there is even a greater merit in the slave when he ignores the wrongs which he suffers and cherishes kindness and good-will to all mankind....Thou art of low caste, but Brahmans may learn a lesson from thee. Swerve not from the path of justice and righteousness and thou wilt outshine the royal glory of queens on the throne."

Although the Buddha urged a life of poverty and overturned the idea of caste divisions, he earned the respect of men of power and influence. King Bimbisara, the virtuous leader of Magadha, warmly hosted him in Rajagrha, remembering the days when his guest had traveled through as a prince. Bimbisara championed the Buddha and his cause, building quarters for him and his followers. The king is still remembered as the first great patron of Buddhism.

Wandering monks of the first millennium B.C. looked for dry shelter every summer, then as now a season of torrential monsoon rains. The Buddha proposed to his followers that they meet and take cover together during the rainy season. For the last 25 years of his ministry, he and others convened annually in the city of Sravasti. There they waited out the monsoon as the guests of a merchant who had heard the Buddha speak. Their host built a seven-story dwelling for them, said to include porches and assembly halls, covered walkways, baths, wells, and lotus ponds. It became the Jetavana Monastery, site of many important lessons given by the Buddha. Traces of the complex remain from his day, including a brick pathway where the Buddha may have walked and meditated. In sites close by, part of the ancient city of Maheth, archaeologists have discovered beads and semiprecious stones including lapis lazuli, agate, and carnelian; copper bangles and an earring; and animal figurines and tiles of terra-cotta. All date to the era of the Buddha's lifetime and vouch for the wealth and busy trade that moved through Shravasti at that time.

Women, as well as men, sought to follow the path of the Buddha during his lifetime. Their place in Indian society at that time would not have warranted such a privilege: Women generally were regarded as the wards and servants of men, handed over from father to husband at marriage. The first woman to speak for women, according to tradition, was the Buddha's own aunt and foster mother, Pajapati Gotami, who proposed to establish an order of nuns parallel to the monks—the ascetic order founded by the Buddha. So dedicated was she to the cause that she shaved her hair, donned monk's robes, and walked the 357 miles from

OPPOSITE: A flower-strewn monument at the Bodh Gaya Monastery reminds Buddhists to walk in the footsteps of the great teacher.

Kapilavastu to the Jetavana Monastery. The Buddha did not immediately accept the idea of a woman's place in his ministry, but his aunt's persistence was finally rewarded. Two other women are singled out in Buddhist tradition as having been accepted as nuns by the Buddha himself: Khema, the beautiful wife of King Bimbisara, and Subha, the daughter of a wealthy goldsmith. Although such precedents laid down a path for bhikkuni, or Buddhist nuns, the lineage eventually died out in the countries that follow the Theravada tradition, and there has been much controversy regarding its reintroduction. An international effort to reestablish the bhikkuni tradition is under way, and in recent years the situation has begun to shift. The lineage of nuns has remained strong in China and Korea in particular, and from there it is spreading to those countries where it was lost or never existed. Today many Buddhist orders consider nuns equal and important participants in the effort to follow the dharma.

In his 80th year of life, the Buddha did not make it back to Shravasti for the rainy season. He was near Kushinagara, about 50 miles south of his birthplace of Lumbini, when he felt severe stomach pains and had to pause in his travels. He ate his last meal, a dish of dried boar meat prepared for him by a generous blacksmith. Knowing that death was approaching, he lay on his side in a shady grove, on a bed that Ananda made for him between twin sal trees, his head pointing north.

The trees burst into unseasonable bloom and heavenly song filled the sky. Ananda and the other disciples grew anxious, not knowing how they could proceed without their teacher. "It is true that no more shall I receive a body," said the Buddha in consolation. "The truth and the rules of the order which I have set forth and laid down for you all, let them, after I am gone, be a teacher unto you." His last words were: "Decay is inherent in all component things, but the truth will remain forever. Work out your salvation with diligence!"

FOLLOWING IN HIS FOOTSTEPS

UPON THE Buddha's death, his disciples prepared his body ceremonially for cremation, anointing it with incense, draping it with flower garlands, and singing Vedic hymns. When they lit the fire, the physical world responded: "The sun and moon withdrew their shining, the peaceful streams on every side were torrent-swollen, the earth quaked, and the sturdy forests shook like aspen leaves, whilst flowers and leaves fell untimely to the ground, like scattered rain, so that all Kusinara [Kushinagara] became strewn knee-deep with mandara flowers raining down from heaven," the gospel recorded. All those present had no doubt that the Buddha had attained nirvana, the state of enlightenment beyond the wheel of life. Ashes and bits of bone collected from the pyre are said to have been divided into eight parts and sent to the cities where the Buddha had already won a following.

Monumental mounds called stupas were built to enshrine the remains of the Buddha. A stupa is an ancient architectural form. The word comes from the Sanskrit for "pile," and originally soil was mounded up over the ashes of the dead, then strengthened, and the whole protected with a covering of stone. From such primitive beginnings, the stupa evolved into a central architectural element of the Buddhist tradition, interpreted with many variations on its design and symbolism. Later stupas included sanctuaries, with room for a visitor to come inside. Eventually Buddhist stupas evolved into magnificent buildings and landmarks of the religion's architecture, varying by culture. Sri Lanka's *dagoba,* Tibet's *chorten,* Southeast Asia's *chedi,* and Japan's pagoda are all variations on the stupa. When a Buddhist visits a stupa, he or she circumambulates it clockwise to show respect and devotion to the spirit represented by the relics housed within it.

Two councils of the sangha, totaling about 500 devotees, took place in the century after the Buddha's death.

OPPOSITE: Carvings on the gate to the fifth-century Great Stupa at Sanchi, India, illustrate the life of the Buddha.

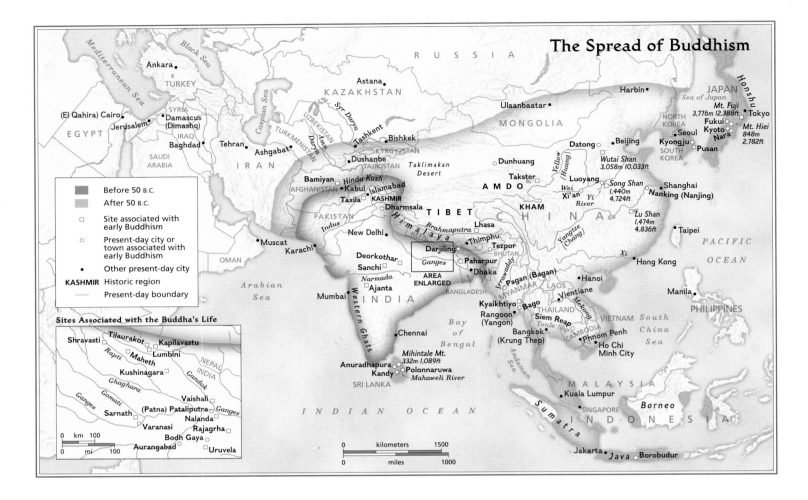

The Spread of Buddhism

Before 50 B.C.
After 50 B.C.

☐ Site associated with early Buddhism
○ Present-day city or town associated with early Buddhism
• Other present-day city
KASHMIR Historic region
--- Present-day boundary

Sites Associated with the Buddha's Life

Shravasti, Tilaurakot, Kapilavastu, Maheth, Lumbini, Rapti, Kushinagara, Ghaghara, Gomati, Ganges, Vaishali, Sarnath, (Patna) Pataliputra, Ganges, Nalanda, Varanasi, Rajagrha, Bodh Gaya, Aurangabad, Uruvela

These councils solidified the central canon of their leader's teachings. Although not a central feature, the Buddhist universe includes gods, goddesses, and demons like those in the Hindu pantheon. They are part of a continuum of beings that extends from the dwellers of hell to the sublime gods, with the realm of human beings in the middle. Sangha members at the councils also established rules of behavior for Buddhist monks. Following the example of the Buddha, monks were expected to lead pure lives apart from the flow of commerce and materialism, but they were not to isolate themselves entirely from the laity. A friendly interchange was expected between those who patterned their entire lives on the Buddha and those who applied his wisdom to a more worldly daily life. Each group was to help the other: A monk was to teach the dharma in lesson and example, while a layperson— whether a poor laborer, a wealthy merchant, or a noble prince—was to provide food, shelter, and clothing to those of the monastic order. This practice of mutual beneficence has continued into modern times.

During the Second Buddhist Council, a philosophical divide emerged that would ultimately split the religion into 18 different sects. The issue was how narrowly to define the promise and practice of Buddhism. The more orthodox council members believed that only the Buddha himself, along with certain remarkable historical predecessors, could reach the state of Buddhahood. The detractors believed that others among themselves or in future generations also could become Buddhas by following the path of the Master. They called these enlightened disciples *bodhisattvas,* or people intent on becoming Buddhas. The more conservative believed in a life of meditation toward the goal of self-liberation. Detractors called that practice too self-centered and insisted that the pious Buddhist must also be part of the world and help others.

By the beginning of the first century, these philosophical distinctions had become various schools of thought with differing bodies of scripture as the basis for their study, although there are many basic ideas held in common: the Buddha as founder and foundation of the religion, the Four Noble Truths, the Eightfold Path, and the importance of a rigorous mental discipline. What began as a philosophical distinction became a geographical one. Theravada Buddhism, for example, predominates in Sri Lanka and the Southeast Asian countries of Burma, Thailand, Laos, and Cambodia, whereas Mahayana Buddhism predominates in Tibet, Bhutan, and Nepal, in China and Taiwan, and in Korea, Japan, and Vietnam. This division has led to the shorthand nomenclature designating Theravada Buddhism as "southern" and Mahayana as "northern."

THE PIOUS KING

THE GEOGRAPHICAL spread of Buddhism in India owes much to an unlikely figure. Ashoka, the king of the Mauryan Empire, which had succeeded the Magadhan kingdom of the Buddha's day, was born in 304 B.C., one of the several grandsons of Chandragupta, first emperor of the realm. Ashoka was ruthless to his brothers, so the records suggest, and killed several of them to attain his father's throne. He led fierce warriors into battle and in 262 B.C. he conquered Kalinga—now called Orissa—adding the fertile delta land to his territory. Apparently the scenes of violence and suffering on the battlefield made a profound impression on him, for after the war he embraced Buddhism with passion. For the remaining 30 years of his life, his drive to conquer territory turned into zeal for spreading Buddhism. He left a legacy across central India in the form of dozens of stone pillars inscribed with edicts to all the people in his newly expanded realm.

"All men are my children," reads one pillar erected in Kalinga. "What I desire for my own children, and I desire their welfare and happiness both in this world and the next, that I desire for all men." Ashoka's edicts, some of them

also carved into cliffsides, can be found from one end of India to the other. Atop many Ashokan pillars stood four roaring lions facing north, south, east, and west, the image that now symbolizes the Indian nation—fitting because, under Ashoka, Buddhism had become the foundation for civilization, linking religion and state.

Emperor Ashoka built many stupas—by then, monumental buildings, not just stones piled on top of soil. Tradition has it that during this massive construction effort, Ashoka removed the eight portions of the remains of Buddha from their sanctuaries and divided them many more times, scattering them throughout his empire.

For each relic, he built a stupa. On a gentle hilltop west of today's Bhopal in central India, for example, Ashoka built eight stupas, including the core of the building that evolved into the Great Stupa of Sanchi. The outer skin of the Great Stupa, a dome measuring 120 feet in diameter, dates from about 150 B.C. Like other sophisticated stupas of that era, it includes a walkway around the dome and a stairway to a *harmika,* or square platform, on top. From the harmika ascends a *chattra,* a multileveled parasol, pointing to the sky. Carvings decorate the four gateways to the stupa. Those of earlier vintage, up to the first century B.C., do not represent the Buddha in human form. Symbols predominate: the lotus, symbol of his birth; the parasol, symbol of his missionary travels; the wheel, symbol of his teachings; the tree, symbol of his enlightenment; and the footprint, symbol of his presence in the world. Ashokan stupas have been found in Shravasti, Sarnath, Lumbini, and on the island of Sri Lanka. Others may yet be discovered. A new central Indian site unearthed in 1999 in Deorkothar, for example, included four brick stupas of the Ashokan era, 30 stone stupas, and monastic buildings.

Ashoka hosted a Third Buddhist Council, from which he sent missionaries in all directions, spreading the word. Some traveled up the tributaries of the Ganges and across the passes of the Himalaya into Central Asia, planting the seeds of belief that would flower centuries later in Buddhist centers such as Bamiyan, Afghanistan. Some

traveled to the west coast of India, and from there by sea to Egypt. Ashokan missionaries also traveled by land and sea to the south and east, carrying Buddhism to Burma and Thailand. Ashoka's son, Mahinda, is said to have brought Buddhism to Sri Lanka. Thanks to these early missionary efforts, Buddhism began to take root in parts of the world beyond India.

THE DECLINE OF BUDDHISM IN INDIA

FOR CENTURIES after Ashoka's reign, Buddhism coexisted with Jainism and Hinduism. There were periods, however, when rulers vehemently faithful to the Hindu religion attacked the Buddhist shrines. The state of artifacts at Deorkothar, for example, suggests that the stupas there were deliberately destroyed, probably soon after 200 B.C. under Pushyamitra Sunga, an advocate of Hinduism. Other rulers benevolently supported Buddhism, including, ironically, the Central Asian rulers who invaded India from the northwest in the first century A.D. From their power base in the mountainous terrain of today's Afghanistan, Pakistan, and Kashmir, the Kushan kings won territory all the way east to Pataliputra, the old Magadhan city. Coins of copper, silver, and gold minted around 100 A.D. pictured King Vima on one side, the Hindu god Shiva on the other. Coins

OPPOSITE: Buddhists have drawn inspiration from the Ajanta Caves' fifth-century murals depicting the life of the Buddha.
ABOVE: Scant light reaches a sculpture of the Buddha stationed at the end of a rock-hewn sanctuary in the Ajanta Caves in India.

made a decade or two later during the reign of the great king Kanishka were imprinted with standing or seated figures of the Buddha. Only five of these rare copper coins are known to exist. They are believed to have been issued in honor of the stupa built by Kanishka near Peshawar and are the only coins ever to bear an image of the Buddha.

The earliest statues of the Buddha come from the Central Asian kingdom of Gandhara during the second and third century A.D. Far from the prototype of the Buddha that one sees today, some of these statues look more like the Greek god Apollo, with fine lips and wavy hair that reveal lasting Hellenistic influences in this region. While statues of the Buddha eventually became important in the practice of the religion, such was not always the case. The lintel of Sanchi's Eastern Gate, dated to 50 B.C., shows the central horse protected by a parasol but riderless. Symbols, such as footprints or the parasol, represented the Buddha, but his bodily presence was conceived as beyond both human sight and draftsmanship. Over time, depictions of the Buddha began to appear in paintings and sculptural tableaux representing his life story. The physical representation of the Buddha continued as a point for debate between the two branches of Buddhism, the early Theravadan orthodox regarding images of the Buddha to be sacrilege. (Modern Theravadans do not hold this belief.) Mahayana tradition held Buddha images to be appropriate, even necessary, objects for focused meditation. A rhetoric of the Buddha's proportions and dress developed, along with an extensive vocabulary of symbolic body and hand positions. As the practice of Buddhism spread, images of the Buddha acquired characteristics specific to each new locale.

A fantastic blend of Theravada and Mahayana aesthetics—and a glimpse into the remarkable lives of the early Buddhist monks—can be found in the monastic cave complexes carved into the mountainsides of the Western Ghats. Cave sites at Ajanta near Aurangabad, like the nearby Hindu and Jain cave site at Ellora—all not one hundred miles apart—give evidence of work over centuries. From about the first century B.C. through the sixth century

A.D., Buddhist monks turned layers of granite, gneiss, and basaltic lava into labyrinthine temples with hundreds of sculptural figures populating their walls. They used techniques that historians can only guess at to carve out pillared assembly halls with intricate vaulted ceilings, meditation cells, and devotional shrines and figurines inside and out. Twenty-nine caves constitute the Ajanta complex alone. Bas-relief sculptures and painted images animate many of the walls inside. Art historians have analyzed the techniques used for these paintings, some two thousand years old. The artisans applied a mixture of mud and cow dung, bound with straw or hair, then whitewashed it with gypsum or lime plaster to create a uniform painting surface. The older cave paintings, dated from 100 to 250 A.D., were painted according to the Theravada ethic, using symbolic and natural motifs without portraying the Buddha's person. In the majority of the caves, though, paintings dating from 500 to 650 A.D. tell the life story of the Buddha, culminating in a figure 20 feet long, reclining in death and preparing for the ultimate passage into nirvana.

Not all Buddhist monks secluded themselves in caves. With the patronage of the Gupta dynasty from the fourth century on, Buddhist universities—busy centers of research, writing, and debate—developed in India. The great educational institution at Nalanda, ten miles downstream from Pataliputra on the Ganges, is often called the world's first university. Ruins testify to the vast scale of the place and the work that went on there. The complex covers almost 35 acres and includes the red-brick remains of monasteries, temples, and stupas set among courtyards and gardens. Monastery buildings, laid out on a north-south axis, follow a similar pattern: an outer square of single cells that open into a courtyard surrounding a central shrine. A seventh-century firsthand account of life at Nalanda helps bring the scene to life:

"There were many courtyards.... Precious terraces spread like stars and jade pavilions were spired like peaks. The temple arose into the mists and the shrine halls stood high above the clouds.... Streams of blue water wound through the parks; green lotus flowers sparkled among the blossoms of sandal trees, and a mango grove spread outside the enclosure. The monks' dwellings in all the courtyards had four stories. The beams were painted with all the colors of the rainbow and were carved with animal designs, while the pillars were red and green."

Ten thousand people—primarily Buddhist monks but also interested patrons and visitors—lived at Nalanda in the early 600s, according to this account. Everyone nearby, from kings to villagers, supported the scholars with clothing, food, shelter, and medicine. The subjects under study were broad and ecumenical: grammar, medicine, mathematics, worldly books, the Vedas and other classics, and the doctrinal literature of both the Theravada and the Mahayana schools of thought.

The foundation of all Buddhist doctrine comes from the Tipitaka, literally "Three Baskets." Originally written on palm leaves and stored in three baskets, these writings, collected during the First Council from people who traveled with the Buddha, come closest to being firsthand accounts of the Buddha's life and teachings. The Tipitaka is divided into three parts: the *Sutra Pitaka,* or discourses arising from episodes in the Buddha's life; the *Vinaya Pitaka,* laying forth monastic rules; and the *Abhidhamma Pitaka,* or higher analyses of the teachings—yet even these are not fully agreed upon among Buddhist schools of thought. Mahayana Buddhism also reveres numerous additional sutras, or discourses, which the tradition itself considers to have been spoken by the Buddha, and which Western scholarship dates from the period between 100 B.C. and 200 A.D. Since all this literature was oral to begin with, and since even the earliest Buddhists spoke different languages, the search for the definitive interpretation of the Buddha's meaning and intent has proved elusive and has propagated volumes of text and commentary.

Scholarly discourse was from early on an important element in Buddhist life. To the northeast, in today's Bangladesh, another impressive monastic community developed, patronized by the mighty kings of the Pala dynasty, who ruled all of northern India from a capital in the Bengal region from the eighth to the twelfth century. The ruins of the Somapura Mahavira monastery at Paharpur can only suggest the magnitude of the royal family's support of the Buddhist religion. One central building begins with an outside wall built in a square, each side nearly 1,000 feet long and divided into 177 monastic cells. Every cell contains a small central pedestal. One can almost imagine a monk kneeling alone in his small, spare, private space, focusing his mind on a Buddhist symbol. Nearly 3,000 terra-cotta plaques have been recovered at the site, some portraying the Buddha and others depicting a variety of animals, Hindu gods, musicians, and snake charmers.

The Somapura Mahavira was the largest but also the last Buddhist monastery built on the Indian subcontinent. From the 11th century on, incoming Muslim emperors saw to it that their Islamic religion prevailed. At times, Muslim invaders destroyed the buildings and icons sacred to the Buddhist religion. By then, though, through trade and migration, word of the religion had traveled thousands of miles in all directions. Elsewhere, Buddhism had taken root and was flourishing in many countries at the very time that it was dwindling in the land of its birth.

ABOVE: *A lotus blossom, a plant that often thrives in poor and imperfect soils, serves as a metaphor for the Buddha and his teachings.*

BUDDHISM IN SRI LANKA

THE STORY of Buddhism on the island of Sri Lanka is told through the dialogue between the Sage and the King. The Sage is Mahinda, sent on travels by his father, the Indian emperor Ashoka, to spread the promise of Buddhism. The King is Tissa, who succeeded his father, Mutasiva, as ruler of the island's north-central region in 247 B.C. and reigned for 40 years.

According to tradition, the Sage and the King met first on Aradhana Gala, a rocky outcropping of the mountain then called Missaka, on the day of the auspicious full moon of May. As King Tissa stood with his bow and arrow beside a mango tree, Mahinda, wrapped in yellow robes, mysteriously appeared to him, then was just as mysteriously joined by four other figures. At first Tissa presumed he was seeing *yakkas*—the spirits of the lakes, rivers, mountains, and trees worshiped on the island. When he inquired of the robed men who they were, they replied *samanas*—wandering monks—and declared, "From compassion for you we are come hither." Sanghamitta, sister to Mahinda, came to Sri Lanka as well, planting there a slip from the Bodh Gaya tree under which the Buddha reached enlightenment and introducing the order of nuns. Soon Tissa embraced the religion brought to the kingdom by these disciples of the Buddha.

Mahinda stayed on in Sri Lanka, living in a cave. Many of the places important to his story were later renamed in his honor. The mountain became Mihintale, the cave Mihindu Guha. A stupa, built to revere his remains, still stands nearby.

Broad stone stairways lead up to the Buddhist community that developed on Mihintale. The school of thought here kept true to its early origins, representing the more orthodox Theravada philosophy. The Tipitaka was first committed to writing in Sri Lanka in 29 B.C. These texts, recorded on fragile palm leaves in Pali, akin to Sanskrit, are the only known examples of that language. Theravada Buddhism still looks to Sri Lanka as the place where its core scripture, often called the Pali canon, was recorded.

By the fifth century A.D., nearly 2,000 monks were living in caves and houses built nearby. Stone tablets from the 10th century, which outlined the rules of the monastery, still stand amid the ruins today. Natural and manmade ponds connect with channels and spouts, suggesting ancient waterworks. Gateposts, railings, and wall ornaments are carved with floral and animal forms, in keeping with orthodox tradition. Distinctive to many of the Sri Lankan sites are exquisite moonstones—ornate semicircular stone steps that begin a stairway leading to a Buddhist shrine. The moonstone at Anuradhapura is carved with several arcs of design: scrolls of leaves, flower petals, four symbolic beasts—elephant, lion, horse, and bull—and, in the center, lotus blossoms folding in and opening out, symbolizing nirvana.

Buddhism spread throughout Sri Lanka through the ministry of Mahinda and generations of monks who followed. Today, 70 percent of Sri Lankans practice Buddhism. They make a pilgrimage of 16 sacred sites on the island, including three said to have been visited by the Buddha—a claim with mythic but not historic veracity. They visit Polonnaruwa, the city that rose to power as Anuradhapura declined. At nearby Gal Vihara, also called Cave of the Spirits of Knowledge, colossal 12th-century images of the Buddha dwell side by side, carved out of a granite cliff. One Buddha stands, 23 feet tall, and the other reclines, twice as long from head to toe. A third sits in the classic Sri Lankan enlightenment posture, left hand cradling the right, palms up, and left ankle bearing the right, both soles up as well.

Pilgrims also travel south to Kandy, where the left eye-tooth of the Buddha is enshrined at Sri Dalada Maligawa, the Temple of the Sacred Tooth Relic. Every summer the festival called Esala Perahera fills the streets of Kandy with music, color, and dance in a popular ritual that dramatizes the intersection of Buddhism, Hinduism, and indigenous

OPPOSITE: A visitor prays at the Mihintale Buddha statue, a site of pilgrimage for Sri Lankan Buddhists during the June full moon.

nature religions on this island. The holy tooth—which has made a dramatic pilgrimage of its own from India, defended fiercely through 15 centuries by Sinhalese kings—travels the streets in a golden casket, carried by a magnificently outfitted elephant. Four other elephants follow the chief tusker, carrying insignia of the four *devalas,* subordinate deities that include the Hindu god Vishnu, benefactor of Sri Lanka. At the final dawn of this two-week festival, four priests representing the devalas meet at an ancient ford and perform a "water-cutting ceremony," slicing the Mahavali River with a golden sword and collecting water to supply the gods for another year.

IN CENTRAL ASIA

ALONG WITH goods, ideas traveled the great Silk Road that connected the Mediterranean and the Middle East with India and China. The history of the spread of Buddhism to the west and to the east can be plotted along its route. The stark, mountainous terrain of the Hindu Kush had already seen the influences of powerful Buddhist patrons by the third century A.D. As in India, here Buddhist monks dwelt austerely in caves carved out of the rock cliffs at the foot of the mountains. One cave community formed in the Lamghan Valley near Bamiyan, Afghanistan, an important oasis and resting spot on the dry and rugged trail linking Kabul to the southern branch of the Silk Road. Bamiyan sits in a rare strip of verdant terrain at an altitude of 9,000 feet, between mountain ranges that shoot straight up to 16,000 feet on either side. It became the symbolic crossroads between India and Afghanistan, and Buddhists left monuments intended to last for all time.

Carving deep into the calcareous rock cliffs, they created two colossal Buddhas, 180 and 127 feet tall. Each stood

ABOVE: *In 2001, Muslim extremists destroyed the fifth-century statue of the Buddha at Bamiyan, Afghanistan, leaving a 180-foot hole.*

enshrined by walls that were vividly painted with ornamental and symbolic imagery. The smaller one was probably completed in the early third century A.D., while the larger one dates from about 200 years later. Eyewitness accounts suggest that these figures were painted with gold and decorated dazzlingly. Tales of Bamiyan carried home by Chinese travelers of the fifth and seventh centuries probably inspired the colossal Buddhas built in China, Korea, and Japan. Bamiyan's remarkable figures stood, weathering over time, until 2001 when Afghanistan's Taliban leadership ordered their destruction, citing them as false idols. Missiles and explosives emptied the rock shrines and damaged the supporting rock cliffs. An international effort is now under way to rebuild the Buddhas.

The Bamiyan figures were Central Asia's most famous Buddhist shrines but not the only ones. Remains of stupas and monasteries have been discovered throughout west Turkistan, and artifacts in museums around the world testify to the Buddhist history of the area. In the wake of the destruction at Bamiyan, another Central Asian colossus came to the attention of the world. In 2001 archaeologists at a new museum in Dushanbe, Tajikistan, announced that they would soon display a 45-foot-long Buddha that had once reclined in the Ajina-tepe monastery in Kayfir-kala, about 185 miles north of Bamiyan. Soviet archaeologists discovered the fifth-century figure in 1966. They had been sending smaller artifacts and paintings from the Ajina-tepe site to Moscow, but they broke this larger piece down into a hundred pieces and sequestered them, driven by politics to hide and protect the artifact. With Tajikistan's new status as a nation and with international support for its efforts, Tajik curators are busy restoring the figure.

THE WAY TO CHINA

SOME OF the liveliest accounts of Buddhism in Central Asia come from China, in the logs of first-millennium pilgrims traveling west to the source of their new religion. Word of Buddhism reached China during the first century A.D. Scholars quickly went to work translating the core scriptures, and by 350 A.D. more than one thousand texts had been rendered into Chinese.

In 399 A.D., at age 65, the traveler Fa Hsien set out on a pilgrimage from the city of Chang'an (today's Xi'an), the ancient Han capital in north-central China at the confluence of the Wei and Feng Rivers. The city had fallen to ruin early in the first century, but it was experiencing a rebirth thanks to its growing Buddhist community. From Chang'an, Fa Hsien walked to Dunhuang, an oasis and military outpost in the far west of China where the Silk Road split into northern and southern routes. The Great Wall reaches its westernmost point here, where it is made not of stone but of coarse clay and gravel layered with tamarisk twigs and reeds. Only the arid conditions of this region have allowed it to last so long. Fa Hsien likely stayed at Dunhuang for a while, honored to reside with the monks at the Mogao Caves, 15 miles south in the Gobi Desert. These monks upheld the legacy of the legendary Bodhisattva of Dunhuang—a man known by two names, Dharmaksema and Zhu Fahu, because of his pivotal work translating Indian scripture into Chinese.

In 1900, that legacy grew in reputation as a custodian at the Mogao site found his way into a new cave. Inside were thousands of Buddhist manuscripts and paintings that had been hidden for a thousand years. A few printed books formed part of this remarkable collection, including the Diamond Sutra, the oldest book bearing its own printed date: "the 13th of the 4th moon of the 9th year of Xiantong," or May 11, 868. Many of the objects in this so-called Cave of the Thousand Buddhas were sold or removed to other countries. Now China's Dunhuang Academy oversees the conservation, research, and display of this cave as well as the other 570 caves, 54,000 square yards of murals, and 3,000 painted statues found nearby.

From Dunhuang, Fa Hsien crossed the Taklimakan Desert with a camel train. "In this desert there are a great many evil spirits and hot winds," he wrote. "No guidance is to be obtained save from the rotting bones of dead men,

A BUDDHIST NUN'S STORY

—LOBSANG DECHEN, *The Tibetan Nuns Project*

EVER SINCE I was a small child in a school for Tibetan refugees in Kullu, India, I admired the life of monks and nuns and knew that I wanted to spend my life practicing Buddhism. Once His Holiness the Dalai Lama visited our school and told us that for the benefit of this life, we had to study hard. From that I realized that education in the school only benefits this life. I wanted to do something that would both ensure happiness in my future lives and also enable me to continue my own path to enlightenment for the benefit of all sentient beings. After learning about the right path in Buddhism, I knew that religious practice would be the only way to achieve that. My final decision to become a nun was made after His Holiness's talk.

I asked our school director to send me to Dharmsala to join the Gaden Choeling Nunnery. One of the two head nuns took me on as a disciple. The nunnery was new with only 10 nuns. They had no organized study program and only occasionally held group prayers. My teacher had me memorize the prayers everybody should know. After three months she went on a pilgrimage, and I was sent to the Tibetan Children's Village (TCV) School in Dharmsala. Because I was a nun, I was allowed to go to the nunnery on Sundays and holidays so that I could join in the special prayers in the nunnery or in the main temple. I found it interesting to see the monks engaged in Buddhist philosophical debate in front of the main temple and wanted to learn to debate like them.

In 1979, I finished 10th grade at TCV and wanted to join an institution where I could learn higher Buddhist philosophy. At that time the only college-level courses were at the Buddhist Institute of Higher Studies in Sarnath. I tried to get admission there, but they would not accept women. Next I sought admission to the recently established School of Buddhist Dialectics in Dharmsala as a day student. At the time nuns were not studying there, and again, I was not accepted.

The TCV director and staff encouraged me to complete 12th grade, because as an educated nun I would be useful to nunneries in the future. In the Tibetan school, we covered

ABOVE: *A silk painting, or* thangka, *of the Buddha draws a crowd of onlookers at Ganden Palace in Lhasa, Tibet.*

some basic Buddhist teachings but not as extensively as it's done in the monasteries. Still, it was a good option. Some of my friends left school and joined nunneries, but because there was no education program, they neither finished their secular education nor were they able to pursue the traditional monastic education. I feel that education in the nunneries is important, and I want to do all that I can to improve it.

After finishing 12th grade, I joined St. Bede's Convent College in Simla, where I completed my B.A., then went on to Chandhigarh for a B.Ed. Upon completion, I taught English and geography at the TCV school for eight years. I enjoyed teaching, but as a nun I felt out of place when rehearsing songs and dances with the children. I also found it a problem that I had to miss the annual spring teachings of His Holiness the Dalai Lama because the school year opened at that time.

On winter holidays I visited the holy places of Buddhist pilgrimage. On these pilgrimages I was reminded of impermanence when I saw places that at one time were important seats of Buddhist learning or wonderful temples that are now simply ruins. One winter I went through my first 100,000 prostrations in Bodh Gaya, the place where Buddha attained enlightenment. It took me one month and 20 days to complete that many prostrations, spending all day in front of the main stupa with brief stops for meals. I have been prone to illness, but this improved my health. I believe that it purified the bad karma that causes illness.

Since the mid-1980s there has been in the Tibetan community in India a growing commitment to prioritizing education among nuns. Meanwhile, in Tibet, after many years of complete suppression of religious practice, there had been some liberalization. Hundreds of people became monks and nuns and set about rebuilding the monasteries. By 1987, this movement had developed into a political struggle for a free Tibet, and nuns held peaceful demonstrations in Lhasa. The Chinese government's response was swift and brutal, and many nuns were arrested, tortured, and imprisoned. When released, they were denied re-admission into their nunneries and were forced to return to their villages. As a result, many nuns undertook the dangerous journey over the mountains to seek asylum in India.

In early 1991, a large group of young nuns reached Dharmsala in distressed condition from the arduous journey. The Tibetan Nuns Project was instituted to look after the new arrivals and establish new nunneries. I was asked to work for the Tibetan Nuns Project, and I accepted.

Education programs are now set up in most nunneries, providing traditional monastic education, religious arts, and secular subjects such as math, science, and English. Once they have completed their education, the nuns will work with confidence in nunneries or in the community.

I myself feel much happier working with nuns since I am in a spiritual environment, and I can adjust my leave so that I can attend the public teachings given in Dharmsala. His Holiness says that we are suffering because our minds are not "tame," that we do not know the real nature of our minds, which are controlled by afflictive emotions carried from life to life. We are so used to this contaminated state of mind that we are not even aware that it is contaminated. The teachings are there to be applied to control our minds, and they help a great deal when I am interacting with people. Though it is difficult, one can experience the changes, slowly, after many years of daily practice. In my daily life, I pray and meditate for half an hour in the morning. If I do it with concentration, I can feel the mental calm for the whole day. Still, I need more time and a quiet place to practice the teachings intensively to be able in a future life to gain enlightenment for the benefit of all.

which point the way." Fa Hsien survived, though, and he made it to Taxila, in modern-day Pakistan, at the foot of the Hindu Kush. From there he traveled south and east, visiting all the significant Buddhist sites along the Ganges River, then completed the circuit by sea, coasting south to Sri Lanka and Sumatra before heading north for Nanking. He arrived home nearly 16 years after he had begun.

More than 200 years later, another Chinese monk headed west. By 627 A.D., when Xuan Tsang set out on the Silk Road, Buddhism had spread its influence through much of central and eastern China, and throughout the coastline and island regions of Southeast Asia. The religion was thoroughly institutionalized in Xuan Tsang's native China. Chang'an, growing into an enormous city of trade, was the home of a major Buddhist university. From there Xuan Tsang traveled to Dunhuang, then took the northern Silk Road passage and visited sites throughout the Indian subcontinent. When he returned to Chang'an, crowds greeted him as a hero. Crown Prince Li Zhi ordered a pagoda specially erected to house the hundreds of sacred manuscripts he brought back with him.

Modern archaeologists used the journals of Fa Hsien and Xuan Tsang in their search for the ancient Buddhist sites of India. The two pilgrims had found Lumbini and Bodh Gaya deserted, but guided by records of land forms and architectural ruins, 19th-century scholars were able to identify the sites.

An already complex religious culture prevailed in China by 500 A.D. Neolithic sites show the prehistoric roots of Chinese ancestor worship, expressed in the care with which burial sites were provided with elegant containers holding food and drink for the passage to the hereafter. Other ancient artifacts manifest 3,000-year-old practices of supernatural divination. Linguists and archaeologists have come up with an explanation for the engraved fragments of ox scapula and tortoiseshell unearthed in the Henan and Shandong Provinces. Apparently a shaman carved a question on the bone, heated it in a ritual fire, then read an answer from the way the heat cracked the bone. Questions and answers, and verification that the answers did come true, have all been deciphered in the pictograph characters carved on these bone fragments.

CONFUCIANISM AND DAOISM

WOVEN IN with China's rich indigenous culture were two organized religions and philosophies, Confucianism and Daoism, both well established by the time of any contact with Buddhism. Confucius—or, more correctly, K'ung Fu-tzu—was born in 551 B.C., nearly the same time as Mahavira, founder of Jainism, and the Buddha. More a philosopher than a religious leader, Confucius offered a view of the world and human beings' role in it that developed into a state religion during several phases of China's long history. Responsibility began in the home, he advised: Children should respect and obey their parents, and from that model, rules for citizenship, decorum, and social order unfolded. "Hold faithfulness and sincerity as first principles," reads a proverb from Confucius's *Book of Analects* (*Lun Yu*), one of the central works of Confucianism. The practical simplicity of these words, with their emphasis on honesty and thoughtfulness, characterizes the philosophy as a whole. Confucius emphasized that respectful behavior in the here and now was the key to achieving the larger goal of social harmony.

It is harder to pin down the history and the message of Daoism. Historically, it was the culmination of several grassroots religious uprisings in China during the first two centuries A.D. Its holy book, the *Dao De Jing,* is ascribed to the legendary, or maybe mythical, Lao Zi, claimed to be an elder contemporary of Confucius. The new religion

OPPOSITE: Visitors ascend the "Stairway to Heaven" leading to the summit of Tai Shan, the sacred mountain home of Daoist gods.
FOLLOWING PAGES: A Buddha's head peers from a cliff in Lu Shan, China, above the Min River, roiling 233 feet below at the statue's feet.

picked up transcendental strains from the ancient nature religions, with the "Dao" meaning both the elusive and unified force of the universe and the path to be followed. "Man takes his law from the Earth; the Earth takes its law from Heaven; Heaven takes its law from the Dao. The law of the Dao is its being what it is," reads the *Dao De Jing,* composed over a 60-year-period, probably from 300 to 240 B.C. Such beliefs and complementary rituals led by popular priests, not members of the court, held a mysterious appeal. Instead of following rules for externalized behavior, as stressed in Confucianism, people were to become the passive vessels of the universal Dao. While in some ways Daoism represented a challenge, in other ways it simply offered a complement to Confucianism. Buddhism represented the third thread in the complicated Chinese weave.

BODHIDHARMA

ABOUT 500 A.D., a prince from southern India followed the advice of his Buddhist teacher and traveled to China. Unable to win court approval in the south of China, he ventured north, by legend crossing the Yangtze River on a leaf. His destination was Song Shan, the sacred mountain cluster that rises abruptly and austerely above China's central plains. All three ways of Chinese religion built sanctuaries among Song Shan's rocky peaks: the Daoist Zhongyue Temple, the Songyang Confucian Academy, and the Shaolin Temple and Ancestral Hall of the Chanzong sect of Buddhism.

Bodhidharma, as this somewhat mythic traveler came to be called, remained at Shaolin, where he developed a combination of mental and physical discipline to strengthen body and devotion. Bodhidharma represented the epitome of self-control. To maintain full wakefulness during meditation, so it is said, he cut off his own eyelids. Even today, wide-eyed Bodhidharma dolls represent the concentration he was able to achieve. The dolls come with blank eye sockets. A devotee paints in one eye as he embarks on a difficult task, then paints in the other upon its completion.

Bodhidharma's teachings infuse the Chinese practice of Buddhism to this day. The physical aspect of his teachings developed into the highly ritualized and spiritually charged martial art called kung fu. His intellectual and spiritual teachings came to be called Ch'an Buddhism—in Japanese, Zen; both words mean meditation—and it is the form that has characterized East Asian Buddhist practice ever since. "There is no wisdom, and there is no attainment whatsoever, because there is nothing [literally, 'no thing'] to be attained," says the Heart Sutra, a central Ch'an scripture. "Because there is nothing to be attained, the Bodhisattva…has no obstruction on his mind. Because there is no obstruction, he has no fear, and he passes far beyond confused imagination and reaches ultimate nirvana."

To follow the Buddha's example, according to Ch'an believers, was to turn wisdom upside down and inside out, to seek to realize nirvana, enlightenment, personally and directly, untainted by tradition or expectation. Small moments of awakening provided glimpses of the larger goal. Those moments could come through the discipline of meditation or from the flash of understanding reached by considering a koan, a paradoxical riddle, statement, or gesture that could not be interpreted by rational thought. The earliest koan was posed when the Buddha, preparing to teach an audience of earnest followers, simply sat in front of them and held up a flower. What did it mean? No words could answer that question. In Ch'an Buddhism, one comes closer to true knowledge by contemplating an experience such as this one, assigning neither words nor meaning to it. Ch'an Buddhist teachers became well known for their koanlike responses to their students. One named Tozen was weighing flax seed when a student asked, "What is Buddha?" Tozen answered, "This flax weighs three pounds." Some koans are so striking and simple, they have become part of the general culture, for example, "What is the sound of one hand clapping?"

The Shaolin Temple became an important center for the practice of a combined physical and mental discipline in the service of the Buddhist faith. In the 14th century, the

ruling class of the Manchu, or Qing, dynasty saw the Buddhist monk-soldiers as a threat and banned their practices. Devotions continued to be carried out there, but in secret. Fires set during Chiang Kai-shek's Northern Expedition in 1928 badly damaged the temple and nearby buildings, but the complex has since been rebuilt. Today it is known for its kung fu school as much as for its Buddhist monastery. On its grounds still stand more than 200 stone stupas, the Forest of Pagodas, memorializing monks who lived there in centuries past.

Song Shan, one of five sacred mountains in China, plays a central role in an ancient myth, which described heaven as a hemisphere above and earth as a square below. At the center of that square stood Song Shan, mirroring the center of heaven and surrounded by four sacred mountains in the four cardinal directions. Since before recorded history,

the Chinese people have revered their mountains as sacred dwelling places of the gods and spiritual destinations for the seeker. The very language used in Chinese to say pilgrimage, *ch'ao-shan chin-hsiang,* means "paying one's respect to a mountain." These mountains reveal layer upon layer of religious history.

In the north, Wutai Shan is a constellation of five prominent peaks amid a 75-mile-long ridge, the tallest reaching 10,000 feet above sea level. Forty-eight temples cluster near these peaks or in the sheltering valleys. They include Nanchan Si and Foguang Si, two of three surviving wooden temples from the Tang dynasty. In Longquan Si, the Dragon Spring Temple, dozens of Buddha images grace the halls, most notably Pu-tai, the Laughing Buddha, a distinctively Chinese figure with bare belly, begging bowl, and traveling satchel, said to have been inspired by a monk who

ABOVE: *Spring arrives at a temple on Pu Tuo Shan, one of five peaks considered sacred by Chinese Buddhists.*

BUDDHISM

SELECTED SCRIPTURES

FOR BOTH the Theravada and Mahayana traditions the basic form of scripture is the sutra, in which a particular point of doctrine is deliberated. Theravada Buddhists revere the Tipitaka (Three Baskets), the total canon of their school, named for the containers in which Ceylonese monks placed their palm-leaf scrolls when Buddha's teachings were written down in the first century B.C. The most important Theravada sutras accompany the discourses attributed to Buddha. The Mahayana Buddhists share much of the Tipitaka, but add sutras that set forth doctrines on the bodhisattvas. Other sects offer their own versions of scripture.

FROM THE TIPITAKA

ON NIRVANA

This monk of wisdom here, devoid of desire and passion,
attains to deathlessness, peace, the unchanging state of nirvana....
The steadfast go out like this lamp....
Where no-thing is the Isle of No-Beyond.
Nirvana do I call it—the utter extinction of aging and dying.

ON COMPASSION

Never in this world is hate
Appeased by hatred.
It is only appeased by love—
This is an eternal law.

Victory breeds hatred
For the defeated lie down in sorrow.
Above victory or defeat
The calm man dwells in peace.

AVATAMSAKA SUTRA *(The Flower Garland Sutra)*

I will be a good physician for the sick and suffering. I will lead those who have lost their way to the right road. I will be a bright light for those in the dark night, and cause the poor and destitute to uncover hidden treasures.

ON RETURNING GOOD FOR EVIL

A foolish man, learning that the Buddha observed the principle of great love, which commends the return of good for evil, came and abused him. The Buddha was silent, pitying his folly. When the man had finished his abuse, the Buddha asked him, saying, "Son, if a man declined to accept a present made to him, to whom would it belong?" And the man answered, "In that case it would belong to the man who offered it."

"My son," said the Buddha, "I decline to accept thy abuse, and request thee to keep it thyself. Will it not be a source of misery to thee?... A wicked man who reproaches a virtuous one is like one who looks up and spits to heaven; the spit soils not the heaven, but comes back and defiles his own person."... The abuser went away ashamed, but he came again and took refuge in the Buddha.

wandered through these lands and showed himself to be a bodhisattva by his unceasing good humor.

Buddhism's hold in China originated in the north, but over the centuries it spread east and south. Between the devotion of influential monks, poets, and teachers, and the patronage of regional patriarchs, as many as ten new and distinct schools of Buddhist thought arose in China during the first millennium.

When a local ruler embraced Buddhism, he often did so not only with his heart but also with his treasury. In 454 A.D., for example, Tao Wu Ti and four succeeding emperors in the northern realm of China carried out a massive building project that resulted in a five-story temple and five 16-foot-tall standing statues of the Buddha, cast in gilt-bronze. These projects are estimated to have required more than 122 tons of copper alone. One statue of the Buddha made in this period was recorded to stand 43 feet tall, made of 49 tons of copper and more than a quarter ton of gold. In 515 A.D., there

were nearly 14,000 Buddhist temples in China, 1,367 in the city of Luoyang alone. Each project topped the one that came before, culminating in a nine-story pagoda. The pagoda stood 1,000 feet tall, including its ringed spire, until a lightening strike destroyed it.

This same sort of imperial initiative resulted in a number of exquisitely sculpted Buddhist shrines in caves in northern China. The Yungang Caves comprise 42 sandstone grottoes just west of Datong; the Longmen Caves, farther south, contain more than 97,000 statues carved into limestone cliffs along both banks of the Yi River. In one cave sculpture dating from the sixth century, a Buddha figure

sits on a many-petaled lotus flower, his right hand raised protectively. Above him, trees are in flower, bodhisattvas mirror his pose, and celestial figures hover on high. This is the Buddha Amitabha, the Buddha of Unlimited Radiance, in his home of eternal bliss—the better life hereafter promised to all by Pure Land Buddhism. To the poor laborer, such a vision provided hope, and Pure Land Buddhism, which emphasized chanting or meditation upon the Buddha's name—"staying mindful of the Buddha"—spread especially fast among the laypeople of China. The new ideas of Pure Land Buddhism stood in contrast, and sometimes in conflict, with those of Ch'an Buddhism.

Pure Land Buddhism is often traced back to a Buddhist monk named Hui-yuan who lived on Mount Lushan in Jiangxi Province. With glistening pools, plunging gorges, flower-strewn paths, and mist-enveloped mountainscapes, the beauty of this land warrants its mythic reputation. Although Mao Zedong led a revolution in the 20th century intended to extinguish religious belief and practices among the Chinese people, still he chose this paradise on earth as his home. His former residence at Mount Lushan, the Lulin Villa, became a museum in 1984.

Buddhism flourished in China from the 1st century A.D. into the 13th century, when a new wave of Confucianism became the predominant religion. Buddhism came from India, but the Chinese made it their own. The religion would not be what it is today without the influences pressed upon it during those centuries in China. Buddhism has remained over the centuries a strong strand of the tripartite Chinese religious tradition—with Daoism and

ABOVE: A Sung dynasty painting shows Daoist philosopher Lao Zi riding a water buffalo, preparing to leave civilization behind.

FOLLOWING PAGES: Holding an offering of burning incense, an elderly woman prays in solitude at the Nan Pu Tuo Temple in Xiamen.

Confucianism—and as the political climate has relaxed in China, is undergoing a great resurgence in popularity.

BUDDHISM IN INDONESIA

IN THE last two decades of the seventh century A.D., the Chinese pilgrim Yi-jing spent 20 years in scholarly pilgrimage, visiting Buddhist sites throughout India and Central Asia and collecting sacred scriptures to carry home to translate. His itinerary included stays in the Indonesian kingdom of Sriwijaya, already an important Buddhist center whose power extended northward into the Malay Peninsula. In central Java soon thereafter, the Saliendra kingdom rose to power, leaving as its legacy the remarkable Buddhist architecture of Borobudur.

Volcanoes and earthquakes have reshaped this landscape over time, but the Temple of Borobudur appears to have been auspiciously sited: lying an even distance within the hills, overlooking a lake at the confluence of two rivers. Architecturally, Borobudur is a three-dimensional square mandala—a sacred design—symmetrical around its central stupa. Sculptures in Borobudur show the pilgrimage of the devout, paralleling stages in the life of the Buddha.

The pilgrim to Borobudur walks clockwise through the lower galleries. Relief sculptures along the way depict the story of the Buddha in this and previous lifetimes. Only after passing through the lower galleries, which represent the *Kamadhatu,* the Sphere of Desire, can one reach the next round of galleries, called the *Rupadhatu,* or Sphere of Form—in Buddhist philosophy, the stage beyond worldly concerns. Sculptures along these walls depict the archetypal pilgrimage, overseen by Maitreya, a bodhisattva who stands for the promise of a heavenly future. Having circled this portion of the temple, the pilgrim may ascend into the next one, the *Arupadhatu,* or Sphere of Formlessness. Atop this level sits the central stupa, which some experts believe was deliberately left empty to signify nirvana, the bliss beyond all reckoning.

Borobudur appears to have been abandoned abruptly just before 1000 A.D., possibly as the result of a volcanic

eruption. The temple lay buried under ash and overgrowth for nearly a millennium, until Dutch archaeologists discovered it in the early 20th century. Despite such a glorious Buddhist past, only one percent of Indonesian people practice Buddhism today.

THE WAY TO KOREA

AROUND 375 A.D., Chinese Buddhist monks were invited to the royal houses of two of Korea's Three Kingdoms. By the seventh century, when the Three Kingdoms were unified under the Silla royal house, its leadership had embraced the Buddhist religion as well. Seventh-century philosopher Uisang offered the vision of a harmonious community found in Pure Land Buddhism. He described his own Korean homeland as a Buddha land replete with holy places, and helped the Korean people conceptualize their land as a single sovereignty.

A practical blend of Buddhism and Confucianism served as the state religion from the sixth century on. Bulguksa, a Buddhist temple built in the ancient Silla capital of Kyongju, still stands today. Originally founded in 535, the temple was completed in 751 under the supervision of the king's prime minister, Kim Dae-seong. The temple is divided into two courts, one centered in the Hall of the Buddha and the other in the Hall of Paradise.

Not far away, Kim Dae-seong also established a hermitage for Buddhists seeking a place for solitude and meditation. An hour's walk from Bulguksa, up the steep eastern slope of Mount Toham, the granite sanctuary of the Sokkuram Buddhist Grotto opens out to the Sea of Japan. In the cave complex's antechamber, eight congregated devas—gods of India who have heard the Buddha's call—and two musclebound stone guards animate the entryway. A devotee then passes deeper into the cave through a short corridor peopled with four terrifying heavenly kings, traditional Korean figures representing the cardinal directions. Each stands firm, trampling demons underfoot. Deeper yet, in the inner sanctum, a Buddha carved of

white Korean granite sits in full lotus position, eyes closed. A bas-relief of attendant bodhisattvas encircles the Buddha.

While the creators of Sokkuram very likely took their inspiration from Chinese Buddhist cave works like those in Dunhuang, they faced a different geological challenge. The Chinese worked on low-lying cliffs of soft stone—limestone and sandstone—whereas the Koreans took on the challenge of a solid granite mountain 2,500 feet above sea level. Chunks of granite shorn out of the mountain cave were stacked without mortar to form floors, walls, and ceilings. Natural ventilation preserved the statuary through techniques not recorded. Sokkuram was left to decay under Confucian regimes up through the 19th century. Well-

meaning preservationists in the early 20th century removed the artwork and encased the entire cave in concrete, which caused water leaks and erosion and even caused moss to grow on the sculptures. Further work done in the 1960s has solved many of the grotto's humidity problems. Pilgrims to the shrine must overlook the trappings of modern technology in order to relive the experience of Korean Buddhists of nearly 1,500 years ago.

Today, among Koreans who practice religion, Buddhism is a predominant faith, especially the Jogye Order of Buddhism, a tradition of meditation and enlightenment like Ch'an and Zen. Founded by Taego Pu, a Korean monk who traveled to China in the mid-1300s, the

ABOVE: *Light strikes Buddha statues in the cave temple of Sanbangsa, a Buddhist sanctuary on the Korean island of Chejo Do.*

Jogye Order especially reveres its "Three Jewels": the monasteries of Tongdo-sa, Haein-sa, and Songgwang-sa. Tongdo-sa, the largest of the three, built on Yongjuk-san Mountain near Pusan, boasts no statue of the Buddha. Instead, its central shrine looks out upon a stupa containing relics of the Buddha brought long ago from China. A visitor reaches the temple only by crossing over the "windless bridge" and through the forest of "windless pines," a passage that symbolizes the purification of the senses needed to approach the divine.

BUDDHISM IN JAPAN

IN 523 A.D., a stout log of camphor wood washed ashore on one of the islands ruled by the Yamato emperor of Japan. Recognizing its value, attendants brought the log to their master. It was a fine example of *Cinnamomum camphora*, a wood favored by court sculptors for its dense grain, pungent fragrance, and natural resistance to boring insects. Seeking the highest way to honor this gift from the sea, the emperor requested that it be carved into the shape of the Buddha. As a model, he allowed his artisans to view the gilt-bronze figurine he had received the year before from emissaries of the court of Baekje, the southernmost of Korea's Three Kingdoms.

Whether or not this story is true, it is a way of telling the early history of Buddhism in Japan. Korean sovereigns, already committed to the Buddhist religion, conveyed sculptures, scriptures, and banners to their Japanese counterparts in the sixth century A.D. It was as much a diplomatic as a missionary effort.

At first, the only converts to the new religion were the nobility: Yomei, named as the first Japanese emperor to practice Buddhism; his sister, Empress Suiko; and his son, Prince Shotoku. Under them the city of Nara became the imperial capital. Shotoku saw to the founding of more than 40 Buddhist temples, including the Horyu Temple, which still stands in Nara and is considered to be the world's oldest wooden building.

Two hundred years later, just outside Nara, Emperor Shomu built Todaiji—its name means "large temple to the east." Measuring about 280 by 165 feet, the temple equaled the imperial palace in size and included Daibutsu Den, the Building for the Great Buddha Statue. Shomu mustered all his country's manpower, wealth, and dedication to build the temple and the massive Buddha statue it enshrined. The sculpture stood 55 feet tall, from the many-petaled lotus on which the Buddha sat to the flaming halo of bodhisattvas that encircled his head. Shomu's building collapsed in flames during a civil war in the 12th century. It was rebuilt, only to be destroyed during battle another 400 years later. The present building was completed in 1705.

SHINTOISM

BY THE 18th century, Buddhism was the religion of the Japanese people, but only because it had adapted to popular religious beliefs of old, such as the Shinto religion. The ancient Japanese world was animated by gods known as *kami,* numbering eight million, according to the eighth-century Shinto epic *Nihon Shoki.* Kami include deities residing in specific places, spirits of natural phenomena and wild animals, ancestral spirits, and the gods, goddesses, heroes, and heroines of popular myth. Some are local and particular while others spread a broad influence, such as the sun goddess Amaterasu, the rice god Inari, and the guardian god of Japan and its emperors, called Okuninushi. By the time of Prince Shotoku's ascendancy, Shinto was a developed religion, diverse enough to encompass many practices throughout the islands of Japan and organized enough to join people in common practices and beliefs. Shinto never separated from its origins in nature, and an auspicious formation, such as a very tall tree, a massive boulder, or an abundant spring, could become a shrine to the resident kami.

OPPOSITE: A torii gate welcomes pilgrims to the Itsukushima Shrine, sacred to both Shintoism and Buddhism, on Miyajima Island, Japan.

At these sacred sites the Shinto faithful erect *torii*, sacramental gateways constructed of two posts and a lintel, to mark the passage from the mundane into the spirit realm.

To Shinto believers, the Buddhist religion at first appeared a threat from the outside. Monarchic struggles between those who espoused the new religion and those who insisted on the old took place through the next century. Gradually, however, with the Shinto willingness to believe in a diversity of spiritual embodiments, the Buddha in his many attitudes and with his attendant bodhisattvas came to be revered among the Japanese people. Buddhist teachers represented the two religions as harmonious, not mutually exclusive.

Buddhist temples were built alongside Shinto shrines. By the end of the first millennium, a religious movement called Ryobu Shinto, "Double Shinto," systematically linked Shinto and Buddhist deities, explaining that each of the kami dreamed of his or her *bosatsu*—the Japanese word for bodhisattva. Even today, a Japanese household very likely includes both a Shinto shelf to enshrine family deities and a Buddhist altar to honor the spirits of the ancestors, the Buddha, and several bodhisattvas. Some call their deities *kami-hotoke,* combining the words for kami and Buddha into one.

As the Japanese embraced Buddhism, the universe of bodhisattvas multiplied, changing the nature of Buddhist beliefs and practices significantly. The historical Buddha was more often called Sakyamuni, from his tribal name. Avalokiteshvara—who usually takes feminine form as Kuan-yin in China and Kannon in Japan—is the bodhisattva of infinite compassion who had postponed his own Buddhahood in order to help others. Maitreya, kind and loving, is the heavenly Buddha who will revitalize the Buddhist teachings in the future.

Each of these bodhisattvas—and many others—came to be known by characteristic postures, colors, clothing, or accoutrements. Kannon's head, for example, is sometimes topped with ten more, which spilled out when the bodhisattva's head split with grief over the number of beings in the world yet to be saved. The female Kannon is evoked as the goddess who aids in fertility and eases childbirth, but Kannon can be manifested in any of 33 transformations. Four established pilgrimage routes—eastern, western, inside Tokyo, and just outside Tokyo—present a map of 33 holy places of Kannon for the devotee to visit.

In a country where volcanic peaks dominate the landforms, it is not surprising to find mountains regarded as the holiest of places. Snow-capped Mount Fuji reigns supreme, taller than 12,000 feet above sea level, and is considered the dwelling place—or perhaps the very being—of a Shinto goddess, revered in annual pilgrimages. Two rugged mountains to the west symbolize two major sects founded within a year of each other. Saicho and Kukai, two young Japanese noblemen, traveled to China to study Buddhism together in the early ninth century. When they returned, each established a mountaintop monastery, Saicho's on Mount Hiei, near Kyoto on the island of Honshu; and Kukai's on Mount Koya, to the south on the Kii-Sanmyaku Peninsula on the island of Shikoku. Saicho's Tendai Buddhism offered Buddhahood

ABOVE: *Long red hair and a white face are hallmarks of a Kabuki performer, an actor in dramas created by Japanese Buddhist monks.*
OPPOSITE: *Visitors to a temple on Japan's Shikoku Island make an offering of incense to Yakushi-nyorai, the Buddha of healing.*

MIRRORING THE BUDDHA
A Daily Practice

THE FUNDAMENTAL practice of Buddhism consists in private meditation and prayer. The intercession of a priest or a visit to the temple is not necessary. Buddhists of all traditions observe special rites on the new, full, and quarter moon days, when they might fast and meditate at home or at the temple, make offerings of flowers, incense, or food, and attend readings and lectures. Among Theravadan Buddhists, found in South and Southeast Asia, lay people and monastics observe the three-month monsoon season as a special time of purification and prayer, but among Mahayanists, in Central and East Asia, only monks and nuns tend to do so. This custom emulates the Buddha, who gathered his sangha, or community of followers, in a retreat every rainy season.

Beyond those routines, however, Buddhists read, pray, and meditate to shape their behavior ever more closely to the model of the awakened one, the Buddha. They mentally take refuge from suffering in the Buddha, the enlightened teacher symbolized by images and living teachers; by the dharma, his teachings as recorded in the scriptures; and by the sangha. Theravadans aspire to mental and spiritual liberation, whereas Mahayanists also seek enlightenment for the sake of others. Various vows unfold into an ethic of nonviolence, calm, temperance, and simplicity that may be summarized as: "Help other beings, if you can; if you can't, at least do them no harm."

One goal of meditation, which can be practiced while sitting, standing, or walking, is to focus the mind within, withdrawing attention from the clutter of worldly concerns to find a mindful quiet and inner peace that reflect the state of enlightenment—a state that rare beings such as the Buddha and the bodhisattvas attained in life. Nuns and monks are the most dedicated practitioners. Many Theravadan Buddhists spend time in a monastery without making it the lifelong commitment common among Mahayana nuns and monks. A monastic lifestyle reduces worldly distractions and presents an environment conducive to meditation and enlightenment. Monks and nuns shave their heads; wear unadorned clothing, often dyed a saffron yellow; and take vows of renunciation and celibacy. Men and women live separately. Monastics wake early and begin the day together with prayer, silent meditation, and scriptural recitation. They spend many hours in study, working with teachers to memorize, discuss, and understand the Buddhist holy books. Evenings end with prayer, recitations, and meditation. They may consume nothing but liquids after midday. Each community supports the local nuns and monks with food and alms, in thanks for their devotion for the sake of them all.

to all but required 12 years of discipline from those who chose the monastic path. The Shingon Buddhism of Kukai (renamed Kobo Daishi after his death) emphasized ritual chanting and visual contemplation of mandalas as methods for quieting the mind and attaining enlightenment. An active Tendai monastery still operates on Mount Hiei. Pilgrims following the Shingon path today travel to Shikoku and repeat Kobo Daishi's 900-mile journey around the island and its 88 temples.

ZEN BUDDHISM

OF ALL the Buddhist practices that evolved in Japan, none have been as influential around the world as those of the Soto school. Founded by the monk Dogen Zenji, the school's teachings are the precursor of today's Zen Buddhism. Dogen was born in 1200 A.D. and understood early on what impermanence of life means, when he was orphaned at seven years old. He first practiced Buddhism on Mount Hiei. Seeking greater understanding, he traveled to China, still regarded at the time as the repository of Buddhist wisdom. He studied and meditated, and by the age of 28 is said to have attained "the bliss of Buddhist truth," emphasizing simplicity and discipline, which he brought back to Japan.

Dogen sought to unify the focus of Japanese Buddhists, finding the common thread among all schools and sects. He wanted to bring believers' regard back to the Buddha himself. Attendant bodhisattvas, scriptures and commentaries, rituals and sacred objects—these were all externalizations. They could be helpful tools in the faith or they could be tempting distractions, becoming ends in themselves that led a practitioner astray from the true path to enlightenment.

The best way to approach the Buddha, he taught, was through seated meditation, *Zazen*. He described the state in Zazen as "mind and body dropped off." Using the sort of paradoxes central to Ch'an Buddhism, he said: "This state should be experienced by everyone; it is like piling fruit into a basket without a bottom, like pouring water into a bowl with a pierced hole; however much you may pile or pour, you cannot fill it up. When this is realized, the pail bottom is broken through. But while there is still a trace of conceptualism which makes you say 'I have this understanding' or 'I have that realization,' then you are still playing with unrealities."

Dogen's monastery, Eheiji, still operates in the mountains near Fukui, on the north-central coast of Honshu overlooking the Sea of Japan.

This monastery and many other Buddhist sites survived through a period in modern Japanese history when the Meiji rulers banned Buddhism in favor of the more nationalistic Shinto faith. Today the two religions intertwine once again in the daily lives of the Japanese. It is not uncommon for a Japanese family to follow Shinto rituals for a marriage, then observe Buddhist rites for a funeral. This is a preference that goes back to ancient times, since in Shinto the dead body could be considered impure, whereas in Buddhism the dead body received a priest's highest regard. Japanese Buddhists uphold the tradition of mammoth shrines. In 1252 the Great Amida Buddha was built in Ushiku, 30 miles north of Tokyo. Called the "High-rise Buddha," it rises 400 feet, the world's tallest bronze.

BUDDHISM IN SOUTHEAST ASIA

THROUGHOUT SOUTHEAST Asia, as in Japan, Buddhism wove its way into a world already animated with primeval spirits, organized by local ritual, and colored by the earlier influence of Hinduism. Theravada missionaries approached by land and sea from India and Sri Lanka as early as the first century; Mahayana missionaries traveled south from China after 700 A.D. Some regions absorbed the religion more deeply than others, but the regional variations on the Buddhist stupa testify to the presence of Buddhism in the landscape of Southeast Asia.

The hybrid energy of the region's religious heritage still pulses through miles of ruins in northwestern Cambodia. Now overtaken by vines and tree roots, these remains mark the site of a majestic metropolis built where the Siem Reap River pours into the Tonle Sap, the Great Lake. First called Yashodharapura, this city served as the administrative and religious capital of the Khmer, whose empire grew from the ninth through the twelfth century to include most of the Southeast Asian peninsula. Palaces, residences, and governmental buildings constructed of wood perished long ago, but the temples, built of sandstone and laterite, have been worn but not destroyed by time.

At the heart of the city, both physically and spiritually, stood Angkor Wat. This magnificent temple's design reflected the symmetry of the universe in its layout and mirrored the mountain of the gods with its pyramidal orchestration of pillars and spires. An encircling moat delineated the sacred space. Divine faces beamed out from walls and corners. Serpent shapes lined the walkways and entwined the railings. The spirit world inhabiting Angkor Wat and its attendant temples included *naga*—snakes— or local spirits of nature; humans, engaged in many labors and pleasures—fishing, planting, trading, and dancing; Hindu gods, devas, and demons, and especially Shiva, seen as the empire's protector; bodhisattvas and Buddhas, including the Buddha himself; and a succession of rulers, many elevated in sculptural narratives to a level at or above that of the gods.

More than a hundred temples span this 40-mile stretch of Cambodian jungle, representing centuries of leadership

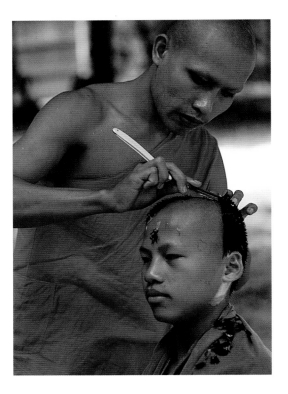

and shifting religious convictions. The Thai army invaded the region in 1431, marking the end of the Khmer Empire. Buddhist monks may have maintained a spiritual life in the abandoned city, but Angkor appeared deserted to French explorer Henri Mouhot when he came upon the ruins in 1858. International efforts coalesced in the 20th century to save the site from the ravages of decay and human warfare, and Buddhist monks have quietly moved back in.

A glorious Buddhist dynasty reigned in Burma (now called Myanmar) from the 11th to the 13th centuries. Anawrahta, first in the line of Pagan kings, took his inspiration from Sri Lankan Theravada Buddhism and unified the south and north of his country. He is said to have been responsible for building thousands of Buddhist chedis (stupas) and temples in his city of Pagan (today's Bagan), built along the Irrawaddy (now called the Ayeyarwady) some 400 navigable miles upriver from the Andaman Sea. Two thousand of these monuments still stand, their glistening spires pointing to the sky. Two of Pagan's stupas house relics of the Buddha: the Shwe Zigon contains a tooth received by Anawrahta from the king of Sri Lanka, and the Shwe Sandaw, or the Pagoda of the Golden Holy Hair, contains a strand given by the Buddha himself to two merchants, who sailed with it to the city of Bago and presented the precious gift to their king.

Another hair of the Buddha is preserved in a pagoda perching precariously on Kyaikhtiyo Mountain. There the

ABOVE: *A young Buddhist monk shaves the head and eyebrows of a fellow devotee before initiation, as he sheds any form of individuality.*
OPPOSITE: *Venerated for its beauty, Thailand's Phra Phuttha Chinnarat Buddha draws pilgrims from all of Southeast Asia.*
FOLLOWING PAGES: *Banyan tree roots claim a section of the twelfth-century temple of Ta Prohm in Siem Reap, Cambodia.*

22-foot-tall structure sits on top of a granite boulder of about the same height, both covered brilliantly with gold leaf. The boulder balances on a rocky ledge in Myanmar's south-central Paunglaung Range, looking as if it might fall at any minute—and so it has looked for centuries. Legend says that the hermit Tissa, possessor of this precious hair, agreed to leave it here only atop a boulder resembling his own head. The lord of the *nats*—Myanmar's indigenous green spirits—dove deep into the Andaman Sea to fetch this ovoid boulder. For centuries, pilgrims trekked through steep jungle paths to reach it.

Mongolian invaders led by Kublai Khan in 1287 brought the building of the many Buddhist marvels to a temporary halt in Myanmar. The Pagan sovereigns had taken steps to ensure their Buddhist stronghold, though, by acquiring and preserving the ancient Pali scriptures, central to Theravadan Buddhism.

Centuries later, in 1871, those scriptures brought 2,400 Buddhist monks to Mandalay, then Myanmar's capital, to the Fifth Buddhist Council. Territory to the east and the west had been colonized by the British, but the interior of the country remained independent, ruled by King Mindon. The king, a Buddhist, wished to preserve the Pali canon for all time. The council monks set about transcribing the scriptures from palm leaves to marble slabs and produced an important revised edition of the Tipitaka. In 1954 a Sixth Buddhist Council was convened by Premier U Nu. Ruling governments since then have not espoused Buddhism, although 89 percent of the people of Myanmar are Buddhist, including opposition leader and Nobel Peace Prize winner Aung San Suu Kyi.

Thailand, like Cambodia, builds upon a rich Buddhist past. Unlike Cambodia, it declares itself a Buddhist nation. Ninety-five percent of Thais today practice Buddhism. Many Thai men, including the longtime king of this constitutional monarchy, Bhumibol Adulyadej, devote several years of their early adult life to becoming a Buddhist monk. Bhumibol was ordained in 1956 at the age of 29, nearly a decade after he had been crowned King Rama IX. Monastic and government officials administer national affairs together in Thailand.

Daily life is filled with many ceremonies arising from the Buddhist tradition. As elsewhere, the monks are supported by the community with gifts to the temple. In the early morning, the saffron-robed monks wander through town with their begging bowls to collect food from the faithful. Because monks may not eat after noon, almsgiving takes place in the morning. Buddhists gather on holy days commemorating events in the Buddha's life. Carrying candles and chanting the ancient Pali scripture, they circumambulate their neighborhood temple or shrine. The temples are not meant as homages to the Buddha as a god, but as places for meditation. Offerings of food or flowers, pilgrimages, alms to maintain a monastey—these are acts of merit to help toward rebirth in a better life.

Even a simple "hello" in Thailand has a religious meaning: People greet each other with a *wai,* a gesture of pressing palms together, closing eyes, and bowing head in an echo of the reverence they would pay the Buddha.

A couple choosing to marry according to Thai Buddhist tradition makes lengthy, mindful preparations for the day. The ceremony itself begins with the arrival of nine monks who seat themselves in a semicircle opposite the bride and groom. As the monks chant Pali scripture, the couple prepares an altar, lighting a candle and incense and placing an alms bowl, half full of holy water, before an image of the Buddha. Next the couple conducts an important merit-making ceremony, offering sumptuous food to the monks and to their family members present. As the senior monk continues chanting, the couple pours holy water from one cup to another one drop at a time, thinking of their ancestors and their obligations to one another. They kneel together and a *monkol,* or white yarn, is wrapped around and between their heads, symbolizing their unity.

OPPOSITE: *Light reflects from the golden spire of Shwe Zigon in Myanmar, a pagoda revered for its tooth relic of the Buddha.*

At the same time a white yarn is stretched around the room, starting at the right hand of the Buddha, passing from monk to monk, then looping around the house to bless the marriage. In some versions of the ceremony, the monks' yarn is cut into short lengths handed out to family elders, who tie them around the wrists of bride and groom with wishes for happiness and many children.

A number of the symbols present in the Thai Buddhist marriage ceremony return at a Thai funeral. Buddhist traditions surrounding death emanate from a belief in the cycle of reincarnation. A Buddhist hopes to be reborn human, or advance to a higher plane, and those around a deathbed recognize this as their last chance to help the dying person attain the best future life possible. They whisper the names of the Buddha, encouraging him or her to chant along, or they write them down and place the paper on the dying person's tongue. After death, the body is promptly bathed, dressed, and placed in a coffin, often with food and flowers, candles and incense. Thus prepared, the body may rest for days or longer so that visitors may bring merit-making offerings on behalf of the deceased. A procession of monks accompanies the coffin to the cremation grounds near the temple. Often leaves and flowers are strewn in the doorway, since the dead should not use an ordinary exit. The monks hold onto a yarn that extends from inside the coffin and symbolizes the connection between the dead and the present-day world. Until they let loose of that yarn, the prayers and gifts of mourners earn merit for the sake of the dead. Because the Buddha dictated that his cremated remains should be honored, the ashes of family members also are gathered and enshrined at home or in a temple stupa.

BUDDHISM IN TIBET

ACCORDING TO one legend, the people of the remote central Asian plateau region of Tibet trace their ancestry back to the union of an ape and an ogress. The ape, so they say, was an emanation of Avalokiteshvara, the bodhisattva of compassion; the ogress was an emanation of Tara, his companion and savior-goddess. It is a legend that crystallizes the Tibetan sense of being primevally connected with both the natural and the spirit worlds. Geographically, Tibet's origins lie along the mighty Yarlung Tsangpo. This river originates in the high plateau and courses eastward, broadening along the north edge of the Himalaya before it flows south, now called the Brahmaputra, into the Bay of Bengal. Tumuli, or mounded ceremonial graves, at Chongye, together with roadways, walls, and tools of Neolithic design provide evidence of civilization in this region thousands of years before.

The city of Lhasa, situated on a tributary of the Yarlung, was the first metropolitan capital. The seventh-century king Songtsen Gampo built his palace some 425 feet above the river on Marpo Ri Hill, on a rise from which he could see miles into the Himalayan distance. He expanded his territory by marrying princesses from China and Nepal. The women piqued his interest in Buddhism, and soon emissaries were traveling from Lhasa to India to learn more. To house the Buddha images belonging to his new wives, Songtsen Gampo built two temples: Jokhang, facing west toward Nepal, and Ramoche, facing east toward China. The three buildings—the palace, later named Potala Palace, and the two temples—still draw Buddhist pilgrims today.

Hundreds, eventually thousands, of Buddhist monasteries came to be built in the remote reaches of Tibet. The first monastery was Samye, Tibetan for "edgeless" or "unimaginable." Completed in 779 A.D., it is an amalgam of architectural forms that show the confluence of Indian and Chinese influences in a Tibetan setting. Upon its opening, the first Tibetan Buddhist monks there were tonsured as part of their ordination.

A rich tradition of translation, scholarship, and debate developed among the monasteries. Using Chinese techniques of papermaking and wood-block printing together with a sacred alphabet derived from Sanskrit, Tibetan monks produced volumes of sacred literature. One of them is the famous *Tibetan Book of the Dead,* a practical and visionary discussion of the process by which a consciousness departs from a dying body. Colored flags were also printed with sacred verse and hung on buildings, even on mountain heights, in the belief that as they fluttered, the wind carried their prayers to the gods.

Colorful customs, costumes, and ceremonies distinctive to Tibetan Buddhism developed in the monasteries. Tibetan Buddhist devotees paint, print, or embroider *thangkas:* tapestries on linen, wool, and sometimes silk, with elaborate iconographic arrangements of the Buddha, bodhisattvas, and other deities.

Tibetan monks train their voices to perform an otherworldly form of chanting, much lower in pitch than most humans can sing, and accompany their haunting meditations with bells, horns, and gongs derived from Himalayan folk instruments.

For special occasions, monks work together for days to create a mandala out of colored sand. A mandala is an intricate design, circularly symmetrical, that is a symbolic representation of a Buddhist universe. Learning to accurately visualize a mandala in all of its detail is an important aspect of certain meditation practices. Tibetan monks work together for days, meticulously dropping sand in fine lines and tiny shapes to create a magnificent work of art. Once the mandala is complete, after meditation and prayer on behalf of the enterprise, a chief monk disperses the sand, an object lesson in transience and non-attachment. By tradition, the participants offer the sand to a river, mindful of the one that flowed alongside the Buddha's resting place when he reached enlightenment.

Buddhism faded in India during the Middle Ages, but it rose in glory in neighboring Tibet. At the invitation of Tibet's rulers and translators, Indian scholars came to Tibet, traveling into the country from the northwest through Kashmir and the south through Nepal. They brought precious scriptures with them, many of which were saved for all time thanks to precise and careful translation into

Tibetan. In Tibetan monasteries, debates were waged, interpretations unfolded, and four different schools of Tibetan Buddhist thought branched out. Ultimately, those following the Gelukpa tradition emerged as leaders, and in 1642, Ngawang Lobsang Gyatso assumed secular and spiritual rule over all of Tibet. His sect considered him the fifth Dalai Lama, or "ocean teacher," a name suggesting his immense wisdom. A Dalai Lama embodies Avalokiteshvara, the bodhisattva of compassion, who puts aside his own achievement of nirvana in order to help others. Dalai Lamas are spiritual leaders always and political leaders when the times require them to be.

The position of Dalai Lama is passed on not by bloodline but rather, according to Tibetan Buddhist beliefs, by incarnation. After the 13th Dalai Lama died in 1933, a search party of Tibetan elders set out looking for the newborn child in whose body the bodhisattva had been reborn. They met a two-year-old, the fourth son of a peasant family, in the village of Takster in the eastern province of Amdo. He said and knew things that indicated to the search party that he was the 13th Dalai Lama's reincarnation. The elders negotiated with his family and village administrators and brought Tenzin Gyatso, at age four, back to Lhasa as the next Dalai Lama.

The 14th Dalai Lama was only 14 years old when the People's Liberation Army of China entered Tibet. Tens of thousands of troops crossed the Yangtze River into the eastern province of Kham in October 1950. Secular leaders surrendered, but the Dalai Lama and many lay people resisted the effort to reclaim the Tibetan land as part of China. For ten years, as the Chinese military occupied more of the country, the Dalai Lama represented his people in negotiations.

In March 1959, protestors filled the streets of Lhasa. Under cover of the demonstrations, the Dalai Lama, disguised as a soldier, left Lhasa. Guided by a group of Khampa guerrilla fighters, it took his party—made up of

FOLLOWING PAGES: All-seeing eyes of the divine stare from the Swayambhunath Stupa, the holiest of Buddhist sites in Katmandu, Nepal.

government officials, high lamas, and members of his family—a month to walk across the Himalaya, entering India at Tezpur, an eastern city on the Brahmaputra River. Many more made the same trek. Nearly 87,000 Tibetans followed him into exile at the time, and in the years since, a steady trickle of refugees has continued to escape across the Himalaya.

Tibetans now count the number living outside their homeland at 120,000. Most are concentrated in India and Nepal, but they are also scattered throughout the world. While the Dalai Lama heads a Tibetan government in exile in Dharmsala, India, China now calls his former home Xizang, an autonomous region of the republic.

Out of this struggle, the 14th Dalai Lama has become a world figure, standing for peaceful negotiation and the rights of indigenous peoples. He received the Nobel Peace Prize in 1989. "The Dalai Lama has developed his philosophy of peace from a great reverence for all things living and upon the concept of universal responsibility embracing all mankind as well as nature," wrote the Nobel Committee in awarding him the prize. The committee applauded his "constructive and forward-looking proposals for the solution of international conflicts, human rights issues, and global environmental problems." After centuries of geographic isolation in the Himalayan hinterlands, then through decades of brutal political conflict, Tibetan Buddhism has come to symbolize humanitarian energy and compassionate ethics throughout the world.

BUDDHISM IN THE WORLD TODAY

ATTENTION TO the Tibetan cause has been buoyed by a respect for, even a commitment to, Buddhism in regions beyond those Asian countries where it was born and first flourished. Buddhism has spread in large part through the dissemination of its ideas and the appeal of its practice. Madame H. P. Blavatsky and the late 19th-century theosophy movement in England and the United States popularized ideas inspired by Buddhist mysticism. Daisetz T. Suzuki, a Japanese scholar trained in Zen, wrote seminal books on Buddhism in English and deeply influenced American artists of the mid-20th century, including poets Allan Ginsburg and Gary Snyder. Centers for Buddhist meditation and study, many taking their names and inspiration from places sacred to the religion's past, operate throughout the United States and Western Europe.

A groundswell of world concern for the ancient sites of Buddhism has helped restoration efforts. At the Buddha's birthplace, an international committee organized as the Lumbini Development Trust is now restoring the site to include a sacred garden, two monastic enclaves, and a cultural center with a museum and research facilities.

In another important way, Buddhism has been reborn in its homeland. Bhimrao Ramji Ambedkar, born into India's lowest caste in 1891, educated himself in the United States and the United Kingdom before returning to his homeland, committed to extending human rights to those of all castes. In the 1930s, he campaigned on behalf of the untouchables, renaming them Dalits, from the Sanskrit for "cut," "oppressed," or "destroyed." His effort to allow elected Dalit representatives in the Indian government was quashed by Mohandas Gandhi himself. Twenty years later, Ambedkar publicly converted to Buddhism, blaming the intransigent caste system of India on the nation's dominant religion. "I renounce Hinduism which is harmful for humanity and impedes the advancement and development of humanity because it is based on inequality, and adopt Buddhism as my religion," he declared. Following his lead, nearly five million Dalits in India have converted. The mission of Siddhartha Gautama, to show all people the way to enlightenment, continues. □

OPPOSITE: A Bhutanese teenager stands beneath a wild-eyed tiger fresco guarding entry to the monastery in the village of Tongsa.
FOLLOWING PAGES: A rainbow tops the Potala, the hillside shrine and traditional home of the Dalai Lama, the spiritual leader of Tibet.

HEWING TO TRADITION

CARRYING A toddler, a Tibetan woman wearing bright clothing and hair wrapping *(above)* maintains the look of old Tibet. Since 1950, when the Chinese took control of their country, Tibetans, who follow a unique path of Buddhism, have rightfully complained that their culture and religion have been suppressed.

Modernization in China, however, has brought about a slight softening of control that Tibetans have felt empowered to exploit. Many Tibetans have returned to practicing some of the old Buddhist pageantry and rituals, such as these traditionally attired young monks *(opposite)* who play the ceremonial Tibetan horn in a parade through the streets of Lhasa.

Others *(following pages)* prefer to practice Buddhism more privately in their devotions, with little more than a prayer wheel and prayer beads to aid them.

THE DALAI Lama *(left)*, the spiritual leader of Tibetan Buddhism, visits with an elderly couple outside the Tashi Lhunpo monastery in southern India. In 1959 the Dalai Lama escaped to India, barely avoiding the Chinese

Army. Establishing a government in exile in Dharmsala, the Dalai Lama has spent half a century drawing world attention to the plight of Tibetans and exerting pressure on the Chinese to give his homeland a greater amount of autonomy. The number of monks in Tibet has been greatly reduced by the Chinese, and many face persecution for behavior viewed as being overly nationalistic. Still, many monks continue to follow in the Buddha's path *(above)*.

JUDAISM

I am the Lord your God, who brought you out of the land of Egypt, out of the house of slavery; you shall have no other gods before me.

— EXODUS 20:2

JUDAISM

ACCORDING TO Genesis, the first book of the ancient Jewish Scriptures, human life began in a garden. The garden lay at the confluence of four rivers, two of which still flow through lands we know today.

And a river went out of Eden to water the garden;

and from thence it was parted, and became four heads.

The name of the first is Pishon; that is it which compasseth

the whole land of Havilah, where there is gold; and the gold

of that land is good; there is bdellium and the onyx stone.

OPPOSITE: *Preserving ancient Hebrew custom, a Yemeni girl wears a traditional bridal costume.*

PRECEDING PAGES: *Moonrise dimly lights a barren desert hill on the outskirts of Jerusalem, the holiest city of Judaism.*

And the name of the second river is Gihon;
the same is it that compasseth the whole land of Cush.
And the name of the third river is Tigris;
that is it which goeth toward the east of Asshur.
And the fourth river is the Euphrates.

THE TIGRIS and Euphrates Rivers converge 200 miles southeast of today's Baghdad, near the city of Nasiriyah, Iraq. Streams and tributaries approach and intersect one another the entire length of the way. Although none is called Pishon or Gihon, it is likely that tributaries now run dry once joined these mighty rivers downstream from where they converge today. The surrounding land is a treeless desert.

The Jewish people look back to Adam and Eve, placed by God in that garden, as their ancient forebears. In so doing, they link themselves to the Sumerian civilization that developed in these lands called Mesopotamia. During the fourth millennium B.C.E. (before the Common Era, in Jewish usage), city-states developed along the two rivers and grew wealthy through agriculture and trade. Ur, for example, was a walled city with fired-brick buildings along paved streets, a metropolis whose glory peaked between 2100 and 2000 B.C.E. The remains of Ur can still be visited in the Iraqi city of Mughair.

Abundant archaeological finds portray the organized political and religious practices out of which Judaism arose. In the center of Ur, as in other Sumerian cities, stood a majestic ziggurat—a tiered pyramidal building—that served many purposes: granary and barn, factory for spinning and weaving, administrative center and temple. Third-millennium B.C.E. graves near Ur suggest that powerful individuals believed they would continue a life of privilege in the afterlife. One king's burial pit also contained the remains of six soldiers, two wagons and oxen to pull them, and more than 50 other servants, including a woman ready to play music on a lyre of gold and lapis lazuli.

The Sumerian civilization invented a form of writing: first, wedge marks pressed into wet clay to keep a tally of goods bought and sold; later, an abstract-symbol system,

leading not only to more complex record keeping but also to chronicling history, law, and religion. Each city revered its own family of nature gods and goddesses, such as An, god of the heavens; Ki, goddess of the earth; Nammu, goddess of the sea; Nanna-Sin, god of the moon and patron of the city of Ur; and Enlil, son of An and Ki, god of winds and storms, and patron of the city of Nippur, upriver from Ur. Out of the neighboring city of Uruk came history's earliest work of literature, *The Epic of Gilgamesh.* This narrative, dating from about 2000 B.C.E., tells of a king who "knew the countries of the world," who "saw mysteries and knew secret things," and who "brought us a tale of the days before the flood"—the same flood, many believe, into which Noah sailed his ark.

Noah—according to Genesis, an eighth-generation descendant of Adam and Eve—lived through a cataclysmic event, a 40-day-long deluge that wiped out human, animal, and plant life where he lived. The scriptures offer a moral explanation: Dismayed with the violence and corruption of creation, the Lord God intended to "blot [it] out from off the face of the earth." Many scholars have sought a geological explanation, their curiosity piqued by the number of flood stories that appear in ancient literature. Several searches have been conducted on the slopes of Turkey's Mount Ararat, since that place name appears in the Book of Genesis. Recent explorations have plumbed the depths of the Black Sea in search of scientific proof of the flood story.

Noah's first act upon stepping onto dry land was to build an altar and light a fire, onto which he piled "one of every clean beast" and "clean fowl."

His sacrificial act of gratitude drew a blessing from his god, who told him and his three sons to "be fruitful and multiply, and replenish the earth." The Table of Nations, as the tenth chapter of Genesis is often called, lists the offspring of Noah's sons, Shem, Ham, and Japheth. Many of their names can be translated to stand for tribes and places, from the Bosporus to Ethiopia, from Cyprus to the southern shores of the Arabian Peninsula. The list encodes a broad spread of known civilizations, but it may be a compilation

from more than one author and cannot be read as a comprehensive geography from a single moment in time.

ABRAHAM AND THE PATRIARCHS

THE LONG list of names in the Book of Genesis—and the long procession of who begot whom—culminates in Abraham, who descended from Noah's son Shem, source for the term "Semite." Abraham's momentous life journey marked the first steps of three of the world's religions: Judaism, Christianity, and Islam. Most scholars date the life of Abraham to the timeframe between 2100 and 1500 B.C.E. Historic traces point to his being born along the border between today's Syria and Turkey. He is claimed as a native son in the village of Haran and the city of Sanliurfa in Turkey.

According to the Book of Genesis, Abraham departed from Haran, following a command from the voice of God. "Get thee out of thy country, and from thy kindred, and from thy father's house, unto the land that I will show thee," the voice said to him. "And I will make of thee a

ABOVE: Steps lead to the 70-foot summit of the Ziggurat at Ur, a Sumerian temple from the era of Abraham.

FOLLOWING PAGES: Sheep graze along the Euphrates as a shepherd keeps watch in a scene replayed since the onset of civilization.

great nation, and I will bless thee, and make thy name great; and be thou a blessing…and in thee shall all the families of the earth be blessed." Canaan was the land into which Abraham was called—the western reach of the Fertile Crescent, stretching along the Mediterranean coast and east to the Jordan River and the inland Sea of Galilee. Canaan was the only hospitable passage between the two powerful civilizations of Egypt and Mesopotamia; it also bore its own fruitful harvests: wheat and barley, dates and pistachios, and a dye of royal purple derived from *Murex* seashells. In Canaan's Shechem—the city of Nablus today—God spoke again to Abraham, confirming that he was in the Promised Land. Abraham built an altar there and another on a hill nearby. His travels took him into Egypt and back again, into territorial negotiations, and into battle, all at places that can be pinpointed on a map of the modern Middle East.

God assured him that his progeny would be as numerous as the stars in heaven, and eventually Abraham saw the birth of a great number of sons—Ishmael, by Hagar, his wife Sarah's handmaid; Isaac, miraculously, by Sarah, who had passed childbearing age; and six more by a later wife, Keturah. Two of Abraham's sons played important roles. Ishmael would later come to glory in the tradition of Islam, revered as one in the line of prophets leading to Muhammad, the Prophet of Islam and founder of the first Islamic community. Isaac was taken by Abraham to a mountaintop in "the land of Moriah," following God's command. There, the father dutifully prepared the body of his young son to be burnt on a sacrificial altar. An angel stopped Abraham just before he completed the deed. His willingness was proof enough to God of his devotion.

Jews ever since have heard in the dramatic story of Isaac the features that distinguish their one God from others worshiped in those times. This God talked with Abraham, promising the possibility of a directly personal relationship, and valued interior devotions over outward offerings. As a

physical mark of the covenant between humankind and God, Abraham's male descendants were required to be circumcised. Through a series of appearances, God consecrated the land of Canaan. Haran, Shechem, Negev, Bethel, Hebron—in all these places, God appeared to Abraham, assuring him that this was his Promised Land. Finally, God singled out Mount Moriah as the place on which Abraham should make his ultimate show of faith. Abraham's sacramental act was the first of countless more to be performed on the mountain in the middle of the city that would become Jerusalem.

It would be impossible to pin down accurate historical analogues for every detail in the life of Abraham and his descendants. Memories and traditions were preserved orally, then collected and written down by different chroniclers and joined, according to some views, into a single text many centuries later. Scholars see evidence in several literary sources for these early biblical books. These strands coalesce in their portrayal of Abraham as a monotheist: a person who believes in one God to the exclusion of all others. Abraham had traveled out of Sumer, where local deities were worshiped, and through Canaan, where the god Baal symbolized the cycle of the seasons in his annual death and resurrection. Just as Abraham traveled from Ur through Canaan and into the Promised Land, so he also moved from a region of local deities, through a culture with a reigning male weather god, and into a land of one God, not attached to natural forces but transcendent in power.

MOSES AND THE EXODUS

ISAAC'S SON Jacob had a dozen sons, who are taken to represent the Twelve Tribes of Israel. Jacob himself was renamed Israel by God, in one of a series of encounters. After a lifetime of conflict and migration, Jacob journeyed with his family to Egypt to escape a famine. Out of that setting emerged the next great Jewish patriarch: Moses.

OPPOSITE: A 12th-century illuminated French manuscript acknowledges Abraham as the patriarch of Judaism, Christianity, and Islam.

lareth. enoch. matusale. lamech. noe. sem. cham. 7 iafeth

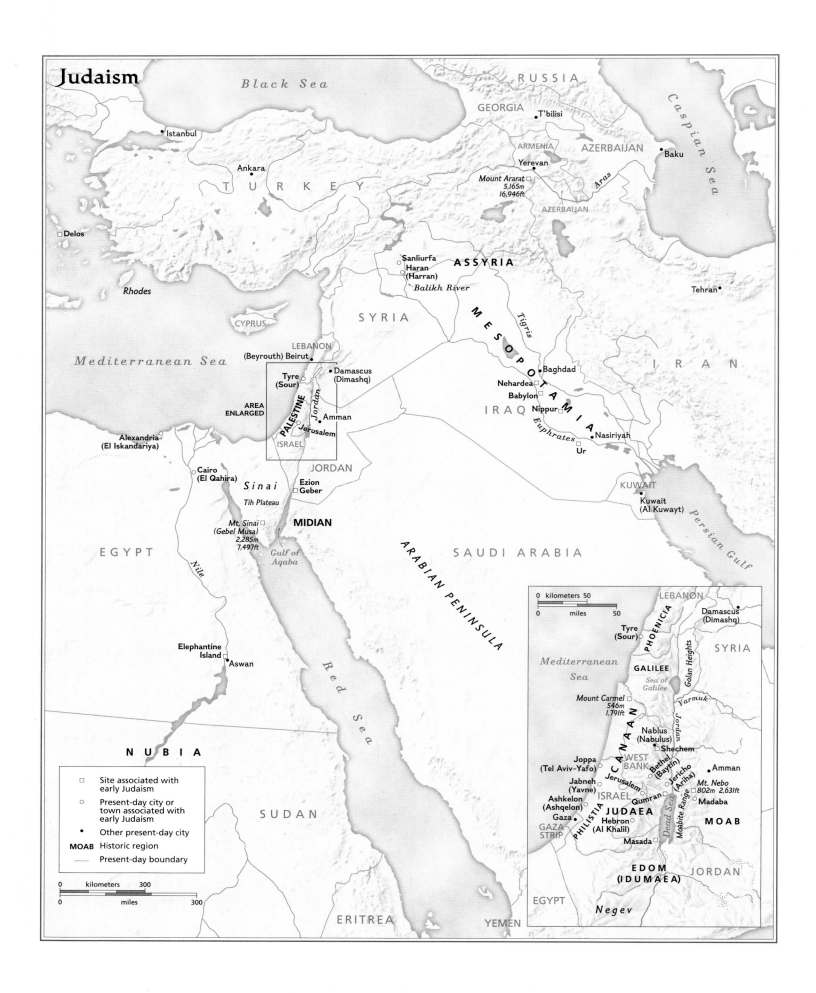

Judaism

Black Sea

RUSSIA

GEORGIA
• T'bilisi

ARMENIA

AZERBAIJAN
• Baku

Caspian Sea

• Istanbul

• Ankara

TURKEY

• Yerevan

AZERBAIJAN

Mount Ararat ☐
5,165m
16,946ft

Aras

☐ Delos

Rhodes

CYPRUS

Mediterranean Sea

Şanliurfa •
Haran •
(Harran)

ASSYRIA

Balikh River

• Tehran

SYRIA

Tigris

MESOPOTAMIA

LEBANON
(Beyrouth) Beirut

Tyre
(Sour)

PALESTINE

• Damascus
(Dimashq)

Jordan

• Baghdad

IRAN

AREA
ENLARGED

ISRAEL

Alexandria •
(El Iskandariya)

Jerusalem

Amman

JORDAN

IRAQ

Nehardea ☐
Babylon •
Nippur ☐

Euphrates

• Nasiriyah

Ur ☐

Cairo ○
(El Qahira)

Sinai

Ezion
Geber

Tih Plateau

MIDIAN

Mt. Sinai ☐
(Gebel Musa)
2,285m
7,497ft

EGYPT

Nile

Gulf of
Aqaba

SAUDI ARABIA

KUWAIT

Kuwait
(Al Kuwayt)

Persian Gulf

ARABIAN PENINSULA

Elephantine
Island ☐
• Aswan

Red Sea

NUBIA

☐	Site associated with early Judaism
○	Present-day city or town associated with early Judaism
•	Other present-day city
MOAB	Historic region
– – –	Present-day boundary

SUDAN

0 — kilometers — 300
0 — miles — 300

ERITREA

YEMEN

Inset map

0 — kilometers — 50
0 — miles — 50

LEBANON

Damascus
(Dimashq)

Tyre
(Sour)

PHOENICIA

SYRIA

Mediterranean
Sea

GALILEE

Sea of
Galilee

Golan Heights

Yarmuk

Mount Carmel ☐
546m
1,791ft

CANAAN

Nablus
(Nabulus)
Shechem

Joppa
(Tel Aviv-Yafo)

WEST
BANK

Bethel
(Baytin)

Jericho
(Ariha)

Jordan

Mt. Nebo ☐
802m 2,631ft
Madaba •

Amman

Jabneh
(Yavne)

Jerusalem

Qumran ☐

Dead Sea

MOAB

Ashkelon
(Ashqelon)

ISRAEL

JUDAEA

PHILISTIA

Gaza

Hebron
(Al Khalil)

Moabite Range

GAZA
STRIP

Masada ☐

EGYPT

EDOM
(IDUMAEA)

JORDAN

Negev

Moses most likely lived during the time of Ramses II, the pharaoh who reigned in Thebes from 1279 to 1213 B.C.E. Ramses' reign was a time of abundance, with great building projects. He had grandiose temples and statues erected, honoring gods and the pharaoh as if one and the same. To accomplish his ambitious architectural efforts, Ramses conscripted thousands of laborers, enslaving the descendants of Jacob and his sons. One document of the time records grain provisions for the '*pr*—short for '*a-pi-ru*—whose job it was to haul stones to build a massive gateway. The Egyptian '*a-pi-ru,* some linguists have suggested, is related to the word *Ibri,* source for our word "Hebrew."

Moses is said to have been found as an infant in a basket, among rushes growing in the Nile River wetlands. Adopted by the pharaoh's daughter, he was born a slave but raised in a royal household.

Early on, Moses took risks that revealed either ethical principles or Hebrew affinities or both: Seeing one of the pharaoh's men beating a Hebrew worker, he rescued his kinsman—in the words of the Book of Exodus, he "smote the Egyptian and hid him in the sand." To escape punishment, Moses fled into the "land of Midian"—in the northwestern corner of the Arabian Peninsula along the Gulf of Aqaba. He traveled from the city of excesses to the countryside, becoming "a stranger in a strange land." There he lived the life of a shepherd until God, whom he called Yahweh, told him to do otherwise.

According to the Book of Exodus, God appeared to Moses "in a flame of fire out of the midst of a bush." (Scholars inclined to a non-literal interpretation have tried to name the exact species. Candidates include *Zizyphus spina-christi,* the jujube of Africa and the Middle East, whose bittersweet red fruit is dried and milled into flour, and *Loranthus acaciae,* a red-flowered parasite that attaches to acacia shrubs. Or, as the monks of St. Catherine's Monastery in the Sinai believe, it may have been the *Rubus sancta,* the holy raspberry, whose ripe fruit and late foliage do glow as if aflame.)

From out of the burning bush, God spoke to Moses, identifying himself as the God of Abraham, Isaac, and Jacob: "I have surely seen the affliction of my people that are in Egypt.... I am come down to deliver them out of the hand of the Egyptians, and to bring them up out of that land unto a good land and a large [one], unto a land flowing with milk and honey." At God's command, Moses returned to Egypt to lead the Hebrews into the land promised once to Abraham and now again through Moses to his descendants, the "children of Israel."

Many routes have been sketched to show how Moses led his people out of Egypt. Where, for example, did Moses command a passageway through a body of water so that several thousand people could traverse it, then recompose the landscape to foil pursuing Egyptian chariots? An early mistranslation of the Hebrew term *yam suf,* "reed sea," into the Greek *erythra thalassa,* "red sea," finessed the whole

ABOVE: A modern rendering of Abraham's family tree shows a direct line to Noah and branches to sons Isaac, Jacob, and Ishmael.
FOLLOWING PAGES: A Bedouin girl finds little refuge in Sinai's wilderness, nearly unchanged since Moses and the Israelites fled from Egypt.

question, and for centuries people have assumed that Moses parted the waters of the Red Sea, whereas it may have been an inland lake or even the marshes of the Nile Delta.

Three routes present themselves as the most likely to have been followed during the Exodus. Considering the hardships they are said to have faced, it is not likely that Moses and his followers took the northern spur on the common trade route. They could have cut through the central Tih Plateau, watered only by fickle desert wadis. Or —the most popular theory—they may have traveled south, into the unpopulated mountainous region of the southwestern Sinai. For each of these hypothetical exodus routes, there is a peak designated as the match for the mountain called Sinai in the Jewish Scriptures. Today the landscape stretching out around Gebel Musa, the southernmost candidate for Mount Sinai, resonates deeply with power and mystery. Rank upon rank of hard rock peaks extend to the horizon, an inhospitable landscape that evokes a mixture of fear and reverence.

Many of Judaism's fundamental practices and beliefs connect to the story of the Exodus out of Egypt. Pesach, the Passover holiday celebrated in spring, recalls in symbolic detail the preparations of the Jews once Moses told them to follow him out of Egypt. Central to the eight-day observation is the Passover seder, a ceremonial meal taken with family members and friends. In preparation, the house is cleaned and the table set elegantly, with wine glasses for all, bowls of salt water to remember the tears of the Hebrew slaves, and a plate piled with three pieces of the crisp, thin, unleavened bread called matzo. Throughout Passover, devout Jews eat matzo rather than leavened bread, remembering that the Israelites left Egypt in such haste, they could not wait for the bread dough to rise. "Why is this night different from all other nights of the year?" the children of the family sing in Hebrew. "On all the nights of the year we eat both bread and matzo, but on the night of Passover we eat only matzo," they sing in reply.

At the center of the seder table sits the *kearah,* a plate arranged with symbolic foods. A blend of chopped fruit and spices, the *haroset* symbolizes the mortar used by Israelite slaves in building. Some green vegetable, such as parsley, is the *karpas,* which stands for the season of spring. Two items on the plate derive from ancient customs of offering burnt sacrifices to the divine: the *z'roa,* the spring or paschal sacrifice, is symbolized by meat on the bone—lamb shank or a poultry neck— while *beitzah,* a roasted egg, symbolizes the festival sacrifice. *Maror,* bitter herbs—usually either horseradish or bitter salad greens such as escarole—stand for the bitter experience of slavery from which their ancestors were about to be freed. The greens are dipped in salt water before they are eaten, emphasizing the sorrows of the ancient Israelites. All these flavors and meanings blend in a ritual event led by the head of the family, who reads aloud the sacred story behind these symbols. "Seder" comes from the Hebrew word for "order." In modern times, variations according to different sects have developed, and each family develops seder traditions all its own, but all still

ABOVE: *Foods for a feast surround a Hebrew prayer on a Passover plate, used by Jews to celebrate their deliverance from Egypt.*

OPPOSITE: *Divine hands deliver the Ten Commandments to Moses in Russian artist Marc Chagall's "Moses Receiving the Tablets."*

follow an underlying sequence of readings, actions, and song, uniting in the ritual with Jews around the world.

The Passover is one of the many commands given to the Jewish people by God through Moses. In every question of right or wrong, Jews refer to teachings conveyed by Moses from God. The people stood at the foot of Mount Sinai, but Moses climbed to the top, where he talked directly with God. He descended carrying two stone tablets on which were written, according to the Book of Exodus, "the words of the covenant, the Ten Commandments." This event is celebrated by the festival of Pentecost, called Shabuoth in Hebrew.

The Ten Commandments form the foundation of moral law for all three religions descending from Abraham: Judaism, Christianity, and Islam. Unique to the times, they begin with the principle of monotheism—"You shall have no other gods before me…for I the Lord your God am a jealous God." They forbid idolatry, require observance of the seventh day as a day of rest, command that parents be honored, and include the laws of social contract against murder, theft, lying, and adultery. The laws voiced by Moses numbered well more than ten. Jewish scribes counted 613 mitzvoth, or commandments, in the Five Books of Moses, the Torah, which define the practice of Judaism. They range from the ethical (not to wrong anyone in speech, not to bear a grudge or take revenge, and to love a stranger) to the practical (not to sow different seeds together in one field) to the charitable (not to harvest the grapes or olives that have fallen to the ground or that lie in the corners of fields, nor gather discarded corn, all of which had to be left to the poor). Some are profoundly metaphysical (to know that God exists and not to entertain the idea that there is any god but

ABOVE: *St. Catherine's Monastery, nestled at the foot of Sinai's highest peak, claims to be the site of Moses' encounter with the burning bush.*

the Eternal), and some are limited by history and circumstance (not to sell a Hebrew handmaiden to another person and to keep the Canaanite slave until he or she is freed, unlike Hebrew slaves, who could only be enslaved for a limited period of time).

From the 613 mitzvoth come rules still central to modern religious practice. Among them are circumcision of the male offspring: The ritual removal of an infant boy's foreskin remains an essential Judaic ceremony by which a child joins the covenant between Abraham and God. To put zitzit, or fringes, on the corners of clothing is another example: Men who practice Orthodox Judaism often drape a rectangular shawl with fringed corner tassels over their shoulders for synagogue ceremonies. Many of the original laws have been reinterpreted for modern times. Numerous mitzvot rules, for example, pertain to sacrifices in the Temple. Today's Jews donate to charity, help maintain their synagogues, and offer up prayers rather than physical gifts to God.

"Six days you shall do your work, but on the seventh day you shall rest," uttered Moses, establishing the law of Shabbat, the Sabbath, or seventh day. In regarding one day a week—traditionally Saturday—as a holy day of rest, Jews emulate God the creator who, according to the Book of Genesis, made the world in six days and rested on the seventh. By law and custom, Jews suspend work from sundown on Friday until sundown on Saturday and attend worship services. In modern times, Orthodox Jews interpret work strictly, refraining from doing such things as turning on electric lights and appliances, driving a car, writing, or watching television. The Sabbath ends, by tradition, when three stars are visible in the night sky.

"You shall not boil a kid in its mother's milk": This simple statement, which also came from God through Moses, underlies one aspect of Jewish dietary laws. Accordingly, Orthodox Jews separate meat and milk in their diets and their kitchens, keeping separate sets of dishes for the two segments of their cuisine. Further laws strictly define food that is kosher—a word deriving from the Hebrew for "proper" or "correct," meaning suitable for ritual ceremony. Only certain animals may be eaten. Those with cloven hooves that chew their cud—cattle, sheep, goats, for example—are permissible, but those without, such as camels, pigs, and rabbits, are not. Fish with fins and scales can be eaten, but shellfish and crustaceans cannot. Animals must be slaughtered humanely, and kosher butchers are trained in technique and Jewish law. Kitchen utensils are cleaned and stored according to special procedures. Not all Jewish families decide to keep a kosher kitchen. In North America today, for example, about 17 percent of Jewish households follow the kosher laws in full.

Moses' experience, as well as the laws he conveyed to the Hebrews, modeled the sort of relationship God would have with believers. The very name of God came to be regarded as unapproachably numinous—beyond human understanding or expression—and it is Jewish custom never to write out the full name of God, acknowledging the limits of human access and expression. Just as God's name could not be written, neither could his image be reproduced by human hands. "You shall not make for yourself an idol, whether in the form of anything that is in heaven above, or that is on the earth beneath, or that is in the water under the earth," God said explicitly. "You shall not bow down to them or worship them." No statuary and no paintings of God or of divine beings have decorated any Jewish place of worship since.

God gave Moses instructions on how to build a tabernacle, a portable altar. The details grew extravagant: acacia wood, a goat-hair tent, tanned rams' leather, bronze and gold clasps, twisted linen cords of royal color, rows of precious stones, the whole anointed with oil and fragrant with incense. This became the Ark of the Covenant: the earthly dwelling place of the Hebrews' God, an object that would allow them to carry their religion with them. In time the Ark would become a mystical focus of reverence and the physical symbol of the Israelites' religion and nation. Once they had built it, "the glory of the Lord filled the tabernacle" and they continued on their journey, carrying it with them.

Although he led the way, Moses never reentered the land promised to the Israelites. It would have been easiest for them to head north on the king's highway, a level and much-traveled roadway that began at Ezion Geber, the port at the northern end of the Gulf of Aqaba. Instead, they likely journeyed farther east, close to today's border between Israel and Jordan, along a line of fortresses built to protect the kingdoms of Edom (Idumaea) and Moab. Fortress remains are still being excavated in this rock-strewn desert.

Tradition has it that Moses led his people as far as Mount Nebo, at 2,600 feet the highest peak of the Moabite Range that rises above the city of Madaba, Jordan. From Nebo's rocky mountaintop, one can look back to the land through which the Israelites wandered into the land they hoped to regain.

SOLOMON
AND THE TEMPLE

THE HISTORICAL return of the Hebrews to Canaan was a gradual event customarily dated to the Late Bronze Age, between 1550 and 1200 B.C.E. They came into a land much divided by tribal boundaries and local rule. In the next period of their history, according to the Hebrew Bible, battles were fought and walls came tumbling down—including the legendary walls of Jericho, the gateway city through which Moses' people must have traveled.

Ten miles northwest of the Dead Sea and fed by a perennial spring, this oasis called Jericho was an ancient settlement site even in the second millennium B.C.E. In its salt-sand soil, date palms flourished, as did trees whose resin was harvested as incense. Today the city is called Tel el-Sultan, after the *tel,* a mound formed by layer upon layer of settlement. Some architectural remains in this city date back 7,000 years. It was an essential entry point from the broad highlands to the east, through the low-lying desert and into the hill country around Jerusalem—"the latch of the land of Israel," according to a fifth-century Jewish scholar. "If Jericho was taken, the whole country would instantly be conquered." Jericho also lies on a significant faultline,

making it subject to earthquakes. The rubble of human and natural history mingles in this powerful place, and archaeologists disagree on whether any findings correspond exactly to the conquest described in the Book of Joshua.

Yahweh singled out Joshua to lead the Israelites after the death of Moses. "See, I have handed Jericho over to you, along with its kings and soldiers," God told Joshua. "You shall march around the city...for six days, with seven priests bearing seven trumpets of rams' horns before the ark." The shofar, a ceremonial trumpet made from the horn of a ram or goat, is blown during Rosh Hashanah, the Jewish New Year. The deep-voiced blasts follow ancient symbolic rhythms said to awaken the sleeping soul.

Fifty-some miles to the west stood the port city of Ashkelon, a stronghold typical of the sort of culture with which that of the returning Israelites would clash. Thick mud-brick walls surrounded this 150-acre city. A massive vaulted archway graced one passageway: Built in 1850 B.C.E., it is the oldest arch in the world. Gateways opened out to roads connecting Ashkelon with other metropolitan centers: Jaffa to the north, Jerusalem to the east, Gaza to the south. Dates and wine, onions and olive oil, wheat and livestock traveled out of this port in abundance. The city's name shares linguistic roots with the word "shekel," a Hebrew coin—a reflection of the lively trade there. Around 1175 B.C.E. a seafaring people called the Philistines invaded Ashkelon. From their tribal name, the entire geographical region came to be called Palestine. Theirs is the city where Samson, who had taken the vows of the austere Hebrew cult of the Nazarites to leave his hair uncut, was sabotaged by Delilah, a Philistine. Theirs is the city of Goliath, the mighty soldier who faced the Israelites in battle in the Valley of Elah, ten miles east of Ashkelon near today's Wadi es Sant. Standing six cubits and a span (about ten feet) and wearing bronze armor that weighed 5,000 shekels (about 150 pounds), Goliath represented the grandeur, wealth, and dominating force of Ashkelon. The story of his unexpected defeat by an Israelite nobody, a young shepherd named David, has inspired readers ever since.

As written in the holy books of Samuel and Kings, David conquered Philistia and many other small kingdoms on both sides of the Jordan, uniting them into the nation of Israel, which he ruled for 40 years. At Jerusalem, with its rocky backbone of hills that allowed surveillance to the west and east, he established the stronghold of Zion by building city walls. There Yahweh was worshiped as the chief deity, but not the only one: Baal, his sister Anat, and his consort Asherah still received sacrifices and praise. Conflict over belief systems heightened over time, as shown in the story of Elijah, a devout believer in Yahweh, who challenged the believers of Baal to a contest on Mount Carmel, 20 miles south of Jerusalem.

The mission to enshrine the Ark of the Covenant in God's Promised Land was fulfilled by Solomon, the son of David. In 970 B.C.E. on the spot where Abraham had offered to sacrifice Isaac, Solomon dedicated a Temple to Yahweh. No physical trace of it remains, although the written record describes a walled Temple, 90 by 30 feet with ceilings 45 feet tall. Its design was likely Phoenician, for craftsmen and materials were sent by Solomon's ally, King Hiram of Tyre, whose builders were renowned. In payment, Solomon granted Hiram 20 cities in the north, in Galilee.

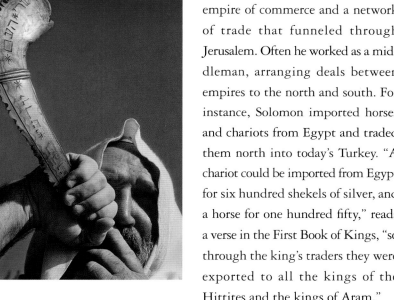

The Temple's walls and foundations were made of stone, its beams of cedar, its floors of cypress. The timber was cut in Lebanon, shipped along the coast, and hauled onto land at the harbor of Joppa, north of Ashkelon. The Temple design contained pagan elements. A huge bronze basin, for example, filled with rainwater, represented Yam, the sea god who contended with Baal.

The Temple's inner sanctum was built to house the Ark of the Covenant. Called Kodesh Kodashim, or Holy of Holies, this chamber was equally extravagant. Two 15-foot-tall cherubim carved of olivewood and covered with gold were placed over the Ark itself. The room for the tabernacle was 20 cubits (30 feet) in all dimensions, a perfect cube. Cedar paneling was carved with floral designs; the interior walls were inlaid with gold.

The Temple was one of Solomon's many building projects. Materials and manpower imported from afar distinguished each of them, reflecting Solomon's success at building an empire of commerce and a network of trade that funneled through Jerusalem. Often he worked as a middleman, arranging deals between empires to the north and south. For instance, Solomon imported horses and chariots from Egypt and traded them north into today's Turkey. "A chariot could be imported from Egypt for six hundred shekels of silver, and a horse for one hundred fifty," reads a verse in the First Book of Kings, "so through the king's traders they were exported to all the kings of the Hittites and the kings of Aram."

Trade was an essential element in the alliance between King Solomon and the Queen of Sheba. She ruled a kingdom at the southwestern tip of the Arabian Peninsula roughly equivalent to today's Yemen. "She came to Jerusalem with a very great retinue, with camels bearing spices, and very much gold, and precious stones," says the First Book of Kings. She returned home with goods of equal value, one imagines: The Scripture says Solomon fulfilled "every desire that she expressed." The partnership with Sheba allowed him to do

ABOVE: The mournful sounds of the shofar, or ram's horn, summon Jews to services on Yom Kippur, the Day of Atonement.

FOLLOWING PAGES: An archaeological team digs in the ruins of Ashkelon, the ancient capital of Jewish kings and the biblical hero Samson.

business with "all the kings of Arabia and the governors of the land." Until then, precious Arabian commodities such as frankincense and myrrh—used in ritual, as perfume, and for embalming— had come overland by camel, with steep tariffs exacted by the Midianites to the south as the goods entered Israel. Solomon established a seaport at Ezion-geber, at the head of the Gulf of Aqaba, and the Queen of Sheba agreed that he could export Arabian products out of her port of Muza. Israelite ships traveling up the Red Sea also visited ports in Africa, bringing aboard rare goods from that exotic land: "Once every three years the fleet of ships…used to come bringing gold, silver, ivory, apes, and peacocks."

The glory that was Solomon's Jerusalem died with him. Underlying tribal differences split the nation in two: Israel in the north and Judaea in the south. Assyria, a kingdom in the upper reaches of the Tigris River, was at that time growing in power and gaining in territory. It vied for power throughout the Middle East with Babylonia, centered farther south on the Euphrates. As a result, Israel fell into Assyrian hands in 722 B.C.E.

The religion of Judaism evolved through this period of nationalistic turmoil, as reflected in the books of the Tanakh, or Hebrew Bible, all of which represent the struggle of Jewish monarchs to behave within the bounds of God's definition of right and wrong while battling their aggressors and leading their people. "Be good, devote yourselves to justice, aid the wronged, uphold the rights of the

orphan, defend the cause of the widow," advises one verse from the Book of Isaiah.

Power shifted from the Assyrians to the Babylonians in 626 B.C.E., but that did not lessen the threat to the Israelites. Jeremiah, the son of a priest, a young man, who grew up just outside the city of Jerusalem, sensed approaching doom. "Out of the north disaster shall break out on all the inhabitants of the land," he said, "and they shall come and all of them shall set their thrones at the entrance of the gates of Jerusalem, against all its surrounding walls and against all the cities of Judaea." In Jeremiah's eyes, the invasion was punishment for those who worshiped gods other than Yahweh. The God of Israel decreed the fall of Israel, Jeremiah warned sternly. In December of the year 604 B.C.E., Nebuchadnezzar of Babylon invaded and destroyed Ashkelon. Four years later, he marched into Egypt. In December 586 B.C.E. he led his forces into Jerusalem, destroyed the city and razed the Temple.

Thousands of Israelites were captured and transported to the city of Babylon— the epitome of earthly splendor, with its gates and walkways, temples and gardens. Nebuchadnezzar had expanded the city's monumental ziggurat and now it stood 300 feet tall, honoring Marduk, the local god. Little record remains of how or where the Israelites lived during their exile. They now called their homeland Yehud, its name in Aramaic, the language of their oppressors, and they called

ABOVE: A window at Notre-Dame Cathedral in Paris depicts the first meeting between the Queen of Sheba (center) and King Solomon.

themselves Yehudim, Jews, united by their belief in Yahweh, their history, and their vision of a Promised Land.

The Book of Job showed to what extremes one's faith should stretch. Job was a good man, in fact "blameless and upright, who feared God and turned away from evil." Satan, the embodiment of evil, wanted to prove to God that Job's faith came only from his being so happily blessed. All those blessings were taken away—his house was destroyed, and his children died in a tornado; he was afflicted with boils all over his body; his wife lost faith and told him to curse God. Through it all, Job's faith was solid. "I know that you can do all things, and that no purpose of yours can be thwarted," he said finally to God. "Therefore I have uttered what I did not understand, things too wonderful for me, which I did not know.... I had heard of you by the hearing of the ear, but now my eye sees you; therefore I despise myself, and repent in dust and ashes." The God of the Jews was demanding and terrifying at times, but in the end, just. He accepted Job's prayer and mutiplied his blessings. The Prophet Job came to stand for the human condition in the Jewish world view: Despite extremes of suffering, the Jewish person faithful to God will ultimately win his blessings.

When Cyrus of Persia gained control of Babylon, the exile was ended. "I returned to [these] sacred cities on the other side of the Tigris, the sanctuaries of which have been in ruins for a long time, the images which [used] to live therein [and] all their [former] inhabitants," reads the so-called Cyrus Cylinder, a clay object on which the great Persian leader imprinted his version of history. In 538 B.C.E. some Jews began to return to Israel. The vast majority stayed in Babylon and built several communities such as Nehardea on the Euphrates, which became an important center for Jewish scholarship in the third century C.E. From this moment on, the Babylonian community remained the largest Jewish center in the world until well into medieval times. The influence of the Jews of Babylon, which then became part of the Persian Empire, is to be seen in the celebration of the Purim festival each year. This reflects the attempt of Haman, during the reign of Ataxerxes, to destroy

the Jewish community. Thanks to Mordecai and Esther, as recorded in the biblical Book of Esther, the Jews were saved. To this day Purim is celebrated throughout the Jewish world as a day of fancy dress, banquets, and gifts to the poor. The Megilla, the scroll of Esther, is read in synagogues in a festive atmosphere.

Those who did go home returned to Jerusalem with increased passion, ready to rebuild their city, their Temple, and their nation.

EZRA'S REVIVAL

INITIALLY THE return to Judaea was fraught with difficulty, and several attempts to rebuild the Temple and Jerusalem failed. Only later, under the joint leadership of Ezra and Nehemia, did another "return" succeed in reestablishing a vibrant Jewish community in Judaea. Jerusalem was slowly rebuilt and a new Temple erected. Ezra also brought about a major religious revival. In particular he reformed the priesthood, but he also introduced innovations to make Judaism less exclusively a Temple-based religion. Typical of his reformation was the reaffirmation of the biblical Feast of Tabernacles, Sukkoth, as a festival for everyone, not just the priests.

A crowd gathered at Jerusalem's Water Gate—the city's east entrance, which opened onto the hillside nearest Gihon Spring. It was one of the massive new gates built into the much expanded city wall. People watched with anticipation as Ezra, a Temple scribe, climbed up onto a wooden platform erected in the city square. Next to him stood other Temple elders: the Levites, descended from the tribe of Levi, considered teaching priests. Two of them held a pair of wooden spools, onto which a scroll of parchment was wound. This was the Torah—the Hebrew word for "law," now used to name the holy books of Judaism. Throughout history, Jewish religious leaders have repeated the ceremony of carrying a scrolled Torah, opening it, and reading from it aloud.

Ezra began by addressing the crowd in Aramaic, the language most of them used. Then he began to read the ancient Hebrew written on the scroll. He paused now and then to let another man explain the meaning of syllables now unrecognizable to the people of Jerusalem. From the Torah, he read Moses' song of praise:

> The Lord is my strength and my might,
> and he has become my salvation; this is my God,
> and I will praise him, my father's God,
> and I will exalt him. The Lord is a warrior;
> the Lord is his name. Pharaoh's chariots and
> his army he cast into the sea.... Who is like you,
> O Lord, among the gods? Who is like you, majestic
> in holiness, awesome in splendor, doing wonders?
> In your steadfast love you led the people
> whom you redeemed; you guided them
> by your strength to your holy abode.
> You brought them in and planted them on the
> mountain of your own possession, the place,
> O Lord, that you made your abode, the sanctuary,
> O Lord, that your hands have established.
> The Lord will reign forever and ever.

The people listening had heard these songs and stories before, and they were moved to tears. Ezra consoled them and encouraged them to celebrate instead. "Go your way, eat the fat and drink sweet wine and send portions of them to those for whom nothing is prepared," he said, "for this day is holy to our Lord."

It was the harvest time, and they brought the best of their crops to the Temple: olives and grapes, wheat and barley, sheep and goats, wool and leather. In preparation for the holiday the people brought branches of "wild olive, myrtle, palm, and other leafy trees" into the city. They lashed them together to build flimsy booths in which they lived for seven days, recalling how their ancestors lived while wandering through the wilderness with Moses. There was singing and dancing and joy all around as the people of Jerusalem celebrated Sukkoth—the Feast of Tabernacles. Modern Jewish communities still observe this autumn holiday by building twig booths and by waving the palm branch (called the *Lulav*) , citron, willow and myrtle to usher in the rainy season.

NEW CONQUERORS

DURING THE second half of the first millennium B.C.E., Palestine was a pawn in the games of larger powers: the Persians, the Egyptians, and the Greeks. During the fourth century, Alexander's forces swept through the Mediterranean, North Africa, and Central Asia, all the way to India. After defeating Darius, the Persian, at Issus in southern Turkey, Alexander moved down the Syrian coast to Tyre, to destroy the island fortress half a mile off the coast of today's Lebanon. At the same time, his forces a hundred miles south brutally stormed the fortress of Gaza, on the coast. Possession of Palestine gave Alexander access to Egypt.

In Egypt, the city of Alexandria rose in grandeur, a pivotal point in the cultural and commercial exchange between the Mediterranean and the Near East. Some Jews had escaped the Babylonian domination of Jerusalem by fleeing to Egypt, forming colonies like the one on Elephantine Island. Largest of the islands in the Nile near Aswan, at the river's First Cataract, Elephantine's role as a trading post stretched back in time. The ancient Egyptians called it Abu, "elephant," probably for its great rounded granite formations. From here, officials during Egypt's Middle and New Kingdoms, from 1975 to 1070 B.C.E., managed Nubian territories to the south. While temple remains testify to worship of nature gods, including the ram-headed creator god Khnum, and his consort, Satis, who wore a crown of gazelle antlers, written remains testify to the worship of Yahweh.

A rich cache of papyrus documents written in Aramaic around 400 B.C.E. and discovered in the late 19th century show a lively and literate Jewish community in Egypt. "To our lord, Bagohi, governor of Yehud, [from] your servants: Yedaniah and his associates, the priests who are in the fortress of Yeb," reads one, requesting that authorization and money come from Yehud, or Judaea, to rebuild the Temple

JUDAISM

SELECTED SCRIPTURES

JUDAISM FOR generations passed along orally its sacred traditions, beginning with Abraham. In time sacred lore became sacred writ. The Torah is God's law, both written and oral. It comprises the first five books of the Old Testament: Genesis, Exodus, Leviticus, Numbers, and Deuteronomy. A vital part of the Torah, the Shema, or confession of faith, includes three scriptural texts from Numbers and Deuteronomy. It is integral to morning and evening prayer. The Talmud is Jewish oral law made in Palestine and Babylon. The Amidah is a series of 19 benedictions, drawn mainly from the Bible and the Talmud, which are the main sections of morning, afternoon, and evening prayers, recited while standing.

FROM THE TORAH

THE SHEMA expresses the essence of Judaism, that God must be loved and obeyed at all times.

Hear, O Israel: The Lord is our God, the Lord alone.
You shall love the Lord your God with all your heart,
and with all your soul, and with all your might.
Keep these words that I am commanding you today in your heart.
Recite them to your children
and talk about them when you are at home and when you are away,
when you lie down and when you rise.
Bind them as a sign on your hand,
fix them as an emblem on your forehead,
and write them on the door posts of your house and on your gates.

LEVITICUS 19:17-18

Do not hate your brother in your heart.
Reprove your fellow human so that he does not continue to sin.
Do not avenge or bear a grudge against your people
and love your neighbor as yourself, I am your God.

FROM THE TALMUD

ETHICS OF THE FATHERS 3:13

Where the spirit of people is pleased with a person's behavior
then the spirit of the Omnipresent will be pleased;
but when peoples' actions do not please the spirit of others
then the spirit of the Omnipresent will not be pleased either.

of Yahweh in Yeb, or Elephantine. "In the month of Tammuz, in the fourteenth year of Darius the king,...the priests of the god Khnub, who is in the fortress of Yeb, conspired with Vidranga, who was administrator here, to destroy the temple of Yahu [Yahweh]." The letter described the attack: Soldiers arrived with weapons, burned the temple, smashed stone pillars, and demolished gateways. Gold, silver and other items of value were looted. The priests assured their governor from afar that they still observed the holy days, fasting and abstaining from sex and wine. "If it seems good to our lord, remember this temple to reconstruct it," they requested. "Look to your clients and friends here in Egypt."

Alexandria grew into a cosmopolitan center of learning. When King Ptolemy II Philadelphus established a library of the world's great books, he wanted a copy of the Jewish Scriptures. He sent delegates to Judaea with his request. In return, 72 Jewish scribes—6 from each of the 12 tribes, according to the story—came to Egypt, bearing a magnificent Torah encased in an ornamented box. They settled on the island of Pharos near Alexandria, where Ptolemy built his tremendous lighthouse, and in 72 days they had translated the ancient Hebrew Scriptures into Greek. While some of the details of this account may be myth—the magical recurrence of the number 72, the location at the foot of the lighthouse—by the end of the second century B.C.E., a Greek-language version of the Jewish holy books existed. Called the Septuagint after its 70-some translators, it quickly circulated throughout the Mediterranean. It was the text from which early Christians learned Hebrew history and the basis of numerous subsequent Christian Bibles. Jewish rabbis rejected the Septuagint in the second century C.E., considering that too many errors had been introduced, and retained the Hebrew originals.

Jews could build a community in a foreign city such as Alexandria. The influential Greeks introduced the concept of naturalization: Despite ancient ties to a foreign state, a person could attain rights of citizenship through time and commitment to a new land. Jews looked back on a long history of wandering and exile. The symbolic objects of their religion—the Ark of the Covenant, the Torah—had been designed as portable. Jews still looked to the Temple in Jerusalem as the most sacred place in their religious world, but a new type of religious assembly hall developed where Jews could meet on the Sabbath to read and study the Torah. People came together at a *bet ha-keneset,* a "house of assembly" or synagogue. It was a social space, a community center open to all, Jews and non-Jews, men and women, rich and poor. Shef Ve-Yativ was the first, according to tradition, built in Nehardea on the Euphrates during the exile with bricks made from the soil of Jerusalem. The earliest archaeological evidence of a synagogue comes from Alexandria: An inscription carved into marble in the third century B.C.E. dedicates a synagogue in Alexandria to Ptolemy III and his queen. Roman documents from the second century B.C.E. mention a synagogue on the Greek island of Delos.

After the death of Alexander in 323 B.C.E., Egypt and Syria vied for Palestine. The Syrian ruler Antiochus IV Epiphanes came to power around 175 B.C.E. and wreaked havoc on the Jewish people and their practices. He forbade the study of the Torah, passed laws requiring homage to pagan gods, and sacrificed pigs, forbidden by Jewish law, on the altar of the Temple of Jerusalem. Some Israelites, partisan with the Hellenistic ruling class, supported Antiochus's efforts to change religious practices in Jerusalem. Others resisted, particularly the Hasidim, a sect dedicated to strict traditions. A daring revolt led by a family of five brothers, under the command of Judah, ousted the Antiochus forces and regained the Temple for the practice of Judaism.

In the Temple stood a seven-branched menorah, or candelabrum, that had to be kept alight continuously. The oil used had to be ritually prepared by the priests. It is said that when Judah returned to the Temple he found only enough

OPPOSITE: Photographed in 1914, a Yemeni Jew, from a tribe tracing its origins to Jacob's son Gad, reads from a scrolled Torah.

FOLLOWING PAGES: Common scenes of Jewish life serve as the subject of the murals of the third-century synagogue of Dura Europos in Syria.

sacred oil to last one day. Miraculously, it lasted eight days until the new oil arrived. This is the basis of one of the most popular of Jewish festivals, Hanukkah, the eight-day Feast of Dedication commemorating the cleansing and rededication of the Temple. During Hanukkah, one light is added each day until the special eight-branched Hanukkah menorah, often called the Hanukkiah, is fully lit.

Judah came from the Hasmonean family of priests, who later took the title Maccabee, literally "the Hammerers" of the Syrians. Within Judaea at the time there was a major schism involving the priests and their practices. The Sadducees, descendants and followers of Zadok, one of the first Temple priests, founded their beliefs on the literal letter of the Torah. They were opposed by the Pharisees, who claimed a lineage of learning, not blood. The Pharisees granted credence to the oral tradition as well as to the written word of Jewish law and loosened the hold of Temple priests on devotional practice. Pharisaic leaders were innovative and more in tune with the needs of the populace. They reconfigured marriage law to offer more protection to wives and permit divorce more readily.

Some visionaries of the time predicted that human history would soon take a radically different turn and that Yahweh would send a *mashiach*—a Messiah, a leader of the caliber of David—who would fulfill the promised glory of Israel as a nation, a people, and a faith. The Messiah originally referred solely to an anointed king and the hope that the Davidic line would be restored. Later it came to express the desire for peace and an end to foreign domination. Some sects in Judaism hoped for a supernatural intervention to change the nature of the world and to remove evil. Others argued that it was for humans to strive to improve the world and bring about the "new era." All these ideas found expression in different sectors of Jewish life over the next millennium, and some would indeed lead to schisms and new religions altogether.

THE SECOND TEMPLE

BY THE beginning of the first century C.E., the seat of power in the Middle East and the Mediterranean had shifted to Rome. In 63 B.C.E., the Roman general Pompey had stormed Jerusalem. Some city residents ushered his troops in, but resisters locked themselves inside the existing Temple compound for three months. Pompey's men piled dirt and timber into an adjacent valley to provide a surface for their war machines, then bombarded the Temple on the Sabbath, the one day they knew their targets would not pick up arms to defend themselves. Pompey seized the city and took many Jews home to Rome as slaves. By the year 1 Rome held sway from Spain and Normandy to Greece, Syria, and Egypt. One political strategy that served Rome well was to establish provincial governments in farflung territories, coupling Roman overseers with local rulers. Thanks to that system, a man who began as governor of tiny Galilee, a land less than a thousand miles

ABOVE: *Hanukkah celebrations include the lighting of a menorah to commemorate the rededication of Solomon's Temple in Jerusalem.*

THE PEOPLE OF THE BOOK
A Daily Practice

JEWISH RELIGIOUS practice regulates daily life to make every action meaningful. From waking until going to sleep there are rituals and blessings designed to make a person think before acting. They link daily behavior to the calendar and the cycles of life. In most Jewish denominations the home often plays as important a religious role as the synagogue.

There are prayers three times a day: morning, noon, and evening. They should be said as part of a community and facing toward Jerusalem, but prayers can be recited by individuals wherever they may be. Hebrew is the main language of prayer although some congregations nowadays include the vernacular. During weekday morning prayers the tefillin are worn. These black leather boxes contain essential passages from the Torah. Wearing them is a reminder of those ideals and a way of preparing oneself physically for prayer. The tallith, the prayer shawl, is also important in helping to create a special atmosphere.

The many laws that regulate what a person can eat, based on biblical traditions, and how food is prepared, are intended to make the whole process a more significant and thoughtful one. The more one can do to remember the spiritual, the more one is likely to remember the ethical and broader principles of Jewish life, such as giving to charity and helping those in need.

Saturdays and the festivals—Passover, Pentecost, and Tabernacles—as well as the more serious holy days are all occasions to create an atmosphere that is oriented toward religious and family values. The services in the synagogue are longer and are more social in tone, with extensive readings from the Bible, and more singing and community participation. But the main celebrations take place in the home around the family dining table (except, of course, the annual Day of Atonement, which is a day of fasting).

From birth to death there are important celebrations of life. The circumcision on the eighth day, the Brith Milah, initiates the process that continues with the Bar Mitzvah at 13 for boys or the Bat Mitzvah for girls at 12, when they become responsible for their own religious lives. Marriage and family celebrations play an important religious role in Jewish life. Death requires the community to rally round and help during the week of mourning called shivah. Linking everything, daily study of religious texts is such a crucial aspect of religious life that Jews have been called "The People of the Book."

square, ultimately went down in history as Herod the Great, ruler over Palestine.

Herod was born in 73 B.C.E. in Idumaea, south of Judaea. Although declared king of the Jews, his religious background is murky; one ancient historian called him a half-Jew. In 40 B.C.E., Herod traveled to Rome and won the admiration of Octavian and Marc Antony, leaders after the death of Caesar. They crowned Herod king of Judaea and thus set him up as a contender against Antigonus, a Hasmonean descendant of Judah the Maccabee who was leading rebellions against Rome.

With the aid of a Roman guard, Herod saw to the swift death of Antigonus. He married a Hasmonean, hedging his political bets, then proceeded to execute her grandfather, brother, mother, and finally her, because he felt threatened by their popularity among the Jews. When Octavian gained full power, Herod sailed via Alexandria to Rhodes, ingrati-

ated himself with the man now called Emperor Augustus, and returned with authority over more of Palestine.

It may have been in the wake of this power grab that religious Jews stashed their precious documents in the limestone caves below Qumran, a tiny village in the desolate low-lying region between Jerusalem and the Dead Sea. In 1947, shepherds there came upon pottery jars containing tattered bits of parchment—one of the most remarkable biblical finds in centuries, the Dead Sea Scrolls. The discovery of the Qumran Caves spurred a decade of excavation that uncovered more than 800 papyrus and parchment fragments—civic and religious documents, sacred texts both familiar and never before seen—as well as common objects such as bowls, combs, lamps, and inkwells. Some texts appeared in multiple copies; others were one-of-a-kind, penned in Hebrew, Aramaic, or Greek. A single hoard of coins contained 561 silver pieces, minted in Tyre about 135 B.C.E. Artifacts and a text on parchment provide the earliest evidence of tefillin, phylacteries still worn by orthodox Jews in weekday morning worship: Four quotations from the Torah, written on four pieces of parchment, are folded into two small leather cases that are tied on to the left arm, where they rest against the heart, and on to the forehead, where they lie against the brain. Thus both organs are dedicated to the divine will, following the commandment in Deuteronomy to "keep these words that I am commanding" and "bind them as a sign on your hand, fix them as an emblem on your forehead." The caves contained manuscripts of all the books of the Hebrew Bible but one, as well as many others. In 1965 the Shrine of the Book, part of the Israel Museum of Jerusalem, opened as a repository for the scrolls and related artifacts.

During his 34-year rule, Herod undertook massive building projects, bringing grand Roman architecture to Palestine. Besides the Temple in Jerusalem, he built himself a fortified palace where Roman troops were quartered. The palace was named

Antonia to flatter his patron, Marc Antony. Thirty-five miles south of Jerusalem, on a bleak hill overlooking the Dead Sea, he built another palace. A mile-long wall—20 feet tall, 12 feet thick, with 38 watchtowers—surrounded Herod's grounds at Masada. Two houses stood here, one at each end of the diamond-shaped hilltop. Despite its location in one of the hottest, driest places on Earth, Herod's Masada villa included a large bathhouse, its water provided by rainwater trapped in massive cisterns. Air heated in a furnace nearby flowed into the space under the bathhouse floor.

Herod built parks and other palaces, roads and harbors, waterworks and theaters. He encouraged great athletic and gladiatorial games. To boost commerce, he turned a tiny village into a thriving port city, which he named Caesarea in honor of Augustus Caesar. But the enterprise for which Herod is most famous is the reconstruction of the Temple of Jerusalem, built precisely on the site of Solomon's Temple and known as the Second Temple. To begin with, he expanded the city plaza, so that now the Temple stood on an esplanade 550 paces long and 400 paces wide.

The Temple was planned as a series of courts stretching from east to west, one inside the other, each one more holy and restricted in access than the one before. The broad, outer Court of the Gentiles was open to non-Jews as well as Jews. Here herdsmen from the country brought lambs, kids, and doves to sell to those preparing a holy sacrifice. Here money changers offered to turn foreign coinage into shekels, so that visiting male Jews could present their annual contribution of half a shekel of silver for the running of the Temple and the communal sacrifices. Jewish women could proceed through the massive bronze gate, ornamented with gold, that led into the Court of the Women. Jewish men could go farther, into the Court of Israel. The inner Court of Priests included the altar at which only the priests could make sacrifices to Yahweh. Beyond that, behind a double veil, was enshrined the Holy of Holies. The shrine was entered only once a year by the high priest on Yom Kippur, the Day of Atonement —still observed as the holiest day of the Jewish calendar, a solemn occasion for fasting, prayers, and confessionals.

Taller than any other building in the city and constructed of gleaming white stone, Herod's Temple stood as

OPPOSITE: *Desert landscape fills the view from the Qumran Caves, where the ancient Dead Sea Scrolls were found.*
ABOVE: *Fragments of Hebrew texts discovered in Qumran trace the history of the Essenes, a second-century B.C.E. Jewish sect.*
FOLLOWING PAGES: *Sunset silhouettes a rider on camelback on the shores of the Dead Sea, a locus for thousands of years of Jewish history.*

a beacon, a sign of Jerusalem's role as the Holy City for all Jews throughout the Middle East and the Mediterranean. It infuriated some Jews, though, that Herod had placed a golden eagle at the entrance to the Temple—eagles belonged on pagan temples, not the Temple of Yahweh, who had forbidden graven images. One high noon, a brash group of students knocked the eagle down and demolished it. Soldiers rushed from the Antonia fort and arrested them. The perpetrators and two of their Levite professors were marched to Jericho and burned alive.

The construction of the Temple and seething resentment of Roman rule both continued after Herod's death in 4 B.C.E. Revolts against the Romans, led by Jews called Zealots, from the Greek for "enmity" and "rebellion," resulted in bloodshed, devastation, and mass flight of the Jews from their holy city. Throughout Judaea, Romans leveled towns and laid waste to the landscape. In the year 70 the Roman emperor Titus crushed a revolt of Zealots and attacked Jerusalem. "As soon as the army had no more people to slay or to plunder," wrote the historian Josephus in a first-hand account, the Roman general "gave orders that they should now demolish the entire city and temple, but should leave as many of the towers standing as were of the greatest eminency…and so much of the wall as enclosed the city on the west side." The portion of city wall that Roman soldiers left untouched still stands: the Kotel ha-Ma'aravi,

or Western Wall, the holiest site in Jerusalem for Jewish pilgrims. To this day, the faithful approach reverently, men and women separately. Many write prayers on bits of paper and stick them into the chinks in the wall, believing that in gaining the closest access possible to the Temple of Jerusalem, they are coming as near as possible to God.

One brave band of Jews held fast in the mountaintop fortress of Masada until the Roman soldiers pushed through the walls. Refusing to be taken prisoner, the Zealots threw themselves over the steep hillside, committing mass suicide. "This was the end which Jerusalem came to," wrote Josephus, "a city otherwise of great magnificence, and of mighty fame among all mankind."

DISPERSAL FROM THE HOLY LAND

THE SIEGE of Jerusalem and the tearing down of the Second Temple in the year 70 marked the beginning of the great Jewish Diaspora, the resettlement of Jews throughout the Mediterranean region and, ultimately, the rest of the world.

Jews already lived in communities in Babylon and its surrounding Parthian Empire, in Alexandria and elsewhere in Egypt, in Rome and other cities in Italy, and in Germany, especially the city of Cologne, to which a Roman legion had been sent from Jerusalem, taking with them Jews as slaves. Now, in a mass exodus sadly repeating days of old, émigrés joined freed

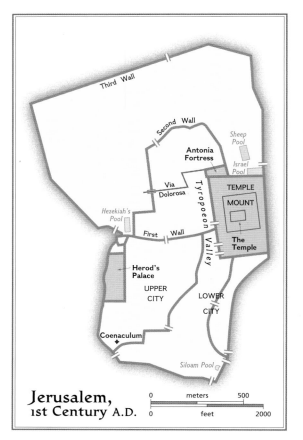

Jerusalem,
1st Century A.D.

Third Wall

Second Wall

Sheep Pool

Antonia Fortress

Israel Pool

Via Dolorosa

Hezekiah's Pool

Tyropoeon Valley

TEMPLE MOUNT

The Temple

First Wall

Herod's Palace

UPPER CITY

LOWER CITY

Coenaculum

Siloam Pool

meters 500
feet 2000

OPPOSITE: Destroyed by the Romans in the year 70, the ruins of the hilltop fortress of Masada remain as a testament to their defenders.

slaves in all the cities of the Roman Empire and began building communities of their own.

The leader of the Pharisee community, Rabbi Johanan ben Zakkai, arranged to be smuggled out of Jerusalem so that he could negotiate a truce that would allow moderate Jews who valued religion more than politics to leave Jerusalem. The Romans allowed him to reestablish religious authority in Jabneh, a little town near the coast, where the Sanhedrin, the council and tribunal, relocated. He founded an academy for the continued study of scripture. The Jews, he believed, could survive without their Temple, but they must preserve the intellectual, ethical, and spiritual lifeblood in the holy word. They were, after all, the People of the Book. He and others labored to write down all that they remembered and understood of Scripture, ceremony, and law.

The role of the rabbis as the primary transmitters of tradition to the nation (as opposed to the purely functionary role now ascribed to the priests) meant that they became in effect the legislative as well as the spiritual authorities and teachers. Through the process of midrash, exegetical and homiletical interpretation of Scriptures, they conveyed the ethical and spiritual tradition of Judaism to the Jewish people wherever they were. Through Halakah, the legal part of the Talmud, they continued the process of developing biblical law within the new cultural and economic circumstances they faced. This body of knowledge, law, and lore, known as the Oral Law, was originally intended to be exactly that—oral. Only the Torah itself was committed to writing.

The Roman Wars signaled the death of the old Temple order, and the generation to follow after the destruction made momentous decisions to preserve Jewish traditions in the wake of the total disappearance of the Temple service.

The primary way in which the Temple service was replaced was through prayer. The rabbis introduced communal prayers to replace the sacrificial system. Some of this had already begun informally during the Babylonian exile and in the ongoing Diaspora, but now it became enshrined by formal dictat. Biblical prayer was always, and remained, simple and personal. The decision was made to write down the oral laws and traditions before they could be lost in the ongoing persecutions and political upheavals. The process had begun around the time of the destruction of the Temple. Then around 200 C.E., the head of the community in Israel, Rabbi Yehuda Hanassi, made the decision to write down and compile the oral law into what became known as the Mishnah. There had been earlier collections, but Yehuda HaNassi's Mishnah became the authoritative text.

The Mishnah was a six-volume compilation of the decisions and discussions that had taken place both about biblical law and about rabbinic interpretation and innovation. Its sections dealt with civil law and politics, marriage and divorce, agriculture, daily life, ritual and authority, purity, and sacrifices. It reflected the whole gamut of life as any constitution would.

No sooner had the Mishnah appeared than the academies of Israel and Babylon began to analyze and often challenge both its substance and its form. There were other traditions, conflicting texts called Beraitot, and incorrect attributions and scribal errors. This discussion on the Mishnah was called the Gemara. There would in time be two Gemaras, with the Jerusalem version completed in about 300 C.E. The much larger and important Babylonian was completed in 500 C.E. Together the Mishnah and the Gemara were given the general name of the Talmud. It has dominated Jewish religious life ever since.

The Talmud became in many ways even more important than the Bible as a repository of Jewish law and custom. Talmudic interpretation consciously tried to differentiate the Jewish Bible from the Christian. The Talmud became the means of Jewish religious survival and resurrection over the coming 400 years, as slowly all but a few embers of Jewish life were extinguished from the ancestral lands. The Talmud and the Jewish Bible became the essential sources of traditional Judaism.

For hundreds of years, through the Middle Ages and the Renaissance up to the 18th-century Enlightenment, Jews also contributed to city life throughout Europe, where they were usually a minority. Nevertheless, the major Jewish community remained that of the East, so that when Islam emerged in the seventh century and began to sweep westward across the Mediterranean, the Jews of Babylonia and the Arabian Peninsula joined the movement. By migrating over generations through Egypt and North Africa, many Jews ended up in Spain and Portugal: Their descendants follow the Sephardic tradition (the name comes from the Hebrew for Spain). Sephardic culture developed through centuries in the later prevailing Islamic culture, which was largely tolerant of other religious practices. Ladino, the Sephardic language, is a blend of Spanish and Hebrew. Today it survives primarily in a body of proverbs and folksongs.

"My heart is in the east, and I in the uttermost west," wrote the Sephardic poet Judah Halevi, who lived in Toledo, Spain, in the late 11th century. "Beautiful land, delight of the world, city of kings," he mourned. "If I could fly to you on the wings of eagles, I would soak your soil with my tears." His poetry rings with the recurrent theme of Judaism: the yearning to return to Jerusalem and the land of Abraham and Moses, made more poignant in the times and places where Jews found themselves the victims of persecution.

Beginning in the tenth century, Jews in Cordoba maintained their own courts and government.

OPPOSITE: A 17th-century engraving shows Roman legions, led by Titus, destroying Jerusalem's Second Temple.

FOLLOWING PAGES: Islam's Dome of the Rock gleams beyond the Western Wall as Jews gather to observe the feast of Shabuoth.

The Andalusian city became a center of Jewish learning that rivaled the Babylonian academies. But a Muslim invasion in 1013 sent Jews fleeing from that city to Seville, Malaga, and Granada. Granada witnessed a similar invasion in 1066, but this time the Jewish community was deliberately attacked on a Sabbath. Four thousand died. It was only the beginning of threats, persecution, and worse for Jews in Spain. As impassioned Muslims and Christians vied for supremacy in city after city, Spain's Jews were caught in the middle, portrayed by both sides as infidels.

One person who escaped Spain in this era was a man named Moses Ben Maimon, born in Cordoba in 1135. After 11 years of secret worship, the Maimon family fled to Fez, Morocco. When Maimon's teacher was executed for practicing Judaism, the family fled again, into the neighborhood of Cairo, Egypt, where they were accepted into a tolerant society. Soon Maimon—known to history by the Greek version of his name, Maimonides, but also affectionately called Rambam—joined Saladin's court as the sultan's physician and rose to leadership in Cairo's Jewish community. His writing turned from logic to theology as he matured. His systematic crystallization of Jewish law, called the *Mishnah Torah,* or the Torah reviewed, remains the authoritative legal text for the Sephardic community to this day. His great philosophical work, *Guide to the Perplexed,* is a classic, valued by readers of all religions and philosophies.

It was Maimonides who first formulated a Jewish theology to match the Christian and Muslim credos. Before him Jewish thought was expressed not in a theological but rather in an informal way. His Thirteen Principles of Faith remain

ABOVE: *Hasidic Jews stand at the foot of the Western Wall, a site for prayer and celebration since the Temple's destruction.*

a simple guide to the essentials of the Jewish faith. They revolve around the core ideas of one God, the Sinai revelation, life after death, resurrection, and messianism.

Maimonides ultimately transcended geographical distinctions, though he arose from the Sephardic line of Judaism. In contrast, those who migrated from Palestine to the north, into France, Germany, and Eastern Europe, represented the Ashkenazic line, named for the Hebrew word for Germany. In these regions, Jews sometimes lived together in a shtetl (from the Yiddish for "small town"). Sometimes they lived in neighborhoods circumscribed by those in authority. These came to be called ghettos, a word derived from the Italian for "foundry," since Jews in Venice were segregated on an island with an iron foundry. The Ashkenazic language is Yiddish, a blend of Hebrew and German that developed in Germany between the 9th and 12th centuries. More than three million people in North and South America, Europe, and the Middle East still speak Yiddish today.

In northern Europe, Jews gained a reputation for excellence in scholarship. Charlemagne, crowned Holy Roman Emperor in 800, included a Jew named Isaac among the ambassadors he sent to Jerusalem and Baghdad to create alliances between West and East. His son, Louis the Pious, appointed a Jew to his court as Magister Judaeaorum, responsible for protecting Jewish rights. This atmosphere of respect did not last long. Religious wars raged between Christians and Muslims over the Holy Land of Jerusalem. In a bitter irony, Jews did not join in the quarrels. Official decrees from Rome gave Christians throughout Europe reasons to mistrust and ways to persecute Jews.

The Fourth Lateran Council of 1215 announced the Third Crusade and also passed sweeping anti-Semitic rules, despite the delegation of Jews from southern France who attended. New laws forbade Jews from holding public office, and all Jews were required to identify themselves by their clothing: a red cape in Italy, a red-and-white circular chest patch in France, a pointed hat in Germany, and, in England, a yellow patch shaped like the Tablets of Law and worn over the heart.

No record of medieval (or modern) Jewish life would be complete without mentioning the Kabbalah. The term itself as applied to mystical literature did not occur until the first millennium. However, the Talmud discusses the esoteric world and refers to types of knowledge that should not be taught to everyone (as opposed to the revealed Torah, which was indeed for all). The first chapter of Ezekiel is the source of this secret tradition but the term used in the Talmud is *Maaseh Merkava* (the Chariot), harking back to the chariot of fire that took the Prophet Elijah up to Heaven (II Kings 2). The rabbis of the Talmud felt that mystical knowledge was too dangerous a tool to be available to everyone indiscriminately and insisted that it should only be studied by a select few taught by trusted masters.

In the centuries before the millennium, many mystical groups flourished both within and without the mainstream tradition, such as the Dead Sea Sects. Some of the earliest texts of Kabbalah, *Sefer Yetzira* (The Book of Creation) and *Sefer Bahir* (The Book of Splendor), may even have dated from this period. But the real expansion of the mystical tradition coincides with a general era of interest in esoteric religion that can be found in Christianity and Islam in the medieval period.

The body of writing that came to be known as the Kabbalah was divided into three areas. The first was an abstract framework for understanding the world, creation, and divine intervention, in ways that were intentionally not bound by the conventions of philosophical thought. It was essentially Jewish in that it expressed complete loyalty to the Talmudic tradition and, initially, used the Talmudic language and conventions.

Then there was practical Kabbalah that wanted to find ways of actually encountering the divine, of using divine power to create life and alter reality, rather like the role alchemy played in the Christian world. The "secret," however, was primarily that of knowing how to harness divine creative energy. One of the goals was to reproduce human life. Medieval rabbinic literature has many discussions about the status in law of such a creation. This was the basis for the famous myth of the Golem of Prague attributed to the great Rabbi Judah Loew, who died in 1609.

Finally there was astrological and magical Kabbalah that sought to ease the pain of the suffering and the insecure by providing a simple scheme that explained the physical world.

With the appearance of the *Zohar,* the great mystical work that is both a commentary on the Torah and a series of lectures on mystical themes, the Kabbalah took its place alongside traditional texts. There remains controversy as to whether Moses De Leon, who lived in Guadalajara in northern Spain in the 14th century, actually wrote the Zohar, compiled it, or simply discovered the long-lost text attributed to the second-century authority Simon Bar Yochai, who is the stated author. Traditionalists accept the earlier authorship and it has acquired a status in the Jewish literary tradition to the point where some study every day a part of the Torah, the Mishnah, the Gemara, and the Zohar.

In 1492 monarchs Ferdinand and Isabella expelled all non-Christians from Spain. A tide of exceptionally talented Jews swept eastward across the Mediterranean to the land of Israel, and the city of Safed in particular. The Kabbalistic approach to Judaism influenced the greatest rabbis of the succeeding generations. Safed, in Upper Galilee, was the center of a reconstructed Spanish Jewish community. It included scholars such as Joseph Caro, whose great work the *Shulchan Aruch,* the *Table Laid,* was a summation of the legal development of Judaism over the previous thousand years.

Safed was also the center of Kabbalah. In the 16th century it was the home of Moses Cordorvero and his more celebrated pupil, Isaac Luria, the *Ari'zal,* as he is known, the lion, one of the giants of the mystical tradition. He and his school were responsible for making Kabbalah more accessible. They used it as a way of adding dimensions to the ritual structure of Judaism, combining it with meditation, contemplation, song, and dance, overturning the solemn traditions that harked back to the pain of the destruction of the Temple and exile. They established norms of religious behavior that led to a more charismatic and popular expression of ecstatic Judaism. This in turn produced a messianic fervor that expected divine intervention at any moment. Luria's influence on prayer and worship was probably greater than any person's since the great era of post-Destruction Judaism. He was a major influence on the new Hasidic movement, which adopted and absorbed a great deal of the Kabbalah into its Judaism.

After the expulsion from Spain, Sephardic Jews established communities in new countries and continents. Theirs was the first recognized synagogue in London, in 1656, and in Amsterdam, in 1671. In Hamburg, Germany, the Sephardic community increased nearly fivefold, from 125 to 600, in the early 1600s. Jewish merchants rode with the rising tide of trade to the New World. Jewish communities formed on many of the Caribbean islands, especially those under Dutch control. Sephardic Jews founded North America's oldest active Jewish congregation, established on Curaçao, Netherlands Antilles, in 1651. In Spanish Town, Jamaica, Jews had a market, shops, and a synagogue on Monk Street in 1704. Peter Stuyvesant was concerned when Sephardic Jews arrived in New Amsterdam in 1654, but the Dutch West India Company insisted that they should be allowed to settle. The records show that, within four years, one of them, named Asser Levy, was conducting real-estate business near today's Albany, New York.

With the flowering of intellectual curiosity that swept Europe in the 15th and 16th centuries, renewed respect was paid the Jewish people and their culture. Christian scholars and artists brought Jewish intellectuals into the fold. In Florence, Italy, Lorenzo the Magnificent gathered a circle of philosophers that included Pico della Mirandola, Marsilius Ficino, and the Jewish mystical poet Judah Abravanel. Abravanel, also known by his Italian name, Leone Ebreo,

OPPOSITE: Glowing with tradition, Prague's 13th century Altneuschul, or Old-New Synagogue, is the oldest surviving temple in Europe.
FOLLOWING PAGES: Candlelight illuminates the names of Czech Holocaust victims on a memorial in Prague's Pinkus Synagogue.

REDLICHOVÁ GRETA 29.VII.1910 EVA 22.VII.1934
SALUS KAREL
RŮŽIČKA FERDINAND 7.V.1906 27.VII.1942
SINGER OSKAR
OLGA 15.III.1885 6.IX.1943 OSKAR 20.IX
VALENTINA 6.IX.1885 EMILIE
RŮŽENA 14.XII.1880 HELENA 1.VI.1914 23.I.1943
HELENA 5.I.1934 23.I.1943
FRISCHMANN JOSEF 7.XI.1878 25.V.1942
WOLLNEROVÁ
PICKOVÁ RŮŽENA 10.VIII.1864 22.X.1942
FUCHS JINDŘICH 2.XI.1852 27.XI.1942
GLASEROVÁ
TELTSCHEROVÁ HEDVIKA 22.I.1908
ROSENBAUMOVÁ
BRUMML JAROSLAV 4.III.1909
ADELA 11.II.18
BLOCHOVÁ LUDMILA 5.VI.1889 20.I.194
GLASER BERNARD 7.III.1862 14.V.1943
BERTA 6.XI
SEIDEL RUDOL
JOSEF 15.X.1932 13.VI
ŠTĚRBOVÁ BERTA

73 FRANTIŠKA 19.II1871 · 1...X...
89 · 28.X 1944 ∗ RUDOLF 8.VI1891 RŮŽENA 18.IX1900 ANNA
.1943 ∗ ROBERT 3.IV1892 · 6.IX 1943 ∗ EDITA 18.IX1903 · 6.IX
88 · 23.II1943 MARTA 18.XII1892 · 6.IX1943 ∗ VIRTOVÁ KA...
R KAREL CHAJIM 9.II1890 ELA 2.V1906 · 15.V1944 LENKA MIR...
VÁ ANASTAZIA 19.VIII1903 · 23.II1943 ∗ PAŠINKA: ŠI...
11 · 16.XI1942 ∗ POLLAK FELIX 21.III1874 · 6.II1943 EMILIE 7.V...
.VII1906 ALICE 13.III1938 · 18.XII1943 ∗ PEČKY: ALLINA...
VÁ RŮŽENA 10.II1891 · 12.VI1942 ∗ STEINOVÁ MARIE 7.XI19...
RTA 6.III1875 · 29.III 1943 ∗ JANDLOVÁ MARKÉTA 1.VIII1905
ARTUR 2.V1893 FRANTIŠKA 8.VIII1897 JOSEF 14.VI1932 MILA
35 · 15.XII1943 ∗ THEINER VÁ ELSA 15.I1905 JOSEFA 4.V1876 · 2
3.X1875 · 9.V1943 PAVEL 7... VIII1902 · 28.IX 1944 IVO 15.X1934 · 23
5.II1920 IVANA 13.XI19... 8.V1944 EVŽENIE 22.IV1875 · 13.IV
4.IX1942 ∗ LÖBNEROVÁ... VIII1898 · 19.X1944 J...
ORA 5.IV1868 · 8.X19... RICHARD 10.I1901 BERTA 4.VIII
ONDY VIKTOR 28.VI... ∗ BÜCHLEROVÁ OLGA 14.II187
.1891 ANNA 9.V189... 6. JAROSLAV 22.II1925 · 20...
· 18.VI1943 ∗ RŮŽEN... 1943 ∗ KRAUSOVÁ OTY...
.VII1898 · 5.VII1943... R 8.X1893 IRMA 6.IV1920 ...
KOVÁ ANNA 7... 2.VLASTA 6.II1920 · 70...
PITKOVI... MARIE 77.IX18...
.25.X1899 · 14.VII...
866 · 22.X1942 ∗
RUDOLF 13.II1882 · 25...
42 ∗ VÍT ∗ 7.5...
.42 ∗ HERTA 17.II...
NET ARNOŠ...

MY JUDAISM

—RABBI JEREMY ROSEN, *London*

I WAS brought up in Great Britain to feel fortunate that my family had survived the Second World War and Hitler. I could not understand why there were people in the world who wanted to kill Jews, but I was reassured that I, at any rate, was safe.

My father, a rabbi and educator, had tremendous respect for British values and loved Western culture. Yet at the same time he was a passionately committed, very traditional Jew who brought us up to enjoy our religion despite its occasional inconveniences. I was vaguely aware of the Eastern European origins of his parents, but my life and self-perception were inextricably bound up with living in the Oxfordshire countryside. I heard anti-Jewish remarks in the local town, but then abuse was also directed toward the city slickers who ventured out of London over weekends. I was constantly aware of "others," but took it as a natural way of things. Living within a warm, protective family cocoon, I did not let it impinge on my life. I was aware that most other Jews

were not as religiously committed as we were, and the Jewish world was full of skeptics of different degrees. But our religious life was a pattern of behavior, a system of traditions, special days, and dietary restrictions that encouraged us to eat, study, and play as well as pray, as a family and as a community. There was no feeling of superiority or exclusiveness. We mixed with all sorts and types. Theology only reared its head when we were asked why we didn't believe in Jesus the way the local Christians did.

When I was in my teens, my father decided that I needed an injection of passionate, scholarly Judaism. And I was sent off (somewhat reluctantly because soccer was my passion, not books) to Israel to study in a yeshiva, defined in Israel as a full-time institution that exclusively taught Talmud and advanced Judaic studies, not from an academic, but from a committed, and nowadays one might say "fundamentalist," point of view. When I arrived in Israel I encountered for the first time the racial and sectarian

ABOVE: A 15th-century manuscript shows a page of the Mishnah Torah, Maimonides' philosophical discourse on Jewish law and tradition.

variety of Jewish life. There were Jews from Africa, India, and Yemen who looked totally different from the European Jews I knew, both in dress and skin tone. Among the Eastern European Hasidim there were various sects, each one wearing a specific style of clothing and headgear that identified their loyalties. I became aware of many different rabbis who were known as specialists in esoteric branches of Jewish spirituality and mysticism.

Many of the traditional oriental Jews, the Sephardim, dressed according to the Arab communities they had come from. There were modern Western Jews who wore head coverings of various sorts and colors, and there were secular Jews who looked like any other Mediterranean person. I felt I had stepped out of a monochromatic Judaism into a kaleidoscope of colors.

I wondered what it was that united all these different varieties of Jews. It certainly wasn't the way they thought of their culture or philosophy. They shared a common sense of having been persecuted, or having been made to feel second-class citizens, and desired to live in a state of their own. What sort of Judaism was it that united the religious?

Judaism is not really a theological system. The first of the Ten Commandments isn't even phrased "You Must Believe" but simply states "I am the Lord your God." There is no formal definition of the divine nature. In response to external forces, Judaism developed more structured ideas about life after death, messianism, and resurrection. Only in response to Christian credos did great rabbis like Maimonides resort to giving Jewish theology a formality. Otherwise it was expressed through teachings that sought to expand on ideas in an informal way, called *Midrash.*

The genius of Judaism lay in its "constitution" known in general as the Torah but more specifically as the Halakah, another word for "law" that literally means "the way to go."

It is a system for every aspect of a person's life, at home, at work, in society at large, as well as in the synagogue. Every daily task is given significance and is modified so as to make one think before one acts. Later mystics added a whole dimension of meditation and preparation that would give greater importance to each act and make it a means of elevation and spiritual growth.

Ideas are important. The nature of God, reward and punishment, revelation, eternal life, and messianism are part of Judaism even though they are not rigidly defined. Various traditions within Judaism understand them very differently. But these ideas supplement and are built on the principle of living the good life and behaving according to the Torah. Love and spirit matter in Judaism above all else. The Jewish emphasis on law is not a dry routine. It offers constant reminders of the noble ideas we aspire to.

Thinking before one eats precisely because there are restrictions, setting aside one day a week for reflection and meditation, preparing for prayer, applying limitations to the whole gamut of physical activity from sex to study, are all designed to enhance the pleasures and meaning of life. One can add the layers of Kabbalistic exercises that are similar to yoga and Eastern meditation and share a great deal with Sufism. But in the end it is the daily pattern of living that defines the Jewish religion more than any other single factor.

My introduction to a universal Judaism in my teens was to a religion of tremendous spirituality and vibrancy, very different from the rather pompous, rationalist formality of much of what passes as Judaism in the West. Judaism offers another paradigm of religious life and experience to enrich the options of human spirituality. But of course, as with all good things today, one has to know where to look.

joined the celebrated Platonic Academy and helped translate the classics of Greek philosophy into Latin. His influence brought works of Judaism, such as the Talmud, the treatises of Maimonides, and the Kabbalah, into the corpus of learning alongside Plato and Aristotle.

Cities across Europe had their Jewish quarters, districts where all gathered at dawn and at dusk to pray and on Friday nights to bring in the Sabbath. Although the home was as important religiously as the synagogue, on the Sabbath in particular people came together to pray, read from the Torah, and study. In Prague, Czech Republic, seven synagogues still standing tell the history of the city's Jewish quarter. Staronová Synagóga, or Altneuschul, the Old-New Synagogue, built around 1270, is the oldest synagogue in Europe still offering services. Pinkasova Synagóga, the Pinkas Synagogue, founded in 1479 by Rabbi Pinkas, shows many layers of Jewish history. Its gallery for women dates from the early 17th century, a harbinger of change in a religion strictly patriarchal up to that time. Outside, in the cemetery founded in 1478, lie the graves of an estimated hundred thousand Jews, buried several deep over the centuries. After World War II, the synagogue became a memorial to Czech Jews killed in the Holocaust. The High Synagogue, Vysoká Synagóga, was financed by Mordechai Maisel, mayor of Prague's Jewish town, who also built Zldoyská Radnice, the Jewish Town Hall, whose clock tower's hands point to Hebrew numerals and rotate counterclockwise, since Hebrew reads right to left. In 1700, a quarter of the city of Prague was Jewish—the largest number of Jews in any city in the world at the time.

In the early 1700s, a Jewish orphan named Israel ben Eliezer, born in a Polish village so small its name no longer shows on the map, veered from rabbinical training and began studying the use of medicinal plants. He could cure people, especially those with mental illness, and soon earned the title Baal Shem Tov, Master of a Good Name, for his ability to work miracles. While he wrote nothing down, his legendary life story and commentaries on it form the groundwork for modern Hasidism, the most mystical branch of Judaism, named by the same Hebrew word for "pious ones" that those resisting the Romans used. For them, God is present in the natural world, immediate and accessible to anyone, no matter what their education or background. "Everything is by Divine Providence," reads the first of Baal Shem Tov's 35 Aphorisms. "If a leaf is turned over by a breeze, it is only because this has been specifically ordained by God to serve a particular function within the purpose of creation." For Hasidic Jews, religious faith dwells in immediate spiritual feeling more than in practice, ceremony, or received tradition, and many find inspiration in the Kabbalah. Hasidic Jews follow a *rebbe,* an enlightened teacher, like Baal Shem Tov. Nowadays they tend to be dynastic. Charismatic Hasidic leaders in the early 20th century inspired communities in places around the world, including Breslau, Germany; Lubavitch, Russia; and Brooklyn, New York. Hasidic men often distinguish themselves by wearing black brimmed hats, following Eastern European tradition, and long side curls or *payos,* following the command of the Torah: "You shall not round the corners of your heads, nor mar the edges of your beards."

Philosophers of the Enlightenment and the American and French Revolutions imprinted a new social consciousness on Western civilization. By the turn of the 19th century, edicts from the Holy Roman Emperor and France's General Assembly decried religious persecution. Napoleon in particular championed the Jewish cause. In 1798 as a military general he led 30,000 troops from Egypt into Palestine, thus assailing the Ottoman Empire but stating that his goal was the reinstatement of the ancient Jewish nation. Once in power in Paris, Napoleon summoned an Assembly of Jewish Notables to correlate new French laws with Mosaic and Talmudic law. Against the advice of other international leaders, he declared Jewish people free and equal citizens of France. His civil code led the way to further reforms in the nations of Western Europe. Jewish intellectual life thrived in 19th-century Amsterdam, Berlin, Breslau,

OPPOSITE: London's Great Synagogue was founded in 1702. An earlier temple built in the city by Sephardic Jews no longer exists.

Vienna, and Warsaw, whereas in Russia, Jews continued to live in shtetls, often threatened by violent raids called pogroms, from the Russian word for "wreaking havoc." The Jewish population of Europe in the late 19th century is estimated to have been eight and a half million, with five million in Russia and nearly two million in Austria-Hungary.

In the spirit of intellectual inquiry, European Jews began reinterpreting their own religion. Beginning in Hamburg and spreading to other cities in Germany, the Reform movement used a Bible and prayer books translated into modern German. "The Talmud speaks with the ideology of its own time, and for that time it was right," said Samuel Holdheim, a German rabbi and leader in the Reform movement. "I speak from the higher ideology of my time, and for this age I am right." The traditionalists opposed many of these developments, advocating strict adherence to the old rules and practices. This arm of the faith became known as Orthodox Judaism.

Most of the divisions in the world's Jewish community of today date back to these distinctions articulated in the 19th century. Synagogues identify themselves as Conservative, Reform, Orthodox, or Hasidic. While all share certain beliefs—most fundamentally, that they all belong to the people chosen by the one God who identified himself to Moses and Abraham—they differ significantly in doctrine and practice. Reconstructionist Judaism, a new branch founded in 1955, defines itself not through theology of the past but through the cultural history that Jews share.

JUDAISM TODAY

A PARIS correspondent in the 1890s, Viennese journalist Theodor Herzl witnessed firsthand the controversy surrounding Albert Dreyfus, a Jewish captain in the French Army unjustly accused of spying. Herzl came to believe that anti-Semitism ran so deep in European cultures, the only way Jewish people could attain full freedom, equality, and dignity was to return to the ancient land of Zion. He published a pamphlet, *The Jewish State in 1896,* which won such

interest that a Zionist Congress convened about it in Basel, Switzerland, in 1897. Supported by a Zionist organization with offices in Constantinople and Jaffa, Jews began migrating out of Russia and Romania and into Palestine. There they found a sparse and barren land, described by Mark Twain when he visited it in 1867 as "a silent mournful expanse" with "hardly a tree or a shrub anywhere. Even the olive and the cactus, those fast friends of the worthless soil, had almost deserted the country." By 1939, half a million Jews were living in Palestine. Their Zionist ideals led them to reestablish a culture based on Hebrew, the universal language of the Jewish people. The promise of a Jewish homeland was finding modern expression.

From the 1890s on, many more Jews migrated to North America than to Palestine. It is estimated that between 1881 and 1931, nearly three million moved out of Europe. Some 427,000 migrated to Canada and South America, especially Argentina; nearly 100,000 settled in South Africa or Australia; but for the vast majority of Jews seeking refuge, the United States was the land that promised a better future. "This country is our Palestine, this city our Jerusalem, this house of God our Temple," stated a rabbi in Charleston, South Carolina, from early on a center of American Judaism. Reform, Orthodox, and—in an American effort at compromise—Conservative Jewish synagogues helped the newcomers make a home. In some cases, America fulfilled its promise as a land of wealth and opportunity; masses of Jews traded the ghettos of Eastern Europe for those of New York and Chicago. Today nearly six million Jews live in the United States.

Modern Jews follow the ceremonies and holidays of old. Eight days after birth, boys are circumcised by a *Mohel,* a person trained specifically for the task, in a ceremony called the Brith Milah (Hebrew for "covenant"). At the age of 13, boys undergo Bar Mitzvah, or confirmation as an adult according to the Hebrew law. Often the boy learns Hebrew and recites a portion of the Torah aloud before the congregation, and at a celebratory meal he makes a speech that traditionally includes words of the Torah. In the Reform and

Conservative and many Orthodox traditions, girls at age 12 undergo Bat Mitzvah, a confirmation and coming of age.

The wedding ceremony dates back more than 2,000 years. It requires the consent of both parties and a document signed by two witnesses, called a *Ketuba,* that outlines the religious, social, and financial obligations of both sides. The ceremony begins with the bedecking of the bride when the groom covers her with a veil. They proceed to the *Chuppa,* a four-poled canopy that represents divine protection. The bride circles the bridegroom seven times, recalling the way Solomon dedicated the Temple. In this way the bride sanctifies her husband-to-be and dedicates him to her. The officiant, who may be a rabbi or a learned layperson, recites the ancient blessing of sanctification over the first cup of wine, and the bride and groom drink from the cup. The groom places a ring on the bride's finger, saying in Hebrew, "Be sanctified to me with this ring in accordance with the law of Moses and Israel." The Ketuba is read, followed by seven blessings relating to marriage, and the second cup is drunk. The ceremony ends with the groom breaking a glass, symbolizing the destruction of the Temple as well as the Talmudic tradition to remember that even on the happiest occasion, there is always some sadness.

Following practices established with the Talmud, men in most branches of Judaism cover their head out of humility and reverence for God, especially during religious services. Many wear a skullcap—called a yarmulke in Yiddish, a *kipa* in Hebrew—which can differ in size and material according to tradition. Most American synagogues are oriented so that to face the center of the sanctuary is also to face toward Jerusalem. Each synagogue has its own Torah, often encased in a recessed wall cabinet and covered by a curtain, replicating the Holy of Holies in the Temple of Jerusalem. At times in the service, the doors are opened and the Torah revealed. In many communities, that is occasion for the congregation to stand.

Unlike other religions, Judaism does not employ visual imagery to convey a sense of an afterworld. Jews find comfort in the belief that their faithful behavior will be rewarded after death. The dead are prepared for burial with simplicity and swiftness, for ancient Jewish law considered corpses unclean. At the time of the burial—and throughout the year for parents, or for 30 days for other relatives—a descendant, spouse, or sibling reads the Kaddish, a prayer that glorifies God and reminds mourners of God amid their sorrow. After the burial a seven-day period of mourning, or shivah, begins, during which family and friends respectfully gather for prayer in the home of the deceased.

Practices such as these, which connect Jews of today with their forebears of more than 3,000 years ago, must have been one of the few sources of consolation during the Holocaust of the 20th century, when Jews suffered the worst genocide ever perpetrated in human history. In four years' time, between 1941 and 1945, as many as six million Jews were executed in concentration camps operated under the Nazi regime of Adolf Hitler. Five death camps in Poland, most notoriously the one in Auschwitz-Birkenau, near the Czech border, were designed to exterminate Jews and others determined by the Nazi leadership as weakening the gene pool of their Aryan nation. Jews throughout Nazi-controlled Europe once again were required to wear identifying badges with the six-pointed Star of David.

The nation of Israel emerged from these horrors, although it had been taking shape throughout the 20th century. The end of World War I saw the fall of the Ottoman Empire, which had ruled Palestine since the 16th century. The League of Nations divided the land into mandates controlled by France and Britain. In its 1917 Balfour Declaration, Britain indicated that it viewed "with favor the establishment in Palestine of a national home for the Jewish people," but believed it important to ensure "that nothing shall be done which may prejudice the civil and religious rights of existing non-Jewish communities in Palestine." By 1946 Syria, Lebanon, Jordan, Iraq, Egypt, and Saudi Arabia were all sovereign states. Only Palestine remained a mandate, technically ruled by Britain but possessed by those who lived there: Arabs, many of them Palestinians with ancient roots there, but also newcomers; and Jews, many of them recent arrivals with Zionist zeal. At that time, roughly a million Arabs, half a million Jews, and about 150,000 members of other religions lived in Palestine. Several efforts at dividing the land into an Arab and a Zionist state failed.

In February 1947, Britain surrendered the Palestinian question to the new United Nations. In November, the United Nations announced a partition plan that divided the land into Arab and Jewish territories. The Arab state proposed was much larger and contained the city of Jerusalem in its entirety, but Palestinians, backed by other Arab nations, rejected the partition plan. Fighting broke out almost immediately. In May 1948, as the British mandate expired, the Nation of Israel declared itself in language that indicated how much its religious history formed a part of its identity: "Eretz-Israel [the Land of Israel] was the birthplace of the Jewish people. Here their spiritual, religious and political identity was shaped. Here they first attained to statehood, created cultural values of national and universal significance and gave to the world the eternal Book of Books."

An armistice in 1949 resulted in newly drawn boundary lines. The city of Jerusalem straddled the line between Israel and Jordanian-controlled Arab land. In one way, the Jewish people had regained their promised land and ended their wandering. In another way, their struggles had just begun. Military and diplomatic conflicts continued over certain key territories—especially the strip of land around the city of Gaza, the West Bank of the Jordan River, and the Golan Heights northeast of the Sea of Galilee. Jerusalem maintained an uneasy balance as the holy city claimed by three religions, Judaism, Christianity, and Islam. Meanwhile, Jews around the world continue to immigrate to the country in which their religion gives them immediate citizenship. More than one million Jews moved to Israel between 1990 and 2001. An estimated 13 million Jewish people live in the world today, with about 5.8 million in the United States and 4.8 million in Israel.

When Israel declared itself the rightful nation of the Jews, another country nearby harbored an unrecognized people who claimed direct links to Moses and David. Jews in Ethiopia may have numbered 100,000 when a Scottish explorer in search of the source of the Nile met them in 1769 and named them Beta Israel. Some claim that these are a lost tribe of Israel, descendants of Dan, whereas others believe that they are the descendants of Solomon and the Queen of Sheba. Caught in civil and tribal wars in recent decades, tens of thousands of Ethiopian Jews have immigrated to Israel.

The ties that bind all Jews together arise from their shared history and the laws commanded to them by their god, Yahweh. As human beings have tried to make sense of those laws, turning them into ceremony, ethical rules, and political action, disagreements and divisions have occurred. Such conflict was epitomized in 1995 when an extremist law student, an Israeli and a Jew, assassinated Israeli Prime Minister Yitzhak Rabin, ostensibly for his willingness to compromise with Palestinians. This land sits precariously at the crossroads of three continents and three religions. It continues to be a land of promise and a land of conflict, of exile and belonging.

Throughout the world, Jewish life today faces two contradictory forces. On the one hand, assimilation and marriage out is reducing the overall Jewish population in most Western communities. On the other hand, there has been a significant return to traditional religious practice in all denominations of Judaism. And, as with all religions, there has been a revival of fundamentalism. It is probably true to say that there are more schools and higher institutions of study of traditional Judaism now than at any time since the destruction of the Second Temple. In addition, the Yiddish language, once considered all but dead, is making a surprising comeback, particularly in the Orthodox world. For all the problems that beset them, including a resurgence of anti-Semitism, most Jews look to the future with optimism. □

OPPOSITE: Jewish settlers in the embattled territory of Gaza rejoice during Israel's Independence Day celebration.

FOLLOWING PAGES: A lone mourner prays among Jewish tombs stacked on a hillside of the Mount of Olives in Jerusalem.

IN THE
FOOTSTEPS
OF ABRAHAM

TRADITIONAL CLAY homes in Haran, Turkey, built in a conical style that has remained unchanged for 5,000 years, now sport electrical power and satellite dishes. Except for the modern conveniences, these homes *(opposite)* look much the same as they would have in the days of Abraham, the patriarch of three religions, whose deeds have offered lessons for readers of the Bible, Torah, and Qur'an. According to Scriptures, it was while Abraham was living in Haran that God told him to seek out a new land for his people. From Haran, Abraham's divinely inspired journeys took him to the Canaan Valley and the civilizations bordering the Dead Sea *(following pages),* and further south to Mecca, in what is now Saudi Arabia, before his return to the lands of modern-day Israel.

AN ANGEL stays the hand of Abraham *(opposite)* before he can deliver the fatal blow to his son in Rembrandt's "Sacrifice of Isaac." The 17th-century Dutch masterpiece depicts what for many is the most powerful lesson from

the life of Abraham: His faith in God's word was such that he was willing to sacrifice his own son. Islamic tradition holds that Abraham was commanded to take the life of Ishmael, his firstborn son by his wife's handmaid, Hagar. In Jerusalem's Islamic mosque, the Dome of the Rock, sunlight strikes the sacred stone of Mount Moriah *(above),* said to be a remnant from the spot where Abraham showed the world the meaning of true faith.

CHRISTIANITY

For God so loved the world that he gave his only Son,

so that everyone who believes in him may not perish but

may have eternal life.

–JOHN 3:16

CHRISTIANITY

†

IN PALESTINE in the year now designated 1 A.D., the region of Galilee was known for its agricultural abundance. According to first-century historian Flavius Josephus, "their soil is universally rich and fruitful, and full of the plantations of trees of all sorts, insomuch that it invites the most slothful to take pains in its cultivation by its fruitfulness; accordingly, it is all cultivated by its inhabitants, and no part of it lies idle."

OPPOSITE: *On the Via Dolorosa in Jerusalem, where Jesus shouldered his cross, women carry goods as in biblical times.*
PRECEDING PAGES: *Farming, fishing, and faith flourished here, on the fertile banks of the Sea of Galilee.*

A TYPICAL family lived in a mud-brick house, roofed with reed mats. Along with a field of grain, an olive grove, and a vineyard, the family tended a garden of onions and garlic, cucumbers and chickpeas. A few sheep and goats provided milk, cheese, and wool. Meat was a rare dish, reserved for feasts and sacrifices, but bread and wine graced many a meal. In most years, farmers harvested enough wheat to carry some to city markets.

The small town of Nazareth, built on a gentle rise with a view of Mount Tabor five miles to the east, lay on the road between Jerusalem and the port of Acco. The town's one spring limited its growth. Its first-century population is estimated at about 500.

In these humble surroundings, according to Christian Scripture, a child was born. Named Jesus, the Hellenized form of the Hebrew Yeshua or Joshua, the boy was raised in the faith of Judaism. He grew up to become a carpenter, then a prophet and a miracle worker, and the inspiration for a world religion. His father, Joseph, came from Bethlehem. "In those days a decree went out from Emperor Augustus that all the world should be registered," relates the Gospel of Luke. "All went to their own towns to be registered," including Joseph and his pregnant wife, Mary, who gave birth in Bethlehem.

The emperor's decree came as the result of changing administrative relations between Rome and its provinces of Judaea and Samaria. Shortly after King Herod's death, Caesar Augustus established direct Roman control. He deputized Publius Sulpicius Quirinius as procurator of Judaea and commanded him to assess the population and their economic value.

The people of Judaea could barely tolerate the new regime. They were looking for a different kind of leader, one of their own, who remembered the covenant between God and their people and who would respect the ancient Jewish ways. They were seeking a Messiah—a holy leader, literally "an anointed one"—who would reshape Judaea into the Promised Land of the people of Yahweh. Many changes had happened in their homeland over the last two or three generations. The Romans had captured Jerusalem. Herod had built roads, waterworks, temples, and fortresses all over Judaea. He had restored the Temple in Jerusalem, although he had built even more temples to the pagan gods worshiped by Romans. It was a time of extravagant development, but also—as many pious Jews were warning—a time of materialism, idolatry, and greed.

Meanwhile, the Jewish faithful had divided into factions nearly as rancorous as political parties. Into this fulcrum of religious debate and political power shifts, Jesus was born. His parents, traveling to Bethlehem, discovered that "there was no place for them in the inn," according to Luke. They spent the night in a stable where Mary gave birth to a son "and laid him in a manger." Tradition locates this manger in a stone-walled grotto: It was common for a first-century householder to use nearby caves as storehouses and stables. Skeptics have questioned Bethlehem as the site of Jesus' birth, suggesting Nazareth instead, but Christians from the second century on have revered this town five miles south of Jerusalem as the place of his nativity. A Bethlehem birthplace conferred a mighty legacy: Rachel, favorite wife of Isaac's son Jacob, is buried two miles away; David, first king of Israel and ancestor to Jesus, was born here, too.

Living in Caesarea, the Palestinian port city, the third-century scholar Origen knew of the designated grotto. It was already a tourist attraction. "There is shown at Bethlehem the cave where He was born, and the manger in the cave where He was wrapped in swaddling-clothes," wrote Origen. "This sight is greatly talked of in surrounding places, even among the enemies of the faith." The grotto was excavated and transformed into a church sanctuary during the fourth-century reign of Roman Emperor Constantine. When Samaritans living in Bethlehem revolted

OPPOSITE: *In a landscape illumined by a star, shepherds tend their flocks near Bethlehem.*
FOLLOWING PAGES: *A fresco of the birth of Jesus adorns a ceiling of a cave church in today's Turkey.*

against Roman rule in 529, that building was destroyed. Another was soon built at the same site, fitted with a hole under the altar through which the grotto can be glimpsed. Architects of the 12th century laid down white marble floors and encircled the spyhole with a 14-pointed silver star. Today 15 lamps burn continuously around the altar, tended by the three branches of the Christian religion that share responsibility for the Church of the Nativity: Greek Orthodox, Armenian Apostolic Orthodox, and Roman Catholic. As of 1995, Bethlehem was placed under the Palestinian Authority, locating it—and its Jewish and Christian shrines —in the crosshairs of 21st-century political conflict.

The Gospels provide few details of Jesus' childhood. Then, coming of age, Jesus made the Passover pilgrimage to Jerusalem with his family, where he began to reveal his extraordinary spiritual understanding:

"When he was twelve years old, they went up as usual for the festival. When the festival was ended and they started to return, the boy Jesus stayed behind in Jerusalem, but his parents did not know it. Assuming that he was in the group of travelers, they went a day's journey. Then they started to look for him among their relatives and friends. When they did not find him, they returned to Jerusalem to search for him. After three days they found him in the temple, sitting among the teachers, listening to them and asking them questions. And all who heard him were amazed at his understanding and his answers."

As an adult, Jesus participated in a ritual immersion ceremony in the Jordan River, some say at the Hiljeh Ford, four miles north of the Dead Sea. The man who performed the rite, called John the Baptist, appears to have belonged to one of the evangelical sects of the era. He had spent some time in "the wilderness"—the dry and barren land of soft, sand-colored rock weathered into cliffs and gorges east of Jerusalem. He wore camel's hair and a leather belt; he ate locusts and honey, reverting to nomadic independence.

John's asceticism represents a theme that would carry through Jesus' entire ministry: the reinterpretation of the physical as a spiritual world. "I baptize you with water," John said, but, he predicted, someone else soon "will baptize you with the Holy Spirit." After his baptism, Jesus spent 40 days in the Judaean wilderness where, according to Scripture, he was tempted by the devil—the embodiment of evil, bent on persuading humans to sway from the path of purity and goodness. Facing physical hunger, Jesus found spiritual sustenance. "It is written, 'One does not live by bread alone, but by every word that comes from the mouth of God,' " he said, summoning the willpower to fast for those 40 days. Christians long ago located an inhospitable mountain of striated rock northeast of Jerusalem as the site of his six-week temptation. Its local name, Jebel Quruntal, comes from the Latin *quaranta,* forty. Sixth-century Christians built a monastery in these rocky heights.

Jesus' lifetime ministry lasted only about three years, and his travels covered distances that a person could easily traverse by foot or donkey—no more than a hundred miles north to south through the towns and countryside of Judaea. Events of those three years are told in the books called Matthew, Mark, Luke, and John. These four books begin the New Testament, the collection of Scripture which, when combined with the Tanakh, or Hebrew Bible—called the Old Testament by Christians—composes the Christian Bible.

THE GOSPELS

EACH OF the four books, termed the Gospels, has a history of its own. The original language was Greek, the cosmopolitan and erudite language of the day. The Book of Mark is considered the oldest. Apparently it was written by someone living in Rome, who may have witnessed the city ablaze in 64 A.D. during Nero's reign. The origin of the

OPPOSITE: In a Renaissance painting, John baptizes Jesus with water from the Jordan River.

FOLLOWING PAGES: In a rockbound Judaean wilderness such as this one, Jesus fasted and prayed for 40 days.

Book of Matthew is harder to pinpoint. The book probably represents stories collected during the last decades of the first century from those who witnessed events in Jesus' life 50 or 60 years before, but it may consist of the expanded notes by the tax collector Matthew, one of Jesus' 12 closest followers, called the disciples.

The Book of Luke is most likely by a man of that name: a physician converted to Christianity in his lifetime, writing late in the first century, perhaps in the city of Antioch—today Antakya, Turkey, then the Roman administrative post in Syria. Unlike the others, this Gospel is specifically dedicated to "you, most excellent Theophilus," very likely a high-ranking Roman. The same Luke wrote the Acts of the Apostles, the fifth book in the New Testament, which tells of the early efforts by representatives of Jesus—the word apostle means "one sent forth"—who carried on the religion after Jesus' death and miraculous Resurrection. Since certain episodes of the life of Jesus reappear in Matthew, Mark, and Luke, they are called the Synoptic Gospels. The fourth Gospel, John, varies in detail and style. It was probably written last, but before 200 A.D.

In his time, Jesus performed many miracles: He restored the sight of a blind man in Bethsaida; he brought a young man back to life in the town of Nain; he spirited demons out of two men and cast them into the bodies of swine in Gadara; and he healed the servant of a Roman centurion in Capernaum. Many miracles took place on or near the Sea of Galilee. Jesus walked on the surface of the water. By stepping into a boat, Jesus calmed a storm. He preached from a boat to a crowd on shore, then advised the helmsman to cast out his net. "Master, we have worked all night long but have caught nothing," Simon replied, but he cast out his net and caught so many fish, they strained the net. Such miracles evoked awe, fear, and humility in those nearby. "Do not be afraid," Jesus said to his fishermen friends. "From now on you will be catching people."

Christian pilgrims from early times went looking for the sites of such miracles, sometimes with little to go on. Today's map of the Christian Holy Land is filled with shrines, and it can be difficult to separate myth from history. Some features are certain, though. Settlements dotted the 33-mile-long coast of the Sea of Galilee, a freshwater lake 685 feet below sea level. To the east, the land rose sharply from the water's edge, building into rocky cliffs. To the northwest, it sloped gently into the Plain of Gennaseret, forming natural harbors. Of the towns clustered along the shore, Tiberias and Bethsaida were the largest. Very likely it was these shores where John the Baptist was imprisoned and beheaded at the whim of Salome. The Gospels identify Bethsaida as the birthplace of three disciples, Peter, Philip, and Andrew. Smaller, but more important to the story of Jesus and his disciples, was Capernaum, on the north coast of Galilee. The ruins of an elaborate Hellenic synagogue still stand in the town, probably at the site of a more ancient synagogue, perhaps the one in which Jesus commanded an "unclean spirit" out of a madman. After that, according to Mark, "his fame began to spread throughout the surrounding region of Galilee."

As that fame spread, more and more people flocked to hear Jesus' parables, simple stories of daily life that displayed the relationship God wanted with human beings. Jesus' message often overturned common sense. In his parable of the prodigal son, a young man finally returns home after squandering everything and earns greater praise than his brother, who had done all as he should. "He was lost and has been found," Jesus explained. In another parable, a man attacked by robbers is ignored by a priest and a Levite, leaders in his own religion, but tended back to health by a Samaritan, a foreigner whom most Jews would shun. "Which one was the real neighbor?" asked Jesus. "The one who showed him mercy.... Go and do likewise."

In his own behavior, Jesus broke the social rules, suggesting there were higher rules to follow. The prevailing Jewish culture segregated the sexes in religious practice; Jesus welcomed women. The Jewish Bible called victims of leprosy unclean; Jesus tended lepers in their homes. Watching the rich make large gifts at the Temple, he congratulated the widow who could only donate a *lepton*—

a copper coin, smallest denomination in circulation. Tax collectors and prostitutes, the poor and disabled: All these were just as likely to please God as those who were offering sacrifices and following the protocol prescribed by the Temple priests. God, Jesus assured his followers, cared less about formalities and more about feeling. God as portrayed in the Gospels was immediate and personal, loving and forgiving. God was a shepherd and believers were his sheep, apt to go astray but welcomed back into the fold; God was a vineyardist and believers were grapevines that needed pruning to bear sweet fruit. To the common man, these ideas inspired hope. To the authorities, they spelled trouble.

The dramatic events of the last week of Jesus' life have been told countless times. As Passover approached, he and his 12 disciples traveled to Jerusalem to observe the holiday at the Temple. They spent their nights near the Mount of Olives. They rested at Gethsemane, a walled garden, or perhaps an olive grove, from which they could look west across the Kidron Valley to the city. As they celebrated the

Passover seder meal, Jesus broke unleavened bread and shared it, saying, "This is my body." He offered glasses of wine, saying, "This is my blood of the covenant, which is poured out for many."

Those words, and the implicit offer from Jesus to die for the sake of his followers, have been repeated in churches through the ages. In the ceremony of Communion—also called the Eucharist, from the Greek for "thanksgiving"—worshipers share bread and wine, reenacting the sacrifice of Christ, his death, and Resurrection. It is the holiest and most universal of all Christian sacraments, celebrated in some traditions daily, in others only on certain Sundays during the year. Several interests merged in the arrest and execution of Jesus. He had threatened the power of the priests by questioning their rules and principles. He had openly criticized the Pharisees, the established Jewish elders. He had aroused Roman suspicion by attracting crowds. Civic administrators could not tolerate the possibility of a revolt. As Jesus prayed in the grove of Gethsemane, he was fully aware,

ABOVE: *Jesus entered Jerusalem in triumph, but five days later, he faced a crowd crying for his death.*

according to the Scripture, of what was to come. Suddenly he was surrounded by "a crowd with swords and clubs, from the chief priests, the scribes, and the elders," who carried him to trial before the council of priests in the Temple.

In the early morning, Jesus was crucified outside the city walls of Jerusalem.

The Gospel of John describes how the body was prepared, wrapped in linen with myrrh and aloes. Jesus was buried in a cavelike tomb, its entry sealed with a stone.

Three days later, the Gospels tell us, the boulder was moved and the tomb was empty, save for the linen the body was wrapped in. As the men and women who cared for him wondered what might have happened, "Jesus came and stood among them, and he said, 'Peace be with you.'" It was the first of many appearances after Jesus' Crucifixion—appearances that his followers took as proof that he had been resurrected, his body raised into an eternal spiritual afterlife in heaven with God. These appearances confirmed for believers that Jesus was the Son of God, a divine being who temporarily took on a human body, pain, and mortality. His lessons and example conveyed an ideal of human behavior up to the very end, as he compassionately suffered betrayal and death, saying, "Father, forgive them; for they do not know what they are doing."

He was the promised Messiah—the Christ, in Greek— a leader among Jews who now took his place with Abraham, Moses, and David.

The story of Jesus' Crucifixion and Resurrection defines Christianity. All Christian denominations believe that Christ died for humankind, in an elevated version of sacrifice—according to God's will—to suffer human pain and death to reach a greater reward. In his lifetime, Jesus' beliefs and behavior provided a model of humanity free of sin. No mortal could compare, but all could emulate his strength in the face of humiliation, betrayal, and death. In this way, Christians believe that Jesus offered redemption: His death paid for the sins of all. By following Jesus' example, Christians share his passion—his attitude of submission—his deep faith in the face of suffering, and his promise of Resurrection.

THE WORD SPREADS

AT THE time of Jesus' death, roughly 30 A.D., a handful of men and women in Judaea, probably no more than a hundred, were followers of Jesus. They believed he was born of a virgin mother and conceived by the Holy Spirit, an emanation from God. At his birth, shepherds heard angels announce the birth of "a Savior, who is the Messiah, the Lord." Three kings traveled from afar—probably Arabia—and brought gifts of incense and gold to the newborn, whom they regarded as a king more glorious than themselves. Witnesses to Jesus began to spread the word among their fellow Jews that the promised Messiah had come to earth and that thanks to him, access to heaven was closer at hand. Soon these early believers traveled to lands outside Judaea, carrying their message with them. By the time the Romans destroyed Jerusalem's Temple in 70 A.D., a man named Saul had traveled thousands of miles throughout the eastern Mediterranean, bearing news of the new religion to which he had just converted.

Saul grew up in Taurus, Cilicia, on the southeastern coast of today's Turkey. He appears to have been sent by his family to study with the Pharisees in Jerusalem. A devout Jew who saw the upstart Christians as a threat to his religion, he was, as he wrote, "circumcised on the eighth day, a member of the people of Israel, of the tribe of Benjamin, a Hebrew born of Hebrews; as to the law, a Pharisee; as to zeal, a persecutor of the church; as to righteousness under the law, blameless." Working on behalf of the Pharisees, he set out for Damascus, Syria. Saul swept the countryside for Christians, rounding them up and bringing them to Jerusalem for punishment, perhaps death.

Then as he was going along and approaching Damascus, suddenly a light from heaven flashed around him. He fell to the ground and heard a voice saying to him, "Saul, Saul, why do you persecute me?" He asked, "Who are you, Lord?" The reply came, "I am Jesus, whom you are persecuting. But get up and enter the city, and you will be told what you are to do."

The episode left Saul blind. He found his way to Damascus, where a man named Ananias laid hands on him, restored his sight, and baptized him a Christian. From then on, Saul—soon called by his Roman name, Paul— dedicated his life to spreading the religion of Jesus.

Between about 45 and 65 A.D., Paul made three or four missionary journeys, virtually a round-trip tour of the Greco-Roman world. His starting point was the city of Antioch, the third largest city in the empire after Rome and Alexandria. "So it was that for an entire year they met," according to the Book of Acts, and "it was in Antioch that the disciples were first called 'Christians.' " Paul also welcomed gentiles, or non-Jews, into the religion. He was also willing to disregard Jewish laws such as the requirement for circumcision and dietary restrictions. These disagreements forced the first-century break between Judaism and Christianity.

On his first journey, Paul sailed to the island of Cyprus. In Paphos he converted the Roman proconsul, Sergius, making Cyprus the first province in the Roman Empire to be ruled by a Christian. In Lystra, near today's Konya, Turkey, Paul healed a man crippled from birth. "The gods have come down to us in human form!" cried witnesses. They believed his traveling companion, Barnabas, to be the Greek god Zeus, and Paul, Hermes, messenger of the gods. Even so, the two men were stoned and left for dead when outraged Jews swayed the crowds. Despite such troubles, they won converts in Asia Minor.

On Paul's second journey, he traveled through the Taurus Mountains to the port of Troas. After a vision in which he received a call to come to Macedonia, Paul sailed via the islands of Samothrace and Thasos into Neapolis. He walked the Egnatian Way—a Roman road that stretched across Greece to the Adriatic—to cities including Philippi and Thessalonica, meeting with opposition from both Roman officials and Jews. In Athens Paul walked past ruins that still draw visitors today: the Agora, or marketplace, and the Acropolis, topped by the Parthenon. According to the Book of Acts, he felt "deeply distressed to see that the city was full of idols." He stood in the Areopagus, Mars's Hill, an open-air courtroom, and warned the Athenians, "We ought not to think that the deity is like gold, or silver, or stone, an image formed by the art and imagination of mortals." Finally Paul returned to Antioch. He had traveled 2,800 miles, twice as far as on his first journey, and had been en route for about three years.

On his third missionary journey, Paul revisited many of the towns where he had helped plant the seeds of

OPPOSITE: Daisies grace the Garden of Gethsemane, where an angry mob seized Jesus.

FOLLOWING PAGES: A pilgrim prays at the Praetorium, where Jesus may have been jailed before the Crucifixion.

Christianity. He spent much time in Ephesus, a city at the mouth of the Cayster River near today's Selcuk, Turkey. The Temple of Artemis at Ephesus, built around 550 B.C., earned a place on a list of seven wonders of the world compiled by a librarian in Alexandria in the second century B.C. By Paul's time the temple had been destroyed and rebuilt again, its persistence signifying how strongly the cult of the goddess prevailed in the city.

Throughout his travels, Paul corresponded with those in the churches he had founded. Those letters now form an important part of the New Testament. The last we know of his life is that he returned to Jerusalem. Once more antagonizing Jewish authorities, Paul was arrested by Roman soldiers and ultimately, at his demand, sent to Rome to plead his case before the emperor. In Rome, Paul lived under guard but could receive visitors freely. He died around 67 A.D. He may have taken yet another journey from Rome to Spain, but even without that additional journey, Paul had traveled nearly 10,000 miles in his lifetime, personally spreading the news of Christianity throughout the eastern Mediterranean and leaving a written legacy that shaped the religion henceforth.

NEW LEADERSHIP

DESPITE JESUS' pastoral origins, early Christianity was an urban phenomenon. By the year 100, more than 40 Christian communities existed in cities around the Mediterranean, including two in North Africa, at Alexandria and Cyrene, and several in Italy. Some had been founded in Judaea by Peter, the disciple Jesus designated as the founder of his church. Like Paul, Peter traveled, hoping to convert Jews and gentiles to Christianity. He also ended his life in Rome, although the dates of his arrival and his death are uncertain. Peter is said to have been martyred for the cause, sentenced to crucifixion by the Romans and, because he felt unworthy to emulate Jesus Christ, nailed to a cross upside

down. As the generations passed, fewer leaders gained authority from direct personal connection to Jesus or his Apostles. Leaders rose from within congregations. Soon a three-tiered system developed, consisting of bishops, presbyters, and deacons. Each church was led by a bishop. A presbyter, or priest, led the services and preached; deacons read lessons and conducted Communion. With affection and filial reverence, followers began calling their bishop *papa* in Latin, *papas* in Greek. By the fourth century, the term referred to the bishop of Rome. (It was also used, and still is today, for the patriarch of the Coptic Church of Egyptian Christians.) Once the position was institutionalized, historians looked back and recognized Peter as the first pope of the Christian church in Rome.

Common beliefs based on personal testimony linked the far-flung Christian churches in the first century. The situation left much room for interpretation. Sects such as the Gnostics, whose religion included elements from Babylonian astrology and Greek philosophy, proposed that their beliefs and practices represented the true path of Christ. Churches agreed on the canon of the Old Testament, or Hebrew Bible, but many books circulated through the Mediterranean world and were regarded by one locale or another as authoritative expressions of the new Christian religion. In the second century a list was compiled in Greek of most of the canonical books that form the New Testament. The 27 books of the New Testament were subsequently listed together by Athanasius, a fourth-century bishop in Alexandria. Soon thereafter, the bishop of Rome assigned a scholar named Jerome to the task of translating both the Old and the New Testament into Latin. That translation, which came to be known as the Vulgate, circulated throughout the Roman Empire from 392 on. In 1592, it was officially adopted as the standard Bible of the Roman Catholic Church.

Some disagreements over practice rose to a level of controversy, such as the date on which to observe Jesus' Crucifixion. Following the Gospel of John, the churches in

OPPOSITE: Spreading Christianity, Paul preached at Ephesus, in today's Turkey, site of the Temple of Artemis.

Asia Minor celebrated the day on the Jewish holiday of Passover, or Pesach. Elsewhere, churches followed the lead of the other three Gospels, which suggested that Jesus was crucified the day after the Passover meal, his Last Supper, and was resurrected two days later. Following the Jewish Passover, the celebration of Christ's death and Resurrection was originally called Pascha. In Rome, church leaders later determined the date more naturalistically, probably following pagan tradition. They assigned Easter—a name derived from Eos, the pagan goddess of the dawn—to the Sunday following the full moon after the spring equinox. When the bishop of Rome decreed that all churches had to follow his practice, those in the East refused. To this day, Eastern Orthodox Easter does not coincide with that of the Roman Catholic and Protestant churches, although that discrepancy also has to do with calendar adjustments made by Pope Gregory XIII in 1582.

ROME EMBRACES CHRISTIANITY

FOR GENERATIONS, Christians suffered sporadic persecution. By the mid-third century, persecution became empire-wide. Depending on the ferocity of the emperor, many Christians were imprisoned, exiled, or killed for their faith. They refused to worship the Roman gods they derided as pagan—Jupiter, Mars, Apollo, Venus—and to glorify Roman rulers as if they were gods themselves. They refused to cremate their dead. In 303, Emperor Diocletian ordered that no Christians were allowed to meet in Rome. Their church buildings were to be destroyed, their Bibles burned. During these times, along roads leading out of Rome, Christians excavated hundreds of miles of catacombs—underground crypts carved in soft tufa stone, inscribed and ornamented with symbols standing for the new religion: the fish, the dove, the shepherd.

Near the end of his reign, Diocletian established a new system of leadership, divided between four rulers called the Tetrarchy, to govern the far-flung empire.

One of the four, Emperor Galerius, issued an edict of tolerance on his deathbed in 311. Emperor Constantine rose to power through military leadership in Britain, Gaul, and Spain. Approaching Rome with a plan to assert his leadership there, he dreamed of the two Greek letters chi and rho, a symbol of Christ. Emboldened by the vision, he marched on Rome in 312 waving banners of the Christian faith. He met with Emperor Licinius near Mediolanum—today's Milan, Italy—and they issued a joint edict granting "to the Christians and others full authority to observe that religion which each preferred; whence any Divinity whatsoever in the seat of the heavens may be propitious and kindly disposed to us and all who are placed under our rule."

In 324, Constantine met Licinius again, this time in battle at Chrysopolis (now Üsküdar, Turkey) and in winning, Constantine became sole emperor of the Roman Empire and an irrepressible agent for consolidating Christianity from Britain to Palestine.

In Rome, despite complaints that Christians built "memorials to human corpses," Constantine erected shrines to Christian martyrs and built Christian houses of worship, called basilicas, from the Greek for "king's hall." Their design echoed Roman public buildings: rectangular hallways leading to an apse, or circular bay, topped with a dome. Often a clerestory above the central hallway brought in more light.

Constantine's building enthusiasm renovated the imperial capital in the East, the ancient Greek city of Byzantium, called by most Constantinopolis, Constantine's city. Twenty thousand people lived in Constantinople—now Istanbul—in its early years. By the sixth century, its population had swelled to half a million. All pagan monuments disappeared, replaced by Christian ones. A jewel-studded cross was mounted conspicuously in the palace to which Constantine relocated the seat of imperial power.

In the spirit of Christianizing the Roman Empire, Constantine endeavored to recover the Palestinian sites important in the life of Jesus. He sent his mother, Helena, and his mother-in-law, Eutropia, to scout out places where

"our Lord's feet had trod." Citizens of Jerusalem led the two women to a site outside the old city walls. Soldiers with them began to dig and unearthed three crosses. To determine which was the Christ's, they brought the body of a man just dead and marveled as he revived when touching one of the crosses. This, Helena declared, was the True Cross. Splinters from the Cross were dispersed as relics throughout the Christian world. At that site, Constantine ordered a church of "rich and royal greatness" sure to "excel the fairest structures of any city of the empire," the earliest version of today's Church of the Holy Sepulchre, completed in 333. Helena also dedicated churches on the Mount of Olives and in Bethlehem, and Eutropia founded a church near Hebron.

Attempting to unite the church intellectually as well, Constantine convened an empire-wide council of Christian leaders in Nicaea—now Iznik, Turkey—in 325. Some 300 bishops attended, coming from as far as Cordoba, Spain;

Antioch, Turkey; Alexandria, Egypt; and Caesarea, Palestine. The assembly decided on an administrative and geographical system, dividing the church into dioceses, each headed by a patriarch, and subdividing the dioceses into provinces, each headed by a bishop. Five dioceses rose to prominence in later years: Rome, Constantinople, Alexandria, Antioch, and Jerusalem.

In closing, the august group agreed on 20 canons of faith and a statement of belief, which stilled some of the debates concerning the Trinity of God, Jesus, and the Holy Spirit. The Nicene Creed, still spoken in many Christian churches, asserts belief in "one God, the Father Almighty, Maker of heaven and earth"; in "one Lord Jesus Christ, the only begotten Son of God," who "shall come again." In 381 another council convened by Constantine added new sentences to the creed that expressed belief in "the Holy Spirit, ...who proceeds from the Father and the Son." New lines

ABOVE: Converted by a dream, Constantine proclaimed Christianity in Rome in 312.

also recognized "one holy catholic and apostolic Church," known by its practice of "one baptism for the remission of sins," and united in the belief that Jesus will return to the earth from heaven and oversee "the resurrection of the dead, and the life of the world to come."

By the end of Constantine's life in 337 A.D., a number of Christian practices had been established that still are followed. Sunday, the first day of the week, was identified as the Lord's Day. On that day Christians gather at their houses of worship for prayer, a reading of Scripture, and the ceremony of the Eucharist, the solemn partaking of bread and wine that recalls Christ's sacrifice, death, and Resurrection. The attitude in prayer was discussed by bishops during Constantine's time, some favoring a kneeling posture with hands folded, and others, a standing position with arms outstretched, mirroring Jesus on the Cross. The focal point of each church was the altar: a central table for elements of the Eucharist and other ritual necessities. Worshipers enter a church with reverence, for it is considered the dwelling place of God. Special gestures of Christian blessing developed. The sign of the cross, traced with the right hand, could be conferred by a priest on a worshiper in blessing or could be traced on one's own upper body in devotion. This practice, in place as early as 200 A.D., was often performed in daily life as a call for God's help. In all but the most nontraditional churches, a cross hangs above the altar. Catholic crosses include a depiction of the crucified body of Jesus, whereas Protestant churches simply display a cross. The Roman Church developed the practice of counting prayers in meditation with appeals to the Virgin Mary and the recitation of the Lord's Prayer, by means of a string of beads, called a rosary. Monks in the Greek Orthodox Church similarly counted genuflections and signs of the cross on a rope with a hundred knots.

The sacred act of baptism with holy water by a minister of the church brought an individual into the fold and conferred the blessings of God and Jesus. Only those who had been baptized could be "saved," or gathered by Jesus into heaven after death. "We indeed descend into the water full of sins and defilement," wrote a second-century Christian, "but come up, bearing fruit in our heart, having the fear [of God] and trust in Jesus in our spirit." Many people believed that baptism should occur as early in life as possible, to ensure salvation in case of an early death. According to Hippolytus, a third-century Roman presbyter, a person should stand nude for baptism. Early churches often included baptisteries, rooms with built-in tubs that held enough water to immerse a person. Prior to baptism, the presiding bishop asked the candidate, "Do you believe in God the Father Almighty?" to which the response was "I believe." From these early baptisms came another statement of faith, the Apostles' Creed.

Christmas was confirmed church-wide as a sacred holiday in the fourth century. No one was sure of the date of Jesus' birth. Western Christians celebrated the day in late December, already a festival time among pagans marking the increase of daylight after the winter solstice. Eastern Christians celebrated 12 days later. Some early Egyptian Christians wanted to observe the day in the spring. In compromise, Christmas was set on December 25 and Epiphany 12 days later, on January 6, celebrating the arrival of three kings to worship the newborn Jesus. Plays to reenact the mysteries of Jesus' birth were performed at Christmastime in Europe in the Middle Ages and represent an important early stage in the history of drama. From them, Christmas carols—songs both serious and joyous—evolved.

Once Easter was fixed according to the moon phase, other observances fell into place and developed over the centuries. The 40 days before Easter Sunday, a period called Lent, originally were a time of preparation for baptism. They have evolved into a period of fasting and repentance, recalling Jesus' 40 days in the wilderness. Lent begins on Ash Wednesday, a date Christians observe with services, when they receive the mark of the cross made with ashes on their forehead, as a sign of humility. In Catholic regions of France, Germany, Italy, the Caribbean, and Latin America, a carnival celebration occurs just before the beginning of Lent, climaxing in Mardi Gras, a day and night of revelry.

CHRISTIANITY

SELECTED SCRIPTURES

JESUS GREW up with Jewish Scriptures and knew the first five books of the Bible, or the Old Testament. Later, his own teachings were recorded by his disciples Matthew, Mark, Luke, and John, and were spread a century later through the teachings of Paul and other followers. These teachings were added to the existing Bible as the New Testament. These additions went through centuries of interpretation. In the 4th century, St. Jerome's Vulgate Bible gave the New Testament the basic shape it has today, one that has been revered in scores of translations.

FROM THE NEW TESTAMENT

JOHN 1:14

The Word was made flesh and dwelt among us and we beheld his glory,
glory as of the only Son from the Father.

MARK 12:29-31

You shall love the Lord your God with all your heart, and with all your soul, and with all your
mind, and with all your strength; this is the first commandment. And the second is,
you shall love your neighbor as yourself.

FROM CHRIST'S SERMON ON THE MOUNT, MATTHEW 5:3-12

Blessed are the poor in spirit, for theirs is the kingdom of heaven.
Blessed are those who mourn, for they shall be comforted.
Blessed are the meek, for they shall inherit the earth.
Blessed are those who hunger and thirst for righteousness, for they shall be satisfied.
Blessed are the merciful, for they shall obtain mercy.
Blessed are the pure in heart, for they shall see God.
Blessed are the peacemakers, for they shall be called sons of God.
Blessed are those who are persecuted for righteousness' sake, for theirs is the kingdom of heaven.
Blessed are you when men revile you and persecute you and utter all kinds of evil against
you falsely on my account.
Rejoice and be glad, for your reward is great in heaven, for so men persecuted the prophets
who were before you.

FROM THE OLD TESTAMENT

ISAIAH 53:4

Surely he has born our griefs and carried our sorrows; yet we did esteem him stricken, smitten of God,
and afflicted. But he was wounded for our transgressions.

The week before Easter, Holy Week, begins with Palm Sunday, a celebration of Jesus' entry with his disciples into Jerusalem. On Maundy Thursday, Communion ceremonies recall the last supper shared by Jesus and his disciples. On Good Friday Christians attend services to remember the Crucifixion. Easter Sunday, which some observe at dawn, is the most triumphant celebration day of the liturgical year, for on that day Jesus was resurrected.

CHRISTIANITY, EAST AND WEST

IN CONSTANTINE'S time one important aspect of Christianity took root: the primacy of Rome and Constantinople as religious and political centers. In time, the two cities would vie as capital of all Christendom, leading to a schism that continues to divide the religion to this day.

In 380 Emperor Theodosius I declared Christianity the empire's sole religion. In less than a century, Christians went from being the objects of persecution to practicing the one legally sanctioned religion in the empire.

Under Justinian, the Byzantine Empire and its capital grew in splendor. In 537 he rebuilt a great church that had been burned to the ground in a riot, dedicating it to Hagia Sophia—Holy Wisdom. Then the largest church in all Christendom, it is still one of the world's architectural masterpieces. From the fifth century on, Byzantine emperors were crowned here—an indication of how tightly religion and political power were interwoven in the empire. The church's great dome rose 183 feet above the floor. Mosaics of colored stone lined the floors. Slabs and detailing of marble, porphyry, and basalt decorated the walls. When a tenth-century Russian prince sent envoys out in all directions to help him decide what religion to follow, they returned with praise of Hagia Sophia, saying, "We did not know whether this was heaven or earth.... We are sure that God dwells there among men, and that this is the best form of worship."

Fierce intellectual battles raged over the question of icons. New churches displayed physical images of Jesus and Mary and the people now called saints: martyrs who had given their lives, Apostles who had spread the religion. Byzantine churches displayed stylized portraits: static, idealized images before which the devout would bow and pray. The icons outraged some church leaders, who insisted that just as no human hands could fashion a picture of God, it was idolatrous to paint Jesus, Mary, or the saints. Others countered that the illiterate could approach God and the saints through images. Ironically, the arguments elevated the importance of icons later in Byzantine Christianity.

In the fifth century Nestorius, patriarch of Constantinople, taught that Jesus Christ had two distinct persons, one human and one divine. Cyril, patriarch of Alexandria, disputed this claim as heresy. The argument led to a split in the church.

Monophysites—those who believed that Christ had one nature—spread their religion from Syria, an early, major center of Christianity, north into Anatolia and Armenia, and farther east. Syria, which had adopted Christianity early on, spread not only the faith but also its language. Fragments of a psalm written in Syriac in the ninth or tenth century were found in Uzbekistan; other Christian traces in Syriac showed up at the border of the Chinese Empire. In 301 Armenia had become the first country to adopt Christianity as its official religion. Christianity also spread south into Latin-speaking North Africa. The Coptic Church of Egypt and the churches of Ethiopia, Eritrea, and parts of Sudan developed independently.

Nestorians—who believed in the dual nature of Christ—had an important center in Nisibis, Persia, today's Nusaybin, Turkey, and moved eastward, establishing churches along the Silk Road. By the middle of the sixth century, Nestorian churches had been founded in India and Ceylon, Mongolia and China. The line of Nestorian churches continues to this day as the Assyrian Church, with congregations in the Middle East, India, and the United States.

In the ninth and tenth centuries, the religion of Constantinople—now called Orthodox, from the Greek for "correct teaching"—continued to spread. Missionaries traveled west from Greece to Serbia, Bulgaria, and Moravia, north and east into Russia. Cyril and Methodius, two brothers devoted to the Christian faith, traveled from Thessalonica north to the Danube River, earning a reputation as the apostles to the Slavs. During their missions they invented an alphabet for the Slavic language, so they could share the Bible with those they met. That alphabet is still used for Russian, Bulgarian, and other Slavic languages. Its name commemorates one of the brothers: Cyrillic.

In these Eastern Christian churches, in Greece, in the Slavic countries, and in the Middle East, the worshiper was surrounded by icons, painted on walls and columns, and mounted on a screen (called an "iconostasis") that stretched between the sanctuary and the altar. In daily life icons were mounted on doorways, placed in a corner of the main room, worn on necklaces, and hung in prison cells and ships' cabins. The icons remain important today. They are not simply pictures to admire, but sacred objects of veneration that bring the person depicted on the icon into the presence of the believer. As icons are carried in procession, people kneel; on entering the church, they kiss them; at home, they light candles before them.

THE WINDS OF CHANGE

BY THE eighth century, the influence of the Byzantine Emperor began to diminish in Western Europe. In addition,

ABOVE: *A priest celebrates the rites of the Eastern Orthodox Church, which split from Rome in 1054.*

the new religion of Islam (see chapter 6) , which had formed in the Middle East during the seventh century, began to spread, and the original Christian lands became subject to alien rule.

The city of Rome had faced waves of invasions by tribes from the north. These interactions had sapped Rome of power but conveyed the Christian religion to Britain, Ireland, France, and Germany. Christian monastic communities formed and became important centers of intellectual advancement and religious leadership, following the example of Anthony of Egypt, who in the third century had established an ascetic way of life in spiritual seclusion. Either solitary or communal, the monastic life required vows of celibacy, poverty, and simplicity in diet and lifestyle. Women founded their own Christian communities, or nunneries, beginning in the fourth century. Often a woman joined in a wedding-like ceremony binding her not to a human husband but to God, Jesus, and the church. On the Greek peninsula of Halkidiki, a 35-mile-long finger of mountainous land stretching into the Aegean Sea, Christians from various traditions built dozens of monasteries. In the year 1050, an estimated 7,000 monks lived amid these

OPPOSITE: *Built as a Christian church, Hagia Sophia — or "holy wisdom" — later became a magnificent mosque.*

ABOVE: *The sleek Bosporus Bridge links Europe and Asia in Istanbul, crossroads of religions and cultures.*

FOLLOWING PAGES: *Reaching toward heaven, Rousanou Monastery crowns towering rocks in Meteora, in northern Greece.*

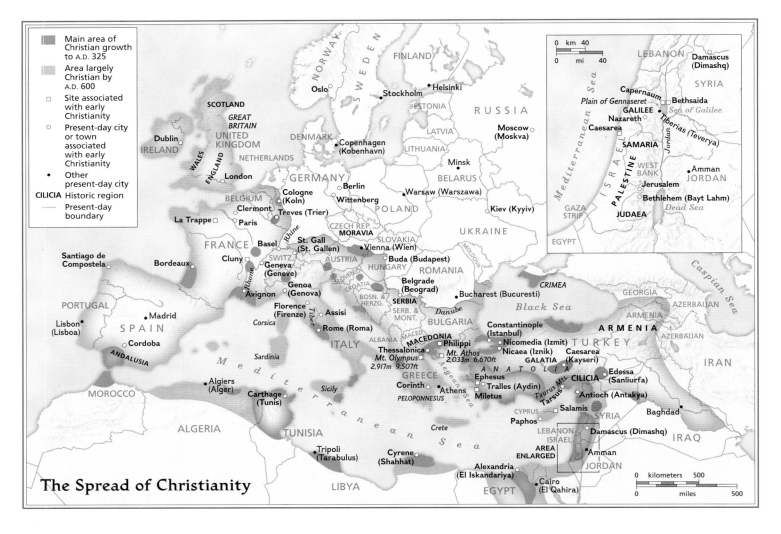

The Spread of Christianity

inaccessible precipices. Twenty monasteries still operate on the peninsula today, including one on Mount Athos, open only to male residents and visitors.

In northern Europe local feudal systems emerged as power structures. Landowners answered to their regional monarchs, and the serfs who worked the land answered to the landowners. In this new order, Christian churches and monasteries still played important roles. In Germany, local lords built private chapels for their families, called *Eigenkirchen*. Villagers from nearby attended services at these chapels, and strands of power held by lord and abbot—the head of an abbey or monastery—intertwined.

In the late 400s, a Roman named Benedict moved out of the city hubbub to a small town with a church dedicated to St. Peter. There, he and fellow Christians lived a humble and holy life together. Occasionally Benedict would retreat even from their company to meditate alone, but he would always return to the society of fellow believers, working hard and doing right. His rules for living, which he described as "the strong and bright armor of obedience," served to establish not only the Benedictine Order but also the general pattern for monasteries and nunneries in Western Europe.

By 900, monasteries were flourishing in Ireland and Britain, France and Italy. In Cluny, France, the Duke of Aquitaine founded a monastery and gave it dominion over his land. There monks prayed, sang, wrote, and held liturgical services. They built a network of dependent monasteries in France, spreading also into Germany, Poland, Italy, Spain, England, and Scotland. Cluny, the first example of a hierarchical monastic organization, was supported by Rome as an example of a just and elegant religious institution. Four distinguished Cluniac monks rose to the position of pope between the 11th and the 14th centuries.

In the early 13th century, St. Francis of Assisi, Italy, preached on the necessity of penance and founded an order for men, the Franciscans, as well as one for women, the Poor Clares, named after St. Clare, the order's first mother superior. Subsisting on the alms of the faithful, these men and women vowed to live by his rules: "in obedience, without property, and in chastity." Francis assigned many of the brothers to missionary travel, establishing a new tradition for orders to come. St. Dominic, born in Spain but influential in France and Italy as well, founded the Dominican order, known as the Friars Preachers. Like the Franciscans, they were a mendicant order. They dedicated themselves to teaching the gospel in everyday language, and ministering to the poor at home and abroad. From these orders arose some of the great thinkers of the theological schools, Roger Bacon from the Franciscans and Albertus Magnus and Thomas Aquinas from the Dominicans.

In 1534 the Society of Jesus was founded by Ignatius of Loyola, who was born in Spain. The Jesuits, as they came to be called, were unique among religious orders in dedicating their work to missions abroad at the behest of the pope. They educated the young and the poor, and ministered to the disenfranchised. Their influence was especially felt in the New World: They traveled with explorers and conquistadores, ministering to the indigenous peoples, and later founded distinguished schools and universities. Numerous other monastic orders for men and women were founded through the early centuries of the second millennium.

Christian monks produced many prized artifacts of medieval culture. From a tiny island monastery off the Northumberland coast of Britain came the Lindisfarne Gospels. These brilliantly illuminated manuscripts on vellum, bound in leather and adorned with gems and gold, were created between 715 and 720. Other significant illuminated manuscripts came out of Western European monasteries, representing a vital stage in the history of books. Liturgical music thrived there, too. Modern-day musical notation dates back to ninth-century manuscripts of Roman chants penned by monks in the Benedictine abbey of St. Gall, in Switzerland.

The bond between religious and secular leadership in Western Europe strengthened in the year 800, when Pope Leo III crowned Charlemagne, king of the Franks, as Holy Roman Emperor. Charlemagne had formed a new realm by combining sections of the old Roman Empire—largely Gaul—with new areas beyond the Rhine, in what is Germany today. The great ruler practiced Christianity and saw in himself a new version of David, king of the Israelites. He came to worship on Christmas Day in Rome's Church of St. Peter, as the story goes, and the pope surprised him by sweeping from the altar and placing on his head the Holy Crown of Lombardy. The crown was said to have been made of a nail from Jesus' cross. According to an eyewitness, "all the faithful Romans, seeing how he loved the holy Roman church and its vicar and how he defended them, cried out with one voice: 'To Charles, most pious Augustus, crowned by God, great and peace-loving emperor, *salus et victoria*—health and victory!' " Then Leo prostrated himself, touching his head to the ground three times to express reverence for the emperor.

Charlemagne's reign presented an ideal of political consolidation and harmony between throne and papacy that could not be maintained. Through the coming centuries, struggles continued among regional leaders for the imperial throne, while favoritism and corruption marred the papal nominating process. In 1046 the German king Henry III became emperor. A solemn Christian, he nixed competition among several papal candidates by nominating his own cousin, Bruno, as the next pope. In keeping with tradition, Bruno took on the name of a great past pope and became Leo IX. In his time, the role of priests in the Roman church solidified. Every morning they conducted Mass—a ceremonial recitation of prayers, Scripture, and creeds called the liturgy, spoken entirely in Latin, and performance of

FOLLOWING PAGES: Seeking God in solitude, a hermit prays in Simonopetra Monastery in northeastern Greece.

the Eucharist. They listened privately to confessions of sin from church members and responded as counselors, outlining acts of penance to be undertaken to receive absolution, or cleansing of those sins. These remain the core responsibilities of priests of the Roman Catholic Church.

By the 12th century, a papal bureaucracy called the college of cardinals had developed in Rome. These "princes of the Church" served the pope as advisors and diplomats. They convened as electors at the death of a pope in the search for the next one. As the Roman church grew in power, they gained in importance. Popes appointed cardinals with an eye to extending the geographic reach of their religion. Prerequisites for cardinalship date to the 16th century: Any man ordained into the priesthood who has shown outstanding piety, prudence, and doctrinal understanding can be named a cardinal. Today, 195 cardinals serve the pope and his Church of Rome.

By the year 1000, two distinct church establishments existed, one loyal to Rome, another to Constantinople. A third region in the Middle East remained independent. In its second thousand years, Christianity would enflame wars of conquest, inspire thrilling explorations, and spread its gospel into parts of the world as yet unknown. The impact of Islam, however, would test the balance of power.

THE CRUSADES

CHRISTIANITY'S SPREAD throughout Western Europe resulted in a complex map of small churches and larger cathedrals. Regions identified their own patron saints. Dionysius, also called Denis, was sent by a third-century pope to be the first bishop of Paris. After enemies of the church executed him on the hill now called Montmartre, he is said to have walked the streets of Paris, carrying his head. The Church of St. Denis stands atop his grave. Ever since, St. Denis has been patron saint of Paris. Patrick, a fifth-century Briton kidnapped into slavery in

Ireland, spent years as a shepherd, a wanderer, and a monk, before the pope sent him back to Ireland, where he persuaded the king to turn away from Druidic paganism and embrace the cross. St. Patrick, now considered the patron saint of Ireland, proposed the three-leafed shamrock as a symbol of the Trinity of Father, Son, and Holy Spirit.

Sacred relics—physical keepsakes from the bodies or lives of holy men and women—were treasured. The cathedral in Cologne, Germany, displays a jewel-encrusted box containing bones from the three kings who worshiped the newborn Jesus. Pope Clementine sent Patrick back to Ireland with relics of St. Peter and St. Paul, to ensure that Ireland's church would have a holy centerpiece. Bits of the crown of thorns placed on Jesus' head during the Crucifixion found their way to Germany, France, Spain, and England, but the full crown of thorns was enshrined in Paris when Louis, King of France, founded the Sainte-Chapelle in the 13th century. The relic was rescued from the violence of the French Revolution and secured for a time in the Bibliothèque Nationale, then deposited in the Cathedral of Notre Dame in 1806.

Throughout medieval Europe, cathedrals soared with vaulted ceilings, spires reaching to heaven, flying buttresses for support, and colorful stained-glass windows. These expressions in stone to the glory of God often took decades, sometimes centuries, to build. Inside and out, carved figures of Apostles and saints watched solemnly over the faithful. In some cathedrals, carvings of beasts and demons reminded Christian attendees of the horrors of hell, to which they were destined after death if they did not live righteously, attend worship services, tithe to the church, and confess their sins regularly. The Florentine poet Dante detailed the geography of the Christian afterworld in his three-part epic poem, *The Divine Comedy,* written between 1306 and 1321. Those who sinned would be banished to one of the nine circles of hell, the realm of Satan, described in the *Inferno*—the more heinous the sin, the deeper the

OPPOSITE: *Russian monks built the five-domed Cathedral of the Transfiguration on Valaam Island.*

descent and more excruciating the eternal torture. Those who had a chance at salvation spent time after death at a cleansing ground, described in the *Purgatorio,* and those whose earthly thoughts and behavior recommended them for eternal salvation ended up, like Dante's beloved Beatrice, with God in heaven, as he described it in the *Paradiso.*

Fom the fourth century on, Christians traveled to special shrines and cathedrals. By making a pilgrimage, they were gaining indulgences—banking up forgiveness for their sins. Especially important was a visit to sacred relics, which could confer blessings, bring good health, and even work miracles. It is said that a sarcophagus containing the body of James—one of Jesus' disciples—miraculously floated from Palestine to Spain. When, in the ninth century, a hermit was wandering in the Finisterre region, "the end of the Earth," in Spain, he saw a light shining in the woods and named the place *campus stellae,* Latin for "field of stars." A bishop determined that here was the secret

grave of St. James, called Santiago in Spanish. Soon pilgrims from France and northern Spain were flocking to Santiago de Compostela. A 12th-century pope promised total forgiveness to all who made the pilgrimage in a year when St. James's special day, July 25, fell on a Sunday. Modern pilgrims still walk one of four major routes to the magnificent cathedral there, with its silver reliquary containing the remains of St. James.

The holiest of all Christian pilgrimages was the one to Palestine. The first pilgrim to record his journey began in Bordeaux, in Roman Gaul, and reached Palestine by land in 333. He described the churches Constantine had built at the Mount of Olives and Bethlehem, but he also saw simple details, charged with religious meaning: the palm tree, for example, the fronds of which were strewn in Jesus' path on his arrival in Jerusalem, now commemorated as Palm Sunday, the Sunday preceding Easter. By the late fourth century, pilgrims followed along sites that symbolized the fateful progress of Jesus' life and Crucifixion. Called the stations of the cross, the procession is replicated in imagery and statuary at churches and monasteries throughout the world.

Following Old and New Testament sites, and sites of miracles and of everyday life in biblical times, Christians carved out their own Holy Land. Even the desert became Christian soil, as monasteries built amid rock and sand attracted those who wanted to live like Moses and Jesus in the wilderness. Justinian founded a monastery later dedicated to St. Catherine, claiming for Christianity a southern Arabian site where he believed God spoke to Moses out of the burning bush. Mar Saba Monastery still stands on a bluff above the barren landscape east of Bethlehem. A thousand or more men lived at Mar Saba in the seventh century; today ten Greek Orthodox monks make their home there.

Christians continued to live in and visit the sites of Palestine even as the land came under Muslim rule. Military conflicts between soldiers of Christianity and Islam occurred as early as 636 at the Battle of Yarmuk, on today's Jordan-Syria border. In 638, Muslims led by Caliph Umar seized Jerusalem from the Persians. By 656, the Middle East

ABOVE: Saints surround the Virgin and Child in a 13th-century rose window of Notre-Dame Cathedral in Paris.
OPPOSITE: On their way to win Jerusalem in the First Crusade, Christians battled Muslims at Antioch.

including Palestine, Egypt, and Mesopotamia had been brought under Muslim rule. By 750, Islamic rulers controlled the north coast of Africa and the southern half of Spain. Through these centuries, Jewish and Christian practices were tolerated in Palestine. The eighth-century caliph Al-Walid called Syria, including Palestine, "the country of the Christians." Their churches were beautiful, their adornments "a temptation," so he intended to build a mosque in Damascus "which would attract [Muslims] away from these churches." The same impulse inspired Caliph Abd al-Malik to build the magnificent Dome of the Rock on the site of Jerusalem's Jewish Temple, near the closest Christian shrine, the Church of the Holy Sepulchre. Conditions in Muslim-controlled Palestine were such that in 785 Christians could build a new church at Um er-Rasas in today's Jordan. Excavating this church in the 1980s, archaeologists discovered floor mosaics that mapped the Holy Land and 24 towns including Jerusalem, labeled the Holy City.

On the other hand, fights erupted when 7,000 Muslim soldiers stepped onto Spanish soil in the spring of 711 and advanced northward. Thus began seven centuries of effort on the part of European Christians to regain Spain. The Muslims—or Moors, as they were known in Spain—were willing to coexist with the Christians, as in Palestine, but they did not tolerate missionary efforts. In 859 a priest in Cordoba was executed for trying to convert Muslims to Christianity. Far more conversions occurred in the other direction: By the 12th century, Christians were in the minority in Andalusia, the southern realm of Spain.

The so-called Crusades started on Italian soil. In 915, Pope John X sent soldiers out into the Roman Campagna—the plains outside Rome—to fend off Muslim invaders. In 1015, ships sailed from Genoa to Sardinia to rout out Muslim pirates. Pope Nicholas II made land deals with noblemen to defend Sicily from other Muslim onslaughts.

Doctrinal issues had long soured relations between Rome and Constantinople, but a common enemy, whether Turkish Muslims in the East or Moors in Spain, brought the two powers closer. Pope Urban II journeyed from Italy to convene a council at Clermont in France. Although he faced issues within the church, and between the church and European rulers, his more important concern was the recent seizure of the city of Jerusalem by the Seljuks—Turkmen, who spoke Persian and ruled from Esfahan, south of today's Tehran. Speaking in 1095 to an audience of European noblemen and knights in their service, Pope Urban declared the First Crusade. According to one account, he exhorted his audience to take up arms "for your brethren who live in the east. ...I, or rather the Lord, beseech you as Christ's heralds to ...persuade all people of whatever rank, foot-soldiers and knights, poor and rich, to carry aid promptly to those Christians and to destroy that vile race from the lands of our friends."

For more than a hundred years European Christians engaged in armed pilgrimage, traveling by land and sea to Constantinople and Palestine, those "lands of our friends" that they considered rightfully Christian. *Dieu li volt!* was the crusaders' cry—God wills it! The First Crusade climaxed in 1099 with the capture of Jerusalem, a gory scene of devastation, with Christians slaughtering Jews and Muslims mercilessly. Crusader states ruled by European nobility were established in the Middle East, with some lands returned to Byzantine rule. The return of the Turks into Edessa, one of the new states, prompted the Second Crusade, relatively unsuccessful incursions around Turkey and into Syria between 1146 and 1148.

During the Third Crusade, waged from 1188 to 1192, two historic leaders, Saladin and Richard I, met in battle again and again along the Palestinian coastline. Saladin—the anglicized version of his name, Salah ad-din Yusuf ibn Ayyub—belonged to a powerful family of northern Syria. He established an alliance with the Byzantine emperor. Richard, the son of King Henry II of England, traveled with King Philip II of France by sea via Crete to Palestine. The

OPPOSITE: Four major pilgrimage routes lead to the Cathedral of Santiago de Compostela in northwestern Spain.

warring forces ultimately reached a compromise over Jerusalem: Muslims would maintain control of the city, but Christians could make peaceable pilgrimages there. During a Fourth Crusade six years later, crusaders captured and destroyed the city of Constantinople. The resulting Latin Empire was founded with an allegiance to the church of Rome and briefly renamed Romania.

Meanwhile, Muslim caliphs still controlled the south of Spain. The Christian countries united by the Crusades solidified efforts to drive out the Moors. In a tight alliance between religious and governmental authorities in Spain, a ruthless hunt for heretics resulted in the Spanish Inquisition, which was begun officially during the reign of Ferdinand V and Isabella in the late 15th century. Anyone suspected of following a faith other than Christianity—and this meant Judaism or Islam—was arrested, questioned, tortured, and, if proved a heretic, enslaved or put to death. Vestiges of this practice, long upheld by Rome, remained until a political revolution shook Spain's monarchy in 1820.

ROME AND REFORM

CONSTANTINE HAD erected a large basilica near the Tiber River on Vatican Hill, on the site revered as the grave of Peter, first bishop of Rome and first pope. As the power and glory of the Roman church grew, buildings popped up around it: residences for the pope and his retinue, guest housing for pilgrims, stores to provide for all their needs. It was in St. Peter's that Constantine was crowned Holy Roman Emperor.

In 846, pirates from among the Saracens—Muslims residing in Sicily and southern Italy—raided Rome and its churches. Pope Leo IV, wanting to protect the Holy See, saw that 40-foot walls were built and 15 watchtowers added to guard St. Peter's.

During the 14th century, St. Peter's was abandoned by the papacy for 68 years: Pope Clement V preferred working from France, and a Palace of the Popes was built in Avignon. In 1377 Pope Gregory XI returned to Rome and, after a brief contest with Avignon, Rome's Vatican again became the home of the pope. Through the next two centuries, a triangle of influence formed: powerful Italian families—the Borgias and the Medicis; determined and visionary popes—Julius II, Sixtus IV; and talented artists—the architects Bramante and Bernini, the painter and sculptor Michelangelo. These alliances turned St. Peter's into a masterpiece of the Italian Renaissance. Michelangelo's work represents the zenith of Christian iconography: the ceiling painting of God creating Adam, in the Sistine Chapel; the towering sculpture of the nude figure of David, the shepherd, reminiscent of a Greek god; and the poignant *Pietà*, the Virgin Mary cradling the body of Christ.

Today the Vatican is an independent sovereignty with international diplomatic significance. When Italy consolidated into a nation in 1870, it seized the property long considered the Papal States, thus bringing to a head questions about the relationship between Italy and the Holy See. In protest, popes refused to travel outside the Vatican until 1929, when Benito Mussolini and Cardinal Gasparri, representing Italy's King Victor Emmanuel III and Pope Pius XI, negotiated the Lateran Treaty and designated 108.7 acres as Vatican City State.

After the Council of Trent, which determined the doctrines of the church, the Western church that remained faithful to the bishop of Rome was called the Roman Catholic Church. The word "Catholic" comes from the Greek, *katholikos,* meaning "universal." Its use to describe the church dates back to the second century, but in those days it expressed the primacy of Christianity over other religions. Not until protesting branches of the Christian faith developed, did "Catholic" specifically mean the church in Rome. Those voices came from several northwest European countries, nearly simultaneously, in the 16th century.

FOLLOWING PAGES: Michelangelo's dome crowns St. Peter's Basilica in Rome, one of the world's largest Christian churches.

✝

GIVE US THIS DAY
A Daily Practice

MOST CHRISTIANS attend a church service once a week, usually on Sunday morning. Entering the house of prayer from the back, they see rows of benches, or pews, on which they sit to face the altar in the front. There a priest or minister, often attended by others, conducts a holy service. Over the altar may hang a crucifix—in many Protestant churches a simple cross, but in other Christian churches an image of the crucified Jesus Christ. In many churches, statuary, murals, paintings, and stained-glass windows depict other holy figures and scenes from the Bible.

The minister conducts the Sunday service, following a liturgy, a ritual pattern that varies according to church or denomination. The tone and content of Sunday services follow an annual cycle that mirrors the progress of the life of Jesus and his ministry, from his birth (Advent, Christmas, and Epiphany) through his Crucifixion (Lent and Easter) and the early forming of the church (Pentecost). Special rituals and celebrations mark the major church holidays, especially Christmas Eve or Christmas—no matter what day of the week—and Easter, which always falls on a Sunday.

Often a Sunday service begins with a call to worship and a hymn sung by a choir or the congregation. Many services include a shared statement of confession and a response from the priest, although confession in the Catholic tradition takes place privately in a booth, the confessor speaking unseen and the priest responding from behind a screen. Confession of sins may bring forgiveness from God, expressed through the priest. All people sin, Christians believe, but only those who repent, confess, and are forgiven will be rewarded in heaven after death. Sometimes a confessor must perform penance, such as saying prayers, to become cleansed of sins.

Recitation of verses from the Old and New Testament provides Christian worshipers with texts to consider for the coming week. The focus of many Christian services is the sermon—a lecture written and delivered by the minister to interpret those texts and apply them to daily life. Other services focus on ceremony: the procession of church officials into the sanctuary, the call to worship, the confession and forgiveness, prayers spoken aloud, and Communion.

Communion is a universal Christian ceremony in which participants reenact the Last Supper shared by Jesus Christ with his disciples just before his Crucifixion. As they eat bread or wafers, church members partake of the body of Christ; drinking wine, they drink the blood of Christ.

THE PROTESTANTS

IN 1517, in Wittenberg, Germany, a young monk and biblical scholar took issue with the Catholic Church. Martin Luther rebelled against oppressive dogma and rejected monasticism and celibacy for priests. He criticized abuses such as the selling of indulgences—taking money in exchange for the forgiveness of sin. Most importantly, he formulated a doctrine of justification by faith:

"Though I lived as a monk without reproach, I felt I was a sinner before God with an extremely disturbed conscience.... I began to understand that the righteousness of God is that by which the righteous live by a gift of God, namely by faith. And this is the meaning: the righteousness of God is revealed by the gospel."

Thus, he emphasized faith based on Scripture, not the authority of the church hierarchy in Rome. These ideas foreshadowed the modern concept of individual freedom, which ultimately influenced German politics and culture. Luther translated the Bible into everyday German and won the public's admiration with unwavering resistance to official church efforts to shame and punish him. His influence spread quickly from Germany west and north into Holland, Denmark, Norway, Sweden and the Baltic states.

Politically structured as a loose confederation of cantons, or republics, since the late 13th century Switzerland was technically Catholic but served Rome primarily as a source for mercenary soldiers. Basel and Geneva were ancient seats of learning, more likely to foster free thinkers rather than dogmatists.

In Basel, Desiderius Erasmus published a Greek New Testament, competition for the Latin version controlled by Rome. Huldreich Zwingli persuaded the town council to ban fees for burials and baptisms, strip churches of icons and images, and change the rule of celibacy for monks and nuns, because none of these Catholic practices were grounded in Scripture. Swiss Anabaptists pointed to baptism as the key ritual of biblical Christianity. Followers took their ideas in different directions, theoretically and geographically, resulting in branches of Christianity ultimately important to North America: the Mennonite, Amish, and Hutterite Churches. In Geneva, John Calvin articulated principles of reform in his great *Institutes of the Christian Religion,* out of which developed the Dutch Calvinist and Scottish Presbyterian churches. French and Flemish Christians influenced by Calvin, respectively called Huguenots and Walloons, fled their homelands during periods of institutionalized intolerance, relocating to Germany, Switzerland, Britain and, later, North America.

England's path to reform was forged by political leaders, although the ground was prepared by scholars such as William Tyndale and Miles Coverdale, who translated Erasmus's Greek Bible into English. When Henry VIII (r. 1509-47) began to believe that his first wife would not bear a son and heir, he petitioned Rome for a divorce—unsuccessfully. His response was to appoint Thomas Cranmer, an advocate for church reform, as archbishop of Canterbury, and Thomas Cromwell, formerly secretary to England's Cardinal Wolsey, as chief minister. Cromwell encouraged widespread destruction of Catholic cathedrals and monasteries, a policy now epitomized in the haunting ruins of Tintern Abbey, the 12th-century monastery in Wales. For a while England tottered between the new Protestant religion and Catholicism, but Anglicanism took firm root through Elizabeth I's administrative and military actions. Cranmer's Book of Common Prayer established Anglican practices and prayers. Elizabeth's successor commissioned a new English translation of Scripture, and the King James Version of the Bible was published in 1611.

Some English Christians felt that the Anglican reform did not go far enough. These Puritans, as they were nicknamed, saw too much "popery" in Anglican practice: the priestly vestments, the use of the cross, the continued observation of special days honoring saints. Soon political

OPPOSITE: Outlawed, Martin Luther took refuge in Wartburg Castle, Eisenach, and translated the New Testament into German.

struggles between Puritans and Anglicans grew as bitter as those between Catholics and Anglicans generations before.

The wave of intellectual and political revolt swept through Europe and the Roman Catholic Church. "From the time of St. Peter there has not been a pontificate so unfortunate as mine," mourned Pope Paul on his deathbed in 1559. An ambassador sent to investigate the problems reported that "in many countries, obedience to the pope has almost ceased, and matters are becoming so critical that, if God does not interfere, they will soon be desperate." An international council of cardinals and bishops convened in Trent, Italy, deliberating for 14 years without great progress, then meeting again in 1561 in an effort to clarify the relationship between the church and European heads of state. In the long run, the Protestant Reformation evoked a Catholic Counter-Reformation, with vast renovations in the church's self-definition and mission. At the vanguard of change stood the new Society of Jesus, which presented a model of social commitment and intellectual rigor that challenged the stereotypes of priestly indulgences and political conniving. Symbolizing the revitalization of the church in Rome, Pope Sixtus V completed St. Peter's Basilica, but also initiated civic-minded works, including aqueducts and a hospital for Rome.

By the middle of the 17th century, the map of Europe's religious affiliations had been redrawn. The Middle East, Turkey, and North Africa had been transformed by Islam. Eastern Orthodoxy still prevailed in Greece, the Crimea, the Balkans, and Russia; Roman Catholicism ruled in Portugal, Spain, France, Italy, Eastern Europe, and in the south of Ireland. Lutheran views were embraced in parts of Germany and Scandinavia. Calvin's Reform Christianity had swept Northern Ireland, Scotland, and Switzerland. The Anglican Church formed the religion of England and Wales.

A NEW WORLD VIEW

SCIENTIFIC ADVANCES shook the foundations of the Roman Catholic Church from the 16th century on. Nicolaus Copernicus of Poland and Galileo Galilei of Italy generated new maps of the universe that jarred the concept of Earth at the center.

Swept up by the ideas of the Counter-Reformation, various religious orders joined expeditions from Portugal and ventured forth to spread their faith in distant lands. In 1541 the Spanish Jesuit Francis Xavier was appointed to go on a mission to India, where missionaries were not welcome. Even so, he established several Christian communities there and continued his efforts on the islands of Indonesia and Japan. Likewise the Italian scholar Matteo Ricci traveled from Portuguese Goa to China in 1582 and founded several Catholic missions. Other explorers sailed west from Portugal and Spain, expecting to find a passage to China, and instead found new continents where unknown races worshiped unknown gods. The first challenge was harder to tackle than the second, for soon church, throne, and investors realized the harvests they could reap in the New World: gold, sugar, and souls.

Considering a world larger than had been imagined—and assuming that it was the job of the Catholic Church to survey it—Pope Alexander VI drew a vertical line of demarcation west of the Azores, declaring all land to the west to be Spain's, all land to the east Portugal's. Adjustments a year later gave Brazil to Portugal. Francis I of France angrily demanded to be shown the clause in Adam's will excluding his nation from claiming new discoveries.

No priests sailed with Christopher Columbus on his first journey west in 1492, but several came on his second in 1493. Columbus himself saw religious conversions as an important outcome of his journeys. "I have to say, Most Serene Princes," he wrote from Cuba to his patrons, Isabella and Ferdinand of Spain, "that if devout religious persons know the Indian language well, all these people would soon become Christians." He prayed that the monarchs would "appoint persons of great diligence to bring to the Church such great numbers of peoples, and that they will convert these peoples." Unfortunately, he and his companions seemed unable to convert without making prisoners, slaves, or enemies of the people they met. Soon Spaniards came as militant conquistadores, conquerors as well as converters of the heathen inhabitants. As with the Crusaders, the conquistadores believed that God willed their mission. The mindset is crystallized in Pedro de Cieza de Leon's *Chronicle of Peru:* "And to think that God should have permitted something so great to remain hidden from the world for so long in history!" In 1511 the pope established three American sees: Santo Domingo and Concepción de la Vega, on the south and north coasts of today's Dominican Republic, and San Juan, on the east coast of the island Spaniards named Porto Rico (now Puerto Rico), rich port.

In 1519, prompted by reports of cities and gold, Hernán Cortés led 600 men on 11 vessels out of Cuba and around the Yucatàn Peninsula. He named his east-coast landing site Veracrúz—true cross. Word of his arrival reached Moctezuma, the Aztec king, in his palace in Tenochtitlan.

Moctezuma sent gifts: disks of gold and silver, one "as large as a cartwheel"; ceremonial finery, including feathered headdresses and jewelry of gold, turquoise, and jade; and food: maize, eggs, guavas, cactus fruit, avocados, manioc, some speckled with sacrificial blood. When Cortés approached the royal city, Moctezuma appeared to greet him arrayed in a crown of gold, turquoise, and shimmering feathers of the quetzal. Cortés gave him a necklace of Venetian glass beads.

Within a fortnight the generosity turned to enmity as Cortés's men, bolstered by native allies, stormed the

Great Pyramid at the center of the city's ritual precinct, beginning a two-year siege that ended with the decimation of the Aztec civilization. When Prince Cuahtemoc, the Aztec commander, surrendered on August 13, 1521, Spain had conquered Mesoamerica's largest civilization. The Spanish occupied Tenochtitlan, renaming it Nueva España, New Spain, and built churches out of *tezontle,* the same red volcanic rock used by the Aztecs for their temples. Visitors to Mexico City, in 2004 the world's 12th largest city, can view remains of the Aztecs' Templo Mayor alongside the Spaniards' Catedral Metropolitana, built in the 1520s.

Soon after the fall of the Aztecs, the scenario repeated itself as Francisco Pizarro led the conquest of the Inca Empire, which stretched for 2,500 miles along western South America. In 1531 a bishop reported that he had personally overseen the destruction of 500 temples and 26,000 idols. Once mainland footholds were established, Spanish missions penetrated North and South America. Following a 15th-century pope's ruling that "Saracens and pagans and any other non-believers" might be enslaved, the Spanish colonists forced natives into servitude. Jesuit priests reacted and founded "reductions"—safe havens for Christian Indians—in the region shared by Paraguay, Argentina, and Brazil. Their mission angered the Spanish, who expelled them in 1767. More than 500 Jesuits abandoned one Paraguay reduction at the time, leaving 100,000 Indians behind.

Religious missions also played a part in French expeditions to North America. More significantly, religious

ABOVE: An Indian artist-reporter depicted Hernán Cortés brandishing sword and cross to conquer the Aztecs.

FOLLOWING PAGES: Testimony to the zeal of Spanish missionaries, a church shines as a beacon of faith in Iruya, Argentina.

differences drove English Puritans to North America in the 17th century. These were believers in search of a new home for their faith. Ostracized in their own homelands, they called America a newfound Eden, a place where religious practice could return to its pure beginnings. "Wee shall see much more of his wisdome power goodnes and truthe then formerly wee have beene acquainted with," wrote John Winthrop, an English Puritan who sailed to Massachusetts in 1630. Winthrop founded the city of Boston on a rise overlooking its natural harbor. "Wee shall finde that the God of Israell is among us," Winthrop believed, and "hee shall make us a prayse and glory, that men shall say of succeeding plantacions: the lord make it like that of New England." Like the Israelites of old who built a temple on Mount Moriah in Jerusalem, he decided, "wee shall be as a Citty upon a Hill, the eies of all people are uppon us."

Other Christian sects moved to North America, seeking the freedom to worship as they pleased. With their anti-materialist and pacifist principles, the Society of Friends, or Quakers, was a troublesome nonconformist sect to those in power in Anglican-dominated Britain. One member, William Penn, collected a debt from King Charles II in the form of New World land. In 1682 he founded the colony called Pennsylvania, establishing its guiding principles in the document called the Great Law, intended to "best preserve true Christian and Civil Liberty." The law protected all who "professeth him or herselfe Obliged in Conscience to Live Peaceably and Justly under the Civill Government" and protected them from being "Compelled to frequent or Maintaine any Religious Worshipp place or Ministry whatever Contrary to his or her mind." A century later, a similar law was passed in Virginia. Drafted by Thomas Jefferson and promoted by James Madison, Virginia's Statute of Religious Freedom was grounded in the Enlightenment faith that "truth is great and will prevail if left to herself." These colonial and state laws form the groundwork for the First Amendment to the U.S. Constitution—first of the ten

called the Bill of Rights—which states that "Congress shall make no law respecting an establishment of religion, or prohibiting the free exercise thereof."

As idealistic as these principles sound, one in five people living in the United States in 1810 did not enjoy the rights articulated in the Constitution. More than a million people of African birth or descent worked as slaves to support the agricultural economy of the new republic. Many more remained in the Caribbean islands, through which most had traveled from Africa. The Atlantic slave trade began in the 15th century. Over the next 300 years, between 10 and 20 million Africans were sold into slavery and transported to the New World.

Slave-trade ports clustered in the south-facing harbors of the Gulf of Guinea, a region whose economic history forged such place names as the Ivory Coast, the Gold Coast, and the Slave Coast. Rich spiritual traditions infused tribal life, involving veneration of ancestors and nature spirits, collectively called *orisha,* and worship of a supreme being. Vestiges of these religions still exist in the practices of voudon in Haiti—the word means "deity" in Fon, the native language of Benin; in Cuba's Santería, which mingles Roman Catholic and African practices; and in the root medicine practices found in African-American communities of New Orleans and the rural South. Even responsive worship—the call from a preacher and spontaneous responses from worshipers—arose from African rituals. In Brazil every New Year's Eve, thousands dress in white and flock to beaches to send little boats filled with flowers into the waves, offerings to the gods of Candomblé, a modern version of the ancient Yoruba religion of Nigeria as influenced by Catholicism and indigenous Indian practices.

Early American Christians believed it was their obligation to convert the African slaves. Much of the early demographic knowledge of slaves, especially in New England, comes from baptism records. Cotton Mather, pastor at Boston's Old North Church, was as well known

OPPOSITE: A Haitian boy is blessed with grain and water in a voudon rite that combines Christian and African traditions.

✝

CHRISTIANITY: AN AFFAIR OF THINGS

—ROBERT LOUIS WILKEN, *University of Virginia*

THE RHYTHM of my life as a Christian is set by two practices, the daily reading of the Psalms and weekly participation in the Church's offering to God, variously called the Eucharist, the Mass, the Divine Liturgy, the Lord's Supper.

On arising each morning the first thing I do (before having a cup of tea and reading the newspaper) is recite Morning Prayer, or "lauds" as it used to be called from the Latin *laudare,* to praise. Morning Prayer begins with Psalm 95, opening with, "O come let us sing to the Lord, let us make a joyful noise to the rock of our salvation, let us come into His presence with thanksgiving."

Whatever my mood on awaking, whatever thoughts may exercise my mind or cares weigh heavy on my heart, my day always begins with songs of praise to God. Contrary to popular conception, prayer is most rewarding when habitual. The repetition each morning of the phrase "let us come into His presence with thanksgiving" puts me in mind that I begin the day in the presence of God and bids me consecrate what I will do to the service of God. For me this period of prayer and meditation is an oasis of solitude and serenity, a time for centering of thoughts and feelings as I lean into the tasks before me.

Morning Prayer, however, is not simply an act of private devotion, an occasion for me to speak to God and listen for God's voice. The words of the psalm are "let <u>us</u> come into His presence." Thus, as I offer my prayers I become part of a vast company all over the world offering praise and thanksgiving.

Sunday is a different experience. On the first day of the week, the day of Christ's Resurrection, Christians come together to celebrate Christ's presence in the Eucharist. Here the setting is communal and social, the mood joyous and festive.

The Eucharist is divided into two parts. The first includes prayer, praise, and instruction. Its high point is the reading of a selection from one of the four Gospels, ancient accounts of the life and teaching of Jesus of Nazareth, followed by a sermon or homily, an exposition of what was read and an exhortation to imitate those noble things.

ABOVE: *In a 13th-century fresco at Studenica Monastery, Serbia, Jesus celebrates the Last Supper with his Disciples.*

Then the focus shifts to a large table or altar covered by a white cloth. Bread and wine are brought forth and the presiding minister speaks a prayer of blessing that includes the words of Jesus, "Take and eat, this is my body" and "Do this in remembrance of me." When the prayer over the offerings of bread and wine is completed, we recite the Lord's Prayer and greet each other with the words, "The peace of the Lord be with you." As the minister prepares the consecrated bread for distribution, the congregation sings: "Lamb of God who takes away the sins of the world, have mercy on us. ...Lamb of God who takes away the sins of the world, grant us peace."

The people begin to file forward to receive Communion. As we wait, there is no chatter, no sound except the shuffling of feet and perhaps the strains of a hymn. There is only a line of people, old and young, hearty and infirm, parents clutching young children, all waiting to receive what is given. The Eucharist concludes in a very personal and individual gesture.

This simple ritual has been observed now for 2,000 years, yet it never loses its power to awe. There is a palpable heightening of intensity in the congregation as the priest begins the prayer over the gifts. For the words that are spoken are not simply words to be understood, they effect something. When a person receives the bread, the priest or lay minister says, "The Body of Christ," and he or she responds, "Amen." When the consecrated wine is received the words are "The blood of Christ," and the response is again "Amen." In the Eucharist we come into intimate relation with Christ through what can be seen and touched.

Christianity is an affair of things. The central Christian belief is that God appeared on earth and lived among us in the person of Jesus of Nazareth. "No one has ever seen God," wrote the author of the Gospel according to John,

"the only Son, who is in the bosom of the Father, he has made him known." In the Christian Creed (from the Latin *credo*, "I believe") confessed by most Christians each Sunday, we not only profess faith in "one God, the Father almighty, maker of all things visible and invisible," but also in "Jesus Christ, the Son of God."

Like the two other religions tracing their beginning to Abraham—Judaism and Islam—Christianity trains the minds and hearts of men and women to worship and serve the one God. Jesus taught: "You shall love the Lord your God with all your heart and with all your soul and with all your might." For Christians, however, the way to God passes through the things of this world. God is known not only through words, such as those of the Bible, through the beauty and order of the world, and through mental or spiritual exercises, but through a human being of flesh and blood. In the language of theology, Christianity is a "sacramental" religion. Centuries ago Augustine of Hippo defined a sacrament as "a visible form of an invisible grace." The form can be bread and wine as in the Eucharist, water as in Baptism, oil as in the anointing of the sick or dying, even a holy site, a place of pilgrimage such as Jerusalem where Christ suffered and died, or the burial place of saints, such as the ancient shrine of Peter in Rome. As pilgrims file past his statue in the Basilica of St. Peter, they reach out, in an act of tactile piety, to rub their fingers across his feet.

We tire of abstractions and crave visible signs. The bread and wine of the Eucharist are palpable evidence that God has come near. If bread and wine make Christ present, we are able to live in fellowship with God. Just as one cannot look at the sun with the naked eye, so, we believe, one cannot know God through the mind alone. First one must kneel and turn one's face to the ground to see the beams reflected on the earth.

among his contemporaries for writing *The Negro Christianized* (1706) as for participating in the Salem witch trials. In the long run, Christians—especially those of the Quaker faith—took the lead in abolition movements in Europe and the United States. "Amazing Grace," one of the best-known Christian hymns of the English language, was written in 1772 by John Newton, an English slave trader reformed by a religious experience into becoming an abolitionist: "I once was lost but now am found, was blind but now I see." In the 20th and 21st centuries, black Christian leaders within Africa continued the crusade against racial prejudice. The Rev. Desmond Tutu, the pioneering Anglican archbishop who led the fight against apartheid in South Africa, received the Nobel Peace Prize in 1984 for his worldwide activities toward, in his words, "a democratic and just society without racial divisions."

By the end of the 18th century, African-American Christians were founding their own churches, only loosely associated with existing denominations. Twenty-seven-year-old Richard Allen studied Methodism—a religion based on inward feelings of personal salvation inspired by Englishman John Wesley and taken up at first by the working classes in the late 18th century. Although a slave, he converted his owner, bought his freedom, and preached throughout Pennsylvania, Delaware, and New Jersey. Barred by church officials from worshiping in Philadelphia's St. George's Church, he started holding religion classes in a blacksmith's shop in 1787. Mother Bethel African Methodist Episcopal Church still stands on the site, proudly claiming its heritage as the first church of its denomination, now two million strong.

In the South, the Baptist tradition presented opportunities for African Americans. Many of these churches formed independently of an overarching hierarchy. Often they were small groups of Christians united in a belief that consensual adult baptism brought salvation. Entire communities would wade fully clothed into a river, undergoing full-body baptism while onlookers sang spirituals such as "Shall We Gather at the River?" and "Are You Washed in the Blood of the Lamb?" A Negro Baptist church had begun meeting in South Carolina at the time of the Declaration of Independence in 1776. Black American Baptists took on missions of their own, founding sister churches in the Bahamas, Jamaica, Nova Scotia, and Sierra Leone in the 1780s.

In 1820, a vision appeared to John Smith, a teenager in Palmyra, New York. On a spring day in a grove of trees, God and Jesus appeared to him and told him that all the creeds of the present-day Christian sects "were an abomination." Soon another heavenly messenger led Smith to buried gold plates, which he translated and called a new and authentic Scripture, the Book of Mormon. Smith's followers considered him a prophet; his church was called the Latter-day Saints. He and his 20,000 followers began moving west and settled in Commerce, Illinois, which he renamed Nauvoo. In 1844, when Smith announced his candidacy for U.S. president, detractors accused him of ambition and criticized his practice of polygamy. The turmoil ended violently, and Smith was murdered by a mob. One practice of the Latter-day Saints was to ordain priests from among the laity, so a devout young man named Brigham Young replaced Smith as leader. Young, too, practiced polygamy: Ultimately, he and his 20 wives had 47 children. He led thousands of Mormons westward, reaching the Utah Territory before the Transcontinental Railroad, and founded Salt Lake City, still the headquarters for the religion. In the century and a half since, the Church of Jesus Christ of Latter-day Saints has grown to a membership of 11 million, and now has temples in every continent of the world.

European imperialism brought Christianity to continents other than North America. Although it is believed that the Apostle Thomas sailed to India and founded churches there, the British East India Company tried as well, but failed, to convert Indians in the 17th and 18th centuries. Missionary societies formed in the late 18th century, with Protestant churches combining charity with conversion efforts. The London Missionary Society, representing four

denominations, sent representatives to Tahiti in 1796. The Foreign Missionary Society of Paris developed missions in Indochina. China missions did not begin in earnest until about 1860, when many Presbyterian and Methodist couples from the United States followed "the call" to spread the faith, along with education, and social and medical services. Through their work, Christianity gained considerable influence in China. The evolution of the Communist Party in the early 20th century put a stop to any further missionary work, and the church declined. In Japan, American Protestant missionaries attracted a following from the samurai upper class, but the church has remained small. Of all the countries in Asia, Korea welcomed Christianity the most warmly, despite a Catholic interpretation of the

ancient practice of ancestor worship as idolatry. Christianity came to Korea mainly through Japan and China until 1884, when Western missionaries also established schools to teach religion and reading. Today one-third of South Korea's population is Christian.

David Livingstone, a medical missionary born in Scotland in 1813, was determined, in his words, "to open up Africa or perish." He braved lion attacks, desert thirst, ill health, and separation from his wife and family. He navigated the Zambezi River and reported for the first time many landmarks of Central Africa—Zambezi's Victoria Falls, Botswana's Lake Ngami, Zambia's Lake Bangweolo. He provided annotated maps to the Royal Geographical Society, but his emphasis on exploration caused a fair

ABOVE: *A gilded statue of the Angel Moroni perches atop Salt Lake City's Mormon Temple.*

amount of skepticism in the Missionary Society. Nevertheless, Livingstone kept returning to Africa, preaching the gospel and healing the sick with medicine, faith, and knowledge. He died in 1873 in his tent in an African village near Lake Tanganyika and is buried in London's Westminster Abbey.

CHRISTIANITY TODAY

WHETHER FOR enlightenment, charity, or conquest, two millennia of missionary efforts succeeded. By 2004, one-third of the world's six billion people followed the Christian faith. While in some countries, such as the United States, the three arms of Christianity—Eastern Orthodoxy, Roman Catholicism, and Protestantism—coexist, they tend to fall on the world map in geographical patterns. The Orthodox church remains dominant in Greece and Eastern Europe, despite efforts by the former Soviet Union to shape a Marxist society beyond religion. Northern Europeans and North Americans by and large practice Reform Christianity. So do the majority in Australia and New Zealand, following the Anglican tradition. In the nations of western and southern Africa, many inhabitants follow the Protestantism brought there by missionaries. Catholicism is the primary religion in Southern Europe, sub-Saharan African countries, Mexico, and Central and South America.

In countries where the poor greatly outnumber the rich and powerful, distinctive traditions have emerged that appeal directly to the disenfranchised. Our Lady of Guadalupe appeared as Mary, mother of Jesus, to a poor Indian in central Mexico in 1521, speaking to him in his native Aztec language and telling him to build a chapel in her honor. Millions throng to the Basilica of Our Lady of Guadalupe in Mexico City each year, especially on her special feast day of December 12. She is considered the patron saint of Mexico, of the Americas, and of unborn children, so she has become a symbol of the Catholic prohibition against contraception and abortion, a divisive issue as the world's population multiplies. Not only in Mexico but throughout Latin America, worship and supplication address incarnations of the Virgin Mary. Images of the Blessed Mother appear in homes, schools, public buildings, and graveyards, her face somber yet compassionate, encircled by a golden halo.

Some Latin American leaders, such as Cuba's Fidel Castro, held the Marxist notion that "religion is the opiate of the masses"—a tool of the rich elite to mollify and enslave the poor and uneducated. Cuba's 1976 constitution forbade any religious opposition to the revolution. It took a 1991 amendment to allow a religious believer membership in Cuba's Communist Party. In 1998, Pope John Paul II made a historic visit to Cuba. Just before his arrival, Castro allowed the people to treat Christmas as a holiday for the first time since his regime took power in 1959. In Cuba, the pope publicly advocated an end to the decades-long U.S. trade embargo on Cuba and repeated the Catholic prohibition against abortion, legal in Cuba since 1965. The famous meeting did not result in compromise, but it did represent a new era of communication.

Pope John Paul II's Cuba visit was one of many missions undertaken in the spirit of the historic Second Vatican Ecumenical Council, convened in 1962 by Pope John XXIII and concluded in 1965 by Pope Paul VI. "I want to throw open the windows of the Church so that we can see out and the people can see in," said John, who had surprised the Roman Catholic world by calling for the council. As with the 20 other ecumenical councils of the past, bishops came from all corners of the world. But their demographics symbolized the changing face of the religion. Of the 2,860 attending, fewer than half came from Europe. Catholicism had become an international religion, a religion of many races and cultures: 489 bishops came from South America, 404 from North America, 374 from Asia, 300 from Africa, 84 from Central America, and 75 from Oceania. For the first

OPPOSITE: In the 12th and 13th centuries, Ethiopia's King Lalibela built churches hewn from rock.

time, women and non-Catholics attended a Vatican Council as observers. All these changes portended the spirit of the decrees coming out of the council, as sweeping a renovation as that of the 16th-century Council of Trent.

One historic outcome of the Second Vatican Council was a growing rapprochement of the Eastern and Roman churches, which had been alienated since the 11th century, and reached out beyond the Catholic and Orthodox folds as well. *Lumen Gentium*, a council constitution, granted that those who "do not profess the faith in its entirety or do not preserve unity of communion," even those who "have not yet received the Gospel," can still receive the gifts of the Holy Spirit. The council clearly stated the Roman Catholic Church's respect for the individual and for religious freedom, "which men demand as necessary to fulfill their duty to worship God."

Such freedom of religion was possible only through "immunity from coercion in civil society," a bold statement representing a churchwide commitment to human rights around the world, with a promise to "cooperate in a brotherly spirit with other Christians, with non-Christians, and with members of international organizations." Now the Mass could be celebrated in everyday language rather than Latin, since "easy access to Sacred Scripture should be provided for all the Christian faithful."

As Vatican II was encouraging immediacy and access, other Christians were joining the charismatic or evangelical movement, experiencing religion in an emotive and ecstatic way in the belief that *charisms*, or gifts from the Holy Spirit, are as available today as they were to the Apostles of Jesus. Some charismatics call themselves Pentecostals, in memory of the day when the Apostles were touched by tongues of fire and founded the Christian church. Evangelical religions grew tremendously in the second half of the 20th century. Evangelical gospels flowed out over American airwaves, as celebrity leaders such as Billy Graham and Jerry Falwell adopted radio, television, and the Internet as the newest ways to harvest souls. Transcending old denominational divisions, evangelical Christianity is the world's fastest-growing religious movement, gaining in numbers primarily through conversion and estimated to be growing 3.5 times faster than the world's population.

The Christian church has developed through two millennia, branching out into dozens of denominations and sects. From Roman Catholic to Eastern Orthodox, Episcopal to evangelical—the Christian religion includes fundamentalists, who believe in the literal message of the Bible; Unitarians, who do not believe in the Trinity but in one supreme God, with Jesus as teacher; and Seventh-Day Adventists, who forecast the imminent return of Jesus and a final judgment day. Christian sects distinguish themselves through many points of disagreement over theology and practice, yet a few core principles allow them to transcend differences and unite in their hopes for future redemption through the sacrifice embodied in Jesus Christ.

The poor, the diseased, the degraded, the outcast, the forgotten—these were the people to whom Jesus ministered, shocking those with wealth and power. As Christianity evolves in an overpopulated world with one in six living in poverty, the mission continues. Christianity has been the religion of the elite, despite its lowly origins. Moving into the 21st century, though, its complexion is changing as the religion gains more adherents in Africa, South and Central America, and the Far East, at the same time that its numbers are dropping in Western Europe. The demographic center of Christianity is now in the Southern Hemisphere. Like the life and parables of its founder, its history is full of paradox, best seen as a dialectic between triumphant conquests and humbling reminders that to suffer and lose all is to secure entry into heaven. ☐

OPPOSITE: Lithuanian pilgrims flock to the Hill of Crosses, symbol of resistance to oppression since the 14th century.
FOLLOWING PAGES: Traditional resting place of Noah's Ark, Mount Ararat looms over Khor Virap monastery in Armenia.

✝

A PILGRIMAGE

RISING IN a perfect cone, Ireland's Holy Mountain, Croagh Patrick *(above)*, towers 2,510 feet over fields and sea near Westport in County Mayo. On the last Sunday in July, "Reek Sunday," tens of thousands of pilgrims wind up the mountain's rocky trail in the footsteps of St. Patrick, who fasted and prayed on the summit. Like pilgrims everywhere, they climb for different reasons— to ask for cures, to give thanks, to pray for victims of the violence that has long troubled Ireland. Said pilgrim Paddy O'Brien: "Last year I had arthritis in my hip, and this year it's gone. I came back to thank Him and do penance."

Bare feet on rough stones for some pilgrims, the faithful struggle up a scree-strewn path toward the summit *(opposite)*. Along the way, many pause to ask the blessing of Ireland's patron saint *(following pages)*.

AT THE windswept, mist-shrouded summit *(below),* a
barefoot woman prays at a newly erected cross "in memory of all who died in Ireland through violence," a toll that
continues in Northern Ireland's religious strife.

After a four- to five-hour-climb, the pilgrims *(opposite)*
parade around a small oratory, reciting "Hail Marys"
and "Our Fathers." They will enter the chapel to confess
their sins, receive communion, and laud St. Patrick in an
Irish-language hymn to "he who overcame the Druids."
Archaeological evidence suggests that, even before
Christianity, the mountain, then known as Crochan Aigh,
"the mount of the eagle," served as a holy site.

ISLAM

In the Name of Allah, the Compassionate, the Merciful,

Praise be to Allah, the Lord of the Worlds.... Only You

do we worship, and only You do we implore for help.

— QUR'AN 1:1-5

ISLAM

☪

THE ARABIAN Peninsula stretches more than a million square miles with not one permanent river flowing through it. It may once have connected the Sahara to its west with the Plateau of Iran to its east, but within human memory it has had its own discrete desert identity. Only its far southwestern corner benefits from monsoon rains. Since ancient times that corner nation, Yemen, was a separate domain, wealthy with fragrant spices and tree resins such as frankincense and myrrh. The Romans called it Arabia Odorifera.

OPPOSITE: *Abstract art festoons the King's Palace in Fez, Morocco. Islamic law forbids depiction of the human form.*
PRECEDING PAGES: *The Ottomans, who spread Islam to Byzantium, built this now crumbling castle in Turkey.*

FROM THERE, trade proceeded by ship from the Gulf of Aqaba, at the northern end of the Red Sea, and also the Gulf of Aden, at its southernmost end, or by caravan up the western reaches—called the Hijaz, or barrier—where volcanic mountains parallel the coast. Valley passes and oases made the Hijaz more hospitable than the desert to the east. By the sixth century, trade routes to the major cities of the Middle East—Cairo, Jerusalem, Damascus, Baghdad—passed through Mecca and Yathrib, a market city. Situated in a bowl surrounded by mountains, Mecca was the place, according to tradition, to which Adam migrated after arriving on earth at Mount Budh, in India or Ceylon. Adam called Mecca the navel of the earth and the center of God's throne. Near its generous spring, named Zamzam, Arabs of old established a shrine. Pilgrims visited annually.

The culture of Arabia was dominated by the nomadic ways of the Bedouin. These people's ancestors had centuries before migrated from the land between the Tigris and Euphrates Rivers. They herded sheep and goats, and sometimes cattle; they survived on dates, milk, and occasional feasts of meat. They lived in tents and wore loose robes woven from their animals' hair. Occasionally they traded meat and milk for fruit and bread, since as nomads in the salt-sand desert, they raised no crops. They preferred to provide for themselves, though, for they considered their way of life superior to that of sedentary farmers.

A fierce ethic of tribal solidarity infused the Arab culture. A householder owned his tent, animals, a few possessions, and his wife or wives. His first loyalty was to his clan, those people who traveled with him. An elder male among the clan was chosen as leader—a meritorious yet democratic designation. A blood bond connected clans into a tribe, the bond of highest allegiance and the foundation for the politics of sixth-century Arabian life. A male elder was chosen to serve as sheikh, head of the tribe. He conferred with a council of elders when making decisions.

At once hospitable and hostile, Arabs considered it acceptable for one tribe to perform a *ghazwa,* or raid, on another, as long as warriors followed the ethical rules of the desert, unwritten and yet fully understood, which included a ban on raids during four holy months. A ghazwa meant a swift camp attack, to steal camels and cattle, other property and women, but without bloodshed. If the attacked clan was left helpless, it might become a client, thus increasing the stronger clan in wealth and numbers. When elders approached to request such an arrangement, they were welcomed and offered food, water, and shelter in the Arab tradition of hospitality. A violent response on the part of the victimized clan, though, would bring on a vendetta. Blood for blood, life for life. The Arab world view emphasized the here and now, with no promise of rewards or punishments beyond this lifetime.

MECCA

EACH ARAB tribe worshiped its own gods. Fearsome gods, embodied in the sacred phenomena of nature—a stone, a tree, a spring, or a well—exacted tribute in the form of sacrifices and pilgrimages. The calendar divided the year into twelve months, of which four were sacred, including Dhul-Hijjah, the month for *hajj,* the pilgrimage. No matter what god they worshiped, thousands would come to Mecca, leaving aside all tribal differences. They followed the rituals of prostration, then circumambulation around the Kaaba, or cube—the shrine of granite in the center of the city, draped ceremonially with the finest fabrics.

Many gods were invoked at Mecca, including Manaf, the sun god, and Nasr, the eagle. The Kaaba was dedicated to Hubal, a deity from the north. A carnelian idol of Hubal stood prominently inside the shrine, but there also stood idols sacred to every tribe, 360 altogether—perhaps one for each day of the Sumerian calendar year, perhaps one for each tribe. Pilgrims approached with reverence, hoping to touch the Black Stone enshrined in the Kaaba. One tradition says that it is a white hyacinth, blackened by human sin. Modern rationalists, including the 19th-century English explorer Richard Burton, suggest that it is a meteorite that the ancients revered as a missive from heaven.

Beyond their many tribal deities, Arabs worshiped Allah in common. Allah, which means "the god," was the supreme creator of all, but an impersonal god, distant and unapproachable. He was the father of three goddesses, Lat, Manat, and Uzza, represented in the Kaaba, but Allah was so removed from daily life no one worshiped him or made a pilgrimage on his behalf.

Polytheistic beliefs infused the sixth-century Arab world, yet monotheistic faiths were well established all around. Locally, Jewish communities influenced Arabia's agricultural towns. Christian communities dotted the Hijaz, and Yemen was ruled by a convert to Judaism known for persecuting Christians. Across the Red Sea from Yemen lay Axum, today's Ethiopia, whose kings had practiced Christianity for nearly two centuries. That region of northeastern Africa is still a stronghold of Coptic Christianity.

In the larger sphere, sixth-century Arabia felt the pressure of conflict between the monotheistic powers nearby. The Christian Byzantine Empire, with its capital in Constantinople, included Turkey, Greece, Central Asia, and the eastern Mediterranean as well as Egypt. The Sassanian Empire encompassed Persia from the Euphrates River east and stretched to the Caucasus in the north, the Hindu Kush in the east, and north almost as far as Tashkent in today's Uzbekistan. The Sassanians practiced Zoroastrianism, since the third century the official religion of Persia.

These primarily urban cultures created a climate of belief and practice that was influencing Arab culture. Despite differences, the three surrounding religions— Judaism, Christianity, and Zoroastrianism—shared common elements: monotheism, or the belief in one and only one

ABOVE: Trade by camel caravans brought Islam to North Africa, where 9 out of 10 people today are Muslims.

supreme power; faith in prophets, inspired human beings through whom God conveys the divine truth; and reliance on Scripture, the holy word, written down by humans but originating from God.

MUHAMMAD

IN THAT time, the Quraysh tribe dominated the city of Mecca, tending the Kaaba and Zamzam, the spring. The tribal patriarch was Abd al-Muttalib, father of 16. According to Muslim tradition, as his favored son, Abdallah, was walking to his wedding, a woman stepped into his path, drawn by the blaze of light she saw between his eyes. She offered herself to him, but Abdallah declined. That night, he consummated his marriage with Amina. When the other woman saw him again, his face had lost its light. Muslims understood: He and his wife had conceived Muhammad, the Prophet. Abdallah died before his son's birth, but Abd al-Muttalib proudly carried his grandson to the Kaaba on the first day of his life, the 12th of Rabi al-Awwal, the first month of spring, around the year 570 A.D.

Women from Mecca preferred their children to be brought up in the open air of the desert, so Muhammad spent his first years with a Bedouin family near Taif, east of Mecca. As soon as his foster mother, Halima, began caring for him, her fortunes changed. The camels gave milk, the donkeys ran fast, and she nursed both Muhammad and her own son abundantly. One day, his foster brothers reported, two angels in white descended upon four-year-old Muhammad, cut open his chest, and washed his heart with snow. Halima rushed the boy back to Mecca, but his mother responded calmly, knowing that her son was destined for an extraordinary life.

Soon Muhammad's mother and grandfather died. Muhammad went to live with his uncle, now chief of their clan. A serious, trustworthy young man, Muhammad had a special place in his heart for the poor and downtrodden. In his work, though, he came into contact with the wealthy, fast-paced world of traders who often passed through Mecca. Commerce connected Africa and the Mediterranean with India and Asia by sea—via the ports on the Red Sea and the Persian Gulf— and by land, via the trade routes connecting to the Silk Road. Muhammad may even have driven caravans up to Syria, for in his mid-20s he was hired by a rich widow, Khadijah, to carry merchandise for her. Soon he married Khadijah, although she was 15 years his elder. Of their four daughters and two sons, only the girls survived. After 22 years of mutual devotion, Khadijah died. Muhammad married a number of other women in his lifetime, polygyny being the Arab custom, adopted but limited by Islam. Through those bonds he secured political alliances, but no later wife evoked the level of heartfelt commitment that he had felt toward

OPPOSITE: Veiling the faces of Muhammad and his mother, a 14th-century artist depicted the Prophet's birth.
ABOVE: Appearing to Muhammad in a cave, the angel Jibril, or Gabriel, hailed him as "Messenger of God."
FOLLOWING PAGES: Surrendering to Allah, Muslims pray at the Prophet's Mosque in Medina, which enshrines Muhammad's tomb.

Khadijah. Two of the first women to proclaim faith in Allah, Khadijah and her youngest daughter, Fatima, represent the ideal of women in the Islamic faith.

By the age of 40, Muhammad began retreating to a mountain cave. He sensed turmoil, spiritual confusion, and materialism in the marketplace of Mecca and sought a reprieve in silent meditation. He walked steep ravines to the black desert sands around Mount Hira. On Hira's south-facing slope, Muhammad found a cave. Its entrance had the appearance of great slabs of stone tumbling over one another. The space was tall enough to stand in, with a floor of golden sand, a place still visited by pilgrims to Mecca.

On the 26th night of the month of Ramadan in the year 610, Muhammad sat alone in the cave. Muslims call that night Muhammad's Night of Power. He heard a voice commanding "Recite." He cowered, and the angel—later identified as Jibril, Arabic for Gabriel— pressed down on him until words began to form.

> Recite, in the name of your Lord who created,
> He created man from a clot,
> Recite, by your Most Generous Lord,
> Who taught by the pen
> He taught man what he did not know.

After this, Muhammad recounted, "it was as if the scripture were written on my heart." These five lines represent the beginning of the Qur'an, the Holy Book of Islam, which was revealed over time by God through the angel Gabriel to the Prophet Muhammad.

THE QUR'AN

THE WORD Qur'an comes from the Arabic *qaraa,* which can mean either "to read" or "to recite." The ambiguity carries meaning. Muhammad was receiving, then reciting words from a divine source, the eternal truth that existed in an ineffable form. Arab people joined Jews and Christians as people who received God's revelation. The Quran has been

read and studied, recited and chanted aloud, ever since. Memorizing the Qur'an is one of the greatest acts of devotion a Muslim can undertake.

The Qur'an consists of 114 chapters called *suras*— Arabic for "rows"—made up of verses, *ayat,* meaning "signs" or "miracles." Scribes helped Muhammad later in his life, but the earlier suras were memorized and passed on orally. Not until the middle of the seventh century was the entire collection written down, although the order of the chapters is believed to have been revealed to Muhammad in the order of Gabriel's instructions from God. Suras are numbered and titled for help in recitation. Scholars associate many suras with episodes in Muhammad's life, but it is difficult to reckon an internal structure within the collection. Some point out that they go from longest to shortest or from early (Meccan) to late (Medinan) revelations. Some suras speak of God in the third person, while others are written in the first-person singular or plural not only for poetic style but also for semantic effect. Every sura opens with a prayer: "In the Name of Allah, the Compassionate, the Merciful." Patriarchs and prophets of Judaism and Christianity are revered in the Qur'an: Abraham, Isaac, and Jacob; Moses, David, and Solomon; Jesus and especially his mother, Mary. The Qur'an has been translated into dozens of languages, starting with Latin in the Middle Ages and exploding into many modern languages in the 19th and 20th centuries. Early handwritten copies of the Qur'an—such as the 1,400-page leather manuscript, one and a half feet thick, preserved in the al-Hussein Mosque in Cairo—remain masterpieces of Islamic art, inked in the graceful forms of the Arabic alphabet and decorated with intricate designs in the margins.

Muhammad received the Qur'an over a span of 22 years. At first, the experience overwhelmed him. Tradition says that after the Night of Power, he raced home and asked Khadijah to cover him with a cloak, he was so awe-struck and frightened. Illustrators ever after have depicted a white cloth covering Muhammad's face to symbolize that he was receiving a revelation. But soon Muhammad knew

he must spread the message. "O thou enveloped in the cloak, Arise and warn!" reads one of the early suras. "Thy Lord magnify, thy raiment purify, pollution shun!" Heeding the assignment to cleanse his people of their pagan and materialistic ways, Muhammad began preaching the message that there was only one god, Allah, the creator and lord of the universe and judge of humankind.

"The unbelievers, among the people of the Book and the idolaters, shall be in the Fire of Hell, dwelling therein forever. Those are the worst of creatures. Those who have believed and did the righteous deeds—those are the best of creatures. Their reward with their Lord will be Gardens of Eden, beneath which rivers flow, dwelling therein forever. Allah is well pleased with them, and they are well pleased with Him. That is the lot of whoever fears his Lord."

Some of the Qur'an's verses address Muhammad's tribe directly. "Covetousness has distracted you, till you visited the graveyards," he warned. Neither riches nor power nor tribal history elevated one person or group over another. What did matter was the commitment to Allah. It was a chastening message: Put aside the pagan gods; when tested with wealth and power, do not neglect your sacred duties, and heed the majesty and demands of the one and only god, Allah. The proper attitude toward God was captured in the name of the new religion. Islam, literally an act of surrender, is related to words for peace and reconciliation. A Muslim is one who surrenders to Allah, who seeks to follow and implement God's will.

A few people became believers—his wife, his daughters, his slave. They began meeting for prayer, following the

ABOVE: In exuberant Arabic script, the Qur'an spells out the laws, prayers, customs, and stories of Islam.
FOLLOWING PAGES: Minarets of the Namira Mosque stand tall on the Plain of Arafat, where Muhammad preached his last sermon.

practices conveyed to Muhammad by Gabriel: standing, bowing, kneeling, prostrating themselves in prayer and total submission to Allah. Several stories are told of Meccan skeptics who miraculously converted once they heard the poetic words of the Qur'an. Muhammad condemned "unmindful" materialism and usury; he defended the rights of orphans, widows, and the poor. He claimed that after death the righteous would be rewarded in a heavenly paradise, while those who ignored these laws from Allah would be punished in hell. On the other hand, many Meccans were outraged. Muhammad's prophecies threatened their age-old social structure. The Quraysh's control over the Kaaba had brought considerable income and prestige to the tribe. Muhammad's uncle and protector advised him to keep quiet, but he could not. Soon many of the

powerful citizens of Mecca, even those of his tribe, began jeering and persecuting him. Muhammad sent some of his followers to Axum, where Christian leaders agreed to protect them. His message and its power grew so threatening, he was targeted for assassination.

In the early 620s, Muhammad fell asleep after his evening prostrations. That night, it is said, he was carried on horseback by the angel Gabriel through the heavens to Jerusalem, 800 miles north. "Glory be to Him Who caused His servant to travel by night from the Sacred Mosque to the Farthest Mosque, whose precincts We have blessed," reads the 17th sura. Muhammad alighted on the Temple Mount, the Temple of the Israelites, where Abraham, Moses, Jesus, and other prophets welcomed him into the circle. Offered goblets containing wine, water, and milk,

ABOVE: *A Muslim woman walks near the spot in Jerusalem where Muhammad was transported by an angel.*

Muhammad selected the one with milk—a sign of the middle way of Islam, neither indulgent nor austere.

From that spot, Gabriel led Muhammad up a ladder into heaven, where God greeted him and told him that the devout must pray 50 times a day. On the way down the ladder, Moses advised him that daily prostrations could number as few as five but still fulfill God's wishes. The Qur'ran has upheld the tradition of having believers pause five times a day for prayer and worship: at sunrise, noon, afternoon, dusk, and before sleeping. Briefly mentioned in the Qur'an but detailed by Ibn Ishaq, Muhammad's eighth-century biographer, the Night Journey represents a mystical high point in the Prophet's life. It drew him into the community of the prophets of Judaism and Christianity. All now shared Jerusalem as a holy city.

MEDINA

WHILE MECCANS by and large tried to drive Muhammad out, leaders in Yathrib heard the promise of peace in Muhammad's message. A green oasis surrounded by desert and rock, Yathrib was an agricultural settlement, a place where Jewish and Arab nomads, making the transition to a pastoral existence, regarded each other with tribal disdain. Invited north, Muhammad and a friend slipped out of Mecca in the night, making the historic journey now called the *hijra.* Soldiers sought them, but a spider web spun across a cave entrance after they had entered it kept their whereabouts secret. Avoiding the well-traveled roads, the two men reached their new city, which was renamed Madinat al-Nabi, city of the Prophet—Medina today. The Muslim calendar counts the years beginning with the hijra, considering Muhammad's arrival in Medina as the start of Islamic history. Twelve lunar months constitute a year, and years are named by number followed by "A.H.," from the Latin *anno hegirae,* year of the hijra.

Muhammad made his home in Medina and built nearby an "alighting place," considered the first mosque of Islam—a large square building reminiscent of the Kaaba, with a courtyard of black sand, eight supporting palm trunks for pillars, and a thatched roof. Muhammad designated an area inside for the poor and infirm, who received food, shelter, and Qur'anic consolations. In centuries to come, it was said that while Muhammad's religion finally relocated its center in Mecca and that city's Kaaba, Muhammad's heart belonged to the mosque in Medina.

At Medina Muhammad served as religious and political leader *(imam),* prophet and statesman, military leader and judge. At first he instructed his followers to pray facing Jerusalem, but later revelations reasserted the importance of Mecca as his people's sacred city. The hajj to Mecca became central to prayer and worship as Muslims were redirected in prayer toward that city and its Kaaba—a momentous shift, an inward declaration of the triumph of Muhammed's revealed monotheistic religion over the tribal polytheism of his birthplace. Around the world ever since, Muslims observe the same *qibla,* or direction in prayer. Five times a day they face Mecca as they worship Allah, effectively making the city and its Kaaba the geographical and sacred center of their universe of faith.

Turning from Jerusalem to Mecca did not represent a separation from Judaism and Christianity but rather established a deeper, more ancient link. Muhammad now traced his people's spiritual lineage back to the earliest monotheistic patriarch honored by Christians and Jews. He had learned through revelations that the Kaaba stood where God in ages past had told Abraham to build a temple. All three religions share the story of Abraham's long wait for an heir: the birth of his first son, Ishmael—in Arabic, Ismail—to his wife's handmaid, Hagar; and the birth of another son, Isaac, to his elderly wife, Sarah. All three honor Abraham's willingness to sacrifice his son to God. According to Islamic tradition, though, it was Ishmael whom Abraham was about to offer, an event that occurred on a mountain next to Hira, where Muhammad experienced his Night of Power. As Abraham lifted the knife, an angel intervened and presented him with a ram to kill instead. In gratitude, Abraham and Ishmael built "a place of assembly for mankind and of safety" in Mecca, on the site where the Kaaba later stood. The Black Stone, according to tradition, came from the foundation of the patriarch's original temple.

Bearing this ancestry in mind, Muhammad stripped the temple in Mecca of its idols and purified it of paganism, to reconnect it and its rituals to its original precepts established by Abraham and Ismail, and to commemorate God's Oneness, *tawhid,* in Arabic,

THE RETURN TO MECCA

MUHAMMAD'S CITY of Medina had its geographic bounds, but Muhammad envisioned a larger world of Islam. It is said that he sent messages to rulers in Yemen, Abyssinia, Egypt, Persia, and Byzantium, inviting them to consider the way of the Qur'an. Meanwhile, Mecca beckoned. Caravans heading to and from the city had to travel through Medina. Muhammad's followers were in a strong position to raid Meccans, a step toward regaining the holy city. Catching wind of Muhammad's intention to seize their caravans moving south from Gaza, a thousand Meccans marched north to defend them. The caravans skirted Medina by traveling along the coast, but Muhammad sent what forces he had—about 300 men—to meet the approaching Meccans at Badr, a town important for its wells. After a night of reciting the Qur'an in prayer, Muhammad and his forces defeated the Meccans. The Battle of Badr in 624 was a turning point in the history of Islam.

Thus Muhammad became a military leader, battling the Quraysh and endeavouring to arbitrate between contentious Arab and Jewish tribes inside Medina who were contractually part of the Medinan community. He intercepted tribal leaders up and down the Hijaz, preferring negotiations to military conquest whenever possible. Conflict between the Muslims and Meccans climaxed in 627 with the so-called Battle of the Ditch. Meccans and Bedouins banded together to assault the Muslims in Medina, who defended themselves by digging trenches to interrupt the attack. Despite being outnumbered once again, the Muslims rose victorious. Their defeat of the Quraysh won them respect and allegiance from many tribes of the region and a truce from the Meccans. In 628, Muhammad led his Muslim followers on the hajj to Mecca. Soon thereafter the Meccans broke the truce by killing one of Muhammad's followers. He responded militarily, the Meccans submitted, and the Muslims took over Mecca and the Kaaba.

That year Muhammad led 2,000 pilgrims to Mecca. Astride a camel, he made the seven holy circumambulations of the Kaaba, each time touching the Black Stone with his camel crook. He thus assimilated the ancient ritual into the practice of Islam. He ordered the idols destroyed, proclaiming a verse from the Qur'an. "The truth has come and falsehood has perished." Muslims must worship only the one true God. From that time on, no mosque or Islamic center has contained representative statuary or paintings.

From the Kaaba, Muhammad traveled east and stood on a mountainside to deliver what is remembered as his farewell sermon. "O People, lend me an attentive ear, for I know not whether after this year I shall ever be amongst you again," he began. He exhorted them to "regard the life and property of every Muslim as a sacred trust," leaving behind them forever the Arab ethics of raiding and vendettas. "Hurt no one so that no one may hurt you," he continued. "Remember that you will indeed meet your Lord, and that he will indeed reckon your deeds." Likewise, he added, "beware of Satan, for the safety of your religion." He specifically described egalitarian relations between men and women: "O People, it is true that you have certain rights with regard to your women but they also have rights over you." He also specifically spoke of race relations, saying "an Arab has no superiority over a non-Arab nor a non-Arab has any superiority over an Arab, also a white [person] has no superiority over a black [person] nor a black has any

FOLLOWING PAGES: While thousands wait in the wings, pilgrims circle the sacred stone, or Kaaba, seven times during the hajj.

ISLAM

FROM THE QUR'AN

THE QUR'AN, the sacred scripture of Islam, is regarded by Muslims as the infallible Word of God, a perfect transcription of an eternal tablet preserved in heaven and revealed to Muhammad. The Qur'an consists of 114 chap-

CHAPTER 1 (VERSES 1-7)
THE PRAYER

This verse is repeated in every one of the five daily prayers. It is also recited during important occasions.

In the Name of Allah, the Compassionate,
the Merciful,
Praise be to Allah, the Lord of the World,
The Compassionate, the Merciful,
Master of the Day of Judgment,
Only You do we worship, and only You

Do we implore for help.
Lead us to the right path,
The path of those You have favored
Not those who have incurred
Your wrath or
Have gone astray.

CHAPTER 2 (VERSES 261-265)
ON CHARITY

Those who spend their wealth in the Way of
Allah are like a grain {of wheat} which
grows seven ears, each carrying one hundred
grains. Allah multiplies {further} to whom
He wills. Allah is Munificent, All-Knowing.

Those who spend their wealth in the way of
Allah, and then do not follow what they spend
with taunts and injury, their reward is with
their Lord. They shall have nothing to fear
and shall not grieve.

A Kind word and forgiveness are better than
charity followed by injury. Allah is
Self-sufficient and Forbearing.

Oh believers, do not render vain your charities by
taunts and injury, like him who spends his
wealth for the sake of ostentation and does not
believe in Allah and the Last Day. He is
like a smooth rock covered by earth; when
heavy rain falls on it, it leaves it completely
bare. Such people get no reward for their
works. Allah does not guide the unbelievers.

But those who spend their money in order to
please Allah and to strengthen their souls are
like a garden on a hill which, when heavy
rain falls on it, its produce is doubled, and if
no heavy rain falls on it, then a shower
(suffices). Allah is aware of what you do.

CHAPTER 33 (VERSE 35)
FOR MUSLIM MEN AND WOMEN

For Muslim men and women,
For believing men and women,
For devout men and women,
For true men and women,
For men and women who are patient and constant,
For men and women who humble themselves,
For men and women who give in charity,

For men and women who fast (and deny
themselves),
For men and women who guard their chastity,
And for men and women who engage much
in Allah's praise,
For them has Allah prepared forgiveness
and great reward.

superiority over a white—except by piety and good action." No new prophet or faith would come after him, announced Muhammad. He specified the two things he left behind for his followers: the Qur'an and his Sunnah—the word of God and the example of his messenger.

Muhammad's pilgrimage in A.H. 10—632 A.D.— was indeed his last. He had, by example, alliance, and conquest, brought virtually the entire Arabian Peninsula into the *ummah,* the community of Islam. As many as 30,000 had embraced Islam by that time. Religious unification now transcended tribal diversity, with a commitment to peace— *salam* in Arabic. The religion pointed the way to a new morality, breaking the vendetta cycle and suggesting heavenly rewards for earthly virtue.

Muhammad had befriended Christian leaders in Aqaba, Jewish leaders in Transjordan, and was planning a march to Syria when he began to feel weak with headaches. He rallied momentarily during a visit to the mosque. He came home to Medina, laid his head on his wife's lap, and uttered his last words: "Let me meet the Most Exalted Friend!" Tradition has it that Gabriel and a host of angels came into the room to ask permission for the Angel of Death to take Muhammad, which the dying prophet granted. "Peace be upon thee, Apostle," said his friends, as do those who have visited his grave ever since. A tomb was built inside his wife's house. Eventually it was incorporated into a separate mausoleum, and then the Prophet's Mosque, whose green dome now protects Muhammad's tomb.

THE FIVE PILLARS OF ISLAM

IN HIS farewell sermon, Muhammad crystallized the obligations of Islam in a five-part code of behavior, called the Five Pillars of Islam. The first Pillar is the *shahada,* literally "bearing witness"—the affirmation of belief in Allah and Muhammad as his prophet. Its essence is expressed in the universal statement of faith: "There is no god but Allah and Muhammad is the Messenger of Allah," the first words spoken by Gabriel to Muhammad in the cave of Hira. To say them is to reveal a heart with good intentions and genuine love for Allah and Muhammad, and therefore all the Prophets that came before him as the "seal of the Prophets." Saying these words constitutes the sole requirement for conversion to Islam. During daily prayers, Muslims hear this statement 17 times. They say it into the ear of a newborn and try to make it the last thing they say before dying.

The second Pillar of Islam is *salat,* group prayer or worship. Group prayer is more blessed than individual prayer, and Muhammad suggested Friday as the day that Muslims would gather to pray. Five times a day at mosques around the world, the muezzin calls Muslims to prayer, just as the first muezzin, Muhammad's Abyssinian slave, Bilal, did in Medina and during the great hajj of 632. Whether in a group or alone, Muslims prepare their space and body with rituals of cleanliness, washing with sand if water is not in reach. Worshipers perform prostrations—standing with hands clasped at the waist, bowing to the knees, prostrating themselves, then standing again—and often repeat this cycle, or *raqa,* several times before assuming a seated or kneeling position for recitation and meditation.

The third Pillar of Islam is *zakat,* a word that means "purification" but has evolved to designate tithing and almsgiving. "Who is he that will lend Allah a fair loan, that He might double it for him; and he will have a generous wage," reads the 57th sura. On the other hand, a later verse states, "he to whom God has given goods and who has not paid his tithe" will face a horrifying consequence on the ultimate day of judgment. God "will make his goods appear in the form of a python with a bald head and two excrescences of flesh," which "will coil itself around the neck of that man" and "seize him in its jaws and say: 'I am your goods, I am your treasure.' " Modern Muslims give 2.5 percent of their assets annually to worthy causes or to poor relations.

OPPOSITE: Targeting the devil, Muslims stone one of three pillars during the hajj in Mina, Saudi Arabia.

The fourth Pillar of Islam is the *sawm*, the fast during the month of Ramadan, the ninth month of the Muslim calendar. For that month, Muslims refrain from food, drink, and sex during daylight hours. Traditionally, the fast starts with the appearance of the first sliver of the new moon and continues for the full lunar cycle. It is a holy month, a month of purifying thoughts and behavior. "When Ramadan begins," said Muhammad, "the gates of heaven open, the gates of hell are closed, and the demons are chained up." It is a joyful month, as well, in the Muslim community. Friends and family gather together to break the fast with a generous meal, then visit the mosque for evening prayer. Often prayer leaders will recite the entire Qur'an, divided into 30 parts, one for each night of the month. On the 27th night, Muslims celebrate the Night of Power. Ramadan ends with the Eid al-Fitr, the Breaking of the Fast, a happy holiday when cards are sent and gifts exchanged.

The fifth Pillar of Islam is the hajj, the pilgrimage to Mecca, a sacred duty and transcendent opportunity. All who are physically and financially able perform the hajj once in their lives, many more often. As expressed by 20th-century Iranian sociologist and philosopher, Ali Shariati, "as you circumambulate and move closer to the Ka'aba, you feel like a small stream merging with a big river. Carried by a wave you lose touch with the ground. Suddenly, you are floating, carried on by the flood. As you approach the center, the pressure of the crowd squeezes you so hard that you are given a new life.... You have been transformed into a particle that is gradually melting and disappearing. This is absolute love at its peak."

Muslims arrive in Mecca roughly 60 days after the end of Ramadan and spend five days in worship, traveling to sites in and around Mecca and to the tomb of the Prophet in Medina. Men wrap two lengths of unstitched white cloth around torso and shoulders. Women wrap themselves in plain cloth, too, covering all but face, hands, and feet. Many stay in tents erected for the occasion in Mina, six miles south of the city. After entering the center of Mecca, they make their way seven times around the Kaaba. On at least one of those circles they pause to kiss the Black Stone, embedded in the Kaaba's east-facing corner in a niche.

After the circumambulation, many pilgrims perform the *sa'y*, running seven times between two small hills in Mecca to remember the time when Hagar, sent into the desert with Ishmael, searched desperately for water. It was part of Muhammad's revelation that she plunged a stick into the ground and discovered the spring Zamzam. Briny water still bubbles there. Pilgrims consider it holy and collect it in small vials to take home.

On the second day of the hajj, pilgrims travel east to the Plain of Arafat, where they climb in prayer and devotion up the sand-colored rocks of the Mount of Mercy, from which Muhammad delivered his farewell sermon. On the way back, they spend the night at Muzdalifa and gather pebbles there. On the third day, an animal sacrifice is performed, remembering the ram substituted for Ishmael. During the fourth day, Muslims throw the stones from Muzdalifa at three upright rock slabs that symbolize Satan. The hajj ends by a final circling of the Kaaba.

Pilgrims come from all directions, don the same humble clothes, and unite in an international community of worship. The numbers arriving in Mecca have soared exponentially from the middle of the 20th century on. In 1950, an estimated 100,000 people made the pilgrimage. In the early 1980s, the number reached one million. By the end of that decade, the Organization of Islamic Conference —a pan-Muslim group of 57 nations—established national quotas. The Saudi government and commercial interests throughout Mecca have poured billions of dollars into making the hajj a comfortable event, with five-star hotels, air conditioning along the route, and escalators in the mosque. By the early years of the 21st century, the annual number of pilgrims had swelled to two million or more.

Overcrowding and emotions heightened by world politics resulted in stampedes and deaths during the hajj on several occasions in the 1990s and 2000s. Wary of repercussions after the attack on the United States on September 11, 2001, masterminded by Muslim extremists,

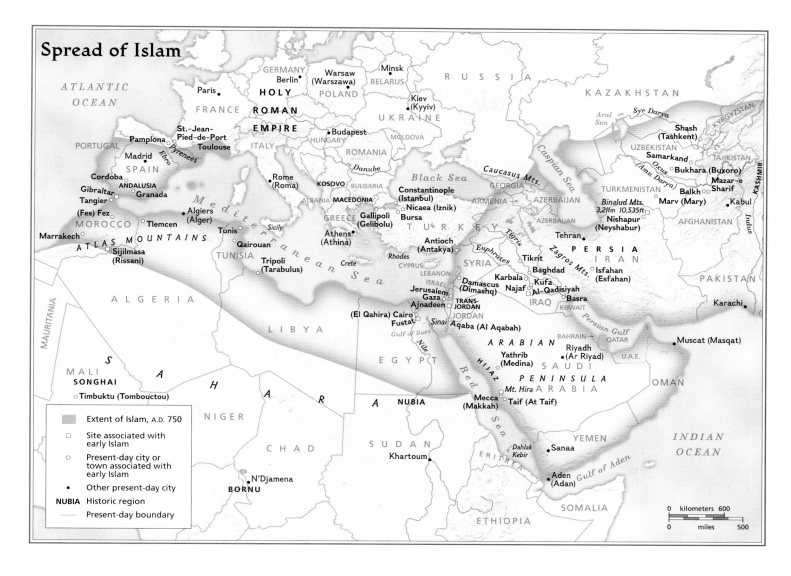

Spread of Islam

ATLANTIC OCEAN

GERMANY
Berlin•
Paris•
FRANCE
HOLY ROMAN EMPIRE
ITALY
PORTUGAL
St.-Jean-Pied-de-Port
Pamplona
Toulouse
Pyrenees
Madrid•
SPAIN
Ebro
Cordoba ○
ANDALUSIA
Gibraltar □ Granada ○
Tangier □
(Fes) Fez ○
MOROCCO
Tlemcen ○
Marrakech •
ATLAS MOUNTAINS
Sijilmasa
(Rissani) □
ALGERIA
TUNISIA
Qairouan ○
Tripoli (Tarabulus) ○
Mediterranean Sea

Warsaw (Warszawa)
POLAND
Minsk•
BELARUS
Kiev (Kyyiv)
UKRAINE
MOLDOVA
Budapest•
HUNGARY
ROMANIA
Danube
Rome (Roma)
KOSOVO BULGARIA
ALBANIA MACEDONIA
GREECE
Gallipoli (Gelibolu)
Athens (Athina)
Sicily
Crete
Rhodes
CYPRUS

RUSSIA
KAZAKHSTAN
Aral Sea
Syr Darya
Shash (Tashkent) ○
Samarkand ○
UZBEKISTAN
TAJIKISTAN
Bukhara (Buxoro) ○
Amu Darya
Oxus
Mazar-e Sharif •
Balkh ○
Black Sea
Caucasus Mts.
Caspian Sea
Constantinople (Istanbul)
Nicaea (Iznik) □
Bursa•
GEORGIA
ARMENIA
AZERBAIJAN
TURKEY
AZERBAIJAN
TURKMENISTAN
Binalud Mts. 3,211m 10,535ft □
Marv (Mary) •
Nishapur (Neyshabur)
Tehran•
PERSIA IRAN
Isfahan (Esfahan) ○
Kabul•
AFGHANISTAN
Indus
PAKISTAN
KASHMIR
Karachi•
Tigris
Euphrates
Antioch (Antakya) ○
SYRIA
LEBANON
Damascus (Dimashq) ○
Jerusalem ○
ISRAEL
Gaza ○
Ajnadeen □
TRANS-JORDAN
JORDAN
Karbala ○
Najaf ○
Kufa ○
Al-Qadisiyah ○
Basra ○
IRAQ
KUWAIT
Tikrit ○
Baghdad •
Zagros Mts.

MAURITANIA
MALI
SONGHAI
Timbuktu (Tombouctou) ○
S A H A R A
NIGER
CHAD
N'Djamena •
BORNU
LIBYA
EGYPT
(El Qahira) Cairo ○
Fustat □
Gulf of Suez
Sinai
Nile
SUDAN
Khartoum •
ETHIOPIA
Aqaba (Al Aqabah)
Red Sea
HIJAZ
Yathrib (Medina) •
Mecca (Makkah) □
Mt. Hira □
Taif (At Taif) •
ARABIA
ARABIAN PENINSULA
SAUDI
Riyadh (Ar Riyad) •
BAHRAIN
QATAR
U.A.E.
OMAN
Muscat (Masqat) •
YEMEN
Sanaa •
Dahlak Kebir
Aden (Adan) •
Gulf of Aden
ERITREA
SOMALIA
INDIAN OCEAN

Legend:
▨ Extent of Islam, A.D. 750
□ Site associated with early Islam
○ Present-day city or town associated with early Islam
• Other present-day city
NUBIA Historic region
— Present-day boundary

0 kilometers 600
0 miles 500

---

the Saudi government required advance proof that all visitors coming into the country for the hajj were pilgrims. Authorities have attempted to time the movement of crowds to avoid bottlenecks at key passage points. In response to violence, Islamic leaders emphasize Muhammad's message of peace. "The world must know that Islam is the religion of peace and mercy and goodness," said Abdul Aziz bin Abdullan Al Sheik, a Saudi Muslim leader, "a religion that prohibits all forms of injustice and the shedding of blood without genuine reason."

THE SPREAD OF ISLAM

As a religious, political, and military leader, Muhammad left a legacy that would be a source of inspiration and

imitation for future generations. He had reasserted the ancient religion of Abraham, and with that faith he had united all of Arabia. His survivors passionately followed his path, and on all three fronts—religious, political, and military—Islam spread rapidly. Muslims saw themselves as agents of *jihad,* literally "effort" or "exertion," fighting evil and carrying the righteous rule of Islam to the far ends of the earth. They respected the rights of Christians and Jews to follow their own paths of worship. They sought ways not to ban others' practices but to adapt them to Muslim ways. Islam traveled by word of mouth as Arabian trade continued to flourish. Muslim influence spread through political alliances and the establishment of educational centers.

First, the region of Arabia itself was solidified. Then Syria and Palestine, under Byzantine control, were secured.

353

From Syria, Muslim believers rode north into Armenia, east into Persia, and west into Egypt. In 637, a historic Muslim victory at al-Qadisiyah, today's Kadisiya in southern Iraq, marked the beginning of the end for the Sassanian Empire. In less than two decades after Muhammad's death, his followers ruled lands from Yemen to Armenia, Egypt to Iran, and expansion continued in every direction. Garrison outposts became important Islamic centers: Kufa and Basra in today's Iraq, Fustat in Egypt, Marv—now Mary—in Turkmenistan, and Qayrawan in Tunisia.

The first great burst of Islamic expansion came under the leadership of Muhammad's four successors, called caliphs. Together these four men are called the Rashidun, the rightly guided. The first caliph was Abu Bakr—the father of Aisha, the youngest of Muhammad's wives, who left her reminiscences of the Prophet in writing. He confronted regional leaders who had begun to fall back into tribal divisiveness. Umar ibn al-Khattab, the second caliph, reunited the ummah by rousing those leaders to join in campaigns of expansion. In 636, after a year of military siege led by Umar, Damascus, a Byzantine center recently looted by the Persians, became a Muslim city.

One temple in Damascus tells the entire history of religion in the Middle East. Built in the second millennium B.C. in honor of an Aramaean deity, Hadad, it was rededicated by Romans to Jupiter in the first century, then converted by the Byzantine Emperor Theodosius to the Church of St. John the Baptist in 379 A.D. After the Arab invasion in 636, the south wall of the church became part of a mosque, built to grandeur between 708 and 715 by the Umayyad caliph Al-Walid. At the same time, Al-Walid saw to it that Christians could build four churches elsewhere in the city. Today the Umayyad Mosque, much expanded over the centuries and still in active use, is considered Islam's oldest monumental mosque.

DIVISION

THE THIRD rightly guided caliph, Uthman ibn Affan, faced challenges of organization and leadership. From the first, there were those who believed that leadership should reside within the family of the Prophet and thus that Ali ibn Abi Talib, cousin to Muhammad and husband to Fatima, should have been the Prophet's first successor. Some of Ali's advocates fomented an uprising in 656, during which Uthman was killed. Ali was appointed the fourth caliph, but contention over lineage escalated into the First Civil War, which raged from 656 to 661. It ended in the Battle of the Camel near Basra in today's Iraq, a victory for the shiat-u-Ali, the party of Ali. An opposition party formed, led by Muawiyah—a general, governor of Syria, and Uthman's nephew—and included Aisha.

Dating from the seventh century, these two factions represent a split more political than theological that still divides the religion of Islam today.

With headquarters in Kufa, in modern-day Iraq, the shiat-u-Ali—also called Shii or Shiites—met their opposition in battle and negotiation. Ali commanded Muawiyah to vacate the Syrian governorship and make room for his own appointee. Muawiyah resisted, and soldiers under Ali stormed Damascus to no avail. Disappointed by failure, one party of Ali's followers broke off from the rest. They came to be called Kharijites, for "those who go out" or "secede." They condemned both Muawiyah and Ali for behavior that did not fit the righteous model expected of a leader of Islam. The Kharijites believed that they both had committed a grave sin, departed from "true" Islam and thus were to be fought and killed.

In 661, Kharijite assassins targeted both Ali and Muawiyah. They killed Ali, but Muawiyah survived to become the next caliph, ruling over a Muslim community now divided into three parts: Kharijite, Shiite, and the majority group based in Medina, called Sunni because they believed they most closely followed the *Sunnah,* or practice, of Muhammad himself. Over time, the differences between these groups hardened, based primarily on claiming the right of succession.

The Kharijites believed that leadership should be conferred on the man who showed the highest level of piety. The Shiites believed that leadership was inherited through the line of the Prophet, from Muhammad to Fatima and Ali and their descendants, based in Baghdad. The Sunni argued that the caliph should be selected by the people of the community. In practice, however, when the Sunni leader Muawiyah became caliph, he became the father of the hereditary Umayyad dynasty, which ruled from 661 to 750 A.D.

Eventually, the three divisions within Islam grew to have geographic and religious meaning as well as political import. The Kharijites' severe egalitarian message drew converts in eastern Arabia and North Africa. Their version of Islam fueled conflicts both intellectual and military, especially among the converting traders and farmers of the region, the Berbers (non-Arabs). Vestiges of Kharijite Islam remain, especially in Oman and Morocco.

Conflicts between the followers of Muawiyah's son, Yazid, and Ali's son, Husayn, cemented the divide between Sunnis and Shiites. After Ali's death, Shiite Muslims in Kufa called for Husayn to become their leader. In 680 Umayyad forces battled with Husayn and his army at Karbala and slaughtered them. Shiites around the world still remember and commemorate his martyrdom. They regard the 40 days beginning with the first day of Muharram, the first

month of the Islamic calendar, as a period of mourning, highlighted by Ashura, the tenth day of the month when Husayn was killed. Shiite men reenact the suffering of Husayn in a passion play, parading to the beat of drums and flagellating themselves to draw blood and personally experience the suffering of their hero.

Karbala, the place of Husayn's martyrdom, is among the most sacred cities of Shii Islam. As is the city of Najaf, the burial place of Husayn's father, Ali. A caliph of the late eighth century, it is said, was deer hunting in the area when his quarry stopped and stood transfixed upon a mound of earth. The caliph's horse stopped, too. The hunter felt a deep sense of awe. Questioning what had happened, the caliph learned from locals that the mound was the gravesite of Ali. There the caliph built a magnificent tomb, later enhanced with a brilliant dome made of 7,777 golden tiles and enlarged into an exquisite mosque. Wanting their beloved to rest in peace near Ali, Shiite Muslims have for centuries buried their dead in a Najaf cemetery near the mosque, by outsiders called the City of the Dead but by believers called al-Wadi es-Salam, the Vale of Peace.

During the last centuries of the first millennium, the Shii spread their influence broadly. They divided into subsects along the way, always united by the conviction that their leader should, like Muhammad, be the imam, the religiously inspired political leader of the community. At its full extent, Shiite Islam held sway along the coast of North Africa and exerted influence throughout Arabia and Persia. Today Shiites represent about 10 to 15 percent of all Muslims, with a much higher proportion in Iran, Iraq, Lebanon, Bahrain, and Azerbaijan, where they represent a majority of the population.

SUNNI DYNASTIES

AGAINST THIS background of dissenting minority Muslim groups, the dominant community was the Sunni majority, from whose line came the two great caliphates: the Umayyad and the Abbasid, which followed from the 8th

THE CALL TO WORSHIP
A Daily Practice

FIVE TIMES a day, at sunrise, noon, afternoon, sunset, and evening, muezzins around the world call the faithful to worship, chanting in Arabic, "Come and pray, come and flourish, there is no god but Allah." "Allahu akhbar!" God is most great. In the mosque, at work, and at home, Muslims pause for the ritual and, above all, prayerful consciousness. To pray without niyyah, intention, means less than not praying at all. In some cultures women pray at home, whereas men go to the mosque, but all Muslims—women, men, and children—praise Allah and his Prophet, Muhammad.

Before prayer, Muslims cleanse themselves. Most mosques have a fountain with water for washing face, hands, arms, and feet. A mosque is primarily a great hall, often an open courtyard, in which worshipers assume orderly rows facing the mihrab, the ornamented wall niche that indicates the direction to Mecca. An imam leads the worshipers in prayer, which combines a reciting of verses from the Qur'an with devout motion: standing, bowing, kneeling face down, kneeling, and sitting. The worshipers may be so great in number that the mosque overflows and even the sidewalks outside are lined with straw mats on which men prostrate themselves. At prayer's end, people turn to their right and left, and bid their fellow Muslims to walk in peace with God's blessings.

Praying five times a day is one of the Five Pillars of Islam—the five tenets of pious behavior that all Muslims follow. Congregational prayers are held at mosques on Friday, and many businesses stay closed on Friday afternoons. After Friday prayer, worshipers sit and listen to an imam or other member of the congregation lecture on verses from the Qur'an, illuminating their meaning and applying them to modern daily life.

As early as they begin to speak, Muslim children memorize sacred phrases in Arabic, such as *"Bismillah ir rahman ir rahim"*—"In the name of God, the Merciful, the Compassionate." This phrase, which begins every sura, or chapter, of the Qur'an, invests meaning into every endeavor. Muslims utter it when beginning anything—a meal, a trip, a visit with a friend, when entering a room or a mosque—as a way of remaining mindful of the One True God. Any reference to the Prophet, spoken or written, is followed immediately by an honorific phrase: "Peace be upon him," in English sometimes shortened to "pbuh" in parentheses. With words of prayer and honor at the ready at every turn of the day, Muslims hope that every day will be a God-conscious one.

century and continued well into the 13th. Over time the locus of Islamic power shifted from Medina to Damascus and then to Baghdad, and an Islamic culture flourished.

As Islam spread and developed, early Muslims sought to apply their religion to the realities of their lives, to more clearly determine what they should do as well as to limit the powers of their rulers. The Qur'an and the circulating stories about the Sunnah, or practices, of Muhammad did not provide a code of law comprehensive or specific enough to cover the issues arising as Islam spread into many different countries and cultures. In time legal scholars came to distinguish between *Shariah* (the "right" or "straight" path, the "guide")—the divine law that comes from revelation and is found in the Qur'an—and in the Sunnah of the Prophet—and *fiqh,* laws reached through human interpretation. Islamic law, then, was the product of sacred scripture and human interpretation, developed to serve as the ideal blueprint for society. For generations after the death of the Prophet, Islamic law grew and evolved. Major schools of legal thought originated in the lively centers of Islamic culture. Traditionalists in Medina emphasized the revealed texts. Rationalists, centered in Kufa and Basra, Iraq, relied more on reasoning to articulate law. By the end of the first millennium, four distinct schools of thought evolved from among many and became dominant: the Hanafi school, found today in Jordan, Lebanon, Turkey, Afghanistan, and farther east; the Maliki in Islamic North Africa, Bahrain, and Kuwait; and the Shafii and Hanbali schools in Saudi Arabia and areas of the Gulf. Diverse geographic and cultural differences and customs in contract and inheritance law, crimes and punishments, and dress requirements for women are reflected in the differing interpretations of the Shariah. Since the late 20th century, Muslim lawyers and scholars have convened international discussions aimed to consolidate and unify Islamic law.

Sufism, or mystical Islam, presented an alternative to the question of how to better understand the wisdom of the Qur'an and the Prophet Muhammad. The word Sufi comes from the Arabic *suf,* wool, for the simple coarse, woolen garments worn by early mystics. Sufis were concerned about the new wealth and excesses that accompanied imperial expansion and rule, and its focus on this world rather than the next. They emphasized the importance of a spiritual life of piety, fasting, and prayer. Sufis stressed the spirit over the letter, seeking to experience enlightenment or the presence of God. In place of intellectual or legal understanding, they followed a more mystical path, based on ascetic practice and devotion to God.

Inspired personalities rose to positions of leadership, and each became a sheikh, or founder, of a separate Sufi order. The 13th-century Persian poet Jalal al-din Rumi, born in Balkh, Persia, is best known for his lyrical love poetry. He inspired the Mawlawyiwah order, also known as Whirling Dervishes, whose members wore full skirts that spread wide as they danced in endless circles, chanting verses of the Qur'an and seeking to attain an ecstatic state. From the Middle East, Sufism spread in all directions. Its distinctive blend of mystical symbolism, ecstatic engagement, and ascetic devotion still attracts converts today.

Eventually, geographical spread brought technical advances. Troops and traders from China's T'ang empire had been pushing westward through Tibet into Central Asia. By 750, the Chinese had conquered Kashmir and Kabul. In July 751, Muslims moving northeast into the same mountainous territory met 30,000 Chinese troops near the Talas River in today's Kyrgyzstan. A Muslim victory brought that territory under the banner of Islam, set the western limit of Chinese occupation, and opened up routes of trade between the Far East and the Arab world. Chinese prisoners taught their captors the art of making paper out of plant fibers. Muslim craftsmen began to make fine paper in Samarkand, a strategic city on the Silk Road in today's Uzbekistan. Muslim travelers carried the technology to Damascus and Baghdad, and from there into Europe.

OPPOSITE: Science and scholarship flourished under the Abbasid caliphs of the 8th to 13th century, Islam's golden age.

Samarkand was home to Ismail al-Bukhari, the great Islamic scholar, of Prophetic traditions, *hadith*, which were narrative stories about the teachings of the Prophet. Al-Bukhari identified and put together a collection of authentic narratives of the Prophet's life and practice. For example, to illustrate permissibility of substituting sand where water was not available to perform ablutions, al-Bukhari cited two of the Prophet's contemporaries who reported that he said, "Passing dusted hands over the face and backs of the hands is sufficient for you." Over a period of 16 years al-Bukhari is said to have collected Prophetic traditions, checked their reliability, and crossreferenced them with the Qur'an. His rules for inclusion established standards or criteria followed by subsequent scholars of Islam. His collection of 2,602 traditions filled nine volumes. Together with a similar anthology by scholar Muslim ibn al-Hajjaj al-Nisaburi, they form the central core of the hadith, second only to the Qur'an as the sacred literature of Sunni Islam.

THE CITY OF PEACE

THE ARTISTRY and opulence admired in the great mosques today dates back to the age of the caliphs. Al-Walid, last of the Umayyad caliphs, rebuilt the mosque of Medina to match the grandeur of the Great Mosque that he had built in Damascus. He sent artisans from Byzantium and Egypt, and materials such as gold slabs, and tiles of glass, marble, and other colored stone. To the dismay of the residents of Medina, he razed Muhammad's home and garden, which caused a wall of his mausoleum to collapse and revealed some of its contents. A more solid structure was built to secure

the sanctity of the tomb. The new mosque included a colonaded courtyard. Interior walls were decorated with gold and mosaics in intricate designs intertwining with graceful Arabic calligraphy in a style that inspired the English word "arabesque." Stonemasons built a bench with an arrow carved into it, then placed it where Muhammad was believed to have sat in prayer and pointed the arrow toward Mecca. This essential feature evolved into the *mihrab,* an ornamented niche in the mosque's interior wall oriented so that when believers face it, they are facing Mecca.

Similar aesthetics came into play near the ruins of Ctesiphon, capital of the overthrown Sassanian Empire, when the Abbasid caliphs moved into the town of Baghdad in the eighth century. They established the glorious City of Peace, from which art, science, and literature poured throughout the next five centuries. Baghdad was designed as a circle with three concentric city walls. The caliph's palace stood in the center, with army quarters surrounding it. Citizens lived inside the next ring and merchants traded outside the city wall. Here from 786 to 809 ruled Harun al-Rashid, the caliph whose ruthlessness turned to fascination, thanks to the young wife who told him bedtime tales. Their story lives forever in the book *alf Layla wa Layla,* known to the world as *The Thousand and One Arabian Nights.* The Abassid Palace in Baghdad, near the North Gate of the old city wall, dates to the 12th century. Nothing remains of the original caliph's palace.

Here the House of Wisdom, Bayt al-Hikmah, was founded in 830: it was a lively center of scholarship and science, perhaps the greatest educational center in the world at that time. The great books of science, literature and

OPPOSITE: The Qaraouine, foreground, and Moulay Idris II mosques rise above the urban clutter of Fez, Morocco.
ABOVE: A popular symbol in Moorish art, the bronze hand of Fatima pays tribute to Muhammad's daughter.
FOLLOWING PAGES: Mud-walled masterpiece, a 14th-century mosque in Djenne, Mali, attests to the spread of Islam to Africa.

philosophy from other areas and cultures were collected and translated. Muslim scholars then built upon the wisdom of the past. Studying ancient mathematical works from Greek and Sanskrit, scholars in Baghdad advanced mathematics, developing the numeral system used around the world today. Plato and Aristotle's philosophy, Galen and Hippocrates' medicine, Euclid's geometry, and Ptolemy's astronomy—all were incorporated into the body of learning by the scholars of Bayt al-Hikmah.

A prominent scholar of this period, Ibn Sina, known in the West as Avicenna, lived and worked in tenth-century Baghdad. His medical text remained the standard in the Middle East and Europe for centuries. At one point the city registered 800 pharmacists. Scientists here compiled a world atlas, envisioned a round globe, and measured the solar year and a degree of terrestrial latitude. In the period of European history designated the Dark Ages, Baghdad was a dynamic center of culture. Thinkers and artists drew

inspiration from the ancient Greeks and the Buddhists, the Persians and the Chinese.

Great advances in science and mathematics took place during the Abassid caliphate. In ninth-century Baghdad, Abu Abdullah Muhammad bin Musa al-Khwarizmi published his treatise on "compulsion and comparison," which introduced *al-jabr*—algebra—to the world. The anglicized form of his name, al-Khwarizmi, gives us the word "algorithm." He also published tables for the movements of the sun, moon, and five planets.

A younger Muslim astronomer in Baghdad, Thabit ibn Qurra, studied not only al-Khwarizmi but also recent Arabic translations of Ptolemy and Euclid. He devised an elegant analysis of the rotation of heavenly bodies, the world's first mathematical description of motion.

Muslims living hundreds or thousands of miles from Arabia needed to orient themselves in prayer toward Mecca. Building on these many scientific advances, Islamic astronomers, cartographers, and engineers published manuals and devised portable instruments to pinpoint the proper direction.

Expeditions into North Africa led to the founding of another great institution of learning. In the seventh century, Islam had established a foothold in Egypt at the garrison of al-Fustat. In 969, a general in the caliph's army—a slave from Sicily who had earned his freedom by converting to Islam—founded a new city farther north. He named it Cairo, al-Qahira, triumphant warrior. Much of Cairo's historic Islamic buildings still stand, protected as a UNESCO World Heritage Site. Visitors can climb up the two minarets of Bab Zuweila, the last gate of the old city wall, and visit the mosque and madrasa of al-Azhar. Competing only with Qaraouine in Fez, Morocco, as the world's oldest university, al-Azhar now runs 61 schools at every educational level and educates more than one million students a year.

As Islamic culture flourished, its vast territory began to fracture. Threats from outside—particularly the Seljuks from the southern coast of Turkey and later the Mongols from Central Asia—compounded with internal pressure from newly emerging indigenous groups, meant the decline of the caliphate-centered culture of Islam. By 1095, though, when the first Christian crusaders took up arms against Islam, a rich Muslim culture was firmly established in many parts of North Africa and Central Asia, starting points for the continuing spread of the religion.

ISLAM IN AFRICA

A MAP of Islam's predominance in Africa today tells much of the story of how religion traveled into the continent. Muslims represent more than 90 percent of the population in the nations of Northern Africa, from Mauritania to Egypt, reflecting a spread westward from the Middle East. Muslims represent about half of the population in the band

of nations just south—from Senegal and Guinea to Ethiopia. The exception here is Somalia, primarily Muslim, which early Islamic traders reached by sea. The proportion in the population of Central and South African nations drops significantly, to less than one percent in the southwest countries of Angola and Namibia. Throughout most of the Maghreb—Arabic for "west," meaning the area west of the Middle East: Morocco, Algeria, and Tunisia—Islam became an active part of culture through trade and intellectual influence, migration, and intermarriage.

By 700, Muslims had traversed all of North Africa by land and sea, following routes established by the Berbers, who lived along the Atlas Mountains, a 1,500-mile-long chain that parallels the coast in Morocco, Algeria, and Tunisia. Soon the wealth and cultural influence of the caliphs infused cities on or near the coastline. Cairo, Tunis, Tlemcen in Algeria, Fez and Marrakech in Morocco all became important centers of Islamic learning and art. Political and doctrinal issues complicated relations between Berbers and Muslims, but ultimately the Berbers embraced the faith of Islam as well, spreading the word and founding mosques and communities deeper into Africa. Using established routes that penetrated the Sahara, Muslim traders and scholars began to influence the rulers of West African kingdoms, from powerful Mali and Songhay to tiny Bornu.

As Muslims moved into Africa, they did not actively engage in missionary work. Sometimes they established their own communities outside existing towns. Often they established ties with regional rulers, offering a code of law and administrative structures that appealed to those enlarging their domains. Mali's 13th-century emperor Sundiata and Songhay's 15th-century king Sonni Ali both declared their Muslim faith. Ruling lands where the people still practiced indigenous nature and spirit religions, they turned to those practices from time to time even though they also prayed to Allah. Sundiata's great-nephew, Mansa Musa, a later king

OPPOSITE: The Dome of the Rock Mosque draws Muslims to Jerusalem, Islam's third holiest city after Mecca and Medina.
FOLLOWING PAGES: Spiritual graffiti, palm prints on a wall in Essaouira, Morocco, honor Muhammad's daughter Fatima.

of Mali, impressed the Muslim world with his extravagant pilgrimage to Mecca in 1324. According to an Arab historian, his entourage included 100 camels, each carrying 300 pounds of gold; 500 slaves, each hoisting a staff of gold; and his wife with 500 attendants. For himself, he brought along 14,000 slave girls. He was so profligate during the journey, the value of gold dropped in Egypt.

Mansa Musa poured his energy and devotion into building his cities into centers of Islamic learning. In Timbuktu, a university was built in the vicinity of three great *masajid,* the local word for mosques. Its buildings, still standing today, are typical of African mosques of the Middle Ages. Made of mud brick, they have flat, unadorned surfaces. Wooden beams protruding from exterior walls support scaffolding when repairs are needed. In the 12th century, 25,000 students attended the university. By the middle of the 16th century, more than 150 madrasas in the city of Timbuktu alone served other Africans eager to study the Qur'an and the hadith.

When Muslims were moving into Africa, a large number of those living in Nubia and Ethiopia were devout Christians. Islam entered this region later and more slowly than North, West, and Central Africa. But Dahlak Kebir, the largest island in the archipelago off today's Eritrea, in the Red Sea, became a Muslim stronghold. Slaves were moved out of Africa and into Arabia through this island; Islamic prayers and ideas moved in the other direction. Arab navigators established an Indian Ocean harbor that became Somalia's capital city, Mogadishu. By the early 14th century, it was, according to one observer, "an enormous town," its inhabitants primarily merchants who "have many camels, of which they slaughter hundreds every day for food." Visitors arriving by boat were met with the same hospitality typical of Arabians a millennium before.

"When a vessel reaches the port, it is met by sumbuqs, which are small boats, in each of which are a number of young men, each carrying a covered dish containing food. He presents this to one of the merchants on the ship, saying "This is my guest," . . . then sells his goods for him and

buys for him, and if anyone buys anything from him at too low a price, or sells to him in the absence of his host, the sale is regarded by them as invalid. This practice is of great advantage to them." This description comes from Ibn Battuta, a 14th-century traveler whose pilgrimage to Mecca, from his Tangier birthplace in Morocco, turned into a 30-year journey. He is considered the only person to have visited all Muslim lands of his age. He left behind his *Rihala,* or *Travels,* which offers fascinating insights into a broad world stretching from Constantinople to Ceylon, Mombasa to Beijing. In Mogadishu, he recounted a Friday visit to the mosque built by Fakhr ad-Din, the city's first sultan. He walked from the mosque to the palace with the sultan, whose head was shaded by slaves carrying "four canopies of colored silk, each surmounted by a golden bird."

Other Muslim explorers, sailing west from North Africa in 710, reached a rocky island in a crucial strait, the entrance from the Atlantic Ocean to the Mediterranean Sea. The next year a Berber Muslim, Tariq ibn Ziyad, led a force of thousands onto the island, claiming it for Islam. Called Jabal Tariq, Tariq's Mountain, the name soon elided into Gibraltar. Spain was only a short sail away.

Sijilmasa—Rissani, Morocco, today—was a key oasis and market town, the northern distribution center for West African gold. Muslim factions fought over it for centuries. In 1054, it was conquered by an Islamic Berber tribe, the Almoravids, from the lands now called Mauritania. From Sijilmasa they launched campaigns into Spain. Their tribal name, shortened to "Moor," became the moniker in Christian Europe for all Muslims, and especially for the Muslim culture that flourished in southern Spain.

THE MIDDLE EAST

FROM THEIR first travels out of Arabia, Muslims sought to move north. Early outings in the seventh century saw migrations and battles through Palestine and into Syria. The city of Constantinople glowed before them, a citadel of size and magnificence. Christianity was the religion of power,

with its absolute sense of heresy: Anyone who refused to believe in Christ was an infidel, whether pagan, Jewish, or Muslim. Guilty of capital crimes according to a decree of Roman Emperor Theodosius in 382, heretics could lawfully be captured or banished. Some Christians believed they could and should be killed. In Islam, as in Christianity, actions did not always correspond with revelations. According to the Qur'an, violence and warfare were justified only in defense of one's religion, not as a means to conquer. The Qur'an interpreted King David's slaying of Goliath as a righteous act to cleanse the world of evil: "If Allah had not repelled some men by others, the earth would have been corrupted." On the other hand, the Qur'an stresses that "there is no compulsion in religion." Much of history attests to Muslims' tolerance for other faiths within their lands.

One of the earliest battles resulting in Muslim occupation of lands beyond Arabia occurred in the Holy Land in the time of the first caliph, Abu Bakr. Word of Muslims moving north reached Byzantine Emperor Heraclius, situated in Antioch. He recruited his brother, Theodore, to lead forces south, but that leadership came to a swift end in July 634 as Theodore was killed in the two armies' first encounter, at Ajnadeen, southwest of Jerusalem. After another skirmish, the Christians retreated to the city of Damascus. Heraclius mustered forces from allied states. They numbered 200,000, according to an Arab account of the time, and were many times the size of the Muslim army, which included brave women as well as men. The two sides met on the Yarmuk River, a tributary of the Jordan. The battle, according to al-Baladhuri, "was of the fiercest and bloodiest kind.... By

ABOVE: *The ceiling of the Alhambra Palace in Granada, Spain, is testimony to the Moors' splendid art and architecture.*
FOLLOWING PAGES: *When Christians recaptured Granada, Muslims took refuge in the mountains of southeastern Spain.*

MY FAITH, MY SUSTAINING GUIDE

—HIBBA ABUGIDEIRI, *George Washington University*

AT THE end of the first course I taught on women in the modern Middle East and North Africa, I asked the class of predominantly female students if any would like to live in the Arab world—my area of specialization and place of birth. Other than the two who said they would not mind a visit, none raised their hand. As we discussed their reasons, I discovered that they understood my question not in terms of where they would live, but of how they would live as women. None wanted to live as a Muslim woman. It dawned on me that after three months of studying the complex issues facing Muslim women, whether the veil, personal-status laws, common regional government structures and policies, or employment laws, the picture that I had left them with was dismal. I had failed as a professor, and worse, as a Muslim woman professor.

In challenging the thesis of Muslim women's oppression as more historically exceptional than other women's oppression globally, or highlighting the critical role that secular variables, added to the suspected Islamic ones, have played in creating the problems faced by Muslim women, I had reified a stereotype: Muslim women were oppressed. Somewhere in that statement was the culprit: Islam.

And then it hit me. What was missing in our discussion was the invisible yet mediating role that culture plays in reconciling women to their realities. Most of us do not question that American women are liberated in our consumerist society, which nonetheless depends, in a primordial way, on women's bodies to sell cars, beer, and music. So how could I make visible those intangible aspects of Muslim culture that in mitigating power relations, bring distinction to Islam and its female believers: hospitality, generosity, respect for elders, adoration of children, a strong sense of community, enduring social ties, and family loyalty? How could I give texture to the way Muslim cultures engender a sense of pride in a woman, especially as a mother? How could I make tangible that elusive but powerful sense of belonging, of identity, that only culture can endow? How could I explain the role that faith has played in the lives of women who find inspiration in Islam as a way to redress their personal and societal challenges? Somehow

ABOVE: Worshiping apart from men, women celebrate the end of Ramadan, the Islamic month of fasting.

I had failed to translate the critical dimensions that faith has played in my own identity as an American-Muslim woman. Yet faith has been Muslim women's common sustaining guide of "negotiating patriarchy."

As a child, growing up in the suburbs of Indianapolis, Indiana, I learned in Islamic Sunday school the names of the prophets. They are the examples the Qur'an beseeches Muslims to emulate. I heard about Abraham's willingness to sacrifice his son, of Moses parting the sea, of Jesus healing the sick, and of Muhammad's exemplary community in Medina. These stories, while entertaining to a child with a vast imagination, pointed to a lesson that was not to be forgotten: that God's appointed messengers, despite their trials, remained constant in their belief in His Oneness, and so should we.

Muslims, whether Sunday school teachers or imams, have upheld a view that the prophets, all of whom were male, are models for all to follow. But what about the female archetypes found in the Qur'an: Mary, Bilquis (the Queen of Sheba), and Pharaoh's wife? Are not their stories also about faith in God? Why is their God-consciousness not exemplary to all Muslims? These questions are not benign when considering that, while giving a respected place to wives and mothers in its interpretation of women's roles, orthodoxy has quietly hushed the voices of those women in God's revelation who teach all Muslims lessons about faith, not gender, about steadfastness, not reproduction. Consequently, Muslim women are glorified with, at best, conditional orthodoxical sanction of non-domestic roles.

The Qur'an does not speak only to men. It speaks, quite explicitly, to women. I knew this at a young age, not because I read the Qur'an, but because I talked to God all the time. I knew with certainty that He responded. Maybe this spiritual consciousness was the result of my Sufi ancestry; my grandfather and father were Sufis of the popular Tijaniyyah

order in Sudan. Sufism has historically welcomed women's spiritual connection to God. Or maybe it was because it never occurred to me that my gender could impede a relationship with God. Those conversations taught me that intellect was connected to faith. As an adult, I found it unreasonable that God would prefer men to women in anything, but especially in terms of worshiping Him.

I am not alone in this belief. Muslim women all over the world, despite differing circumstances, have sought refuge in their faith in Him, which reflects their belief that Islam is not to blame; its restrictive, even distorted interpretations are. Knowledge, and Qur'anic literacy, are key to their empowerment—a dynamic that is reminiscent of Muhammad's encounter with Gabriel, who commanded him to recite, to read. Faith and knowledge are inextricably bound in worship. This kind of faith is not passive. It has inspired what I believe is a global women's movement, though silently underway. Although there are no historical connections between women in different parts of the Muslim world that make up this "movement," many—from Egypt, Jordan, Morocco, Sudan, Turkmenistan, Kazakhstan, and Uzbekistan—have found in their faith not only a guide, but a powerful source of contestation. Many groups (which also include men) are calling for a reinterpretation of the Qur'an in hopes of expanding what has been a rigid orthodoxical space for women. Their goal is gender justice. This contemporary "gender jihad" is a struggle, not against men, but for Islamic gender parity. This struggle binds women to the archetypal figures of the Qur'an—both male and female: In the face of hardship, they seek refuge in Him alone.

I love being a Muslim woman, with all the perfections of His Creation and the imperfections of Muslim practice. Because I have what counts most: faith that He is the One; and I am proudly His servant.

Allah's help, some 70,000 [of Heraclius' men] were put to death, and their remnants took to flight." Jews of the region, according to an Arab account, welcomed their conquerors, saying, "We like your rule and justice far better than the state of oppression and tyranny in which we were." Muslims remember the martyrs who died or lost sight or limbs for victory.

From the Yarmuk, it was a short march to Jerusalem, which Muslims already considered their holy city because of Muhammad's Night Journey to the Temple Mount on his way to heaven. The entry into the city was relatively peaceful. According to a tenth-century Christian historian, Umar, the second caliph, assured the citizens that under his rule "their lives, possessions, and churches" would be secure and the churches "would neither be destroyed nor made into dwellings." Umar asked Sophronius, the regional Christian bishop, for a place to build a mosque. The patriarch said, "I will give you a place where you can build a mosque, a place where the emperors of Rome would not allow anything to be built. At this place can be found the rock where God spoke to Jacob and which Jacob called the gate of heaven. Jews called it the holy of holies and it is in the middle of the earth. The temple of the Jews once stood there and Jews venerated it. Wherever they were when they prayed they turned their faces to it. I will show you this place on the condition that you write a document that only this one mosque will be built in Jerusalem."

Scholars have pointed out that 13th-century version projects back to an earlier time of an urbane civility that may not have existed between Muslim and Christian leaders in 636. Muslim accounts state that Umar asked to be shown the site of the Temple of David and Solomon. Sophronius showed him two places that he knew were wrong. "You are lying," Umar is believed to have said, "for the Messenger [Muhammad] described to me the Sanctuary of David and this is not it." The site of the Temple, last renovated by Herod, had been flattened by the Romans in 70 A.D., and both chroniclers describe it as a dung-heap. With the approval of Sophronius, Umar oversaw the construction of a mosque there, using stones strewn about during the disassembly of Herod's Temple. It was named al-Masjid el-Aqsa, the Farthest Mosque, shortened to al-Aqsa.

Al-Aqsa was the start of a Muslim holy site in Jerusalem, which grew to 35 acres of grounds, gardens, and buildings including the famous Dome of the Rock. The sanctuary plan provides a virtual history of Islam in Jerusalem. Umar built an entrance to the sanctuary from the west: massive structural gates with parallel passageways through either Bab ar-Rahmah, the Door of Mercy, or Bab at-Tawba, the Door of Repentance. At the south end, Umar built a mosque big enough for 3,000 worshipers. Not 50 years later, in 685, Caliph Abdal-Malik ibn Marwan sited a second mosque to the north. He built the Dome of the Rock, so called because its central dome arcs 115 feet tall over a rock that protrudes from the floor—the very rock, Muslims say, where Muhammad was greeted by Abraham, Moses, and Jesus and from which Jibril led him up to heaven. With the completion of the Dome of the Rock, the al-Aqsa Mosque was enlarged to nearly double capacity. The open-air Dome of the Chain marks the exact center of the sanctuary and may have replaced a building that predated al-Aqsa. To level the southeast corner, a vaulted passageway was built below the sanctuary in the eighth century.

Growing numbers of the faithful required several mosque expansions up to 1033 A.D. The Dome of al-Nahawiah was built in 1207 as a school of literature. In the 16th century, Ottoman Emperor Suleiman installed stunning mosaics, predominantly a cerulean blue, in the ceiling of the Dome of the Rock. In elegant Arabic script the tiles spell out *Ya Sin*, one of the Prophet's names found in a verse from the Qur'an: "By the wise Qur'an. You are truly one of the Messengers. Upon a straight path. It is the Revelation of the All-Mighty, the Merciful. To warn a people, whose fathers were not warned and so they are heedless." The dome's gold exterior has recently been restored. Two mosques were joined in 1922 to form the Islamic Museum, the oldest museum in Jerusalem, displaying holy books and artifacts from the 11th century to the 20th.

ISLAM IN EUROPE

MUSLIM SAILING vessels transported their people and their message to the islands of the Mediterranean during the seventh century. They landed in Sicily in 652, but not until 831 did the citizens of Palermo surrender, leading to a treaty between Byzantines and Muslims more than a century later. Norman invaders planted their banner of Christianity in Sicily in the 11th century, but they respected the Muslim presence. In the early 12th century the Norman King Roger II of Sicily commissioned al-Sharif al-Idrisi al-Qurtubi to draw a map of the world. Placing south at the top of the page, al-Idrisi created a revolutionarily accurate rendering of the Middle East, North Africa, Europe, and Central Asia. He also created the *Kitab Nuzhat al-Mushtaq,* known as "The Book of Roger": a silver disk with a map of the world encased in a celestial sphere. To this day, street names and layout in the city center of Palermo recall its Arab past. The Norman palace is often called il Cassaro, from the Arabic *al-qasr,* fortress.

Thanks to Tariq and the Berbers of Africa—considered mawali, converted clients of the Arabs—followers of Muhammad crossed the Strait of Gibraltar and entered Spain, then under the rule of Visigoths, Germanic invaders who had set up a regional capital in Toulouse, France. Sometimes battling and sometimes migrating, the Muslims under Tariq moved north through Andalusia, as they called Spain. Their advance meant the defeat of Roderick, the last Visigoth ruler in Spain. In less than a decade, they had overtaken the entire Iberian Peninsula.

As they reached the Pyrenees, the Muslims began to face French resistance. The Muslims won a battle with the Franks at Toulouse but were defeated in 733 in Tours by Charles Martel. In 778 Martel's grandson, Charlemagne, led an expedition into the Pyrenees. He had turned back toward France when Basques native to the region, antagonistic to both the Muslims and the Franks, attacked his forces at the Roncesvalles Pass between Pamplona, Spain, and St.-Jean-Pied-de-Port, France. This battle went down in history thanks to the French epic, *La Chanson du Roland.* Charlemagne's will did not slacken, though, and by 801 he had pushed the Muslim border south of the Ebro River.

A glorious Muslim civilization flourished in southern Spain for the next seven centuries. In the 780s Abd al Rahman, grandson of a caliph of Damascus, escaped Muslim infighting in Syria and fled to Cordoba, Spain, where he built the city's Great Mosque, probably on the site of a Roman temple. Although renovated by Muslims and then transformed into a Christian cathedral in subsequent centuries, the Great Mosque of Cordoba still evokes the mystery of a Moorish house of prayer. Rows of pillars topped with slightly pointed archways recede into the distance, echoed by citrus trees planted in the Patio de las Naranjas, the Court of Oranges. Muslims, Jews, and Christians lived together in Cordoba. The early caliphs of Cordoba exemplified tolerance, but tenth-century leader Abu Amir al-Mansur, called by Spaniards Almanzor, waged campaigns against Christians and their churches.

Scholars and scientists gathered in Cordoba. Abbas ibn Firnas built mechanical wings and attempted human flight, 600 years before Leonardo da Vinci, and constructed a mechanical planetarium, complete with synthesized thunder and lightning. Cordoban geographers created atlases of Spain, North Africa, the Arabian Peninsula, and the world. Significant contributions to the history of philosophy came from 12th-century Cordoban scholar Ibn Rushd, also known by his Latin name, Averroës. He served as physician to the caliphs but is better known for his commentaries on the works of Aristotle and the *Republic* of Plato. He argued that religion and philosophy sought the same end but that reason led more certainly to truth than did revelation—a claim that alienated him from some Muslim clerics.

The elegant splendor of Spanish Islam reached its pinnacle in Granada, in the complex of buildings and gardens known as the Alhambra. Granada was the seat of the one remaining Muslim kingdom in Andalusia. First built on a hilltop as a ninth-century fortress, the Alhambra, beginning in 1238, was embellished into a palace and

mosque, with surrounding gardens and courtyards, the whole amounting to a small walled city. Its many towers provide ample views of the graceful Andalusian countryside. Labyrinthine walkways lead to breathtaking spaces for living, meeting, and worship. The fragrance of myrtle and orange blossoms and the sound of falling water fill the air. Verses of the Qur'an are carved into stone walls; brilliantly colorful mosaic tiling filigrees the walls.

As these opulent quarters were being built, Christian efforts to recapture Spain picked up momentum, driven by the same religious fervor that was fueling the crusaders on their eastward mission to recapture the Holy Land. Christian forces were amassing in the north, beginning their successful sweep through Spain. Cordoba fell to Christians in 1236, Seville in 1248. Moorish leaders remained in power, sequestered inside the Alhambra, for another 250 years. The marriage of Ferdinand and Isabella strengthened Spain as

a Christian nation. They gained control of Granada in 1491 and moved into the Alhambra. From there they commissioned Christopher Columbus to explore the New World. In the same month, January 1492, they published the famous Alhambra Decree of 1492, expelling all Jews and Muslims from Spain. Rabbi Isaac ben Judah Abravanel replied to the edict, asserting the dominion of his people as God's chosen but also condemning the Christian rulers' disregard for Moorish culture. "Yes, you have humbled the Moslem infidel with the force of your army," wrote Abravanel, but added, "by what authority do churchmen now want to burn the immense Arabic library of this great Moorish palace and destroy its priceless manuscripts? In your heart of hearts, you distrust the power of knowledge, and you respect only power." Despite the expulsion of Muslims in the 15th century, their influence remains in the art and architecture, spirit and culture of Andalusian Spain.

THE SELJUK TURKS

AS ISLAM spread, leadership struggles weakened its homeland. Divisiveness between Shiite and Sunni Muslims grew more bitter at the same time that nomads from Turkey, members of the Seljuk tribe and recent converts to Islam, began moving into Iran. They concentrated their power in Isfahan, a city in central Iran. Caravan routes coming from the northwest, the southwest, and the south intersected at this oasis. From there in 1055, Seljuk Turks moved on to claim Baghdad, then fanned out to the west, gaining control of lands in Armenia and southern Turkey and in Syria, Palestine, and Egypt. Outsiders to some of the dynastic conflicts between Arab Muslims, the Seljuk Turks espoused Sunni Islam over Shiite. Over time, they planted Islam firmly into many new territories, especially Turkey and Central Asia as far as the Hindu Kush.

A new wave of invaders from Central Asia challenged Islam in the 13th century. The Mongol warrior Hüleii, grandson of Genghis Khan and brother of Kublai Khan, intended to uphold the family tradition and conquer lands from Persia to the Mediterranean and the Nile. Now the Muslims faced a different threat from that posed by the Seljuks, for Hulegu practiced pagan shamanism, despite strong influences on him from the Nestorian Christian tradition. Leading a cavalry of thousands, he stormed through Muslim territory, vandalizing graves and shrines. His troops confronted a Shiite sect known as the Assassins, sending their survivors into hiding in the area that is modern Pakistan. In 1258, Hüleii conquered Baghdad.

While the Seljuks and Mongols were invading the Middle East, Christian crusaders were traveling in that same direction from all over Europe, determined to wrest what they considered their Holy Land from control of the Muslim infidels. Their mission was driven by political motives as well. Roman and Byzantine leaders united against the Seljuks' effective takeovers in Turkey and Eastern Europe. The First Crusade ended in 1099 as the Christians climaxed a five-week siege by capturing Jerusalem. A French eyewitness later described how Muslims tried to hide in their temples, but they were "unable to escape from our gladiators. Many fled to the roof of the temple of Solomon [the al-Aqsa Mosque], and were shot with arrows, so that they fell to the ground dead. In this temple almost ten thousand were killed." Having accomplished their goal, the Christians retreated.

In the late 1140s a new Muslim leader arose. Born in Tikrit, Saladin was a Sunni Muslim and a member of the Kurdish tribe still predominant at the border of Turkey and northern Iraq. Under the Seljuk Turks, he defended Egypt during the early Crusades, then claimed power from the reigning Shiite caliph and began building a sultanate headquartered in Cairo. He reconquered Jerusalem in 1187, prompting European monarchs to stage a Third Crusade. England's Richard I, called the Lion-Hearted, defeated Saladin in battles at Cyprus and at Acre and Arsuf along the coast of Palestine. He failed to take back Jerusalem, but Saladin allowed Christians to visit the city on pilgrimage.

In this time of shifting politics and constant attacks from outside, the arts of Islam flourished. Ghiyath al-Din Abul-Fath Umar ibn Ibrahim al-Nisaburi al-Khayyami lived in Nishapur, a town in today's northeastern Iraq where the salt desert abuts the Binalud Mountains. A mathematician who published books on geometry and algebra, he is better known as Omar Khayyám, the author of the *Rubáiyát,* a collection of poems written in the early 12th century. His hometown was a center of art and commerce and a welcome oasis on the trade route. There glassblowers advanced their craft and perfected the art of fusing beads of colored glass into kaleidoscopic designs.

Regional warlords in the west of Turkey began chafing against the ruling Seljuks by the late 13th century, their

OPPOSITE: *Shiite Muslims weep to touch the silver bars on the tomb of Caliph Iman Reza in Mashhad, Iran.*
FOLLOWING PAGES: *Spinning toward bliss, Sufi mystics called Whirling Dervishes twirl like tops while chanting Qur'anic verses.*

restlessness leading to the growing power of the Ottoman Empire. Ertugrul Ghazi's ventures initiated the new regime. From Söğüt, 75 miles southeast of the Sea of Marmara, Ghazi and his army rode triumphantly north into Bursa, across the Straits of Gallipoli, then through Bulgaria, Macedonia, and the northern edge of Greece, collecting lands along the way. He claimed Serbia through a victory at the Battle of Kosovo in 1389. His son Osman, for whom the empire was to be named, expanded the family's territory, as did Osman's son Orhan, who conquered Nicaea—Iznik in Turkish. The dynasty remained in power, expanding its territory to the west and south, gathering up all that had been part of Byzantium. Finally Mehmet II, seventh in the line of Ottoman rulers, conquered the Byzantine capital itself in 1453. By 1580 the Ottoman Muslims possessed lands that virtually equaled the old Roman Empire. Christian Constantinople had become Islamic Istanbul.

In triumph, Mehmet II ordered the construction of an Ottoman palace where, in the sixth century, Emperor Justinian had sited his Byzantine palace overlooking the Sea of Marmara. On this same site, Mehmet II built Topkapi, his "palace of felicity." Just across the Bosporus Strait, the city's Jewish district had repopulated in the 1490s, since Mehmet II invited refugees expelled during the Inquisition to come to Istanbul. Topkapi became a citadel with imperial residences, administrative buildings including several treasuries, mosques with minarets, courtyards with fountains, and gardens with private pavilions. Four palaces were built within a decade. Grand gates—of note the Bab-i H'mayum, the Imperial Gate, with its spired watchtowers and crenellated entry wall—provided points of entry.

The crowning glory of Ottoman Istanbul was the transformation of Constantine's Hagia Sofia, the Church of Holy Wisdom, into the imperial mosque, center of the city's religious life. Since 1934 the building has been a museum and, since a 1993 UNESCO mission to inspect the building, it has undergone major renovation and repair, including removal of the plaster that Muslim occupants used to cover the main dome's Christian ceiling mosaics. The Ottomans built many other mosques in the city, notably the Blue Mosque, by Ahmet I near Hagia Sofia as a new imperial mosque in the early 17th century. Its name comes from its interior blue tile work. Towering over all are the mosque and attendant buildings commanded by Sulëyman in the 16th century. Sulëyman was the last great conquering emperor, gaining territory in North Africa, Eastern Europe, Iraq, and in isolated regions of East Africa and Arabia, including Mecca, Medina, and Yemen. At the same time, he solidified the central governing structure from Istanbul. He hired the renowned Ottoman architect Mimar Koca Sinan to build a new imperial palace. The central mosque piles dome upon dome, building to the center, with four minaret spires spaced symmetrically around it. The complex also incorporated four madrasas, a medical school, and a school of Sunnah study—a centralized, state-run multiversity.

The Ottoman Empire reached its peak during Sulëyman's reign, from 1520 to 1566. At its largest, the empire stretched from Hungary to the Crimea, from Turkey to the Caspian Sea and the Zagros Mountains of Persia, and from west of Algiers along the north coast of Africa to the Sinai. Istanbul became the largest and richest city of Europe, and the empire controlled other important ports and trading centers. Ottoman naval bases were located at Algiers in Algeria, Alexandria and Suez in Egypt, Basra in Iraq, Rhodes and Kavalli in Greece, with shipyards on the Mediterranean and the Black Sea. Through Damascus, controlled by Ottomans, traveled caravans and Muslim pilgrims. Out of Ottoman-controlled Cairo came coffee and fragrances via Yemen, spices and fabric from India, and elegant rugs from North Africa. With the rise of European colonialism and sea trade, the Netherlands, Portugal, and Britain presented economic competition. Military losses in Eastern Europe and the Caucasus collapsed the empire's reach. But not until the aftermath of World War I did the empire disappear altogether. The Turkish republic was founded in 1922, the last caliph deposed in 1924; yet the legacy of Ottoman Islam continues to exert an influence, especially in Turkey, Eastern Europe, and North Africa.

ISLAM IN ASIA

LANDS IN Central Asia came early under the influence of Islam. During the Umayyad caliphate, messengers of Islam traveled east from Medina. With battles in 637 at Al Qadisiya, on the Euphrates, and in 642 at Nehavend, in today's Iran, Islam spread to Afghanistan and Uzbekistan, today's Pakistan, and Punjab and Sind in India. Early on, the caliphs enlisted Syrian warriors and sent them east.

Glorious mosques affirm a continuing Muslim presence in Central Asia. Herat, a city in western Afghanistan, stands along the Hari River in the southern foothills of the Paropamisus Range. In the 13th century Muslims built the magnificent Friday Mosque, still a living house of worship, atop the ruins of a Zoroastrian temple. Situated on the Zeravshan, a tributary of the Oxus River in today's Uzbekistan, Bukhara was a city of learning when the Muslims entered. The new rulers maintained that tradition, building four madrasas between the 16th and 19th centuries. In the 20th century, when this region was part of the Soviet Union, the Communist leaders allowed only two madrasas to continue to operate: the Mir-i Arab in Bukhara and the Kukeldash in Shash, the capital of Fergana, now called Tashkent. Upstream from Bukhara was Samarkand, where Timur, or Tamerlane, ruled. Between the two cities stretched the lush Zeravshan Valley, a part of the Silk Road and a vision

ABOVE: *Named for its interior tiles, Istanbul's Blue Mosque was built to outshine neighboring Hagia Sophia.*

of paradise to Arabs from the desert steppes. According to one tenth-century Iranian author, it was "the most fruitful of all the countries of Allah," full of "the best trees and fruits, in every home are gardens, cisterns, and flowing water."

India and Arabia were trading partners even before the time of Muhammad. Word of Islam traveled with traders and with armed forces entering the region of today's Pakistan. The culture they confronted was thoroughly Hindu, although Buddhism had a strong secondary presence. Afghani warlords moved into these lands from the northwest, sacking temples for gold, in the 11th and 12th centuries. Small sultanates became a part of India's religious and political landscape, especially in the west and south. In 1526 the victory of Babur, a descendant of the Mongol Timur, over a sultan in Delhi marked the start of the Mughal Empire, India's ruling culture until the mid-18th century.

Muslim conquerors wreaked havoc on India's ancient monuments, gradually replacing them with mosques. They built graceful palaces, schools, and bazaars in a distinctive architecture known as the Mughal style, culminating in the Taj Mahal, the splendid mausoleum erected by Shah Jahan for his beloved wife. Hinduism and its caste system influenced the social system of Mughal India. Muslims formed the upper class, the *ashraf,* and enjoyed the most privilege. Upper-caste Hindus who converted to Islam did not rank as highly but still received respect and eventually were included in the ashraf. Indians in the lower castes converted, too, but ranked still lower. Sufi orders drew many converts; their mysticism and fascination with symbolism were in harmony with Hindu and Buddhist ways. Some people feared that their philosophy of passive receptivity weakened the fiber of the Islamic community.

Despite the Mughals' power and the social incentive to convert, only one in four Indians followed Islam in the mid-18th century. About this time the British moved into the subcontinent, turning it into an economic vassal by the 19th century. The Mughal Empire was falling apart.

Hindus more easily fit into the British bureaucracy than Muslims, who responded to their declining influence by urging a return to traditional Islam. Resistance to the British was building throughout India. Muslims debated whether to unite with Buddhists and Hindus against the British, ultimately becoming a permanent minority, or to renew the ideal of an Islamic state.

On August 14, 1947, following independence from Britain, the Muslim nation of East and West Pakistan formally split from India in an event called Partition. Millions of people were uprooted as Muslims fled to Pakistan and Hindus there escaped to India. Today Muslims represent 12 percent of the population in India, 83 percent in Bangladesh—formerly East Pakistan and an independent nation since 1971—and 97 percent in Pakistan.

The ancient seaport of Karachi became the capital of Pakistan, until the 1960s when Islamabad was founded in the far north of the country. An immense mosque—capacity 70,000—was built there in 1976, designed by a Turkish architect and funded by Saudi Arabia's King Faisal. This mosque combines traditional elements, such as pointed minarets and a central prayer hall, with a modern tent-shaped central building instead of the usual dome.

ISLAM IN EAST ASIA

LIKE INDIA, China has ancient ties to the Islamic world, although some doubt that Kingzhen Dasi, the mosque in Xi'an—the central Chinese city long called Chang'an, capital for the Han and Ming dynasties—really dates back to the eighth century, as is often claimed. Perhaps a mosque did stand on this site that long ago, for Muslim traders passed through this cosmopolitan city on the great Silk Road. There is evidence that a strong Muslim community had settled there before the 16th century, for by that time Muslims in Xi'an were writing their commentaries in Chinese, not Arabic or Persian. The architecture of Kingzhen

OPPOSITE: *From a minaret in Greece—as from mosques the world over—a muezzin calls the faithful to prayer.*

Dasi reflects how much Muslims had adapted to their Chinese culture by the 17th century, when its present entrance gate was built. Its overall design is traditionally oriented toward Mecca, but little else draws from the Middle Eastern mosque tradition. The prayer hall and the muezzin's tower feature the upswept rooflines of the Far East. Arabic inscriptions inlaid in the walls extol Allah and quote verses from the Qur'an, but their lettering reflects the verticality of Chinese pictographs rather than the looser horizontal swoops of Arabic. Some 60,000 Muslims worship in this mosque today. Many in China practice a distinctly Chinese form of Islam. Calling themselves Hui, they live in communities throughout most of the country, including Tibet, Mongolia, and neighboring Thailand and Burma. Only recently has a sense of religious identity united them.

Since the 12th century, Arab traders dominated the seaways of the Red Sea, the Persian Gulf, the Arabian Sea, and the Indian Ocean. Arab vessels sailed from Africa and the Middle East around India's southern shores and into the Andaman Sea. By the time Europeans laid claim to the Spice Islands in the 17th and 18th centuries, Islam was the religion both of the leaders and of the people in the region.

Muslims formed settlements and managed the trade in spices, rice, sandalwood, and Sumatran gold. By the

ABOVE: *Built by Shah Jahan as a shrine to lost love, the Taj Mahal epitomizes the splendor of Mughal architecture in India.*

16th century, at the start of Portuguese exploration in the region, eight sultans claimed dominion over portions of the archipelago. Clashes at the leadership level pitted Islam against Hinduism in several key spots. Malacca was a major seaport, and many people of the islands had heeded the call of Islam. Native traditions colored the Islam practiced in these islands. Today, for example, Java's most important festival is Garebeg, celebrating Muhammad's birth. In a colorful parade, gamelan musicians and soldiers lead 16 men dressed in red, carrying the *gunungan,* a six-foot-tall pyramid of cookies, eggs, peanuts, peppers, coconuts, and fruit, held together with sticky rice and strewn with flowers. They deposit the gunungan at the mosque, and the faithful grab handfuls to bring home for a ceremonial meal or to plant in their fields to ensure good harvests. Early Muslims designed Garebeg, a pastiche of religious rituals, to introduce Islam and express the reigning sultan's generosity.

Dating from those times, the Kampung Hulu Mosque still serves the Muslims of Malacca. Standing next to the house of prayer with a red three-tiered roof is a single white tower that looks more like a lighthouse than a minaret. After the Portuguese, then the Dutch, landed at Malacca to stake a claim, the Muslims migrated farther south, reestablishing the sultanate in Johor, at the southern tip of the mainland. When the British came to power in the region, they planned to return southern Malaysia to the Dutch, but Stamford Raffles, lieutenant governor of Java, objected. The British stationed him on an island then called Temasek, ruled in 1819 by a Muslim sultanate. Raffles and the sultan came to a business agreement, and the British East India Company bought the island destined to become Singapore.

Continuing trade, Sufi missionaries, and a modern wave of Islamist revival have kept Islam alive here and throughout Malaysia and Indonesia. Today, Indonesia is home to more Muslims than any other nation in the world. Only 88 percent of the population—a proportion topped in many Arab nations—they number nearly 207 million, against, for example, 25 million in Saudi Arabia.

THE NEW WORLD

CONSIDERING THE dominance of Muslims, both politically and intellectually, in the years of New World exploration, it is not hard to believe the hypotheses that Muslims led the way. On his first voyage, Christopher Columbus carried a 12th-century journal of Muslim explorations westward into the Atlantic and heeded the advice of his Moorish navigator, Luis de Torres. A map drawn by Turkish cartographer Piri Reis in 1513 depicts West Indian islands including Cuba and Hispaniola and the northern coastline of South America, but scholars debate whether it compiles other early maps or renders an explorer's firsthand observations. Estevanico, a slave from Morocco and presumably a Muslim, traveled in the vanguard of 16th-century Spanish forays into Florida, Texas, and Mexico. His gift for languages made him the most likely to befriend the Indians met along the way.

Islam traveled across the Atlantic in the minds and hearts of African slaves, as exemplified in Abdul Rahahman, a Muslim transported to Louisiana as a slave and named Prince by his owner because of his claims to royal lineage. Bilali, a legal scholar enslaved on a coastal island in Georgia, was put in command of a slave militia during the War of 1812. Omar Ibn Said, a Muslim teacher in West Africa and runaway slave in North Carolina, wrote verses from the Qur'an in charcoal on the walls of his prison cell. As many as one out of five slaves brought to the United States were practicing Muslims. When Canada and the United States welcomed new workers to their shores, Muslims from many countries migrated to North America of their own will. As early as the 1870s, people from Syria, Lebanon, and Jordan chased the promise of economic opportunity and trusted they would find religious freedom as well. In the 20th century, invitations to Muslim professionals brought scientists, engineers, and doctors from Asia, Africa, and the Middle East to work in American industries and schools. When Israel was founded as a Jewish state in 1948, displaced Palestinians sought refuge in Canada and the United States.

Conversions to the faith, coupled with continuing immigration, made for a growing population of Muslims in North and South America and the Caribbean. The majority of 20th- and 21st-century converts in America have been of African descent. In the mid-20th century, Elijah Muhammad and, for a time, his disciple Malcolm X championed the black separatist movement called the Nation of Islam, urging African Americans to become Black Muslims as a way to develop new self-esteem and community. After Malcolm X's hajj to Mecca, however, he urged the Nation of Islam to follow him in his conversion to Sunni Orthodoxy, and eventually much of the community followed suit. Today African Americans constitute the largest indigenous Muslim population in North America.

ISLAM TODAY

THE DIASPORA of Islam includes every continent of the world. In many places Muslims live and worship in peace, gathering to pray in mosques built alongside churches and temples of other faiths. Nearly 20 percent of the world's population, 1.6 billion people, practice Islam. It is the second-largest religion in the world, exceeded only by Christianity.

Just as many parts of the world have witnessed a resurgence of religion, the resurgence of Islam has also occurred. Islamic revivalism is often labeled, or mislabeled, "Islamic fundamentalism" and simply equated with radicalism and violence. However, in many parts of the world, many Muslims have become more conscious of their Islamic faith and identity, and this religious reawakening has expressed itself both in personal and in public life. Many have become more religiously observant, expressing their faith through prayer, fasting, and Islamic dress and values. A growing number of Muslim women, both overseas and in the United States, have chosen to wear Islamic dress, in particular a headscarf, or *hijab*, as a sign of modesty.

The belief that Islam is a total way of life has led to a call to create and live in a more Islamically oriented society and state. Islam has reemerged in politics and society both in highly visible and in more subtle ways. This phenomenon, often referred to as Islamic fundamentalism, political Islam or Islamism, has had many faces. The majority of Islamic activist organizations call upon those who were born Muslim to become more observant and to work to transform their societies. Many of these activists are professionals in law, medicine, teaching, business, or engineering. The educational and social dimensions of these movements can be seen in the growth of Islamic schools, banks, student groups, publishing houses and media, and social welfare agencies.

At the same time, the most visible activists have been a minority of extremists who have turned to violence and terrorism and used religion to legitimate their actions and mobilize support. In recent decades, they have threatened the stability and security of many Muslim societies, from Egypt to Indonesia and the West. September 11, 2001, was an example of the global dimension of Muslim extremism, epitomized by Osama Bin Laden and al-Qaeda. Such extremism also shed light on the struggle for the soul of Islam that exists between a mainstream majority of Muslims and a widespread and dangerous minority.

Islam today is a vibrant faith, one of the fastest growing of the world's religions. It thrives not only in 56 Muslim nations but also in Europe and America, where it is the second- or third-largest religion. Like all religious peoples, Muslims seek in diverse and sometimes conflicting ways to adapt their lives and religious tradition to the changing realities of modern mores. As in the past, debates persist over the true meaning of Islam—we see diverse interpretations of revelation and differing opinions regarding the nature and scope of Islamic law, and implementation—and how best to follow "the straight path, the way of God" in today's world. □

OPPOSITE: Muslim warriors filtered through passes in the jagged Hindu Kush, or "killer of Hindus," range to invade India.

FOLLOWING PAGES: Imam Reza held out a promise of paradise to pilgrims to his sister's splendid tomb in Qum, Iran.

PRAYERS

HANDS LIFTED to heaven, an imam begins noontime prayers under the searing sun in Mashhad, Iran *(above)*. One of the Five Pillars of Islam decreed by the Prophet, prayer pervades the lives of devout Muslims. At dawn, noon, afternoon, sunset, and after nightfall, muezzins call the faithful to ritual prayer. To prepare their bodies for worship, believers *(opposite)* wash in a fountain at a mosque in Damascus, Syria. When no water is available, Muslims may cleanse themselves with sand.

Praising Allah *(following pages)*, "the Compassionate, the Merciful," pious Muslim women join together in ritual prayer. Muhammad taught that group prayer, or *salat,* is more blessed than individual prayer, known as *du'a.*

ILLUMINED BY a shaft of sunlight, a believer kneels in prayer in the Jami Masjid Mosque in Srinagar in Kashmir *(below)*, a place of sometimes violent strife between Muslims and Hindus.

Wherever they settle, Muslims must live according to the rules and rituals decreed by the Qur'an, fulfilling the obligations of their desert-based religion even in urban settings. When there is no room in the mosque, Muslims prostrate themselves outside, as in the scene *(opposite)* on the narrow, car-lined Rue du Bon-Pasteur in Marseilles, France, where Muslims comprise the second-largest religious group after Roman Catholics.

EPILOGUE

— HIS HOLINESS THE DALAI LAMA

IN THIS new millennium, our world requires us more than ever to accept the oneness of humanity. Many of our world's problems and conflicts arise because we lose sight of the essential truth that binds us as a human family. We forget that despite the superficial differences between us in terms of ethnicity, culture, language, and religion, people are the same in their basic wish for peace and happiness.

From the very core of our being we all desire contentment. Indeed, I believe that the purpose of life is to achieve happiness. From my own limited experience I have learned that since, as human beings, we are not solely material creatures, it is a mistake to place all our hopes for happiness on external conditions alone. The key is to develop inner peace. There is no denying that we need material things for physical comfort, but these alone cannot provide full satisfaction. As human beings, we also aspire to deeper mental and emotional satisfaction. Given that religions represent vital spiritual resources, they remain relevant in the world. If religious faith had not much value in our day-to-day life, I believe we should have the right to abandon it. This, however, is not the case. I feel that even in this highly scientific and technological age, religious faith continues to provide millions of fellow human beings around the world with a deep sense of meaning and inspiration.

Throughout humanity's long history, individuals and communities have looked to their religion and culture as a source of meaning and basic spiritual and ethical values.

It is sad to observe that in today's increasingly material and technological world, there is a lessening of commitment to the fundamental humane values. If human society loses such basic values as justice, compassion, forgiveness, and honesty, we will face greater difficulties in the future.

Therefore, I believe that the world's religions still have an important role to play. There are similarities as well as differences among the various traditions. Each has its own philosophy and unique teachings, while they all share a principal goal of creating better and kinder human beings. What is important is to recognize what is suitable for a particular person or group of people. We should look at the underlying purpose of religion and not merely at the abstract details of theology or metaphysics. All religions make the betterment of humanity their main concern. When we view different religions as instruments for developing such human qualities as compassion, tolerance, forgiveness, and self-discipline, we can appreciate what they have in common.

Religion, for most of us, depends on our family background and where we were born and grew up. I think it is usually better not to change that. However, the more we understand of each other's ways, the more we can learn from each other. All the major religious traditions carry a similar message. For example, their presentations of love and compassion may differ, but the general concept of compassion remains the same. To realize this, and to appreciate its deeper implications, naturally inspires genuine respect for

FOLLOWING PAGES: A Buddhist monk rings a bell atop Adam's Peak in Sri Lanka, a pilgrimage point of four faiths.

other faiths, which also acts as a foundation for the development of harmony between the world's different religions. This, in turn, will certainly help increase greater understanding and peace among peoples throughout the world. I believe this is something to which we all aspire.

By declaring my respect and reverence for all the world's major faiths, I am not advocating any attempt to unify the various traditions into a single "world religion." I firmly believe that we need different religions, because a single tradition cannot satisfy the needs and mental dispositions of the great diversity that is our human community. Even our body needs a variety of food. If a restaurant were to sell only one kind of meal, it soon would have no customers. But because it offers a variety of food, more people come and enjoy it. Everyone feels their own form of religious practice is the best. I myself feel that Buddhism is best for me. This does not mean that Buddhism is best for everyone. Everyone has a right to make his or her own choice. Even so, I do not believe that people should lightly change the religion of their birth. What we need to do is to develop an understanding of the differences in our various traditions and to recognize the value and potential of each of them. Indeed, I believe that one of the greatest benefits of achieving an inner spiritual transformation based on our own faith is that this experience helps us appreciate the value of other traditions.

Cultivating harmony, respect for others, compassion, and tolerance is something that we can each start doing in our own lives and in our own actions. If, on the other hand, we take the differences between faiths as grounds for argument and conflict, there will be no end to it. All of us will be diminished, even if one side does manage to impose its point of view by force. History shows that coercion has rarely yielded positive results, and in the present, no one side will triumph through belligerence. Hostility based on religious differences can have no meaningful or lasting benefit at all.

Perhaps the most significant obstacle to inter-religious harmony is the lack of appreciation of the value of others' faith traditions. Until comparatively recently, communication between different cultures, even different communities, was slow or nonexistent. Sympathy and respect for other faiths was not important or relevant, except where members of different religions lived side by side. But this situation is no longer viable. In today's increasingly complex and interdependent world, we are compelled to acknowledge the existence of other cultures, different ethnic groups, and, of course, other religious faiths. Whether we like it or not, most of us now experience this diversity on a daily basis.

One of the most positive aspects of the time I have spent in exile from my own country is that I have been freer to travel. I have had extraordinary opportunities to meet with other religious leaders and practitioners and hold discussions with them, to visit the holy sites of other faiths, to pay my respects there, and to join in prayers with other pilgrims. Such good fortune is not open to everyone. However, I believe that reading this book, which attempts to present the world's major religions, their histories, holy places, and practices in an accessible way, could be like undertaking a pilgrimage. Its rich illustrations reveal the vibrant visual quality of our diverse faiths, while the personal accounts allow us to experience an inside view. I believe that in a real sense, religion has to do with generating a good heart and a positive mind, both of which ultimately bring us benefits and happiness. It is my sincere hope that readers will come to recognize that there are many ways of accomplishing this, and that if we have faith and put these ways into actual practice we can all contribute to making a more peaceful and kinder world.

2500 B.C. Earliest roots of Hinduism:
Aryan fire-sacrifice cult in Persia.
Indus Valley culture at its peak

2000 Aryans begin migration to India

1750 Abraham leads his clan from
Mesopotamia at Yahweh's bidding

1500-600 Vedas, holy writ of Hinduism,
compiled from oral tradition

1240 Moses receives the Ten Commandments

1000 David reigns in Jerusalem

950 Solomon builds the first Temple.
At his death in 922 the kingdom splits
into Israel (north) and Judaea (south)

600 Birth of Lao Zi, father of Daoism

587 Nebuchadnezzar razes Jerusalem:
Jews exiled to Babylon until 538

563-483 Life of Buddha

551-479 Life of Confucius

540-468 Life of Mahavira, founder of Jainism

520 Jews rebuild Jerusalem's Temple

275 Septuagint, first Bible in Greek

246 Buddhism thrives in India under King
Ashoka and spreads to Sri Lanka

165 Maccabees rid Jews of Syrian rule

63 Roman rule imposed on Palestine

29 Theravada Buddhist writings
compiled in Sri Lanka

6 B.C.-A.D. 31 Life of Jesus

A.D. 45 St. Paul spreads Christianity
among Gentiles

65 St. Mark writes the first gospel

70 Romans raze Jerusalem's Temple:
dispersal of Jews

100 Buddhism spreads into China

200 *Mahabharata* and *Ramayana*, once secular
epics, now sacred Hindu texts

313 Constantine legalizes Christianity

325 First Council of Nicea rejects Arianism,
formulates Nicene Creed

350-800 Golden Age of Buddhism in China

372 Buddhism spreads to Korea

405 St. Jerome completes translation of
Vulgate Bible in Latin

410 Rome falls to Alaric; St. Augustine is
inspired to write his *City of God*

450 Buddhism practiced in Burma, southern
Thailand, Sumatra, and Java

496 Clovis baptized; Franks (dominant
European tribe) converted to Christianity

500 Buddhism begins to wane in India

500 Jewish sages compile the Talmud

529 St. Benedict formulates his rule

552 Buddhism reaches Japan

570-632 Life of Muhammad; Islamic era dates
from his hijra to Medina in 622

596 Pope Gregory I sends Augustine as
missionary to England

632 Abu Bakr is first caliph; successors take
Damascus, Jerusalem, Persia, Egypt

651 Muslim scholars compile the Koran

661 Muawiya begins in Umayyad caliphate

680 Shii Muslims break with Sunnites

711 Muslims invade India and Spain

747 Tantric Buddhism reaches Tibet

750 Abbasids replace Umayyads; Muslim
mystics launch Sufi movement

755 St. Boniface, "Apostle of Germany,"
slain by pagan mob in Frisia

786-809 Caliphate of Harun al-Rashid

800 Charlemagne crowned emperor
by Pope Leo III

910 Fatmids establish a caliphate in North
Africa; conquer Egypt in 969

1054 Christianity splits into Orthodox and
Roman Catholic churches

1058-1111 Life of al-Ghazzali, who reconciled
Sufism and orthodox Islam

1095 Pope Urban II begins Crusades

1100-1300 Mahayana Buddhism flowers
in Japan

1100-1400 Theravada Buddhism spreads
over Southeast Asia from Sri Lanka

1135-1204 Life of Moses Maimonides,
codifier of Jewish law

1209 St. Francis founds his Order

1215 Innocent III convenes Fourth Lateran
Council; papal power at its peak

1225-74 Life of St. Thomas Aquinas

1375 John Wyclif tries to reform the church;
translates the Bible into English

1414-18 Council of Constance ends the
church's Great Schism, which followed
the "Babylonian Captivity" at Avignon

1469-1538 Life of Nanak, founder of Sikhism,
a blend of Hinduism and Islam

1492 Spanish Inquisition decrees baptism
or exile for Jews and Muslims

1517 Martin Luther posts his 95 Theses

1534 Henry VIII establishes the Church
of England

1536 John Calvin publishes his *Institutes
of the Christian Religion*

1540 Ignatius of Loyola founds the Society
of Jesus, the Jesuits

1545-63 Council of Trent ushers in Catholic
Counter-Reformation

1611 King James Bible

1620 Pilgrims land at Plymouth Rock

1692 Puritans in Salem, Massachusetts,
hang 19 citizens as witches

1750 Mystical Hasidic movement
emphasizes joy in Jewish ritual

1772-1833 Life of Rammohun Roy,
Hindu reformer

1791 U.S. Constitution guarantees freedom
of religion for all

1810 First Reform synagogue founded in
Seesen, Germany

1847 Mormons establish church state in
American wilderness

1869-1948 Life of Mohandas Gandhi, Hindu
champion of passive resistance

1870 First Vatican Council proclaims doctrine
of papal infallibility on matters of faith

1896 Theodor Herzl, founder of modern
Zionism, writes *The Jewish State*

1941-1945 Six million Jews are executed
under the Nazi regime in WWII

1947 Creation of Muslim Pakistan

1948 The State of Israel is founded

1948 World Council of Churches formed

1950 World Fellowship of Buddhists

1959 Dalai Lama escapes to India after
Chinese invasion of Tibet

1962-1965 Second Vatican Council marks
shift to modern Catholic Church

1966 Maulana Karenga creates Kwanzaa

1966 Swami Prabhupada founds the
International Society for Krishna
Consciousness

1967 The Six Day War

1967 Israel gains control of East Jerusalem

1968 Liberation theology begins at Second
Latin American Bishops' Conference

1971 East Pakistan secedes from
West Pakistan to become Bangladesh

1975 Incorporation of Sikhism into
Republic of India

1978 John Paul II becomes pope

1978 Louis Farrakhan forms his own sect
of the Nation of Islam

1979 Islamic republic established in Iran
under the Ayatollah Khomeini

1980-92 Falasha migrations from Ethiopia
to Israel

1987 Palestinian Islamic movement Hamas
founded at the beginning of the
Palestinian *intifada*

1989 Dalai Lama receives Nobel Peace Prize

1992 Militant Hindu nationalists destroy
mosque at Ayodhya, the legendary
birthplace of Hindu hero Rama

1994 The Taliban begins its conquest
of Afghanistan

1998 Pope John Paul II visits Cuba

2001 Hindu celebration of Kumbh Mela
in Allahabad, the largest religious
gathering in world history

2001 September 11 terrorist attacks by
Muslim extremists Osama Bin Laden
and al-Qaeda operatives

GLOSSARY

HINDUISM

Agni: fire divinity; intermediary between gods and humans through his form as the sacrificial fire

Ahimsa: non violence

Ashram: refuge, referring either to a place or a stage in life

Atman: the soul

Avatar: literally "crossing over," a god on earth in human form

Bhagavad Gita: 'The Song of the Lord,' excerpt from the *Mahabharata*

Brahma: the one god, the creator

Brahman: highest, or priestly class, in Hindu caste system; also the sacred power that sustains living beings

Caste: class system in Hinduism

Dalit: a member of the lowest social group in India, previously called Untouchables

Dham: divine abode

Dhantal: percussion instrument of Trinidad

Dharma: morality, one of the goals in human life

Dholak: classic Indian drum

Diwali: festival of lights

Durga: goddess; destroyer of demons

Dusserah: Hindu new-moon festival, held in October

Gamelan: Bali instrument, related to xylophone

Ganesha: elephant-headed god; remover of obstacles

Ghat: step

Ghee: clarified butter

Guru: sage, teacher

Hanuman: monkey god; Rama's servant

Harijans: a class of people outside the *varna,* the Untouchables

Holi: spring festival

Incarnation: the embodiment of God in human form

Kali: goddess; representing the terrifying aspect of Durga

Krishna: god; seen as incarnation of Vishnu

Kshatriya: second highest Hindu caste; the warrior class or nobility

Lakshmi: goddess of wealth and beauty

Lingam: Shiva as the phallic emblem, a point of focus in worship

Mahabharata: epic story about the gods

Moksha: ultimate liberation from the cycle of death and rebirth

Mughal: Muslim rulers of India

Murti: image of deity

Naga: snake

Nataraja: lord of the dance

Nirvana: enlightenment

Parvati: goddess; consort of Shiva

Pinda: rice balls, as an offering in worship

Puja: daily worship

Purusha: the primeval being, divided and sacrificed to create the world

Rama: god-hero; incarnation of Vishnu

Ramayana: epic story

Rig Veda: collection of ancient Hindu belief

Sadhu: holy man

Samagree: aromatic paste

Samskara: improvements

Samsara: ceaseless cycle of birth and rebirth

Satyagraha: grasping of the truth

Shiva: principal deity

Sita: Rama's wife

Sudra: fourth and lowest of the castes, a laborer

Swami: holy man

Untouchables: formerly name for lowest social group in India

Upanishads: Hindu scriptures

Vaishya: third Hindu caste, farmers and merchants

Varna: one of four social classes or castes in Hinduism

Veda: see Rig Veda

Vina: string instrument

Vishnu: along with Shiva, one of the two most important gods

Wayang: shadow puppet theater in Bali

BUDDHISM

Anatman: non-self

Arhat: worthy one, follower of Buddha

Bhikkhu: wandering Buddhist mendicant

Bhikkuni: Buddhist nuns

Bodhisattva: enlightened being

Bosatsu: Japanese word for bodhisattva

Buddha: one who has achieved enlightenment

Chakra: disk

Ch'an: a form of Chinese Buddhism, which believes that meditation alone can lead to enlightenment

Chattra: a multilevel parasol in Buddhist decoration

Chedi: word for stupa in Southeast Asia

Confucianism: the philosophy, religion, and government based on the teachings of Confucius in China

Dao De Jing: Daoism's holy book

Daoism: Chinese philosophy founded by Lao Zi

Dharma: the Buddha's teachings, which could lead others to enlightenment

Enlightenment: the experience of liberation from the cycle of birth and rebirth

Kami: spirit beings in Shinto belief

Karma: action and its meritorious or not so meritorious consequence, in this or a future life

Kannon: in Japan, name for the historical Buddha

Koan: a riddle in Zen Buddhism

Mahayana Buddhism: believes that all humans have the potential for Buddhahood

Mandala: sacred design in Buddhism to focus the mind in meditation

Nirvana: the blissful state achieved by a Buddha that releases him from the cycle of rebirth

Pali: Buddhist scriptures

Pagoda: word for stupa in Japan

Samana: wandering monk

Sangha: community of the faithful

Shinto: indigenous religion of Japan

Stupa: Buddhist shrine containing a relic of the Buddha; see also Chedi, Pagoda

Theravada or Hinayana Buddhism: followers of the Buddha's original teaching

Tipitaka: three baskets, Buddhist doctrine, collected from firsthand accounts during the Buddha's life

Tirthankara: ford-builders, who form a bridge from this world to the state of enlightenment

Torii: sacramental gateways in Japan

Wat: word for temple in Southeast Asia

Zen: Japanese form of Ch'an Buddhism

Zazen: Sitting meditation

JUDAISM

Ark of the Covenant: sacred shrine; the earthly dwelling place of God

Ashkenazim: German and Eastern European Jews

B.C.E.: Before the Common Era

Beitzah: Passover symbol: roasted egg

Bet ha-keneset: house of assembly or synagogue

C.E.: Common Era

Chuppa: four-poled canopy for wedding ceremony

Conservative Judaism: American movement of non-Orthodox religious practice

Essenes: monastic brotherhood of Jews from the second century B.C.E. to the second century C.E.

Exodus: the flight from slavery in Egypt; also second book of the Bible

Gemara: discussion of Mishnah, or oral law

Ghetto: a section of a city where Jews had to live

Hannukah: eight-day festival of dedication, commemorating the cleansing and rehabilitation of the Temple

Haroset: a blend of chopped food for Seder, symbolizing the mortar used by Israelite slaves

Hasidism: ultra-orthodox, mystical movement

Kabbalah: mystical tradition

Kaddish: prayer read by a descendant after a relative's death

Karpas: green vegetable for Seder, stands for season of spring

Ke'arah: plate used during Seder, arranged with symbolic food

Ketuba: Jewish marriage contract

Kodesh Kodashim: Holy of Holies

Ladino: language of the Sephardim

Maror: Passover symbol: bitter herbs, stand for bitter experience of slavery

Matzo: unleavened bread

Megilla: scroll of Esther

Messiah: leader

Midrasha: authoritative text of the Bible

Mishnah: a collection of oral law

Mitzvoth: commandments; 613 mitzvoth were handed down, rather than only 10, per the Jewish Bible

Orthodox Judaism: movement faithful to the literal meaning of the Torah

Passover: festival celebrating the liberation from slavery in Egypt

Payos: side curls

Pharisees: a Jewish sect who claimed a lineage of learning, not blood, with strict observance of rites and ceremony of the written law

Pogrom: violent raid on Jewish settlements in Russia, from the Russian word for "wreaking havoc"

Prophet: one who speaks on God's behalf

Purim: festival celebrated on the 14th of Adar in the Jewish calendar in commemoration of deliverance from the massacre plotted by Haman

Rabbi: official Jewish teacher

Reconstructionist Judaism: new branch of Judaism, founded in 1955 and defined as cultural history shared by Jews

Reform Judaism: a non-orthodox movement

Rosh Hashanah: Jewish New Year

Sabbath (Shabbath): day of rest

Sadducees: a Jewish sect who founded their beliefs on the literal letter of the Torah

Seder: literally "order;" Passover feast

Sephardim: Jews who had settled in Spain and North Africa

Shabuoth (Shavuot): festival of Pentecost, commemorating the occasion when Moses received the Ten Commandments

Shema: The Jewish proclamation of faith: "Listen (shema) Israel; Yahweh is our God, Yahweh is the one."

Shiva: period of mourning

Shtetl: Yiddish for small town

Sukkoth: Feast of the Tabernacle

Synagogue: Jewish house of prayer

Talmud: compilation of the Mishnah and Gemara

Tanakh: Hebrew Bible

Teffilin: phylacteries; small black leather boxes containing the text of the proclamation of faith which Jewish men wear near the forehead and the heart during morning prayer

Torah: God's law, the first five books of the Bible: Genesis, Exodus, Leviticus, Numbers, and Deutoronomy

Tzitzit: fringes on a prayer shawl

Yahweh: the name of God in Israel

Yarmulke: skullcap

Yiddish: language of the Ashkenazim; a combination of German and Hebrew

Yom Kippur: Day of Atonement

Zealots: a fanatical Jewish sect during the first century C.E. opposing Roman domination of Palestine

Zionism: movement toward creation of a Jewish state

Zohar: commentary on the Torah

Z'roa: Passover symbol; spring sacrifice: lamb shank or poultry neck

CHRISTIANITY

Anabaptists: broke from the Roman Catholic church; emphasize baptism as the key ritual of biblical Christianity

Apostle: literally "the one sent forth;" the 12 Apostles were the first followers of Jesus

Apostle's Creed: See Nicene Creed

Baptism: the act of bringing an individual into the Church through a blessing by holy water

Bishop: in the church's early hierarchy, the leader of a church. Today, the leader of several churches in an area called a diocese

Calvinist: Branch of reform Christianity, led by the Swiss John Calvin

Canons of Faith: 20 regulations set by Constantine's church for all Christians to live by

Cardinal: the tier of hierarchy second to the pope in the Roman Catholic Church. Groups of bishops report to a cardinal

Christ: the anointed one; the name given Jesus after his divine Resurrection from the dead

Cluniac Order: founded by the Duke of Aquitaine in France, focused on scholarship and culture

Communion, or Eucharist (from the Greek for gratitude): the holiest and most universal of all Christian sacraments, in which bread and wine are shared among worshipers

Confession: private recitation of one's sins to a priest in the Roman Catholic Church, for which prayers or good acts are assigned as penance

Constantine: Emperor of Rome in 324 A.D.; a convert to Christianity, he granted Christians religious freedom and consolidated Christianity from Britain to Palestine

Counter-Reformation: a renovation in the original mission of the Roman Catholic Church, prompted by the Protestant Reformation

Coptic Church: Christian church in Egypt; inspired by monophysite belief

Crucifix: an icon of Christ nailed to a cross

Crusades: a series of four armed missions over several centuries, aimed at driving Muslims from regions that Rome considered rightfully Christian

Deacon: in the church's early hierarchy, the lowest tier of clergy, who read Scripture and distributed Communion

Diocese: an administrative and geographical division, each headed by a bishop

Easter: celebration of the day when Christ was resurrected from the dead

Eastern Orthodox Church: federation of Eastern churches according primacy to the Patriarch of Constantinople and adhering to the Byzantine rites

Eucharist: see Communion

Gethsemane: the walled garden where Jesus celebrated the Last Supper, then was arrested before Crucifixion

Gnostic: Christian sect whose religion included elements from Babylonian astrology and Greek philosophy

Gospels: the first four books of the New Testament

Holy See: see Vatican

Homoousios: the belief that God the father and Christ the son are one being

Icons: physical images adorning Christian churches, of Jesus, his mother, Mary, saints, and angels.

Huguenots: branch of reform Christianity in France, named after Bensancon Hugues, influenced by John Calvin

Iconostasis: a screen hung with icons in the Greek and Eastern Orthodox Church

Lent: the 40 days of fasting and abstinence before Easter

Lindisfarne Gospels: illuminated manuscripts, made by medieval monks of this tiny island off the coast of Britain

Liturgical Year: begins with Advent, the coming of Jesus

Liturgy: formal religious services

Messiah: name given to Jesus as a prophet; he was also called the Christ: the anointed one

Methodism: inspired by John Wesley, a religion based on inward feelings of personal salvation

Miracles: healing and other divine acts performed by Jesus during his ministry

Missionary: one who takes on a mission to espouse Christianity in non-Christian places

Monastery: a specialized cloister where monks follow the vows of celibacy, poverty, and simplicity in lifestyle

Monk: a holy man who chooses to live a life either as a hermit, or in a monastery, a community of those who have chosen to take the required vows of monasticism: celibacy, poverty, and simplicity in life-style

Monophysites: after a division of the original church in the fifth century; disputing the nature of Jesus Christ, they upheld the doctrine that Jesus Christ had one divine nature

Mormons: also called Latter-day Saints, sect founded by John Smith to break from other Christians in 1820

Nestorians: after a division of the original church in the fifth century disputing the nature of Christ, they upheld the doctrine that Christ had two distinct persons: one human and one divine; today called the Assyrian Church

New Testament: the collection of Scripture— 27 books—which, when combined with the Hebrew Bible, or Old Testament, composes the Christian Bible

Nicene Creed: creed stating belief in the Holy Trinity and in certain tenets of Christianity; a canon of faith

Numinous: sacred and transcendent, that which inspires awe or terror

Nun: a woman who takes the vows of monasticism; her initiation involves a wedding-like ceremony binding her to God

Nunnery: the equivalent of a monastery; a cloister for nuns

Old Testament: the Hebrew Bible.

Orthodox: from the Greek for correct teaching; the Christian church that follows Constantine's original canons of faith; spread from Constantinople through Eastern Europe to Russia

Papa: name for the early bishops of the church; eventually the *papa* of Rome, or pope, was recognized as the highest of bishops. Jesus's follower Peter was the first pope

Parables: simple stories of daily life recited by Jesus that displayed the relationship God wanted with human beings

Pentecost: the day, 50 days after Jesus's death, when the Holy Spirit descended upon the disciples and instilled in them the gift of tongues

Presbyter: in the church's early hierarchy, clergy second to the bishop, who led services and preached

Puritans: followers of Anglicanism who broke away to create a stricter version, centered in North America

Quakers: also called Society of Friends; Christian sect with anti-materialist and pacifist principles, who left England for religious freedom in North America

Reformation: Reformation of the traditional Roman Catholic faith

Resurrection: the rising of Christ from the dead

Roman Catholic Church: Christian church with a hierarchy of priests and bishops under the pope in Rome, a liturgy centered on a mass, veneration of the Virgin Mary and saints, clerical celibacy, and a body of dogma including transubstantiation and papal infallibility

Rosary: a string of prayer beads with a crucifix at the end

Samaritan: a foreigner shunned by most Jews; the hero of one parable of Jesus

Sect: a group of believers who branched out from the core faith and created their own version

Synoptic Gospels: Episodes of the life of Jesus that reappear in the Books of Matthew, Mark, and Luke

Transubstantiation: the changing of bread and wine of the Eucharist into the actual body and blood of Christ

Vatican: the seat of power for the Roman Catholic Church; also called the Holy See

Voudon: rites practiced in Haiti, Cuba, and in the root medicine practices found in African-American communities of New Orleans and the rural South in the United States; the word means "deity" in Fon, the native language of Dahomey

Vulgate Bible: The first translation into Latin of the Old and New Testament; standard Bible of the Roman Catholic Church

Walloons: Branch of reform Christianity in France and Belgium, inspired by John Calvin

ISLAM

Ahl al-sunnah: the Sunnis, the majority group of Muslims who follow the Qur'an, the *hadith*, the *sunnah*, and *shariah*

Ayat: a verse of the Qur'an

Bismillah ir rahman ir rahim: in the name of God, the Merciful, the Compassionate; the beginning of each chapter in the Qur'an

Caliph: successor of Muhammad

Dhul-Hijjah: the 12th month of the Islamic year, the month of the hajj

Eid al-Fitr: the breaking of the fast and end of Ramadan to celebrate Muhammad's Night of Power

Fiqh: legal interpretations of the Qur'an

Ghazwa: tribal raid

Hadith: texts collected by Ismail al-Bukhari; second only to the Qur'an as the sacred literature of Sunni Islam

Hajj: the Fifth Pillar of Islam, the pilgrimage to Mecca during the month of Dhul-Hijjah

Hijra: Muhammad's move from Mecca to Yathrib (Medina) in September 622, later to be counted as the first year in the Muslim calendar

Imam: prayer leader; among Shii, also community leader

Islam: Arabic for "surrender to God"

Jihad: effort or exertion; refers to fighting evil and carrying the righteous rule of Islam to the far ends of the earth

Kaaba: Holy Shrine in Mecca

Madrasa: school of Islamic studies

Mihrab: the ornamented wall niche that indicates the direction to Mecca

Muslim: follower of Islam; in Arabic "one who submits to God"

Niyyah: intention, as in praying with good intention

Qaraa: to read or recite

Qiblah: direction of prayer, toward Mecca

Qur'an: sacred scriptures of Islam, consisting of 114 suras, or chapters, divided into ayat, or verses

Prophet: one who speaks on God's behalf

Ramadan: the ninth month of the Muslim year, observed by fasting from sunrise to sunset

Rashidun: the rightly guided; Muhammad's initial four successors

Salam: peace; also used as a greeting

Salat: Second Pillar of Islam, prayer or worship

Sawm: Fourth Pillar of Islam, referring to the fast during the month of Ramadan

Sa'y: running seven times between two small hills in Mecca to remember the time when Hagar, sent into the desert with Ishmael, searched desperately for water

Shahada: First Pillar of Islam, the affirmation of belief: There is no God but Allah and Muhammad is his Messenger

Shariah: the right path, or guide; the law that comes from divine revelation and is to be found in the Qur'an

Sheikh: head of a tribe

Shiat-u-Ali: the party of Ali, or Shii, also known as Shiites, who believe that Ali (cousin and son-in-law of Muhammad), his descendants, and the imams should lead the Islamic community

Shii: see Shiat-u-Ali

Shiite: see Shiat-u-Ali

Suf: wool

Sufi: spiritual mystics

Sunnah: word of God

Sunni: see ahl al-sunnah

Sura: chapter of the Qur'an

Tawhid: God's oneness

Ummah: community of Islam

Zakat: Third Pillar of Islam, tithing and almsgiving

Karen Armstrong, *A History of God,* New York: Ballantine Books, 1991; *Muhammad, A Biograpohy of the Prophet,* San Francisco: Harper San Francisco, 1992; *Islam, A Short History,* New York: Modern Library, 2000

Michael Avi-Yonah, *The Holy Land: A Historical Geography,* Jerusalem: Carta, 2002

Laleh Bakhtiar, *Sufi: Expressions of the Mystic Quest,* London: Thames & Hudson, 1979

Peter L. Berger, ed., *The Desecularization of the World: Resurgent Religion and World Politics*, Washington, DC: Ethics and Public Policy Center, 1999

Jonathan Bloom and Sheila Blair, *Islam: A Thousand Years of Faith and Power,* New York: TV Books, 2000

Earle E. Cairns, *Christianity Through the Centuries,* rev. ed., Grand Rapids, MI: Zondervan, 1981

Joseph Campbell, *The Mythic Image,* Princeton, NJ: Princeton University Press, 1974; *The Way of the Animal Powers,* Vol. I; *Historical Atlas of World Mythology,* London: Summerfield Press, 1993

Owen Chadwick, *A History of Christianity,* New York: St. Martin's Press, 1995

Malek Chebel, *Symbols of Islam,* Paris: Editions Assouline, 1997

Simon Coleman and John Elsner, *Pilgrimage: Past and Present in the World Religions,* Cambridge, MA: Harvard University Press, 1995

Michael D. Coogan, ed., *The Illustrated Guide to World Religions,* New York & Oxford: Oxford University Press, 2003

Harvey Cox, *The Secular City: Urbanization and Secularization in Theological Perspective*, New York: Macmillian, 1965; and *Religion in the Secular City: Toward a Post Modern Theology* (New York: Simon & Schuster, 1984)

David Daiches, *Moses: Man in the Wilderness,* London: Weidenfeld and Nicolson, 1975

Brian de Breffny, *The Synagogue,* New York: Macmillan Co., 1978

J. B. Disanayaka, *Mihintale, Cradle of Sinhala Buddhist Civilization,* Colombo, Sri Lanka: Lake House Investments Ltd., 1987

H. Bryon Earhart, ed., *Religious Traditions of the World,* San Francisco: Harper San Francisco, 1993

David Edwards, *Christianity, The First Two Thousand Years,* Maryknoll, NY: Orbis Books, 1997

Gerhard Endress, *Islam: An Historical Introduction,* 2nd ed., transl. Carole Hillenbrand, New York: Columbia University Press, 2002

Emel Esin, *Mecca the Blessed, Madinah the Radiant,* London: Elek, 1963

John L. Esposito, *Unholy War: Terror in the Name of Islam,* New York & Oxford, Oxford University Press, 2003; ed., *The Oxford History of Islam*, Oxford University Press, 2000; with Todd Thornton Lewis and Darell J. Fasching; *World Religions Today,* Oxford University Press, 2002; ed., Abdulaziz Abdulhussein Sachedina and Tamara Sonn, John O. Voll, eds., *The Islamic World: Past and Present,* Oxford University Press, 2004

Majid Fakhry, *An Interpretation of the Qur'an,* New York University Press, 2004

Bruce Feiler, *Walking the Bible: A Journey by Land through the Five Books of Moses,* New York: Harper Collins, 2001

Israel Finkelstein and Neil Asher Silberman, *The Bible Unearthed: Archaeology's New Vision of Ancient Israel and the Origin of Its Sacred Texts,* New York: Free Press, 2001

Dominic Goodall, ed. *Hindu Scripture*, Berkeley & Los Angeles: University of California Press, 1996

Michael Grant, *Herod the Great,* New York: American Heritage Press, 1971

Manfield Halpren, *The Politics of Social Change in the Middle East and North Africa*, Princeton: Princeton University Press, 1963)

Muhammad Abdel Haleem, *Understanding the Qur'an: Themes and Style,* London & New York: I. B. Tauris, 1999

Bernard Hamilton, *The Christian World of the Middle Ages,* Thrupp, UK: Sutton Publishing, 2003

Brian Innes, *Death and the Afterlife,* New York: St. Martin's Press, 1999

Minoru Kiyota, ed., *Japanese Buddhism: Its Tradition, New Religions and Interaction with Christianity*, Tokyo & Los Angeles: Buddhist Books International, 1987

Emil G. Kraeling, *Rand McNally Bible Atlas,* New York: Rand McNally & Co., 1966

Daniel Lerner, *The Passing of Traditional Society: Modernizing the Middle East*, New York: Free Press, 1958

Tom Loewenstein, *The Vision of the Buddha,* Boston: Little, Brown, 1996

Martha Morrison & Stephen Brown, *Judaism,* New York: Facts on File, 1991

Jan H. Negenman, *New Atlas of the Bible,* ed. Harold H. Rowley, Garden City, NY: Doubleday & Co., 1969

Patrick Olivelle, *Upanisads,* Oxford University Press, 1996

Steven Ozment, *The Age of Reform 1250-1550,* New Haven and London, Yale University Press, 1980

S. K. Ramachandra Rao, *The Icons and Images of Hindu Temples,* Bangalore: Ibh Prakashana, 1981

Pramesh Ratnakar, *Hinduism,* New Delhi: Lustre Press, 1996

Francis Robinson, ed., *The Cambridge Illustrated History of the Islamic World,* Cambridge: Cambridge University Press, 1996

Malise Ruthven, *Islam in the World,* 2nd ed., Oxford & New York: Oxford University Press, 2000

Frederick M. Schweitzer, *A History of the Jews since the First Century A.D.,* New York: Macmillan Co., 1971

Ninian Smart, ed., *Atlas of the World's Religion,* Oxford & New York: Oxford University Press, 1999; *The Religious Experience of Mankind,* New York: Charles Scribner's Sons, 1969; *The World's Religions,* Cambridge: Cambridge University Press, 1989

The Song Of God: Bhagavad-Gita, transl. by Swami Prabhavananda and Christopher Isherwood, Hollywood, CA: Vedanta Press, 1944

Fred R. von der Mehden, *Religion and Modernization in Southeast Asia,* Syracuse, N.Y.: Syracuse University Press, 1988

Madhu Bazaz Wangu, *Buddhism,* New York & Oxford: Facts on File, 1993; *Hinduism,* New York & Oxford: Facts on File, 1991

K. Warikoo, ed., *Bamiyan: Challenge to World Heritage,* New Delhi: Bhavana Books & Prints, 2002

David Westerlund and Ingvar Svanberg, eds., *Islam Outside the Arab World,* Richmond, UK: Curzon, 1999

Robert Wilken, *The Land Called Holy,* New Haven & London: Yale University Press, 1992

AUTHORS

SUSAN TYLER HITCHCOCK, PH.D., is the author of 11 books on history, culture, and nature, including *Gather Ye Wild Things* and *Mad Mary Lamb,* and taught humanities in the School of Engineering at the University of Virginia. As an editor for National Geographic her books include *Revolutionary War, Trail to Wounded Knee,* and *On the Move: Transportation and the American Story.*

JOHN L. ESPOSITO, PH.D., is University Professor of Religion and International Affairs and of Islamic Studies at Georgetown University. His specialties are Islam and Politics, Religion and International Affairs, Islam and Global Terrorism, and the impact of Islamic movements from North Africa to Southeast Asia. He is editor-in-chief of the *Oxford Encyclopedia of the Modern Islamic World, The Oxford History of Islam,* and *The Oxford Dictionary of Islam,* and his more than 25 books include: *What Everyone Should Know About Islam: Questions and Answers, Unholy War: Terror in the Name of Islam, The Islamic Threat: Myth or Reality?, Islam and Politics, Islam and Democracy* (with J. Voll), *Islam: The Straight Path,* and *Women in Muslim Family Law.*

BOARD OF ADVISERS

INTRODUCTION: ARCHBISHOP DESMOND TUTU is author of numerous books including *Crying in the Wilderness. The Struggle for Justice in South Africa, Hope and Suffering: Sermons and Speeches,* and *The Rainbow People of God: The Making of a Peaceful Revolution.* Born in Klerksdorp, Transvaal, he was ordained as a priest in 1960 and received a Master of Theology degree in England in 1966. He taught theology in South Africa, then became assistant director of a theological institute in London. In 1975 he was appointed Dean of St. Mary's Cathedral in Johannesburg, the first black minister to hold that position. From 1976 to 1978 he was Bishop of Lesotho, and in 1978 became the first black General Secretary of the South African Council of Churches. Tutu is an honorary doctor of a number of leading universities in the United States, Britain, and Germany. In 1984 he won the Nobel Peace Prize, based on his work toward "a democratic and just society without racial divisions."

THE REV. MPHO TUTU was ordained in June 2003 at Christ Church, Alexandria, Virginia, continuing spiritual journeys traced by her parents. Born in London, Tutu grew up in South Africa when apartheid still ruled. "I've had the example of two parents who've had very lively ministries of their own," said Tutu of her father, Desmond, and her mother, Leah. "I've always felt that my home is the church. If I didn't feel a call by God to an ordained ministry then I couldn't do it." Before studying theology Tutu worked in the nonprofit sector, administering a scholarship for South African refugees. Last year she completed a three-year Master of Divinity program at Episcopal Divinity School. For the next two years, she will be clergy resident at Christ Church. She is married to Joseph Burris, a sportswriter for the *Boston Globe* and has a seven-year-old daughter, Nyaniso.

ORIGINS: LAURIE COZAD received her Ph.D. in the History of Religions from the University of Chicago Divinity School, where she specialized in Hinduism and Buddhism. She is currently an assistant professor at the University of Mississippi and holds a joint appointment in the Department of Philosophy and Religion and the Croft Institute for International Studies.

HINDUISM: ARVIND SHARMA, PH.D., is a scholar of Hinduism and of issues concerning women and religion. Having taught at the University of Queensland and the University of Sydney in Australia, he is now the Birks Professor of Comparative Religion at McGill University in Montreal, Canada. Among the more than 30 books he has published are *Our Religions, Women in World Religions, Religion and Women,* and *Today's Women in World Religions,* and he is the co-editor of *The Annual Review of Women in the World Religions.*

BUDDHISM: THE VENERABLE LOBSANG DECHEN is a Buddhist nun and co-director with the Dalai Lama's sister-in-law of the Tibetan Nuns Project (TNP), which was initiated under the auspices of the Department of Religion and Cultural Affairs of His Holiness the Dalai Lama, and the Tibetan Women's Association. She received her B.A. from St. Bede's College in Simla and her B. Ed. from Punjab University in Chandigarh. She resides at Geden Choeling Nunnery in upper McLeod Ganj, India.

JUDAISM: RABBI JEREMY ROSEN, PH.D., is a rabbi, teacher, and academic. Born in Britain, he studied philosophy at Cambridge University and received his rabbinic ordination from the Mir Yeshiva in Jerusalem, Israel. He entered the orthodox rabbinate in Scotland in 1968 and was appointed principal of Carmel College in 1971. In 1985 he returned to the rabbinate as the rabbi of the Western Synagogue in London. In 1991 he moved to Antwerp, Belgium, where he taught both at the university level and at the European Union. In 1992 he was appointed professor and then Chairman of the Faculty of Comparative Religion, Wilrijk. Since 1999 he has been Rabbi and Director of YAKAR, a modern Orthodox community center in London.

CHRISTIANITY: ROBERT LOUIS WILKEN, PH.D., is William R. Kenan, Jr., Professor of the History of Christianity at the University of Virginia, in Charlottesville. He is president of the St. Anselm Institute for Catholic Thought and Chairman of the Board for the Center for Catholic and Evangelical Theology. He has taught at Notre Dame, Fordham, the Gregorian University in Rome, the Augustinianum, and Hebrew University, and is author of ten books, including *The Spirit of Early Christian Thought: Seeking the Face of God, Remembering the Christian Past,* and *The Christians as the Romans Saw Them.*

ISLAM: HIBBA ABUGIDEIRI, Ph.D. is assistant professor of History, Honors and International Affairs, George Washington University. She teaches classes on Middle East history, including the modern Middle East survey course and Women in the Arab World. She specializes in gender history and 19th-century Egypt. She collaborated with John L. Esposito and Yvonne Y. Haddad on *The Islamic Revival Since 1988: A Critical Survey and Bibliography* and has published on Arab nationalism, women in Islamic exegetical texts, and colonial medicine. She was born in Sudan.

EPILOGUE: HIS HOLINESS THE DALAI LAMA. Born in 1935, Tenzin Gyatso was recognized at the age of two as the reincarnation of the Dalai Lama, and by age 19 he was negotiating with China's Mao Zedong over the future of Tibet, which China invaded in 1950 and has occupied since. After years of failed peace talks and a violent suppression of Tibet's resistance movement, the Dalai Lama fled in 1959 to Dharamsala, India. There he continues to be the spiritual leader of six million Tibetans and also heads Tibet's government-in-exile. In 1989, the Dalai Lama accepted the Nobel Peace Prize for his work on global human rights—particularly for his ceaseless efforts to free his country from Chinese rule. His followers believe him to be the 14th earthly incarnation of the heavenly deity of compassion and mercy. He works for the regeneration and continuation of the Tibetan Vajrayana branch of Buddhist tradition.

PHOTOGRAPHERS

JAMES P. BLAIR was a National Geographic photographer from 1962 to 1994, during which time he published 47 stories and more than 2,000 pictures, including coverage of Yugoslavia, Czechoslovakia, Ethiopia, West Africa, Iran, Greece, and the United States. His books include *Our Threatened Inheritance* and *Mysteries of the Ancient World.* He has won awards from the Overseas Press Club of America, the National Press Photographers Association, and the White House News Photographers Association. His work has been shown from Teheran to Washington, D.C., where his images are part of the permanent collection in the National Portrait Gallery. He currently teaches in such venues as the Smithsonian Institution, the International Center for Photography, and The Maine Workshops for Photography.

MARTIN GRAY is a photographer and Buddhist monk, who began his career as a photographer of sacred architecture and pilgrimage sites while still a youngster, the son of U.S. diplomats. During his father's posting in India, he visited the sacred caves of India, Nepal, and Kashmir, and studied Buddhism and Hinduism. After graduating from the University of Arizona, he returned to India to become a mountain hermit in the tradition of Theravada Buddhism, and joined a monastic order for ten years. He left the monastery, founded a travel business, then sold it to photograph the world's sacred architecture. Since the 1980s he has photographed more than 1,000 sacred sites in more than 80 countries, and has studied sacred site mythology, the history of religions, and the anthropology of pilgrimage traditions. Currently he lectures at museums, universities, and conferences around the world. His website sacredsites.com holds his extensive collection of pilgrimage photography.

ACKNOWLEDGEMENTS

National Geographic would like to thank the following people for their help in creating *The Geography of Religion: Where God Lives, Where Pilgrims Walk:* Melissa Farris for her cover design; Ngodup Dorjee and Tenzin Taklha, liaisons with His Holiness the Dalai Lama; Elizabeth Napper for paving the way for us to work with the Venerable Lobsang Dechen; and Tracey and Joe Blanton, who brought the work of photographer Martin Gray to us. Jane Coughran set the stage for illustrations research, and we are grateful for her guidance. In addition, we would like to thank Alice L. Laffey, College of the Holy Cross; John O. Voll, Georgetown University; and Charlotte Bell, who contributed to the book's concept. Dan O'Toole and Emily McCarthy assisted in editorial production.

ILLUSTRATION CREDITS

Cover (upper photos), James P. Blair; (lower left), Erica Lansner/Getty Images; (lower right), Dave Bartruff/CORBIS.

Front Matter: 2-3, James P. Blair; 4, Thomas J. Abercrombie; 6, James L. Stanfield; 10 & 12, www.sacredsites.com and Martin Gray.

ORIGINS: 14-15, Chris Johns, NGS; 16, James P. Blair; 19, Ira Block; 20, Gordon Donkin, by permission of the National Library of Australia; 22, NASA and The Hubble Heritage; 23, Robert Frerck/Woodfin Camp & Associates; 24-25, www.sacredsites.com and Martin Gray; 26, Ekdotike Athenon, S.A.; 27, Raymond Gehman/NGS Image Collection; 28-29, Chris Johns, NGS; 30, www.sacredsites.com and Martin Gray; 31, Erich Lessing/Magnum Photos; 32-33, Richard A. Cooke III; 35, Kenneth Garrett; 36-37, Photo by Enrico Ferorelli, Computer Reconstruction by Doug Stern; 38, Kenneth Garrett; 41, George F. Mobley; 42-43, Edward S. Curtis; 44, James P. Blair; 47, Gianni Dagli Orti/CORBIS; 48, www.sacredsites.com and Martin Gray; 51, Richard A. Cooke III; 52, Paul Chesley; 54-55, Chris Johns, NGS; 56, Maria Stenzel; 60 & 62-63, www.sacredsites.com and Martin Gray; 64-69 (all), James P. Blair.

HINDUISM: 70-71, www.sacredsites.com and Martin Gray; 72, James P. Blair; 75, Marilyn Gibbons/NGS Image Collection; 76 (all) & 78-79, James P. Blair; 80, www.sacredsites.com and Martin Gray; 82 & 83, George F. Mobley; 86 © Raghubir Singh/Estate of Raghubir Singh; 88-89, Raghubir Singh; 90, Pierre Perrin/CORBIS SYGMA; 91, www.sacredsites.com and Martin Gray; 92-93, Roy Toft/NGS Image Collection; 94, Raghubir Singh; 95, Prakash Singh/AFP/Getty Images; 96, © Raghubir Singh/Estate of Raghubir Singh; 97, www.sacredsites.com and Martin Gray; 98, George F. Mobley; 100, www.sacredsites.com and Martin Gray; 103, Jehangir Gazdar/Woodfin Camp & Associates; 105, James P. Blair; 106, "Conquest of Kaliya," c. 1760, Metropolitan Museum of Art (27.37); 107, www.sacredsites.com and Martin Gray; 108, Jean-Louis Nou/AKG-Images; 111, James P. Blair; 112 & 114-115, www.sacredsites.com and Martin Gray; 117, James P. Blair; 120, Central Press/Getty Images; 122 & 124-125, www.sacredsites.com and Martin Gray; 126-131, James P. Blair.

BUDDHISM: 132-133, www.sacredsites.com and Martin Gray; 134, Paul Chesley; 137, Raghubir Singh; 138, The British Museum; 140, W.E. Garrett; 141 & 142-143, James P. Blair; 144, www.sacredsites.com and Martin Gray; 147, Hubertus Kanus/SuperStock; 150 & 151, James P. Blair; 153, Jodi Cobb/NGS Image Collection; 155, www.sacredsites.com and Martin Gray; 156, Reuters/Peter Andrews/CORBIS; 158, Steve McCurry; 160, www.sacredsites.com and Martin Gray; 162-163, Ingrid Booz Morejohn/PictureWorks; 165, www.sacredsites.com and Martin Gray; 167, National Palace Museum, Taipei, Taiwan, Republic of China; 168-169, James P. Blair; 171 & 172, www.sacredsites.com and Martin Gray; 174, George F. Mobley; 175, Gordon Gahan; 178, Michael Kuh; 179-187 (all), www.sacredsites.com and Martin Gray; 189, Paul Chesley; 190-191, Galen Rowell/Mountain Light Photography; 192-197, Steve McCurry.

JUDAISM: 198-199, Jodi Cobb, NGS; 200, James L. Stanfield; 203, Georg Gerster; 204-205, Ed Kashi; 207, Giraudon/Art Resource, NY; 209, Art by Marc Burckhardt, Calligraphy by Julian Waters; 210-211, Nathan Benn; 212, Ted Spiegel; 213, © 2004 Artists Rights Society (ARS), New York/ADAGP, Paris/Réunion des Musées Nationaux/Art Resource, NY; 214, www.sacredsites.com and Martin Gray; 217, Ted Spiegel; 218-219, Robert Clark; 220, Bridgeman Art Library; 224, American Colony Photographers; 226-227, Princeton University Press/Art Resource, NY; 228, Jewish Community Center of Greater Washington - Weiner Menorah Collection; 230, Richard T. Nowitz/ NGS Image Collection; 231, Jeffrey Markowitz/CORBIS SYGMA; 232-233, Jodi Cobb, NGS; 234, NGS Maps; 235, James L. Stanfield; 236, © The Israel Museum, Jerusalem/David Harris; 238-239, Richard T. Nowitz/NGS Image Collection; 240, Annie Griffiths Belt; 243, Nathan Benn; 244-245, James P. Blair; 246, The British Museum; 249, Historical Picture Archive/CORBIS; 253, Alexandra Avakian; 254-255, Annie Griffiths Belt; 256-257 & 258-259, REZA; 260, Giraudon/Art Resource, NY; 261, www.sacredsites.com and Martin Gray.

CHRISTIANITY: 262-267 (all), Thomas Nebbia; 268-269, Nicolas Thibaud/EXPLORER; 270, Scala/Art Resource, NY; 272-273, Thomas Nebbia; 275, Scala/Art Resource, NY; 276, Thomas Nebbia; 278-279, Annie Griffiths Belt; 280 & 283, James L. Stanfield; 287, James P. Blair; 288, REZA; 289, Erich Lessing/Magnum Photos; 290-291 & 294-295, James L. Stanfield; 296, www.sacredsites.com and Martin Gray; 298, Bruce Dale; 299, Archivo Iconografico, S.A./CORBIS; 300, www.sacredsites.com and Martin Gray; 304-305, James L. Stanfield; 307, Fred Peer; 309, ©Biblioteca Apostolica Vaticana (Vatican); 310-311, James P. Blair; 313, Carole Devillers; 314-318 (all), James P. Blair; 321 & 322-323, www.sacredsites.com and Martin Gray; 324-329, James P. Blair.

ISLAM: 330-331, REZA; 332, Bruno Barbey; 335, James L. Stanfield; 336, Sonia Halliday Photographs; 337, Bildarchiv Preussischer Kulturbesitz/Art Resource, NY; 338-339, REZA; 341, Thomas J. Abercrombie; 342-343, REZA; 344, James L. Stanfield; 348-349 & 350, Mohamed Amin/Camerapix; 354, Lynn Abercrombie; 355, Artifact courtesy The Hispanic Society of America, New York; Photo courtesy the Arthur M. Sackler Gallery, Smithsonian Institution, Washington, DC; 358, R. & S. Michaud/Rapho, courtesy University Library, Istanbul; 360, Victor R. Boswell, Jr. at Museo Arqueológico, Granada, Spain; 361, www.sacredsites.com and Martin Gray; 362-363, James L. Stanfield; 364, www.sacredsites.com and Martin Gray; 366-367, Bruno Barbey; 369, Bruno Barbey/Magnum Photos; 370-371, Bruno Barbey; 372, James L. Stanfield; 376, James P. Blair; 378-379, James L. Stanfield; 381, REZA; 383, James P. Blair; 384, Bill Ellzey/NGS Image Collection; 387, Thomas J. Abercrombie; 388-389 & 390, James P. Blair; 390-391, Ed Kashi; 392-393, Annie Griffiths Belt; 394, William Albert Allard, NGS; 395, Steve McCurry.

Epilogue: James L. Stanfield.

The Geography of Religion
Where God Lives, Where Pilgrims Walk

by Susan Tyler Hitchcock, Ph.D.

with John L. Esposito, Ph.D.

Published by the National Geographic Society

John M. Fahey, Jr., *President and Chief Executive Officer*

Gilbert M. Grosvenor, *Chairman of the Board*

Nina D. Hoffman, *Executive Vice President*

Prepared by the Book Division

Kevin Mulroy, *Vice President and Editor-in-Chief*

Charles Kogod, *Illustrations Director*

Marianne R. Koszorus, *Design Director*

Barbara Brownell Grogan, *Executive Editor*

Staff for this Book

Karin Kinney, *Editor*

Cinda Rose, *Art Director*

Charles Kogod, *Illustrations Editor*

Suzanne Poole, *Illustrations Researcher*

Karin Kinney, *Researcher*

Suzanne Crawford, *Associate Editor*

Christian Kinney, Ann Oman, *Captions*

Carl Mehler, *Director of Maps*

Thomas L. Gray, *Map Editor*

Matt Chwastyk and The M Factory, *Map Research and Production*

Ric Wain, *Production Project Manager*

Mike Horenstein, *ILA Production Project Manager*

Meredith Wilcox, *Illustrations Assistant*

Cameron Zotter, *Design Assistant*

Margo Browning, *Release Editor*

Robert Swanson, *Indexer*

Manufacturing and Quality Control

Christopher A. Liedel, *Chief Financial Officer*

Phillip L. Schlosser, *Managing Director*

John T. Dunn, *Technical Director*

Alan Kerr, *Manager*

One of the world's largest nonprofit scientific and educational organizations, the National Geographic Society was founded in 1888 "for the increase and diffusion of geographic knowledge." Fulfilling this mission, the Society educates and inspires millions every day through its magazines, books, television programs, videos, maps and atlases, research grants, the National Geographic Bee, teacher workshops, and innovative classroom materials. The Society is supported through membership dues, charitable gifts, and income from the sale of its educational products. This support is vital to National Geographic's mission to increase global understanding and promote conservation of our planet through exploration, research, and education.

For more information, please call 1-800-NGS LINE (647-5463) or write to the following address:
National Geographic Society
1145 17th Street N.W.
Washington, D.C. 20036-4688 U.S.A.

Visit the Society's Web site at www.nationalgeographic.com.

This 2012 edition printed for Barnes & Noble, Inc., by the National Geographic Society.

ISBN: 978-1-4351-4195-7

The Library of Congress has cataloged the 2004 edition as follows:
Hitchcock, Susan Tyler
National Geographic geography of religion:
where God lives, where pilgrims walk /
Susan Tyler Hitchcock with John L. Esposito.
        p. cm.
Includes bibliographical references and index.
ISBN 0-7922-7313-3 (alk. paper)--
ISBN 0-7922-7317-6 (deluxe : alk. paper)
1. Religion and geography.
2. Religions. I. Esposito, John L. II National Geographic Society (U.S.) III Title.
BL65.G4H58 2004   200'.9--dc22

Printed in Hong Kong
12/THK/1